The Parrys

of the Golden Vale

Background to genius

Anthony Boden

TU·NE·CEDE·MALIS

Thames Publishing

London 1998

First published in 1998 by
Thames Publishing
14 Barlby Road
London W10 6AR

Printed and bound in Great Britain
by Whitstable Litho Ltd, Whitstable, Kent

CONTENTS

ACKNOWLEDGEMENTS

I am deeply indebted to Tom and Debbie Fenton at Highnam, and to Laura Ponsonby and Kate Russell at Shulbrede Priory, not only for allowing me unfettered access to the Parry family archives, but also for the unfailing warmth, hospitality and encouragement which they and their families have given to me during my many visits to their homes. Research becomes a pleasure when supported by such friendship.

I am especially grateful to Dr Jeremy Dibble, Dr Dennis Farr CBE, and Peter Burman MBE for advice and for permission to quote from their published works; to John E Parry for sharing with me the fruits of his genealogical research; to Christopher Walker for allowing me to publish quotations from the diaries of his grandmother, the late Helen Richmond; to Jack Farley for his care and photographic skill in copying many of the illustrations in this book; to John Hill, a Parry descendant, my meeting with whom in the British Library India Office in 1994 was the result of pure serendipity; and to Michael Trott, whose early encouragement persuaded me that this book should be written.

Others who have helped me in various ways include: Audrey Ash, Jennifer Beazley, Ronald Bleach, Hugh Cobbe, John and Theresa Comins, Professor J D M Derrett, Suzanne M Eward, Brian Frith, Judith Dickinson, the Revd Jonathan Hadfield, Dr Bernard A Juby, Graham Lloyd, Elisabeth McDougall, Tricia Manners, Jill Robinson, Mary Roebuck, Tony Stocks, Ronald Stratton, Dr K M Tomlinson, Margaret Wilkin and Christian Wilson. I am also indebted to the staffs of the British Library India Office; the Society of Genealogists; the Guildhall Library, London; the Public Record Office at both Chancery Lane and Kew; the Records Offices of the Corporation of London and the Counties of Gloucestershire, Herefordshire, Worcestershire and Warwickshire; and to the Country Life magazine for permission to quote from the articles about Highnam Court by Arthur Oswald which appeared in the editions of 12 and 19 May 1950.

Finally, I must thank my wife, Anne, for her constant support and understanding throughout the past two years.

A N B
April 1998

Hubert Parry (1892). *The Royal College of Music.*

Introduction

In 1905, on taking up his short-lived appointment as Professor of Music at the University of Birmingham, Sir Edward Elgar embarked upon a series of lectures, the first of which bore the optimistic title 'A Future for English Music'; but was there, in those early years of the twentieth century, a gambler who would have risked his money on the proposition that English music had a future at all? The long Victorian era had failed to produce an English composer of the stature of Mendelssohn, and in the previous century the considerable talents of Thomas Arne and William Boyce had scarcely rivalled the glorious achievements of Georg Friedrich Händel. To have believed Oscar A Schmitz's indictment of England as *Das Land ohne Musik* (The Land Without Music, 1914) was to have condemned English music not only to a bleak future but to have ignored its golden past: Tallis, Byrd, Weelkes, Tomkins, Gibbons, Purcell and 'all that noble host' could be discounted.

Elgar knew otherwise. A quarter of a century before his Birmingham lectures a new musical voice had been heard in the west. 'In looking for a practical starting point for anything that may be usefully considered in relation to present day music', he said, 'I think it unnecessary to go back farther than 1880... Some of us who in that year were young and taking an active part in music... felt that something at last was going to be done in the way of composition by the English school'.[1]

Sir Henry Hadow was one of the first to rejoice in what was being done. 'There has arisen among us a composer who is capable of restoring our national music to its true place in the art of Europe', he wrote in 1898:

> At the very nadir of our fortune, when we had entirely ceased to count among the musical nations of Europe, there appeared at the Gloucester Festival in 1880 a cantata entitled *Scenes from Shelley's 'Prometheus Unbound'*... No one seems to have had any idea that, on that evening in the Shire Hall, English music had, after many years, come again to its own, and that it had come with a masterpiece in its hand.[2]

Elgar too acknowledged without reservation the composer of *Prometheus*. His was a name, he told his Birmingham audience, 'which shall be always spoken in this University with the deepest respect and, I will add, the deepest affection – I mean Sir Hubert Parry, the head of our art in this country... with him no cloud

---

[1] See Edward Elgar (ed. Percy M Young), *A Future for English Music and other lectures* (London, 1968), p 33 *et seq.*
[2] See Charles L. Graves, *Hubert Parry*, Vol II (London, 1926), pp 190/1.

of formality can dim the healthy sympathy and broad influence he exerts and we hope may long continue to exert upon us'.[3]

The influence of Parry upon Elgar was profound, and upon his pupils, among whom were numbered Vaughan Williams, Holst and Howells, indelible. A pathfinder, it was Parry who, in the example of his own music and in his brilliant didacticism, laid the foundation-stone of the British Musical Revival.

Vaughan Williams had first heard of Parry when he was still a schoolboy and determined to study composition under the great man at the Royal College of Music:

> I remember saying to my mother that there was something, to my mind, peculiarly English in his music. So I was quite prepared to join with the other young students of the RCM in worshipping at that shrine, and I think I can truly say I have never been disloyal to it...[4]

For Herbert Howells, Parry was, quite simply, the greatest man he ever met:[5]

> His mind was so concentrated on things right outside music, and, at the College, he never tired of making us students remember that if we allowed our outlooks to become hedged in by purely musical matters and refused to allow the wider, broader issues of life – not merely of art – into our minds, we could never become complete human beings.[6]

Or, as Gustav Holst expressed it: 'he gave us...a vision rather than a lecture'.[7] Parry's contribution to his art as teacher, performer and writer was prodigious, but the great glory of his legacy is to be found in his compositions. Sadly neglected for far too long, interest in his music is reawakening, largely as a result of enlightened and enterprising recording projects. Works which have lain silent for three generations are again giving pleasure to listeners who might otherwise have known Parry only for *Jerusalem* and that great masterpiece *Blest Pair of Sirens*. At last it is possible to experience something of the admiration and wonder which prompted Ralph Vaughan Williams to affirm that 'amidst all the outpourings of modern English music the work of Parry remains supreme'.

Hubert Parry was a great composer; but he was also the pre-eminent son of a remarkable family which over many generations had made distinguished and important contributions to British national life. Lineally descended from Sitric, King of the Danes of Dublin, who in 1014 fought against Brian Boru 'and all that obeyed him of the men of Ireland' at the Battle of Clontarf, Parry's ancestors settled in the Golden Vale of Herefordshire, from where, in succeeding generations, they set out to serve the English crown at Agincourt and the Tudor cause at Mortimer's Cross and Bosworth.

---

[3] Edward Elgar (ed. Percy M Young), *op cit.*
[4] Ralph Vaughan Williams, *A Musical Autobiography*, quoted in Ursula Vaughan Williams, *RVW – A Biography of Ralph Vaughan Williams* (Oxford, 1964), p 31.
[5] Memories of Brian Frith, a close friend of Herbert Howells.
[6] Christopher Palmer, *Herbert Howells* (Novello, 1978), pp 13/14.
[7] Imogen Holst, *Holst* (Faber, 1974), p 18.

The reign of Elizabeth I was a golden age of influence for the Parrys. The Queen was served by several members of the family, including James Parry, her Chief Huntsman, and Blanche Parry, Chief Gentlewoman of the Queen's Privy Chamber and Keeper of Her Majesty's Jewels, who had arrived at the Court of Henry VIII in time to see Elizabeth rocked in her cradle, and remained to devote the whole of her adult life in ministering to her royal mistress's needs.

In the closing years of her reign Elizabeth summoned yet another Parry, a cousin of Blanche; one who was to become her favourite chaplain. Henry Parry (1561-1616) was a clever and ambitious man, destined to become Bishop, first of Gloucester and, ultimately, of Worcester. No priest was closer to the Queen; a queen still pictured in official portraits as a clear-eyed woman with lion-coloured hair but who, in reality, was now 'aged, toothless, bald and irascible.' Elizabeth cared for Henry Parry to the extent at least of making him expensive gifts: a china tea-pot and a silver canister. And it was he who was called to her side during her last sickness.

By the end of February 1603, weak and emaciated, Elizabeth had withdrawn into a private chamber at Richmond, where, barely capable of movement, she lay on the floor cocooned in cushions. On 21 March she was at last persuaded to undress and go to bed. From then on 'she began to lose her speech, and from that time, ate nothing, but lay on one side, without speaking or looking upon any person'.

Two days later Henry Parry preached at a service in the chapel at Richmond 'a very learned, eloquent, religious and moving sermon' on the subject of vows. His prayer, 'both in the beginning and conclusion, was so fervent and effectual for her Majesty that he left few eyes dry'.[8]

John Manningham, who had arrived that day, dined with Parry and three other senior clerics. Over the cooked meats and wine they told him that the Queen had :

> yesterday signified by the lifting of her hand and eyes to heaven, a sign which Dr Parry entreated of her, that she believed that faith which she had caused to be professed, and looked faithfully to be saved by Christ's merits and mercies only, and by no other means.[9]

To Henry Parry, then, fell the lot of reassuring the hierarchy of the Established Church that their sovereign, who had retained in her private chapel the vestments, crucifixes and other symbols of the Old Faith, was actually a convinced Protestant. Semi-comatose as she was, the slightest flicker of the eyes was counted proof enough.

Elizabeth died on 24 March 1603. Archbishop Whitgift had remained to pray until late at night, when everyone departed except Parry and a few of the ladies-in-waiting. Between 2 and 3 o'clock in the morning 'mildly like a lamb, easily like a ripe apple from the tree', she took Death's hand. Parry 'sent his

---

[8] Manningham, *Diary* (Camden Society), pp 145/6.
[9] *Ibid.*

prayers before her soul', wrote Manningham, 'and I doubt not but she is amongst the royal saints in heaven in eternal joys'.[10]

Blanche Parry had witnessed Elizabeth's coming into the world; Henry Parry her going out.

Sir Hubert Parry's more immediate forebears were no less distinguished than his early ancestors. His father, Thomas Gambier Parry, was an extraordinary figure: the Victorian counterpart to a Renaissance Man; a pioneer collector of Italian paintings of the *trecento* and *quattrocento* whose knowledge matched his wealth; arboriculturalist, composer, ecclesiologist, philanthropist, water-colourist, and inventor of a technique, previously thought impossible by artists working in the cold, damp British climate: that of successful mural painting.

Thomas Gambier Parry's father and grandfather were both Directors of the East India Company whose colourful lives and intrepid adventures established the fortune which gave Thomas the independence to pursue his interests and creativity; and which, in turn, provided Hubert with the education, upbringing and environment to enable his creative energy to flourish.

This is neither a biography of one man nor an in-depth study of his music. Rather, it is a saga of a remarkable family with roots planted deeply in British earth; of their accomplishments and failures; their joys and clashes, triumphs, tragedies and loves; and of the many inherent strands which impacted upon the mind and character of Sir Hubert Parry; the strands which when woven together in company with his own unique thread of genius gave him a wholly individual voice and made possible an invaluable contribution to the nineteenth-century renaissance of English music.

---

[10] *Ibid.*

I

Patriots and Profiteers

When a determined man of influence decides to obliterate his past it is hardly surprising that a century later the tracks of his childhood will have vanished away. Sir Hubert Parry's father, Thomas Gambier Parry, tried hard and long to find his grandfather Thomas Parry's origins, and his descendants maintained the search well into the present century; but their quest remained unresolved: Thomas Parry (1732-1816) had 'dropt a mysterious veil between himself and his progenitors'.[1] Thomas Gambier Parry was assisted in his search by a distant relative, Francis Charles Parry, a judge in the Court of Bankruptcy at Birmingham and an enthusiastic genealogist who spent many years and a good deal of money in researching the family history of the Parrys. The two men began corresponding in 1844 and continued to do so until 1865, when Francis, at age 86, was still writing of fresh journeyings about the country; of fresh studies which were to throw light on hidden points and, especially, as Hubert's half-brother Ernest was to record, 'on the parentage of that strange man, our great-grandfather, Thomas Parry' who had taken such pains to destroy any record of his father or background – save only one proud pointer to his ancestry: the family coat of arms of the Parrys of Poston in the Golden Vale of Herefordshire, 'Argent a fesse between three lozenges sable. <u>Crest</u>: Three battle-axes erect ppr. <u>Motto</u>: *Tu ne cede malis* (Yield thou not to evils).' That coat of arms and crest had been familiar to Hubert and Ernest from childhood. Embossed on leather book-bindings and blotters, engraved on silver and silver-gilt plate, cutlery, pocket watches, seals, and carved on dining chairs, those three erect battle-axes were all around them in their family home at Highnam Court near Gloucester.

Ernest could not accept that his great-grandfather had been 'in any way connected with trade or that he made his money by energy and enterprise in the course of a long business career', and convinced himself that Thomas 'was always possessed of means'.[2] Thomas Gambier Parry would gaze at the portrait

---

[1] Ernest Gambier-Parry, *Gambier Parry Family Memoranda* (manuscript). Property of Mr TJ Fenton, Highnam archive. (Abbreviated hereafter to 'GPM'), p 109.
[2] GPM p 24.

of Thomas painted by Sir William Beechey and mutter 'it is simply impossible that that man could have been a mere nobody or come from a family of nobodies'.[3] Unable to penetrate the mystery, Ernest was forced to acknowledge that it 'was difficult to say whether this veil was dropped by him with the full intention and purpose of shutting out all history of his family from those who were to come after him; neither can I trace any motive for such action. He was a shrewd, clever man. There can be no doubt of that. But if he deliberately set to work to hide his past and parentage, his shrewdness and his cleverness, judged by his success, must have been more than human... If Thomas Parry acted deliberately in [this] way, how was it he left his arms impaled with others on the family tomb; or how was it he left his fob-seals with his arms again impaled with others there?'.[4]

Ernest seems not to have taken fully into account the one thing of which Thomas had been enormously proud: his ancient pedigree. No doubt he knew about his ancestor, King Sitric, whose great-great grandson, Ideo, Earl of Desmond, forsook Ireland and set sail for Wales, the homeland of his mother, Nest. In Wales, Ideo had entered the service of Rhys ap Tewdwr, Nest's brother, the heroic Prince of Deheubarth (the larger part of South Wales) and in return received a large estate at Llywel. Ideo's second son, Moreiddigh, or Meredith, married Catherine, widow of Baron Thomas Lacy, of the powerful Norman family; settled at Poston in Herefordshire's Golden Vale; and founded a dynasty which after five generations took the name of ap Harry, or Parry.[5] Thomas Parry could not be denied this heritage, no matter how dark the cloud which cloaked his childhood.

Ernest's sister, Beatrice, made an attempt to solve the enigma and made a discovery which must have given her brother's upper middle-class sensitivity quite a jolt. In the City of London freedom admissions she found an indenture witnessing that one Thomas Parry was admitted to the City Freedom through the Girdlers' Company in February 1755, having been apprenticed to Thomas Hall, Citizen and Girdler of London, for seven years from 6 May 1747 for a consideration of five shillings.[6] The document states that Thomas was the son of Henry Parry, a perukemaker of St. Clement Danes, and is signed by Thomas himself.

Beatrice was convinced that this was indeed her great-grandfather, and was confirmed in her view on subsequently finding in Tomkins' *Liveries of London* (1775) that 'Thomas Parry, gent., Berners Street, Oxford Street' was listed as a member of the Girdlers' Company. She may well have been right. Thomas Parry lived for many years at 52 Berners Street; but since he had gone to such lengths

---

[3] GPM pp 45/46.

[4] GPM p 25.

[5] Moreiddigh of the Golden Vale passed his inheritance to his son, Ieuan ap Moreiddigh ('ap' means 'son of'), and five generations later the family surname 'Parry' evolved and became fixed: Philip ap Ieuan, Gwilym ap Philip, Harry ap John, and John ap Harry; the conflation of 'ap Harry' forming 'Parry' in the same way that 'ap Howell' formed 'Powell'.

[6] Corporation of London Records Office, reference: CF1/799 (old no. 96). The Girdlers' Company was one of the City Livery Companies, as the successors to the medieval trade and craft guilds are known, and many of these City Livery Companies still exist today. To be admitted to freedom by servitude a person had to complete an apprenticeship of at least seven years' duration to a City Freeman (four years after 1889).

to conceal his origins might not he also have fabricated the name of his father?

Beatrice knew the date of Thomas Parry's birth: 23 October 1732[7], but was unable to find his baptism registered in any London parish register. The search is somewhat easier today, and the International Genealogical Index shows that six children were baptised 'Thomas Parry' in England and Wales in 1732, four of them in or before the month of May, and none of them with a father named Henry. In fact only one baptism is compatible with the birthdate in October 1732 of a child entitled to use the arms of the Parrys of the Golden Vale: Thomas Parry, son of Walter and Hannah Parry of Barcheston, Warwickshire, who was baptised on 20 November 1732.

Walter Parry was the great-grandson of Richard Parry (d1681) of Broadway, Worcestershire, a dyer, a thriving trade in the Cotswold area, where the woollen industry created an economic boom and was a major source of employment until its decline in the nineteenth century. Walter (c1639-1705) ran a successful fulling and dyeing business at the Fell Mill on the southern bank of the Stour between Barcheston and Honington. Fell Mill Farm is still there today, and strolling between its gates and Barcheston, with its church, rectory and farmhouse (now called 'The Manor'), it is not difficult to imagine the working and domestic life of a prosperous seventeenth-century yeoman. In this quiet rural corner Walter Parry turned wool into riches:

> Innumerable of stains and splendid dyes,
> As are the tiger-moth's deep damask'd wings.

Bishop Henry Parry of Worcester had three sons and a daughter: Henry, Richard, George and Vashter. One of the bishop's descendants, the Reverend John Parry (1639-1714), was Rector of Aston Somerville, Gloucestershire (now in Worcestershire) for over half a century, and it is possible to trace links between his family and Richard Parry of Broadway's successors. Perhaps they were close cousins. Old Walter's third son, Daniel, farmed at Barcheston but failed to achieve the prosperity of his father. When he died intestate in 1744 he had been a widower for seven years. Daniel's son, a younger Walter, administered his father's estate and made a list of his property[8]: four apple mills and two presses, farming implements, a fowling piece and musket, a churn and staff, kitchen utensils, a bible and a few books of religious instruction, two night gowns, two great coats, five frock: good and bad, three coats and waistcoats, four hats, two wigs, eight pairs of stockings, two brass candlesticks... the total value of Daniel's goods was £29. 10s. 1d.

Walter lived for only five more years, dying intestate himself in 1749. Once again, a list of property had to be made, but this time there was no adult son to complete the task. A Mr Robert Lloyd of Blockley was appointed the administrator of all Walter's goods and chattels, the inventory of which was similar to that drawn up for Daniel in 1744 but with the addition of six silver

---

[7] GPM p 25.
[8] Worcester RO.

spoons, presumably the property of Walter's wife, Hannah, who, like Robert Lloyd, had come from Blockley, seven miles from Barcheston. Walter and Hannah had five children in the ten years following their marriage in 1729, two of whom died in infancy. And yet when Walter died in 1749 at the age of 42, the letters of administration make no mention of Hannah or her two daughters, Elizabeth and Martha; only of his son, Thomas, a seventeen-year-old youth to whom Robert Lloyd was appointed 'guardian or curator at law'.[9]

Were Hannah and her daughters already dead? If so, there is no record of their burials in the Barcheston parish register. Had Hannah abandoned Walter, taking Elizabeth and Martha with her? Whatever the circumstances, if Thomas Parry *was* Sir Hubert Parry's great-grandfather, he chose to cancel them out from his mind, preferring to leave behind an enigma to baffle succeeding generations of his family .

Unaided by a modern, computerised genealogical index, Beatrice knew nothing of the Parrys of Barcheston and had no reason to doubt that Henry Parry the perukemaker was her great-great-grandfather. That Thomas Hall's apprentice became Thomas Parry, gent. is almost certain. Apart from the unlikelihood that the address in Berners Street could be a coincidence, the signatures on the Freedom document and on papers signed many years later by the founding father of Hubert Parry's family show pronounced similarities, even allowing for a maturing in handwriting. Furthermore, the records of the Girdlers' Company show that Thomas Parry became an esteemed member. He was elected a Warden of their governing Court in 1772; an honour which he declined, agreeing to pay a fine of fifteen guineas to be spared serving in that office[10], a sum which no humble girdler would have been able to afford.

Thomas was fourteen years old when he began his apprenticeship in 1747, two years before the death of Walter Parry in Barcheston. Notwithstanding Ernest Gambier-Parry's later distaste and supposition to the contrary, Thomas had gone off in search of a trade, as indeed had three of the Reverend John Parry of Aston Somerville's six sons, two of whom, Samuel and Thomas, went to London as seedsmen of the Grocers' Company, and one, Benjamin, as a wax chandler. Perhaps Thomas had no choice if, as seems likely, his family had fallen apart; and it could well be that Henry Parry the perukemaker was one of Thomas's London relatives, and that he gave shelter to a boy who had lost his natural father. A fourth son of the Reverend John Parry was actually called Henry, but he was dead long before Thomas Parry's apprenticeship began.

Even if Thomas *had* begun to train as a girdler, it does not follow that his apprentice years were entirely spent in learning that craft. Girdlers made the belt which was worn to suspend a purse, wallet or side-arms[11], an essential accoutrement at a time when gentlemen carried swords. It was not unusual for young men to embark upon such apprenticeships in order to gain the rights and

[9] *Ibid.*
[10] Guildhall Library London: Minute Book of the Girdlers' Company.
[11] Valerie Hope et al, *The Freedom, the Past and Present of the Livery, Guilds and City of London* (Barracuda Books, 1982).

privileges held by City Freemen, and the Girdlers' Company may have been no more than a passport to the City as far as Thomas was concerned; but however his early London years might have been spent, it is clear that Thomas acquired both a good education and a considerable amount of business acumen at that time. His subsequent career was both successful and remarkable: service with the Royal Navy from 1758 to 1781 and a Director of the East India Company thereafter. Having started out on his working life with barely a penny piece, Thomas had made a fortune by the time he reached his early thirties.

Well before joining the Royal Navy, Parry had made the acquaintance of Daniel Twining of Messrs. Twining & Carter, tea merchants. Family tradition has it that Thomas Parry was taken to London by the Twinings, and it seems far more likely that his commercial experience was gained by contact with a large firm of that sort, with its powerful City and East India Company connections, than with Thomas Hall the girdler.

Although still expensive, until the duty was reduced in 1784, tea was, by the middle of the eighteenth century, ceasing to be a luxury for the privileged few. As a contemporary commentator wrote of customs in Nottingham:

> The People here are not without their Tea, Coffee and Chocolate, especially the first, the use of which is spread in that Degree, that not only the Gentry and Wealthy Traders drink it constantly, but almost every Seamer, Sizer and Winder, will have her Tea and will enjoy herself over it in a Morning.[12]

There was a lot of money to be made from tea – and Thomas Parry was drawn to money as moth to candle. A century later Richard Twining would remember 'the name of Parry as that of one of the oldest and most valued friends of my family. [It] has been familiar to me from my youth up… I have heard my father often speak of it as a friendship of the closest and most unbroken character'.[13]

The wealth of the East, its silks, spices and tea, had drawn explorers from Europe into uncharted oceans throughout the seventeenth century. The English East India Company, incorporated by Elizabeth I by royal charter on 31 December 1600, enjoyed great success from its inception but, driven from the East Indies by the Dutch, gradually strengthened its position on the mainland of India, acquiring trading posts at Madras, Calcutta and, after the marriage of Charles II to a Portuguese princess, Bombay. Charles II also enlarged the charter of the Company, giving it the right to acquire territory, control its own currency, exercise full powers of civil and criminal jurisdiction, make treaties, command armies and wage war. Native rulers were progressively subdued whilst officials of the East India Company, provided they survived tropical diseases, could hope to return home with fortunes of tens of thousands of pounds.

In 1756 the Nawab Siraj-ud-daula seized Calcutta and other Company factories, only to be defeated by Robert Clive at the Battle of Plassey in 1757. The East India Company was now all-powerful in the sub-continent, forcing the

---

[12] Charles Deering (ed. G Ayscough), *Nottingham Vetus et Nova* (1751), p 72.
[13] GPM p 38: extract from a letter dated 21 September 1865 from Richard Twyning to Thomas Gambier Parry.

British Government to accept some colonial responsibility for India. An empire was in the making.

Thomas Parry craved both adventure and wealth. Necessity had already taught him self-reliance. He made it his business to know thoroughly the ways of the City, of investments, of securities, of Government funds. He understood the great national importance of the East India Company and the riches which were to be gained by its monopoly of trade in the east. He saw the East Indiamen riding at anchor on the Thames: cargo-ships as large as any in the world, gilded and carved, fitted out luxuriously for officers and passengers, armed as warships, symbols of British pride.

In the year following the Battle of Plassey, 1758, Thomas Parry joined the Royal Navy as a volunteer Corporal, an assistant to a Master at Arms, and embarked on HMS *Dover*, bound for the Far East to join the *Argo*, a Company ship operating from China. For the next two years his career progressed upwards. He advanced first to Clerk, an essential first step towards Purser: an appointment which he achieved in 1760 whilst sailing to the East Indies with a squadron of ships under the command of a Captain Haldane:

> Pursers were warranted by the Admiralty and were not professionally examined, though they had to provide financial sureties. Their duties were to oversee the supply and issue of victuals, slops (clothes) and other consumable ship's stores, partly as officials responsible for government stocks, partly as private contractors whose affairs were officially regulated.[14]

Parry had landed the perfect position for a man who wished to see the world, serve his country and at the same time sustain a profitable interest in commercial dealings; but the enterprise was not without danger – the Seven Years War (1756-63) had run only half of its blood-soaked course, and every voyage might end in ambush and sinking.

The British had declared war against Spain on 4 January 1762. Some months earlier, Colonel William Draper, commander of a regiment based at Fort St George, Madras, had devoted part of his sick-leave to spying on the defences of the Philippines. He had visited Manila and concluded that conquest would present no difficulty should it be required, and that success could be achieved by using 'only such force as might be spared from India, consistent with the security of the Company's settlements and conquests there'.[15] Back in England, Draper laid this information before grateful ministers. On 23 January 1762 the Earl of Egremont wrote to Major General Stringer Lawrence, Commander in Chief of Land Forces in the East Indies:

> His Majesty, considering the great advantage his trading subjects in those parts would reap from such an acquisition, and the crippling blow the commerce of Spain would sustain from such a loss... has judged proper to dispatch Colonel Draper to Madras to confer with you as well upon the practicability of this scheme as with regard to the

---

[14] N A M Roger, *Naval Records for Genealogists* (HMSO, 1988), p 22.
[15] PRO: CO., 77/20. Earl of Egremont to Major General Lawrence, Whitehall, 23 January 1762.

number of troops which may with prudence be spared from Bengal and the coast of Coromandel.[16]

A combined naval-military operation was decided upon, one of the earliest of its type. Secret instructions for the attack on Manila were sent to Rear Admiral Samuel Cornish, Second Commander of British Ships in the East Indies, whose weather-beaten squadron had anchored at Trincomalee on the east coast of Ceylon for much needed maintenance:

> in the best manner I could to enable me to proceed when the season would permit to give them the necessary repairs at Bombay, being in extream bad condition; and indeed nothing but the necessity of the service and my earnest desire to execute their Lordships commands could have justified my proceeding with them on the expedition, for during my passage to this place [Manila Bay] every day produced new complaints which gave me great uneasiness and I was apprehensive that many of the ships would not be able to return.[17]

Cornish's squadron consisted of eight ships of the line, three frigates and two Indiamen. During an eight-week voyage from Ceylon to Manila, Thomas Parry was appointed Secretary to the Admiral and transferred from his parent ship, the *Medway*, to Cornish's flag-ship, the *Norfolk*, commanded by Captain Richard Kempenfelt. The combined force, including Indian troops, totalled well over four thousand men.

This menacing but leaky flotilla anchored in Manila Bay on 23 September 1762. The next day Cornish received a visitor:

> This morning an officer with a Spanish flag came on board the admiral with letters from the Captain General of the Philippines desiring to know by what authority we entered their bay with such a force without previously advising him thereof, offering us at the same time all the assistance in his power if we were drove there by distress, but assuring us if we came in a hostile manner (which he could not think possible not having heard of any declaration of War between Spain and England) he was determined to defend the honour of the Catholic Crown to the last extremity.[18]

Parry was undoubtedly present when Cornish sent this unfortunate Spanish gentleman back with naval and military escorts to summon the city of Manila to surrender, and from this point the many messages and communiqués signed by the Admiral were written in Parry's hand.

The Spanish, totally unaware until that moment that they were at war with the British, were both unprepared for an attack and unwilling to surrender without a fight. Cornish ordered his frigates close inshore to provide cover for troops landing in long boats. By nightfall on that first day of hostilities the suburbs of Manila were ablaze, ignited by the Spanish themselves.

On 28 February Draper's secretary, Lieutenant Fryer, was sent into the garrison under a flag of truce to escort a relation of the Spanish governor's who

---

[16] *Ibid*
[17] PRO: Adm 1/162 (2), fos 50-1.
[18] British Library India Office Records: HM, 76, pp 55/65.

had been taken prisoner. The defenders' response was to decapitate Fryer and to return his headless body 'maimed in the most inhuman manner with a letter from the governor expressing the utmost horror of such a treacherous act, imputing the fault to the ignorance and barbarity of their natives', who were 'utterly unacquainted with the customs of war'.[19]

The natives were given adequate opportunity to learn the niceties of war in the European manner during the following weeks of bombardment and hand-to-hand fighting. They would see twenty-three of Draper's officers and eight hundred of his men killed, along with numerous wounded whose chance of recovery was negligible. Even so, by 2 November Draper was writing to the Secretary at War in England, much to Cornish's intense irritation, to inform him that Manila was already taken 'with trifling loss'.[20] At the core of Draper's letter was a complaint about the unequal distribution of prize money from the expedition:

> The sea and land forces had so near a connection and co-operated so fully and cordially upon this service that I thought the best way of dividing any prize money that might be taken by us would be to adhere to those rules which His Majesty has thought proper to fix for the sea services and that the officers should share in their respective ranks according to those proportions. The distribution was made in this manner. The field officers shared with the captains of the squadron, our captains of foot and marines with their lieutenants. and so on with the subordinate classes… But the captains of foot have thought the disproportion of prize money between the field officers and them to be too great (a field officer receiving nine times as much as a captain) …as this is the grievance complained of, [I] beg you will receive His Majesty's commands thereon; am in hopes it will not be thought I have acted from any self interested motives, as I am myself a great loser by the method, sharing only as a subordinate flag officer to Mr. Cornish instead of dividing as the Commander in Chief at Land.[21]

The amounts were astonishing. Apart from the taking of two Spanish ships, the *Santissima Trinidad* and the *Philippina*, together worth several hundred thousand pounds, a ransom of four million dollars was levied upon the Spanish. Cash, silver, plate, diamonds, pearls, gold and effects were stripped from the Treasury, the Cathedral and the religious houses of the Dominicans, Franciscans, Augustines and Jesuits. Conquered soldiers and sailors were relieved of their cash and property, and large sums were taken from the Archbishop and several Spanish aristocrats.

In his initial secret instructions to Draper, George III had left the distribution of booty as a grey area in an otherwise specific set of orders:

> With regard to any booty which may be taken at land during this expedition, We are pleased to leave it to you and the Commander in Chief of Our ships to make such agreement with the East India Company or their Officers for the distribution thereof, as you shall judge equitable and reasonable'.[22]

---

[19] *Ibid.*
[20] PRO: WO 1/319, fos 405-13.
[21] *Ibid.*
[22] PRO: CO 77/20. Instructions of George III to Draper, 21 January 1762.

Relationships between Cornish and Draper, and between the officials of the East India Company and Draper, very soon soured. On the same day that Draper had written to the War Office claiming victory at Manila, he had ordered his Aide de Camp to write to Thomas Parry aboard Cornish's flagship at Cavite, asking him to advise the Admiral that he had 'delivered up the City of Manila to Dawsonne Drake Esq., agreeable to His Majesty's instructions'. Dawson Drake was the representative of the East India Company assigned to the task of governing Manila once it had been captured. Cornish, furious at being upstaged, had Parry draft a stinging reply:

> I find myself necessitated to acquaint you that I think you have been rather premature in this act as the conditions of the capitulation are not yet complied with nor are the military stores as yet taken, an account of which by His Majesty's instructions should be deliver'd up with the government. Neither do I think the conquest sufficiently compleat as yet to resign the power from the military to the civil. I must further observe that from my rank here in His Majesty's service I ought to have been consulted before this cession had been made. This step of yours is so very extraordinary that I must represent it home to the Lords of the Admiralty.[23]

Draper's operational high-handedness was a reflection of his resentment at having to share the prize money from the expedition 'as a subordinate officer' to Cornish instead of on equal terms. Had not the concept of the operation been entirely his? And now he was to have neither the glory nor the lion's share of the booty. At the same time, Draper had managed to alienate his subordinates and was ready to admit that his 'method of dividing the prize money has given much offence and made me very unpopular with the captains and subalterns'.[24]

But neither Cornish nor Parry had cause for complaint about *their* shares in the booty. Of like mind and temperament, their unanimity translated into a personal bond of sufficient strength for Cornish, on their return home, to appoint Parry as executor of his will and, more importantly, to introduce him to his own wife's family, the Gambiers, thus establishing the foundations of a mutual family link

Cornish and Parry remained on board the *Norfolk* until her return to Portsmouth in July 1764. Both as secretary to the admiral and as purser, Parry had been a key figure in the financial management of the Manila expedition, but, in spite of personal profit, his role in the disbursement of prize money was to remain a thorn in his side for some years after the dust of war had settled. In the two years 1765 and 1766 he was taken to court by the widows of officers who had lost their lives at Manila, who claimed shares in the prize money, and who applied to Draper, Cornish and Parry for an account of the sums involved. They were to be disappointed. All three men steadfastly refused to divulge any information, and Parry maintained simply that the appropriate amounts had been

---

[23] PRO: Adm 1/162(2), fo 97.
[24] PRO: WO 1/319, fos 405-13.

paid to the estates of the dead men.[25]

As late as 1768 post-Manila litigation still rumbled on. Arthur Cuthbert had been the Purser of HMS *America*, one of the ships in Cornish's squadron. Whilst on the expedition in the east he had asked Thomas Parry, with whom he was, of course, intimately acquainted, to invest £1,000 for him, having, as he put it, 'knowledge of Parry's great correspondence and dealings in London'. This was Parry the wheeler-dealer, respected and trusted by other men of business, a *primus inter pares*. Cuthbert wanted his new-found money invested in safe government funds and securities. Parry remitted it to Daniel Twining with appropriate instructions; but by the time it had crossed half the globe and arrived in London, Twining was dead. As an executor of Twining's will, one John Pardoe of Size Lane undertook to settle the sum invested. Pardoe, a Director of the East India Company, ignored Parry's instructions and Cuthbert's wishes, and invested the money in his own name in a quantity of Capital Old South Sea Annuity.

When Parry returned to England in 1764, Cuthbert, his money lost, appointed him and James King, Parry's business associate, 'his attorneys to receive all due to him'. But Pardoe, as wily as he was devious, escaped by showing that the power of attorney had not been properly authenticated.[26]

Thomas Parry had learned that wealth did not flow from weakness and never allowed sentiment to cloud his financial judgement. George Thornton, a merchant from Blackheath, was to find to his cost just exactly how hard-nosed Parry could be.

In January 1767 Thornton put a load of his own merchandise on board the East India Company ship *Calcutta* and prepared to set sail for the Far East. He had borrowed £1,000 from Parry and King, and had given them a bond. On 9 July 1767 the ship was wrecked off the coast of India 'by carelessness of the pilot'. Thornton himself saved the crippled ship, 'steered her up the Bengal river by night, and eventually to save the cargo ran her ashore'. Two and a half years after he set out, Thornton arrived back in the Thames with the *Calcutta*. When he called on Parry and King he was stunned to receive neither sympathy for his misadventure nor any allowance for his losses. Worse still, they charged him interest on their loan at 5 per cent![27]

*   *   *   *   *   *   *

Soon after his return to England on board HMS *Norfolk*, Thomas Parry commissioned the artist Tilly Kettle to paint a fitting reminder of his recent adventure. The resultant large-scale canvas[28] surprises in both its scale and subject matter. Measuring 144 x 175 cms, the painting is a triple portrait of

---

[25] PRO: Chancery Proceedings for the period 1714 to 1758: Reynolds v Parry (1597) Dec 10, 1765, and Booker v Parry (1599) July 14, 1766.

[26] PRO: Chancery Proceedings: Cuthbert v Parry (887) Nov 25, 1768.

[27] PRO: Chancery Proceedings: Thornton v Parry (74) Apr 6, 1773.

[28] This painting, now in the possession of Mr. T.J. Fenton, was exhibited at the Society of Artists in 1768 (Exhibit No. 58). The exhibition was held in honour of the King of Denmark. Thomas Parry was a witness at the marriage of Tilly Kettle in 1777.

Admiral Cornish, Captain Kempenfelt[29]and Thomas Parry, pictured in the flag officer's cabin on board the *Norfolk*. Kempenfelt stands, appearing to invite the seated Admiral to join him on deck; between the two, Parry, quill in hand, takes down some significant text dictated by his superior. Surely this is the moment before Cornish set out from the *Norfolk* to lay his terms of capitulation before the Governor of Manila at his headquarters in the city. Those terms were written out in Parry's handwriting; this was his moment in history. But what startles is Parry's position in the painting. His face is almost at the centre of the canvas. His eyes gaze proudly out at us. His light-coloured clothing contrasts with the darker uniforms of Cornish and Kempenfelt. It is Parry, the secretary, who is centre stage in this scene. It is his new wealth which has called the painting into being: an icon of his self-esteem .

It is easy to despise Parry the source of his wealth but, of course, he had done no more – and in fact a good deal less – than many of his contemporaries. Only men of quite different values, and they were few in eighteenth-century England, would have judged Parry ill. In his *Life of Samuel Johnson,* James Boswell recalled being told by Capability Brown 'that he was once at the seat of Lord Clive, who had returned from India with great wealth; and that he showed him at the door of his bed-chamber a large chest, which he said he had once had full of gold; upon which Brown observed, "I am glad you can bear it so near your bed-chamber".' It was Captain Thomas Backhouse who revealed that when the British were about to depart from Manila, the English governor, Dawson Drake... took all the furnishings from the Spanish governor's palace and chapel and packed them in crates which he neatly marked, "Rice for Governor Drake". Backhouse informed the Spanish, but it seems that Drake left the Philippines with his private hoard of booty'.[30]

*　　*　　*　　*　　*　　*　　*

Thomas Parry remained in the Royal Navy until 1781, but never again voyaged away from England after his discharge from the *Norfolk* in July 1764. Rather, he was assigned in turn to ships held in reserve at Portsmouth, Woolwich, Deptford and Plymouth. When a ship was in reserve, warrant officers, including pursers, were borne on the Ordinary books of the dockyard and were supposed to employ themselves aboard in the maintenance of the ship. In Parry's case, this probably meant that he was able to continue as a private contractor, visiting the dockyards on business whilst at the same time maintaining his London interests.

---

[29] Richard Kempenfelt and nearly eight hundred men went down with the *Royal George* on 29 August 1782 whilst the ship, of 108 guns, was undergoing a partial careening in Portsmouth Harbour.

> Toll for the brave!
> Brave Kempenfelt is gone;
> His last sea-fight is fought,
> His work of glory done.

> (William Cowper: *Loss of the Royal George*)

[30] Letter of Captain Thomas Backhouse, 1765, in Ridington, *Calendar of Home Office Papers of the Reign of George III,* 589, No 1865; quoted in Nicholas P Cushner, *Documents Illustrating the British Conquest of Manila 1762-1763* (Royal Historical Society, 1871).

Throughout this time he owned a house in the capital, but by 1765 his bachelor quarters in Reeves Mews were becoming too small for his needs and he took a house in Norfolk Street. Thomas Parry's social life was expanding – and soon the prospect of marriage was added to his agenda.

Mary Oakes was the youngest daughter of Mathew Oakes, Victualler to the Navy in Portsmouth, with status second only to that of the Port Admiral. The Oakes were a Cheshire family, and Mary's grandfather was a Master of Foxhounds there. Although Parry would have had dealings with Oakes at an official level, it was probably Samuel Cornish who steered his protégé and trusted ex-secretary into the wealthy Victualler's drawing-room: an eligible bachelor with money of his own.

Thomas Parry and Mary Oakes were married by licence at the Parish Church of St Thomas, Portsmouth, on 2 July 1767. He was thirty-five years old and she a girl of eighteen.

In spite of his own material comfort, Thomas Parry cannot have been other than impressed by the careers and connections of his new in-laws. One of Mary's brothers, Thomas, became a nabob in the East India Company and was appointed Senior Civil Member of the Council at Madras and President of the Board of Trade there. Another brother, George, an officer in the Royal Navy, progressed rapidly from the rank of Lieutenant on board HMS *Prince George* to Captain of HM Sloop *The Savage*, and served with HRH Prince William, afterwards William IV, who also stood godfather to George's son, William. Mary's eldest brother, Richard, rose in the diplomatic service to become Chargé d'affaires at St Petersburg in 1776. He so impressed Catherine the Great that she presented him with a valuable ring, seen on his finger in the portrait of him painted by G Mason Chamberlain RA. Richard was appointed Under Secretary of State for the Northern Department in 1778, but died unmarried in April 1779 in his thirtieth year.

But Richard Oakes was more than a talented and successful career civil servant. He was gifted as poet, musician and artist; enthusiasms which he shared with his sisters and which Mary Oakes passed on to her children. In the age of Haydn and Mozart, of Sheridan and Johnson, of Gainsborough and Stubbs, a love of the fine arts was about to be introduced to the Parry family.

In the twelve years following her marriage, Mary bore nine children, all of whom except the first, Thomas Samuel (b 1768), were baptised in London, where, by 1769, Thomas Parry's splendid new house had been built in Berners Street: an appendix to Oxford Street, perched on the rim of a developing West End; a quiet residential road leading via leafy orchards and fields to Green Lane and the north.

At a time when marriage was entered into at least as much for gain as for love, Mathew Oakes would have provided a handsome dowry for his daughter; a substantial contribution towards the construction, decoration and furnishing of 52 Berners Street. Mary's part in the bargain, by the conventions of the eighteenth century, will have been to obey her husband and provide him with heirs; to make polite conversation; to order the household; to sew a fine seam;

and to grow ever more weary and prematurely aged from repeated child-bearing.

By 1779 Thomas, in his forty-eighth year, could look with satisfaction on the success of his life thus far; on his growing family; and on an association with the Royal Navy of more than twenty years. Although comfortably off he had not yet thought to resign his purser's warrant. And yet by 1781 he was able to quit the Navy; to take a large country house, at Banstead in Surrey; and to apply to become a Director of the East India Company, the qualification for which was possession of £2,000 of India Stock, the equivalent of some £250,000 today; this at a time when a naval officer could expect to earn £80 per annum, a prosperous farmer £150, and a master manufacturer £200.

Mathew Oakes died on 6 November 1779 leaving his wife £100 a year, and £300 to be divided among his surviving children: Thomas, Lucy, George, Fanny, Betsy, Ann and Mary. Oakes also left £10 to each of Thomas Parry's children; but larger by far were the bequests which he made to his five daughters: each was to receive £1,000. Oakes expected his sons to make their own fortunes.

On the passing of Mathew Oakes, Thomas Parry became the patriarch of the family and the principle executor of his father-in-law's will. It was not Parry's style to sit down with his juniors to discuss money matters; he knew best. But before 1779 was out Thomas and George Oakes, and their spinster sisters, Fanny, Betsy and Lucy, brought a bill in Chancery against Parry and his fellow executors, their mother, and their two married sisters, Ann Sowden and Mary Parry and their children, seeking to break Parry's silence on the true extent of their late father's estate. Where, they wanted to know, had the rest of the money gone? Not for the first time, Parry found that 'the sinews of war is money'. Guardians were appointed to represent Ann Sowden's infant son, Benjamin, and the Parry children in court; but then the slow wheels of legal procedure were overtaken by a quite extraordinary succession of deaths within the family.

Richard Oakes, as we have seen, had already died a few month's before the death of his father. Ann Sowden, Mathew Oakes's sixth child and the widow of the Reverend Benjamin Choyce Sowden, died on 29 May 1780. Her mother, Mary Oakes, soon followed, dying intestate on 6 October 1780. Exactly two months earlier Mary Parry had given birth to her ninth child, a girl, and named her Ann in memory of her sister. All of the other Parry children had been brought to baptism within a few weeks of their birth; not so Ann. This had been one pregnancy too many for Mary and one from which she did not recover. Mary Parry died on 13 March 1781.

In a codicil to his will, Mathew Oakes had, without explanation, changed the condition under which just one of his daughters should receive her legacy of £1,000: 'on further consideration it was his will that instead of being paid said sum she was to receive no part thereof till six months after the death of her mother'.[31] That daughter was Mary Parry. No such condition was imposed on the legacies of Oakes's other daughters. Now, not only had that condition been fulfilled, leaving the money set aside for Mary Oakes's pension within Thomas Parry's control, but the beneficiary of one of the major bequests, Parry's own wife, was also dead, her inheritance passing into his hands too.

---

[31] PRO: Chancery Proceedings: Oakes v Parry (1670) May 20, 1782.

On 16 May 1781 Ann Parry, a motherless infant, was baptised at St Marylebone, and on the very next day Thomas Parry obtained an order from the Court of Chancery to pay £2,351 into the bank to be invested in a trust for the infant Benjamin Sowden. It was the second such investment. In December 1780 Parry 'did obtain an order... to pay the sum of £3,150, part of the testator's [Mathew Oakes's] personal estate received by him into the bank... to the credit of the said cause Sowden... and that the same... should be laid out in the purchase of bank three per cent annuities'.[32]

Young Benjamin Sowden gained enormously from Parry's handling of Mathew Oakes's estate, and the amounts invested on his behalf give a clue to what the total value of that estate, controlled by Parry, must have been. Presumably the Oakes heirs were unable to force Parry to reveal his hand until after the proceedings were heard in the Court of Chancery on 20 May 1782. After that there seems to have been no further argument within the family, nor does any record survive of Parry's own personal gain; but these were not the only major money matters which Parry was handling in 1782.

On his return from the Manila expedition, Sir Samuel Cornish had used his prize-money to purchase an estate at Sharnbrook in Bedfordshire from Sir Philip Butler, but he was allowed little time in which to enjoy it. Cornish died, a childless widower, in November 1770, leaving his entire estate in trust to Thomas Parry and James King, the executors of his will, for the benefit of his mother-in-law, Mary Gambier, and after her decease to his nephew Captain Samuel Pitchford RN on condition that Pitchford take the name and arms of Cornish.[33] It seems that Parry and King invested a substantial part of Cornish's money in India. In June 1782 they sought the authority of the Court of Directors of the East India Company to remit one hundred and five thousand rupees from Bombay 'on account of the Estate of the deceased [Cornish].[34]

Less than a year later Parry put down the investment required and took his place as one of the twenty-four Directors of the Honourable East India Company, soon rising to the coveted 'three star' status: a Director holding at least £150,000 of Stock in the Company!

---

[32] *Ibid.*

[33] PRO: PCC Wills: Prob 11/961. Pitchford complied with his uncle's condition, and rose in the Navy to become Admiral Samuel Cornish. He also married a Gambier, Mary, a daughter of John Gambier (1723-82), the second Governor of the Bahamas.

[34] British Library India Office Records: B/98 East India Company Minutes, June 6, 1782.

II

The Company

The arrival of Thomas Parry at East India House in 1783 coincided exactly with the biggest shake-up in the affairs of the Company which its Directors had ever known. Over the course of nearly thirty years 'the Grandest Society of Merchants in the Universe' had, by degrees, transformed itself from a largely commercial concern into a great territorial power, and with that power had come corruption and division. British control of the American colonies had finally crumbled in November 1781 with the surrender at Yorktown of Lord Cornwallis and his army, 'a respectable specimen of mediocrity who will be remembered more for his diligence in devising fiscal reforms than for his ability to wage successful wars'.[1] The loss of influence to the west prompted the coalition government of Fox and North to focus attention on India and on the malaise which was infecting the East India Company, both in the subcontinent itself and in the Company's splendid London offices in Leadenhall Street.

In November 1783 Fox introduced a bill to reorganise and reform the government and administration in India by establishing seven Commissioners named by Parliament to control the Company's affairs. The resultant turmoil set a cat among the Leadenhall Street pigeons; but although passed by the Commons, the personal intervention of George III ensured that the bill was thrown out by the Lords. Fox was finished. The twenty-four-year-old William Pitt became Prime Minister, leading a reinvigorated Tory party which would keep the Whigs out of office for over half a century.

The necessary qualification for admission to the Direction of the East India Company, the possession of a fortune, was by no means an automatic passport to power in Leadenhall Street. Vacancies occurred only on the death or disqualification of a Director, and then competition was exceedingly fierce. Responsibility for electing the twenty-four Directors rested with more than two thousand Proprietors: owners of East India Company capital stock. To obtain sufficient votes involved aspiring candidates in a difficult and possibly costly canvass of Proprietors; but in addition, it was absolutely essential to gain the

---

[1] Thomas Babington Macauley, *The History of England in the Eighteenth Century* (Folio Society Edition, 1988), pp 175/6.

support of one of the great East India Company interests, of which the major two were the Indian interest and the Company, or City and Shipping, interest. The Indian interest was further sub-divided into groups, principally the Arcot interest, made up of the creditors and agents of the Nawab of the Carnatic, and the Hastings interest, which included the personal friends and supporters of Warren Hastings, the Governor General[2], of which Thomas Parry was one:

> Clive had become an empire builder by accident. Hastings was an empire builder by design. His policy was to build up a strong British India, to extend its territories, when opportunity arose, and to knit to this paramount power independent Indian princes by offering them military protection against their enemies.[3]

Hastings's policy of Imperial expansion was immensely expensive and, in the view of the Whigs, morally indefensible. The East India Company had been established for commerce, not dominion, and Hastings's enemies were quick to condemn not only the ends of his ambition but also the severity of his means. Parry, on the other hand, perceived Hastings's policy as one of selfless devotion to essential British and Company interests, and entered into a supportive correspondence with his idol:

London, 25 October 1784

Dear Sir,

I embrace the opportunity by the "Fox" packet to acknowledge the honour of your letter of 6th November last by the "Narbuddah" and duplicate by the "Worcester". Your expressions of thanks for my support I receive with additional pleasure from a conviction of their sincerity, and that it has been justified by the general satisfaction your continuance under the late Act of Parliament of the high office you have so long filled with honour to yourself and advantage to the Nation has offered. On this important event accept, Sir, my sincere congratulations.

I most earnestly hope and trust that by the very honourable support you have received and the happy consequences to be derived from the powers vested in you, you will be induced to continue in the administration of the Government of India till the great and essential work of Reform and Economy is carried into effect.

In the conduct of such vast political and commercial concerns – under the opposition which has been encouraged against your Administration – the World has beheld with admiration your Magnanimity, Perseverance and the great resources of your mind. But, Sir, venerating your character as I sincerely do, and admiring the wonderful extent of your abilities and the disinterested zeal you have evinced in support of the rights and interests of the Company; and zealously as I have given you my support as a Proprietor and Director, permit me to offer it to you as my opinion that your attention to promote the interests of Others has too frequently exposed you to the attacks of your political Enemies; and it is to be lamented that Persons who have derived their consequence and fortunes from your Patronage and support, regardless of their own Characters and the honour of their Patron have defeated on many occasions his anxious endeavour to prevent Acts disreputable to his Government.

---

[2] See C H Philips, *The East India Company 1784-1834* (Manchester, 1961), p 24.
[3] J H Plum, *England in the Eighteenth Century* (Pelican, 1986), p 175.

Under the present support and confidence you have the satisfaction to possess, I trust your Administration will produce Consequences highly beneficial to the Nation and honourable to yourself.

May your health enable you to fulfil every great and good purpose to the end of your Government, and that you may be restored to your Family and Friends in this Country is the very sincere wish of Dear Sir,

Your most obedient humble servant,

Thomas Parry[4]

Hastings resigned the Governor Generalship in 1785, was succeeded by Cornwallis, and returned home to face impeachment. His trial began in Westminster Hall on 13 February 1788 and continued for seven wearisome years of 'examinations and cross-examinations... statements of account... [and] papers filled with words unintelligible to English ears, with lacs and crores, zemindars and aumils, sunnuds and perwannahs, jaghires and nuzzurs'.[5] In 1795 Hastings's honour was cleared and he was acquitted on all the charges brought against him; but, a ruined man, the Court of Directors of the East India Company came to his aid and supported him financially to the end of his days.

Fox's proposals for India had incensed Parry and his fellow Company Directors, but Pitt recognised the necessity to bring India under the political and strategic control of the British Government. The stated aim of his India Act of 1784, referred to by Parry in his letter to Hastings as 'the late Act of Parliament', was 'to give to the Crown the power of guiding politics in India, with as little means of corrupt influence as possible'; but, unlike Fox, Pitt saw that some compromise with the Company was essential if new measures were to succeed. His solution was to leave the patronage of British India, the appointment of writers (civil servants) for the administration of the Company's territories, and of cadets and assistant surgeons for the Company's armies, in the hands of the Directors.

Thomas Parry did not hesitate to use his patronage to secure positions in the Company for his family. His eldest son, Thomas Samuel, sent out to the China Civil Service, had died unmarried in 1794 at the age of 26. None the less, Thomas bundled off his other sons, George, Richard, William and Henry, to serve the Company in the east.

Six of the twenty-four Directors of the East India Company were chosen each year to replace six retiring Directors, the latter being ineligible for re-election until the following April. Each Director therefore remained in office for four years and then 'went out by rotation' for a year in the sure and certain knowledge that he would be re-elected when the year was up. Thomas Parry was out by rotation in 1797, the year in which Pitt had offered Lord Mornington the Governorship of Madras with the reversion of the Governor Generalship. Parry's brother-in-law, Thomas Oakes, was, at that time, serving at Fort St George, Madras, as Senior Member of the Board of Revenue. With a radical

---

[4] GPM pp 35/6.
[5] Macauley, *op cit*, p 191.

overhaul of the Madras administration imminent, Parry was anxious to see Oakes appointed to a seat on the ruling Council there. Advancement for his brother-in-law could, after all, be only beneficial to Parry's own sons in India. So, although unable to exercise persuasion personally at Leadenhall Street, he sent a specially printed letter to each member of the Court of Directors:

> Gentlemen,
>
> Your late Chairman [David Scott], sometime since, gave notice of an intended arrangement for India, and a few days previous to his quitting the Chair, proposed for your consideration, the appointment of Lord Mornington, as President and Governor of Fort St. George, to succeed to the Government General of Bengal on the coming away of Marquis Cornwallis.
>
> In forming such extensive arrangements, I have been naturally led to conclude, other appointments, of a subordinate nature, may come under your consideration, and am therefore impelled to bring to your recollection, the long and faithful services of my relation, Mr. Thomas Oakes, of your Fort St. George Establishment. To the majority of your Honourable Court, it would be an intrusion on your valuable time, to recapitulate his claims of service; but being of opinion, they have not fallen under the notice of the junior Members, I have presumed to annex to this address, extracts from the records of the Company, as taken by order of your Honourable Court. From these extracts it will appear, that since his first appointment to the service, in the year 1770, he has filled several of the most important stations, with advantage to the Company and honour to himself.
>
> Mr. Oakes is anxiously ambitious of holding a station of responsibility in the service of the Company (an ambition, I trust, you will applaud) and should your Honourable Court be pleased to confer on him such a testimony of your approbation of his past services, as a succession to a seat in your Council at Madras, upon any vacancy that may happen, permit me to assure your Honourable Court, as my solemn belief, that Mr. Oakes will discharge the important trust, with honour, integrity, and ability,
>
> I am, with every sentiment of respect,
> GENTLEMEN
> Your most faithful and obedient humble servant
> THOMAS PARRY[6]

Berners Street,
April 19th, 1797

Oakes had certainly proved himself to be a bright star in the Fort St George firmament. He had come to the notice of the Court of Directors in London in 1781 when, as Military Secretary at Madras, he had been sent home with important despatches by the Governor, Lord Macartney. Oakes had embarked on board the *Admiral Hughes* packet with his bundle of secret papers; but the ship was captured by the French and Oakes was taken to Brest as a prisoner. He did not arrive back in England until May 1782, still clutching the precious papers, and was rewarded for his services and determination by the grant of a coat of arms for use by himself, his successors and the descendants of his father, Mathew Oakes.

---

[6] British Library India Office Records: 0/6/3.

On returning to India, Oakes continued to impress his seniors, and was highly commended for his zeal and ability by the Governor and Council in 1792; but none of this, nor Thomas Parry's fawning letter to the Court of Directors, brought Oakes a seat on the Council at Fort St George in 1797.

In the following year Thomas Parry's second son, George (b 1772), a Deputy Secretary in the Military, Political and Secret Department of the Madras Civil Service, returned to England a sick man after serving for eight years in the sub-continent. Barely any better after more than two years leave at home, George returned in 1801 to India, where, before the year was out, he died in Calcutta. George's eldest sister, Harriot (b 1769), a beauty whose portrait was painted by both George Romney and William Beechey, was soon to follow. Harriot had married Edward Simeon of the Isle of Wight, and it was there that she too died in 1801.

The loss of three children in seven years might be thought sufficient to have softened Thomas Parry's obdurate insistence on forcing his sons to serve in the east. Surely when Richard Parry (b 1776) was also invalided home in 1803 his father would demand that he stay in England? Richard had been in Bengal since leaving school and, in spite of a family conviction that he was the most talented of the Parry brothers, had risen no further than a Sub-Treasurer's post in the Board of Trade. In a letter sent in 1805 to his recently-married sister Lucy (b 1773), William Parry, a supercargo at the East India Company's factory in Canton, writes with refreshing frankness about his brother's predicament:

Should my father force him [Richard] back again to India against his will, how much will he have to answer for; and if he does after what he has known him to have suffered from the climate, it will be really cruel.

Mrs. Metcalfe is a great admirer of him, and frequently talks of and makes inquiries after him. She actually declares that when he waited on Sir Henry Russell to take leave, everybody was frightened at his appearance – so emaciated a figure did he present; and so desperate did I conceive to be his case, that I had nearly made up my mind to lose him on the Passage. But thanks to God my fears have been dispelled and he is still spared to us!! How my father can reconcile himself to another separation from such a comforter, from such an ornament, I am at a loss to conceive; and although I am one of the last men in the world to encourage disobedience, or recommend a Child to run counter to the wishes of his parents, I cannot help declaring that were I in Richard's situation and had determined that my Constitution was not equal to the Climate, the accession to the Governor General-ship should not wrest me from home. It is a circumstance doubtless of deep regret that the fair hopes my Father had fondly and reasonably entertained of seeing our Brother rise to the honourable and distinguished Situation of a Seat in Council, to which his eminent talents and reputation gave him the fairest claim, should be thus suddenly arrested; but it would I conceive be the height of weakness, not to say wickedness, longer to indulge in this hope which the will of Providence appears obviously to oppose, and which is not to be attained but at the price of our beloved Brother's happiness. And rather than make a sacrifice of this blessing to the ambitious views of another man, I would engage in any occupation in my Native Country which presented a prospect of yielding me a subsistence, even at the risque of such a determination causing a breach in the affection of my parent.

My father's duty at present is to rest satisfied and be happy in reflecting that so long as the health of our dear Brother enabled him to exist, those brilliant talents and activity of mind wherewith he has been blessedly gifted by nature (and which he has wisely improved by application and study) were uniformly employed to his own honour and in promoting the Interests of his Employers, whereby he rendered himself adored by the Natives of India, admired and looked up to by the Circle of his choice and valuable acquaintance, and distinguished by the favor and liberality of the Governor General.[7]

Predictably, Thomas Parry would not 'rest satisfied' and forced his son Richard back to India; but at least one of his children defiantly refused to bend to his tyranny. Thomas's youngest daughter, Ann, escaped by eloping with her sweetheart, Charles Woodcock, from the Surrey home of her sister Mary (b 1775) and brother-in-law, Daniel Warrington; married against her father's wish and without his consent; and set off for India with Woodcock, a writer with the Madras Civil Service. Ann seems to have been helped in this act of daring by understanding friends, Miss Reynolds and her family, mentioned gratefully in another letter dated 24 February 1806 from William Parry to his sister Lucy:

> I remain in a state of anxious fear lest [my father] should have allowed her [Ann] to leave England without a reconciliation. Should it have happened, I hope my interference with him will have the influence I am so desirous it should meet with. I have written her, and hope she will find on her arrival at Madras the various articles I have forwarded to her which I thought might be acceptable in forming her Establishment. The friendship she experienced from the Reynolds has induced me to write to Miss R. and beg her acceptance of an Ivory Fan, and her family a supply of Tea.[8]

But William was in a weak position to interfere. His high earnings in China were paid directly to his father by the Company; and Thomas gave his son only a small allowance with which to maintain himself. William plunged into debt, did not dare to ask his father for help, and was obliged to turn to friends who, he wrote to Lucy, 'came forward not only with their disinterested advice but with pecuniary aid, and through whose means my affairs, which at one time wore the most desperate and hopeless aspect, have gradually improved. I [now] have every prospect of being nearly on a footing with those who have never yet felt the bitter pangs which have long been preying on my constitution, and totally deprived me of health and peace of mind'.

In February 1806 William had only just learned of Lucy's marriage to Major General Daniel Burr and of her 'long and painful confinement' in the previous year. Writing with love and congratulation he confided in Lucy that:

> To yourself I have sent two beautiful oil paintings of the Emperor and Empress' palace, which have been greatly admired; two boxes of fine powdered Sugar Candy which I thought you would like for Coffee; a box containing 13 curious Tea-pots, two of which are real Japan, an old Commission of your friend Lady Arden… The paintings cost me 80 dollars, but for God's sake say not a word to my Father.[9]

---

[7] Highnam archive.
[8] *Ibid.*
[9] *Ibid.*

Lucy received neither the letter nor the gifts. She died at Flushing in Cornwall on 17 November 1805, requesting that her sister Mary take care of her baby daughter.

The nation was rejoicing in Nelson's victory at the Battle of Trafalgar; Britain had gained undisputed control of the seas; and Richard Parry reluctantly awaited his passage to India.

*   *   *   *   *   *   *

There are several contemporary accounts of a journey to the subcontinent in an East Indiaman late in the eighteenth century, one being by Thomas Twining, a writer who sailed from Deal, the usual port of embarkation for passengers, on 26 April 1792, the same year as Richard Parry's first voyage. Twining landed at Madras on 1 August – a speedy passage in those days. On boarding the East Indiaman, he was conducted to a cabin down a ladder 'to the lower or gun deck, not far from the stern'. The porthole was shut because a heavy sea was running, he could hardly see across the cabin, nor could he stand without grabbing hold of some fixture, and the stench of the close suffocating air was terrible. There were seven bunks in the cabin, which was six feet wide; and on the journey to India 'through the hot climate of the tropics and the rough seas of the Cape of Good Hope, when, the port and scuttle being closed for many successive days and nights, there was no air nor ray of light'. Of seven youths who shared the cabin, Twining was the only one who saw England again.[10]

Fares to India were £70 to £250 according to the rank of the passenger and the accommodation provided. By the time of his return in 1806 to take up his appointment as Secretary to the Military Board in Bengal, Richard Parry could afford and expect to be provided with a private cabin, as could his sister Ann Woodcock and her husband, who had sailed some months before him.

The Woodcocks arrived in Madras at a wretched time for the local population. The years 1806 and 1807 were blighted by the worst famine and depression ever known in the region; many Indians were starving but, as Eliza Foy noted on her arrival in Madras in 1780, first impressions were entirely of 'Asiatic splendour, combined with European taste exhibited around you on every side, under the forms of flowing drapery, stately palanquins, elegant carriages, innumerable servants, and all the pomp and circumstance of luxurious ease, and unbounded wealth'.[11]

Unlike at Fort William, Calcutta, the seat of the Governor General, there was no European town in Madras and only a few houses in Fort St George. British settlers resided entirely in garden houses on the Choultry plain; travelling to the Fort in the morning for business and returning home to rest in the afternoon. But in spite of the stifling heat, powdered hair, tail coat, high collar and cravat, knee breeches, silk stockings and buckled shoes remained the

---

[10] G H Hodgson, *Thomas Parry: Free Merchant, Madras 1768-1824*.
[11] Eliza Foy, *Original letters from India* (Calcutta, 1817), p 221.

prevailing fashion with Europeans. Perukes were still worn by the clergy and army officers; and even as late as 1818, Thomas Parry (no relation), a free merchant of Madras, was importing 'powder, lavender water, pomatum and silk stockings'.[12] Airless nights were unrelieved by the blessing of electric fans; and with sleep came squadrons of hungry mosquitoes.

One bright consolation for Ann Woodcock must have been the welcoming presence in Madras of her uncle, Thomas Oakes. Having no memory of her mother, the close affection of Oakes and of his unmarried sisters, Fanny and Betsy, was especially valued by Ann and her brothers and sisters; but Ann arrived in Madras at a troubled time for her uncle.

For almost two years Oakes had been under a cloud, suspected by the Governor, Lord William Bentinck, of stirring up trouble at Fort St George because of his opposition to the Governor's dismissal of George Garrow, the Collector of the Southern Division of Arcot. In a minute sent to Leadenhall Street in 1804, Bentinck reported that:

> It is necessary to inform the Court of Directors that upon the occasion of Mr. Garrow's removal, a clamour against the justice of the measure prevails in the settlement. It is with reluctance that I feel myself obliged to state, that the example of the first Member of the Board of Revenue [Oakes] in some measure gave countenance to this conduct.[13]

On 6 November 1805 the Court of Directors censured Oakes:

> We feel ourselves called upon to express our concern that a spirit of insubordination should have manifested itself among our Servants by clamour against the proceeding of Government in relation to this Affair; and especially that such a spirit should be countenanced by the example of a Gentleman whose merits we have found reason to distinguish with encomiums. We must here declare our disapprobation of the conduct of any of our Servants, whatever their rank or situation may be, who shall betray such a disposition as is complained of in the present case.[14]

Seething inwardly at what he knew to have been injustices against both Garrow and himself, Oakes determined to remain silent before his noble accuser and to bide his time until truth would out: a wise policy. By April 1806 he was shown to be vindicated and rewarded with the long-awaited seat on the Council of Fort St George which his brother-in-law, Thomas Parry, had tried unsuccessfully to fix almost a decade earlier. Could it be coincidence that advancement for Parry's son Richard followed soon afterwards?

Richard Parry and his youngest brother, Henry (b 1779), were both sent out to the Bengal Civil Service by their father at the age of 16. From 1806 boys of that age nominated by the Directors of the East India Company for writerships overseas were educated at the East India College, Haileybury, where Thomas Malthus was but one member of a distinguished academic faculty. Haileybury was noted for the diversity of its syllabus, which included Latin and

---

[12] G H Hodgson, *op cit*, p 26.
[13] British Library India Office Records: 0/6/3.
[14] *Ibid.*

Greek, political economy, natural philosophy, history and some elements of Indian languages; but nothing of the sort was available to would-be writers in the eighteenth century. Richard and Henry were prepared for their careers at a school run by Thomas Thorne at the Manor House, Chiswick, where the emphasis was on writing, accounts and book-keeping. Richard qualified on Boxing Day 1791 but, inheritor as he was of his mother's artistic temperament and possessed of a fine mind, Thomas Thorne's commercial precepts were hardly likely to satisfy his longing for knowledge. Richard was acutely aware of the shortcomings of his education and determined to make good its deficiencies by his own efforts. He improved himself, as his brother William had put it, 'by application and study' over many years. Henry, on the other hand, seems neither to have craved intellectual enrichment nor to have retained the approval of his authoritarian father.

In his inimitable fashion, Thomas Parry had managed to alienate his youngest son. In one of his letters to his sister Lucy, William Parry had expressed a fervent wish that their brother Richard, whilst in England in 1805, might be able to bring about a reconciliation between Henry and his father, but this seems not to have happened. Henry left Thomas Thorne's school in 1794, three years later than his brother Richard, went out to India, and remained there until 1819, three years after Thomas Parry's death, and thereafter remained surprisingly reluctant to discuss his father, the mystery of whose origins he was unable or unwilling to clarify. Henry lived for thirty-seven years after his retirement from the Bengal Civil Service in 1823, settled at Leamington Spa in Warwickshire and, having remained a bachelor for most of his life, in his old age married the widow of a Colonel G G Denniss.

On his return to Bengal in 1807 Richard Parry found himself in the midst of a hornet's nest of friction between the civil and military staffs. Since 1800 the Department of the Secretary to the Government in Bengal had been divided into four branches: Judicial and Revenue; Secret, Political and Foreign; Military; and Public. Each department was headed by a Sub Secretary, and the Secret, Political and Foreign Department had been put under the control of a Lieutenant Colonel Kirkpatrick, who had previously held the post of Military Secretary, the latter appointment having been conferred on a Lieutenant Hook.

The Court of Directors in London had approved the overall arrangements but were unhappy about the introduction of military personnel into civil posts and directed that Lieutenant Hook's appointment be reconsidered; but the Governor defiantly failed to obey their orders, believing a military officer to be far and away the most appropriate choice for the post, and promptly introduced a second military officer into the Department as Deputy Military Secretary. The Directors were not amused:

> The Court forthwith ordered his removal, and Sir George Barlow having succeeded to the Government, the Court's orders were, in August 1805, carried into effect by him, by the removal of Captain Hook, and appointment of Mr. Richardson, who was succeeded by Mr. Richard Parry in 1807.[15]

---

[15] *Ibid*, 0/6/18(623).

Parry took up his appointment on 12 March 1807 at an annual salary of 39,000 Rupees, but, knowing nothing of military matters, must have had a miserable time in his dealings with professional soldiers.

Almost all of Parry's previous experience in Bengal had been with the Board of Trade, but his heart was never in tune with the commercial world. Richard Parry was a romantic who longed to be a maker of beauty, to express himself in verse, to share his love of music and art with others, but who, caged by his father in a world of the pocket, threw up a barricade of apparent coldness and silent reserve to defend himself from the materialism with which he was surrounded. As one who knew him wrote:

> He had a refined and cultivated mind. His classical acquirements and tastes formed a bond of union between him and the accomplished Marquis Wellesley [the Governor General of India], but whatever [his] inner man held was all shut up by the closest reserve and reticence, and nothing but reciprocity of mind and sentiment called it forth. He lived a recluse life; his Indian habits and interests chiefly engaged him. He seemed to be less acted upon by external forms of attractiveness than anyone I ever knew. All around him – house, garden, furniture, equipages, were maintained in the greatest simplicity and baldness… His manner was cold, almost repulsive.[16]

Little of Richard Parry's poetry survives, and that which does was copied by Ernest Gambier-Parry from the originals, now lost, at the beginning of the present century. None of his translations from Latin, Greek, Italian and French have been preserved, nor either of his long fables, *The Ram, the Hare, the Cat and the Dog* and *The Soldier and the Poet*. The longest fragment which we have is taken from a poem which, Ernest tells us, was of over two hundred lines, headed 'Addressed to my sister Lucy (Mrs. Burr)' and dated June 25 1802, that is, two years before her marriage; 'Mrs. Burr' being added later. The poem, written in Bengal, begins:

> Here 'mid the ardour of Sol's fiercest ray,
> Whose fires shoot forth intolerable day

After lamenting the trials of the Indian climate, a home-sick Parry turns his thoughts to the sea and cliffs of England, and to the Surrey countryside around his father's house at Banstead:

> Bright-bearing, they shall chase the oppressive gloom,
> Again the cheering rays of home illume,
> Shall strew with blooming flowers the painful road,
> And smiling point to Banstead's dear abode.
>
>   *   *   *   *
>
> Methought in Summer's placid air we strayed,
> Beneath the hazel's close embowering shade,
> Dark'ning the favourite lane which winding leads

---

[16] Letter from Frederick Gambier to Thomas Gambier Parry (24 May 1867), transcribed in GPM pp 54/5.

To Lambert's[17] rural seat and flowery meads.
Ne'er, Lucy, with more rapt'rous joy I hung
On the dear accents of thy honied tongue;
Nor e'er by wit refin'd thy pow'rful sense
Flow'd in such streams of winning eloquence.
E'en Nature seemed to lend her magic power,
T'exalt the pleasure of th'exstatic hour.
The Purple Clouds, the Downs' luxuriant green,
The solemn stillness of the circling scene,
(Broke by the tinkle of the distant fold)
The wood's high foliage tipp'd with trembling gold.
Down my flush'd Cheek the tear of rapture stole,
And pleasure's purest transports filled my Soul.

Richard Parry's chosen verse-form for the majority of his poems, the heroic couplet, was introduced into English poetry by Chaucer, used almost invariably by Alexander Pope, and was the predominant measure from the age of Dryden to that of Johnson; but Johnson was no admirer of the poet whose idiom inspired these lines of Parry's: Thomas Gray. Johnson thought Gray's verse 'licentious', citing as example the use of 'honied' as an adjective formed from the noun 'honey'; but Gray – and Parry – were in good company. Both Shakespeare and Milton had used it. Parry was undoubtedly familiar with Gray's great *Odes*, and in 'solemn stillness' he is, of course, quoting directly from the *Elegy written in a Country Churchyard*.

Gray's *Elegy* ends in an epitaph for 'A youth to fortune and to fame unknown'; and it was in a series of epitaphs – *On a coachman; On a painter; On a bricklayer*, etc. – that Richard Parry preserved another quality of which few were aware: his sense of humour, as here in *On an indolent man*:

Here lies a man (if we may call
Him man who never mov'd at all).
*   *   *   *
If all his joys were placed in rest
He sure is now supremely blest
Yet ah! Once more he'll suffer pain
Compell'd to move and rise again.
Heav'n's awful trump alas shall blow,
And rouse him an he will or no.

Parry's is not great poetry certainly, but neither is it the unfeeling utterance of a cold recluse blind to natural beauty. Too little remains for a fair assessment to be made of his verse; but, in any case, Richard Parry's most valuable artistic legacy was the result not of his own authorship but of his enlightened patronage.

Barely had he settled into his office at Fort William, Calcutta, before the promotion at last came through for which he had waited so long and, for his father's sake, had suffered so much. Richard Parry's appointment as Resident at Fort Marlborough, Bencoolen, carried both rank and prestige – his status was the

---

[17] Thomas Parry rented his house at Banstead from the Lamberts, who lived nearby.

equivalent to that of a governor – but the territory over which he was to exercise authority was hardly an extensive dominion. The small British settlement of Bencoolen (now Bangkahula) was little more than a clearing in the dense, malaria-infested, equatorial vegetation of the west coast of Sumatra; and its importance rested on a single commodity – pepper!

Before setting out on the two-thousand-mile voyage from Calcutta to Bencoolen, Parry recruited an Indian artist, Manu Lal, to accompany him on his travels. Manu Lal was to be to Richard Parry the equivalent of a camera to a modern tourist: his means of making a permanent record of the vast range of colourful and rare flora and fauna to be found in the immense oak and teak forests of Sumatra. And the exquisite results which Manu Lal achieved in more than twelve dozen drawings in water-colour may still be seen in the collections of Natural History Drawings at the British Library India Office and at the Royal Botanic Gardens, Kew.[18] They are amongst the best examples of the genre termed 'Company Painting' by historians of Indian art: the work of Indian artists who adapted their style to the taste of East India Company servants in order to satisfy their fascination with the picturesque and the exotic. Company Painting remains a neglected and little known branch of art which well deserves wider study.

Parry arrived in Sumatra on 22 December 1807 and remained for two and a half years of crucible heat and energy-sapping humidity. The opportunities to escape from Fort Marlborough to the interior or to outlying islands with Manu Lal may not have been frequent, but probably helped Parry to survive the intellectual stagnation and physical discomfort of so remote an outpost.

A distinguished successor of Parry's, Stamford Raffles, wrote to William Marsden from Bencoolen in 1818:

> This is, without exception, the most wretched place I ever beheld. I cannot convey to you an adequate idea of the state of ruin and dilapidation which surrounds me. What with natural impediments, bad government, and the awful visitations of Providence which we have recently experienced, in repeated earthquakes, we have scarcely a dwelling in which to lay our heads, or wherewithal to satisfy the cravings of nature.
>
> The roads are impassable; the highways in the Town overrun with rank grass; the Government-house a den of ravenous dogs and polecats. The natives say that Bencoolen is now a *tàna mati* (dead land). In truth, I could never have conceived anything half so bad.[19]

The few letters received by Parry from the Court of Directors in London were hardly calculated to stimulate an otherwise dreary existence. There is not much to be said about the shipping of pepper which would inspire a creative mind!

---

[18] British Library India Office, reference: Add Or/490 'An inhabitant of the Poggy Islands'; NHD2 Nos 286-99, 'Fourteen drawings in water colour depicting 12 birds, 1 mammal and 1 fish from Sumatra; bound in volume measuring 21 by 14 inches. Nos. 288, 290-4 and 297 are inscribed in Urdu, "The painter of this picture is Manu Lal, artist, an inhabitant of Azimabad (Patna City)". The paper is watermarked 1806 and was probably brought from England by Parry on the expiry of his leave'.
[19] Lady Sophia Raffles, *Memorials of the Life of Sir Stamford Raffles* (Murray, 1830), p 293.

It appearing that a considerable quantity of Pepper Dust is always in the Pepper shipped from your Residency, being of an average from 6 to 10 tons per Ship, while the quantity of Dust in the Bombay Pepper is very trivial. The Court have resolved in consequence, to transmit you 20 Sieves and 2 Screens via *Cuffnells* [a ship] for the purpose of Sifting the Dust from the Pepper whereby it may be shipped in a clean condition.[20]

Parry had not fully recovered his health before being forced back to the east by his father, and by 1810 was back in Bengal, too ill to work and 'out of employ'. In January 1811 he was given the job of Secretary to the Salt and Opium Department of the Board of Trade, but was unable to continue for long. He returned home in 1812, rented a house in Cadogan Place, and presented his collection of Manu Lal's work to the East India Company's library:

The Company's first Day Book records the gift, 'June 26th, 1812. Received from the Baggage Warehouse, per *Union*, 202 Drawings of Plants. Mr. Richard Parry. Plants and Animals from Sumatra.' On 2 December 1812, 52 duplicates were returned to him and 150 drawings retained. 125 paintings of plants were transferred to Kew in 1869.[21]

Now, in spite of deteriorating health, Richard Parry took delight in very real happiness. Through his elderly father's long and intimate relationship with the Gambiers, Richard had met Mary, the eldest daughter of Samuel Gambier of Shenley Hall, Hertfordshire, First Commissioner of the Royal Navy (and niece of James Lord Gambier, Admiral of the Fleet, who, as the heroic captain of HMS *Defence*, one of a squadron of ships commanded by Earl Howe, had secured a famous victory against the French in the Bay of Biscay in 1794. He was also to sign the Treaty of Ghent in 1814, establishing peace between the American States and Great Britain).

The Gambiers traced their pedigree back for many generations to a family of the nobility of France, and Mary's great-great-grandfather, Nicholas Gambier, left Caen in Normandy on the revocation of the edict of Nantes, settling in England in 1690. Mary's Aunt Mary Gambier had married Sir Samuel Cornish's nephew, Captain Pitchford, who, under the terms of his uncle's will, had taken the name Samuel Cornish and, like his uncle, also rose in the Navy to the rank of admiral.

Mary, a vivacious girl whose portrait was painted by Sir Thomas Lawrence, was, according to her Uncle Frederick Gambier:

bright, high-spirited – which life-long malady [asthma] could not subdue – warm-hearted, impulsive, generous, affectionate to overflowing, unselfish, – yet devotedly attached to her husband, and holding his high qualities in admiration. I believe her affection was fully reciprocated on his part.[22]

---

[20] British Library India Office records: B35/39.
[21] Mildred Archer, *Natural History Drawings in the India Office Library* (HMSO, 1962), p 87.
[22] As Note 16.

On 23 June 1813, Richard Parry resigned from the East India Company's employ. He had served for twenty years in the Bengal Civil Service, and his age on retirement was only 36. On the following 4 August he and Mary Gambier were married at St Marylebone Parish Church; but even now Thomas Parry failed fully to rejoice for his eldest surviving son. He did not quite approve of the marriage because Richard had chosen the only delicate daughter in the Gambier family.[23]

Richard and Mary Parry set up home in Cadogan Place, dividing their time between there and Banstead. It seems that Thomas Parry moved out of his country house to make way for the newly-weds, whilst he took a house close to his daughter Ann, her husband Charles Woodcock and their six children, who had settled in Croydon on their return from India. One of those children, Thomas Parry Woodcock, was to remember Richard Parry, 'tall and delicate looking', riding over to Croydon from Banstead one afternoon to present his sister with a grand piano of the best quality then made; price 140 guineas.

Internationally and nationally, the early years of the nineteenth century were dominated by the ambitions of Napoleon Bonaparte; by the descent into permanent madness of George III in 1810 and the assumption of the title Prince Regent by Prince George in the following year; and by the worst ever Luddite riots in 1812, a year in which wheat prices rose to their highest nineteenth-century level, and in which Britain went to war against America, 'an unpleasant and unnecessary episode in the greater Napoleonic struggle'.[24] 1812 was also the year in which William Parry was forced to set sail for home from China. Twenty years in the Far East had broken his health, as it had broken three of his brothers, but unlike them, he had secret responsibilities which were to be left behind, and which he was now forced to reveal in his will:

> William Parry, now of Canton, but about to embark for England.
> To my brother, Richard Parry, in trust for my natural son, born of Affie, a Chinese, and christened by the name of Richard, at 21, £4,000. To my friend John Hendrick de Wit, of Capetown, in trust for my natural daughter, Lucy Maria, born of said Affie, at 21, £4,000.
> To my friend Charles Magniac, of Canton, in trust for my natural son, Charles, at 21, £4,000… My brother Richard, £8,000. My brother Henry, £12,000. My sister Mary [Warrington], £5,000. My sister Ann [Woodcock], £10,000. £5,000 in trust for said Affie. Residue to my brother, Richard.[25]

John de Wit, a ship's officer from South Africa, took William Parry's daughter, Lucy Maria, to Cape Town; another friend, Edmund Larkin, took William's eldest son, Richard, back to his home at Tottenham; and the youngest boy, Charles, remained in Canton in the care of a third friend, Charles Magniac of Macao. Nothing is known about the later lives of Richard or Charles; but Lucy remained in South Africa, married a Lieutenant Colonel William Shaw, gave birth

---

[23] Memories of Thomas Parry Woodcock, recorded in GPM p 57.

[24] GM Trevelyan, *History of England* (Longmans, 1934), p 582.

[25] *Genealogical Abstracts from Parry Wills proved in the Prerogative Court of Canterbury down to 1818, with Administrations for the same period,* compiled by Lt Col G Parry (The Society of Genealogists, London).

to three daughters and eight sons, and died at Wynberg in 1886 at the age of 81; and her descendants are still living in South Africa today.

In 1805 William Parry had been so deeply in debt that he was obliged to seek a loan from his sister Lucy's husband, General Burr. On 1 January 1807 he had written to Burr:

> Having every reason to expect that by the time the Ships now despatched return to China I shall have liquidated every outstanding claim against me, I can confidently assure you that should you feel disposed to entrust me with a further loan to the extent of 4 or 5,000£ it will be perfectly safe, having long since discharged all demands of the Chinese, and I will allow you an interest of 8 per cent, which I will either remit or allow to accumulate at compound interest as you shall prefer'.[26]

Within five years William had moved from financial hardship to the possession of a great fortune, and it seems probable that he had invested large sums in America, perhaps with the assistance of John de Wit, who was of American descent. What he had been unable to foresee was that hostilities were imminent between the motherland and her former transatlantic colonies. He embarked on the *Winchelsea* at the end of 1812, and a few weeks into the voyage was obliged to add a codicil to his will:

> 12 Feb 1813, on board ship *Winchelsea*, at sea.
> Whereas the war between England and America must place my property in a state of much uncertainty, I make the following alterations to my Will. To my children and their mother the sums mentioned. If any remains, next to be paid £2,000 to John de Wit, or his wife... £500 to Charles Magniac and £100 to his brother, Hollingworth Magniac... To Mrs. Ann Woodcock, a brooch set in brilliants, containing her own and her children's hair.[27]

Further codicils, added each day from 16 to 18 February 1813, blend afterthoughts with sighed farewells:

> *Winchelsea* 16 Feb 1813. In further alteration of my will I give to R. Parry £500 towards promoting the cause of the Christian religion, £200 of it for the poor of Banstead.

> 17 Feb 1813. Love to all dear friends, Lambert, Reas, Darby, dear Aunt Lucy, etc.

> 18 Feb 1813. In case of the death of my dear Lucy Maria, before her marriage, £1,000 to De Wit, Esq., of Capetown.[28]

William Parry completed his voyage home, arriving in England in a state of complete physical collapse. He died at Marlborough in Wiltshire on 14 September, 1813, in his thirty-sixth year.

Did Thomas Parry know about his son William's half-Chinese children? It seems unlikely. Richard Parry dealt with the administration of his brother's will

---

[26] Highnam archive.
[27] As Note 25.
[28] *Ibid.*

and would have had no cause to add painful scandal to his elderly father's burden of grief. Better by far that Thomas's pride should be left intact and, indeed, boosted. Two events now provided the final joys for which the old man had for so long hoped and waited.

On 16 August, 1815, just a few weeks after Wellington's defeat of Napoleon at Waterloo, Richard Parry was elected a Director of the East India Company and took his seat at Leadenhall Street. The election had been severely contested, the Gambiers taking an active part in the canvass on behalf of their brother-in-law. This success was soon overtopped by even happier news: the birth on 22 February 1816, at their Cadogan Place home, of Richard and Mary Parry's first and only child, a son, Thomas Parry.

It had been thirty-five years since Richard Parry's mother, Mary, had been laid to rest in the vault of the magnificent family tomb which his father had built by the south side of the tower in Banstead churchyard.[29] If the size of that mausoleum was a true measure of Thomas Parry's sense of loss, then his love must surely have been great. In spite of considerable wealth, nothing in his later, lonely life could replace the happiness of his married years. But with an heir to the family name and fortune safely delivered, Thomas Parry, in his eighty-fifth year, finally content, released his shaky grip on life. He died on 9 April 1816.

Richard Parry, steadily fading away, was ultimately defeated by his long illness, probably tuberculosis, on 30 June, 1817. He was 40.

In his old age, Thomas Parry Woodcock could just remember Richard Parry's widow, a young woman of 30, dressed in a white dressing-gown, waving her handkerchief to her little boy in the garden.[30] Young Thomas's own memory of his mother was scarcely any more distinct. Mary Parry died in 1821.

---

[29] The Parry tomb at Banstead bears, at the sides, the Parry coat of arms impaled with the coat of the Oakes family (ie, azure, on a chevron *argent*, between three falcons belled *or*, as many leopards' faces). At the head of the tomb, on a shield by itself, is a badge showing a serpent encircled, tail debruised, head to sinister: an early Christian symbol of immortality.
[30] GPM p 57.

III

A Journey with Bateson

Mary Parry's father, Samuel Gambier, had died soon after her marriage to Richard Parry in 1813, and so, after the death of her husband, she turned increasingly to her Uncle James, Baron Gambier of Iver, for help. Mary and her little boy were welcomed warmly into the house rented by Lord Gambier at Offley in Hertfordshire for his two unmarried sisters, Henrietta and Louisa. Young Thomas Parry's one faint recollection of his mother was at Offley, 'of a white figure bending over him in bed. Of her face he could recall nothing, any more than of the tone of her voice'.[1] When Mary herself died in 1821, the task of bringing him up naturally fell to Lord Gambier, to Mary's mother, and especially to his aunts, Henrietta and Louisa Gambier.

Richard Parry's executor, his brother-in-law Daniel Warrington, clearly had no expectation that this delicate five-year-old orphan would survive for long, and set about selling off the family homes and their contents at Berners Street and Banstead. Very few of their collected treasures were spared: a few items of furniture, family portraits, and the white and gold basin which had been used at the infant Thomas's christening were all that remained.

Thomas always spoke with great affection about his great-uncle, Lord Gambier, and many years later acknowledged his debt of gratitude by inserting the name 'Gambier' into his own: Thomas Gambier Parry. But as a freckle-faced boy at Eton his nickname was 'Trout', and at home he was known simply as Tom.

From Eton, where his tutor was the Reverend Edward Coleridge, where he enjoyed cricket and rowing, and where, more significantly, he received instruction in drawing from William Evans (1798-1877), Tom went up to Trinity College, Cambridge, in March 1833, as a gentleman commoner . By the time of his graduation with a general degree in 1837, he had already travelled widely in the world with his two favourite uncles: his late mother's unmarried brothers, Charles and Frederick Gambier. He had also made his first tentative purchases of

---

[1] GPM p 3.

paintings, a pair of seventeenth-century Roman pictures, one by Salvator Rosa and the other by Lanfranco; neither was outstanding, and both reflected the conventional taste of the time. Tom had not yet discovered the artists of fourteenth- and fifteenth-century Italy, the for long unfashionable 'primitives' whose work was to become his passion; but these two trophies of the Grand Tour hung proudly in his rooms at Trinity, the first fruits of what was to become a remarkable collection of art treasures; a collection which was to include not only pictures but medieval ivories, Limoges enamels, Italian maiolica and Islamic metalwork. Into his Trinity rooms Tom also imported a small cottage piano upon which his contemporaries at Cambridge remembered him playing constantly. In his love of music and art, Tom was undoubtedly his father's son.

In 1836, at the age of twenty, Tom Parry set out once again for Europe, but this time he was not accompanied by his Gambier uncles; his travelling companion was, instead, his Cambridge friend Robert Bateson. Although he maintained journals of his several trips abroad over many years, the hand-written account of Parry's sketching expedition in 1836 is both the earliest and by far the liveliest to survive. In his description of a summer journey through Belgium, Germany and Switzerland is recorded all the exuberance of a young man relishing the unexpected and exciting; a young man setting out on an artist's life.[2]

July 7, 1836 – Journey with Bateson

Let her go ! hard a starboard! now gentlemen I can't wait a moment longer! any body going a shore ?!! were the simultaneous shouts of captain, engineer and boatman, as we left the rank where the dirty steamer was moored, half deafened by the mixture of a hundred voices yelling in discords, a horrid shrill bell tolling some octaves higher than [any] bell one ever cast before, and the clatter of engine, roaring of the black funnel, and splash of the paddles, whose mechanical powers dashed us among crowds of tugs, boats, steamers, and lighters that were floating about in all directions, adding to the confusion of the usual scene. Stop her ! – every minute cried the fellow looking over the paddle box, when some unfortunate wherryman[3] was lugging after him about 3 families, whose heads were full of ideas about a merry party at the tunnel, or were vainly trying to find some friendly vessel chocked up between dozens of others the other side of the river. Before starting I had the luck to be introduced to a Mr Denney who introduced me to his very pretty (whatsoever she was but most likely his) daughter, and his very ugly (most likely) wife. To these there was nothing to talk about but – where are you intending to travel? – to which the answer, to my horror, was "we have not determined yet", and to complain about the abominable stench of bilge water. Indeed these seemed to be the general subjects of conversation through the company; it was a motley group, with cross faces and cross purposes as they run against one another to get out of the way of ropes etc., in the scurry of getting off. French, German and Italian were mixed with the English jabber, and now and then some Irish patois was added to make din of talk still greater; however barring all difficulties, putting up with all bother, and above all, holding one's nose to escape being knocked down by the bilge water, we got safely out, beyond the Nore's-ark [sic] stationed at the mouth of the Thames, and puffed and paddled away at a great rate, like a duck in a thunderstorm.

---

[2] Highnam archive.
[3] A wherry is a light rowing-boat for carrying passengers.

A clatter of pewter spoons, iron forks and knives of some other uncommon metal soon proclaims that a dinner is preparing, or prepared. Vast dishes come smoking along the deck, and except a few now and then capsizing into ladies' laps, or down the hold, all arrive on a long (white I will not say) table cloth; and after a few rounds of "Now Mam, dinner's ready", we sit down 38, trusting to the substantiality of an English steam-cook's dishes. An oldish English woman… volunteered to carve the half-boiled joint of veal, and got no dinner for her pains. Dinner over, the hours passed away as slowly and smoothly as the sluggish waves we seemed to awaken in our splashing through them; the light got fainter and fainter as the sun sank into the mists of the horizon, and now only remained one or two glimmering specks of distant light-houses that twinkled a last farewell, then blended with the watery circle of joined sea and heaven, and left us to track our course in darkness. But such scenes and the ideas that they awakened of past and present and future were soon contrasted with one of the most absurd and ridiculous consequents I ever met with; drowsiness seemed to claim its power over the whole set of passengers, that were either hanging over the side of the vessel, or lolling on the abominably hard benches that the untutored Pagans of owners, and shipbuilders, had dispersed about for Christians to sit upon. At about 10 o'clock it was getting very dark and equally cold in proportion; most of the passengers therefore seemed inclined to turn into their berths, or get out of the way of the cold and the splashing incivility of the paddles that now and then greeted one with a good souse of sea-water that was about as strong an anti-soporific as a man could take. However, the deck was soon spread over with blankets and other soft articles, to save the arms, elbows, and bare bones of the many that were going to court Morpheus on deck. But others (myself and friend included) went below and "turned in", or as I should express it "on" sofas, placed at the back of the boiler, for fear we should be too cold; the other parts of the chilly cabin being already as low as 96 Fahrenheit. Not long had we that got berths, as well as about 20 strewed all about the floor, settled ourselves, before there was a simultaneous shout of "Steward! I say Steward!! (Yes Sir! Yes Sir!) What's this horrid stench?! here! Eau de Cologne for 20! quick!" This clatter of voices soon brought a fat old goody of a woman to the cabin door with "eau de Cologne water" as she called it, with which she commenced sprinkling the company till the bottle was dry. The scene was most ludicrous; lots of people sitting half up in bed and half hidden by the wavy blankets, looking for all the world like scared mermaids or Kelpies[4],holding their noses, or writhing their sleepy faces, to escape the tremendous vibration of the olfactory nerves, caused by the most awful scent of bilge water I, or anybody else, ever encountered. The whole business seemed to tickle the fancy of one of our passengers in a berth (which, by-the-by, he said was nearly his death) close at my heels; and he in turn tickled one's, by the evolution of his bad puns and wretched wit, that made the whole set of us down-below laugh the more.

When I awoke I found myself left alone in the cabin, as all the rest had 'turned out', 'turned up', and 'turned to' at breakfast, that like yesterday's dinner was serv'd up on deck. The picture of the cabin was not tempting enough to make me stay below longer than necessary; the first thing that caught my eye, after winding up about 20 steps, was a duty boy, with fingers as black as the sooty board he sat on, endeavouring to clean some dozens of knives, forks and spoons for the breakfast table. All these were plunged into one broken pitcher, enough to hold 4, but made to wash 40, then wiped either on a black towel, or left for the air to absorb the clammy moisture that clung to them: so much for the delicious cleanliness of our dear Brittanic bipeds.

The banks of the broad Schel[5]may be all very interesting for the modern historian but certainly not for an artist; and hence did not draw away my eyes, as the polar star does

---

[4] Kelpies are waterspirits, usually in horse form.
[5] The Schelde: the river upon which Antwerp stands.

the needle, from an unoccupied place at the breakfast-table. But without talking about dirty apparatus in the shape of lever-like spoons, and milk that was (excuse the simile) like seasick stomachs, rather turned, and the butter and cream that were pretty much in the same state except that they had mutually agreed to change colours, let us suppose ourselves at Antwerp:

> Oh for a pen that e'en could write
> Morn, evening, afternoon, and night;
> That could describe the pretty plight
> Of men and lumber; and the sight
> When the *Braves Belges* with main and might,
> Customed to cut away from fight;
> Their customed cutting with delight
> Commenced upon the cordage, yielding
> Beneath their strokes: Oh Copley Fielding

[The water-colour artist, AV Copley Fielding (1787-1855), was much sought after as a drawing master, and Thomas Parry possibly had lessons with him. Parry refers to Copley Fielding here and elsewhere in his journals, and in the following paragraph addresses him in spirit.]

How I wish you'd been here to express in pencil and paper-language lots of miserable looking, & half-stand-at-ease sort of soldiers, that came jumping double-quick on board the steamer as it bumped up against the quay, and soon turned everything to right about, lugging about bags, hat boxes, trunks, portmanteaus, books, Indian rubber capes, great coats, but more particularly fat ladies' pockets, one of which, to my great amusement, was full of little puppies… till they were tired of fun, gave us our 'exeats', and packed us off, with our half-packed luggage, to find our way to the steam coach [train] that was to start at 2 o'clock for Brussels.

Antwerp. Friday 8 July

The steamer was gone. This gave us time to take a look at the place that neither of us had seen before. No sooner had we got to the cathedral, than a fellow in a blue frock began offering us his services as "commissionaire de l'Hôtel". The cathedral has certainly one of the most imposing façades I ever saw; the height particularly strikes one, and the general effect produced by it. A little time however sufficed for the exterior, that like most other foreign churches of any size, is surrounded by houses so closely, as to have all the basement storey hidden, which is often very good in cathedrals on account of the quantity of buttresses and prominent side chapels, that give so different an effect to them to what we find in the large churches of England.

The picture of the descent from the cross by Rubens is most splendid: I could have stood opposite it for an hour, but the idea of being too late for the four o'clock steam coach gave me a twinge of conscience that allowed one only half an hour for the cathedral. There are a few other pictures by Belgian painters that are well worth seeing, but should not be looked at after the famous Rubens. The architecture of the interior is not very fine.

After a walk round the docks, and a long talk about shipping with the *ciceroni*, the first 'lion'[6] that came in our way was the church of St. Paul, that I should suppose to have been mostly built in the 12th century or a little later. The calvary is a good specimen of Romish (if I may call it thus) idolatry… The interior of the choir is very finely fitted

---

[6] *Cicerone*: a guide who shows or explains antiquities, etc. Lionizing is sight-seeing.

up with old carved oak, silk, gold, silver, and like costly things in great profusion. But the thing of the greatest interest after the cathedral is the church of St. Jacques, where they show the tomb of Rubens, that monopolises a whole side-chapel railed off with a marble palisade, and ornamented within with a very neat altar, beneath a beautiful picture of that illustrious master of his art, and with several marbles storied to his fame…

'There goes the omnibus', said our guide, as we were intently scrutinising a curious old picture that had just caught our attention, 'and if you don't make haste the steamer will be off'. Off we went therefore, *ventre à terre*, spite of heat, crowds of children, dust and other impediments, running was our only means of getting to the *Chemin de Fer* in time, and by way of securing our places, away cut the young fellow that acted guide before us, like any flying sapper… The *Chemin de Fer* does great credit to the Belgians, it is well planned and executed, and well conducted for those who like passing over ugly country quickly and comfortably. The pace is about 20 miles an hour, with distance being 30 miles, which passed over in just an hour and a half .[7]

Brussels, Saturday 9

The first thing on my mind in turning out this morning was the carriage, which we were here to look for, having (fools we were) thought it better to get one at Brussels than have the bother of bringing it by the steamers of land and sea from England.

After ransacking various shops, manufactures and slums, all in vain, the carriage that the host of our hotel offered making up for us out of his own collection of about 3 or 4, was our last resort; a sort of windsail to give us time and place for breathing after the toil of fagging up and down the hill that this town is situated on, under the scorching of an almost Indian sun, and that followed by the consoling reflection that we were roasted in vain. the carriage was all in bits; it was to be put together, painted etc., by Monday night (I confess my idea is that it will not be).
[Parry and Bateson spent the next two days sight-seeing in Brussels.]

Tuesday 12

At 9 o'clock, or a little after, our carriage, to my astonishment, being ready, and we being equally ready ourselves, away we went *à la* unicorn, and after passing through the part of the once large, but now only far famed, forest of Ardennes that grows about 4 or 5 miles from Brussels, we arrived at the most interesting little place, the village of Waterloo. The visit to the church (excuse the Bull) lead me back to the year before I was born [*1815, the year of the Battle of Waterloo*]; on entering the humble portal, I found myself surrounded by above 20 marble monuments, graven in memory of those who never could need such mouldering records of their actions; that serve but to tell that there were those who dreaded not to die for their country, that gained her safety by losing them, although they were of the best and bravest that could bear her name. Some tablets full of names, others full of numbers; some raised by regiments in honour of their dead comrades; some raised by parents; and one, to a young officer, placed there by his own brothers and sisters, made up the long list. They are all English (I observed here and there a German name in the same list as that in which the English names are enumerated). Not a single French monument is there.
[The journey continued on 12 and 13 July via Namur, Huys, Liège and Spa.]

---

[7] The first passenger rail service (iron road) in mainland Europe, from Brussels to Mechelen, opened on 5 May 1836.

Thursday 14

This day has been spent most amusingly. At about half past twelve we started off on queerish horses over queerish roads to see a large cavern, naturally made in lime rock by the rushing mountain torrents, or some great convulsion of the hill in which it now is; that I had already seen before, but was induced to revisit not only for the fun of going with my friend who wished much to see it, but from the recollection of a most amusing trip with a party of 8, my two Uncles Charles and Frederick being of the number, made here about 3 years ago, while we were waiting the necessary quantum of days, at the expiration of which we were to get a sort of passport of health from the Physician here to satisfy the wary Prussians we had not the cholera.

[The two friends left Spa on 15 July and passed the Prussian border on their way to Treves (now Trier), via Malmady and Shonberg.]

Sunday 17th was passed at Treves; in the afternoon hired a hackney coach as it was too hot for walking; drove about the environs of the town, stopping for a few minutes at the Roman Baths, of which a very considerable part remains; at the Roman Amphitheatre, of which very little remains; at the church of ----- outside the walls of the town, where the tower has some of the most curious ornaments and the most fantastic display of Romanesque taste I almost ever have seen. The day was finished in a walk by the river, luxuriously cool, and worth double all the bother of sight seeing; in which however we did not indulge ourselves at Treves by staying Monday there, being anxious to hasten our journey to Switzerland, where Earth's own monumental antiquities would have a stronger claim upon us, than the toe of some Roman statue, or the wretched morsel of a broken kettle, that even Cain or Adam drank out of, or Mother Eve impressed with woman's first little finger nail. Never would I say there is no interest in antiquities, but only would I hesitate in attributing utility to them, except so far as public history is concerned, and so far as the private associations of individuals may be the sources of pleasurable employment.

[On Monday 18 the travellers and their carriage embarked on a boat and sailed down the Moselle to Berncastle, continuing over the following two days, arriving in Coblentz on Wednesday 20, and driving by night from there to Worms, the city in which, in 1521, Martin Luther stood before Charles V to defend his doctrines.]

Worms is a very fine old town with several things to interest one who came to it for the purpose that I did, which was to see one of the finest old Romanesque cathedrals in that part of Germany; and which indeed interested me so much as to keep me drawing its West end for about 2 hours and a half. Here I must say I met with more civility from strangers than I ever met with before. After sketching away with a very heavy book in my hand for about half an hour, a certain pretty looking girl who, or of what name or nature I know not, brought a chair out of a neighbouring house, and left it with me to enjoy the full use of it for as long as I chose to stay – and surely I did stay a long time, and did enjoy the use of the chair to the use of which, if I may be allowed to pronounce on my own drawings , I attribute my making one of the best sketches I ever made or ever had to make in my life. The difficulty of drawing a huge irregular building of the sort I had then before me, seems to arise from the exceedingly perplexing perspective, of which I made a considerable hash, having to draw arches, circles, ornaments, rounds, octagons and squares in as many directions as there were differences of shape, and all that without either compass or ruler, that is with nothing but pencil, knife and Indian rubber.

In the interior of the cathedral, the vast size and boldness of ornament and the wondrous breadth of vaulting struck me exceedingly. The architect has spared as much ornament as was not actually necessary. This is a Protestant cathedral, and hence void of all the gaudy Roman Catholic tinsel that the professors of that faith have the taste to

prefer to the beautiful Gothic ornaments they seem to pride themselves in destroying. In the evening we had a most delightful drive to Manheim [sic].
[On Friday 22 they drove from Mannheim to Heidelberg.]

On Saturday morning early we left [Heidelberg] for Spires, and not without adventure; the town being on the opposite side of the Rhine, and there being no bridge, carriage and horses with all live and dead stock are transported in an immense ferry boat across the stream. Before we got to the river, the clouds that had been collecting all morning began to warn us to shut up the carriage; the wind freshened, and in less than 3 minutes turned directly from North to South East, having blown exactly contrary to the direction whence the clouds came during the whole morning, and gave the boat a fair wind back to its original place where, 10 minutes before, it had a fair wind to come to us. No sooner had we got safely into this boat, that must even have shamed Charon had he gained a sight of it, there came on, I may without exaggeration say, the most tremendous rain shower I ever witnessed; the drops came as nearly horizontal as tempest could drive them and as thick as one could possibly imagine a sea, divided into drops, could be. That was accompanied with several claps of thunder, so directly over our heads as to leave scarce a moment between the flash and the report. Charon had lifted a sail that was as nearly carried away as sail ever was without quite going, but had it gone altogether it would have saved us time, and them trouble; for not only from it were we whirled round like any walnut shell in a basin, but carried by wind and stream altogether out of the right course and quietly deposited in a mud bank!! When we at last got ashore [on] the other side, the storm was over. The poor horses looked more like drowned rats than any other sort of animal, and seemed too much blown, rained and scared to pull us along any more.
[They carried on to Baden that same night, spending the next three days there quietly before continuing to Strasbourg on Wednesday 27 July.]

The Cathedral of Strasburg [sic] baffles description; I could only express all my feeling about it by saying that it is the Cathedral of Cathedrals. It is <u>a perfect</u> (I should rather not say perfect, for this it is not, as but one of the two designed towers are completed) model, inside and out, of elegance and taste; it is composed of parts of different styles, but all combine to make the whole the more beautiful and pleasing from the consequent variety. Rather late in the evening we arrived at Offenburg, a small place about a third of the distance between Baden and Schaffhausen *[where they spent the night of Thursday 28]*.

Friday 29. Immediately after breakfast we went in a sort of Brighton Sociable *[a carriage in which the passengers sat opposite to each other]* to the falls of the Rhine that are about an hour's drive from Schaffhausen, and according to my humble judgement sufficiently grand to please anyone that has not seen the falls in America. *[It is possible that Parry had visited America with his uncles.]*

As soon as the falls had been thoroughly examined from both sides of the river, and near and at a distance, we returned to Schaffhausen intending to go the same day as far as the 2nd Station in the road to Freyburg [sic]. The horses were ordered, and in about half an hour we were off. In going out of the town the streets were rather rough and badly paved, intersected with various little gutters that lead to the Cloala maxima at the side, and that now and then were so deep as to make our old fashioned carriage bump rather low, and rebound equally high, above its right position, giving one the same sensation as that of riding over a broad fence at full gallop. A good many of these waves had we bumped and bounded over when, at last, coming to a rather larger swell, that breaking full on our bows made the whole apparatus reel, and roused my attention from within to what was going on outside. We heard simultaneously a great shout of 'Hullo! hoi! arrêtez! arrêtez! vôtre domestique! Monsieur! arrêter!' That brought me upstanding in a demisemiquaver, and called me to the place whence the noise came, when turning, I saw the rumble [rumble-seat], servant, cloaks, hatboxes and all in the act of falling, and at the same moment come whack down backwards, by which motion the servant was in an instant enveloped in cloaks and great coats, etc., leaving for me to see nothing but the extremities of his arms and fingers stretched out, and his helpless legs dangling from beneath the rumble-apron, with the unhappy drop-box considerably disarranged by the fall, hanging by one screw to its original place, beneath them.

Bateson and myself were out of the carriage without opening either door almost before the rumble was safely lodged with all its baggage safely on the ground and, as quickly, lots of spectators were assembled, and with us and the postillion, set up such a shout of laughing as might well have done for the laughing chorus in *Der Freisch* [*Weber's opera Der Freischütz, first performed in June 1821*]. All this was the operation of a second, but produced such an effect on my visible muscles that I have often, and no doubt often shall, laugh whenever I think of that scene that was much too absurd to forget. The servant was not the least hurt, but laughed as much as the rest. the carriage was then wheeled off to the coach builder's, and we walked to the falls again, wishing to climb up the large rock in the centre of the falls; but the river was too full, and consequently the tide too strong for that. Not contented with two visits to the falls, we went again at moonlight, at about 11 o'clock at night, [and] tried the stream again, but failed.
[By Sunday 31 July they had reached Basel, and began their Swiss tour, travelling to Baden en Suisse on Monday and Zürich on Tuesday; on Wednesday 3 August they set out for Zug.]

Wednesday 3 was a longish day, and tedious from the quantity of hills, up and down most of which I walked almost all day long. We stopped at Zug to dine, and crossed the lake to Art in a boat after dinner. Here we found ourselves just beneath the Rigi, which we meditated ascending at night as it would be cool for walking and we should be in time to see the sun rise, and walk down to Kusnack [*Kussnacht, near Lucerne*] early in the morning...We took the ascent very quietly, starting at half past 11 [at night] with two horses, that were not of much use to us as the road was often too bad for riding, and at about a quarter to 4 gained the top. It was still quite dark, or I should say would have been quite dark except for the very bright moon and stars that appeared brighter than ever on account of the exceeding clearness of the atmosphere. The rooms in the Inn at Kulm were <u>almost</u> fuller than they could hold, and every bit of furniture that could possibly be used to lie down on, even to the bare boards, was occupied by sleepers and snoarers [*sic*], that we found huddled up together indiscriminately in the 2 *salons à manger*, when first we worked our way on entering the house, to get something to refresh us after the long walk. This operation was soon over, and I slunk away (to enjoy that which is, and often has been, the greatest delight to me) to sit alone on the side of the mountain, looking and thinking, utterly engrossed with all the glory of the scene before me.
[On Friday 5 they returned to Kussnacht on foot, and then travelled on to Lucerne. The next day, they took a boat across the lake to Fluelen, visited the William Tell chapel between Gersau and Kussnacht, continued on Monday and Tuesday over Surinen Alp to Engleburg, and through the valley of Hasli to Meyringen.]

Wednesday 10. In the afternoon, we got a carriage and a guide to take us to Brientz to see the Giesback [*sic*], a fine waterfall near it, on the opposite side of the lake. A boat, rowed by 4 women, was our conveyance across. In a volume of Mr. Wordsworth's poems that I had with me, containing 'Memorials of a Tour of the Continent' [*1820*], I found a short description of his trip over the lake in a boat rowed, like our own, by women, that he speaks of as heavenly [*sic*] beings, or such as those found on earth invested with such and such qualities as would make them 'angels incarnate'. *[Not quite. The passage from Wordsworth's poem 'Scene on the Lake of Brientz' to which Parry refers, actually reads:*

> *Pupils of Heaven, in order stand*
> *The rustic Maidens, every hand*
> *Upon a Sister's shoulder laid,*

> *To chant, as glides the boat along,*
> *A simple, but a touching song;*
> *To chant, as Angels do above,*
> *The melodies of Peace in love!]*

I only wish he [Wordsworth] had seen our boat conveyancers, and the groups of many others I found on each shore of the lake, and I think he would have let his poem sink, either in the lake or into obscurity.

[The remainder of August was spent in sight-seeing and sketching extensively in Switzerland. By 5 September, Parry and Bateson were on their way overnight from Bulle to Fribourg.]

Monday 5. The little diligence that only had places for 3, and hence which we 2 and our servant took as if it were a private carriage, brought us to Friburg [*sic*] by about 8 in the morning, and as the organist of the Cathedral commences for an hour upon the organ at 9, we had to scramble over our breakfast at a great pace in order to be in time for him. But, as he had been invited to the wedding of a friend, he could not play before 12 o'clock; at which time we were summoned to the Cathedral, and in about 10 minutes, the organist, a little German, struck up with a fine, crashing *Sanctus* of Beethoven, whose harmonies above those of any other men, are most thrilling and effective. The organ was at its full power part of the time, but without the least harshness. After the cessation of a minute, he began an introduction extempore that turned off to one of Weber's most lovely airs that is my favourite. He played the most beautiful harmonies and bass to it that could be arranged, and played the little simple flowing melody on the stop that imitates the human voice (the stop of the "human voice" is called here the *Tremblant*) that added such trembling sweetness, and such soft expression as I had thought beyond the power even of the organ. Music only running in my head has often overpowered me, whether it be the composition of others, or the natural turn of my mind at the moment, but the effect of this was overflowing sweetness such as no words could express, no, not even poetry, nor such as every soul can comprehend or feel. Perhaps it were better to be such at times, for music is often too much for one.

At 4 o'clock by some lucky chance he played again and, of course, we went to hear him. It rained the whole day, so that the 2 hours of music were delightful breaks to the long hours of finishing, that is to say, touching up old sketches…

Tuesday 6. This morning at 9 o'clock we heard the magnificent organ for the 3rd time and were equally or more delighted with it. It had astonished me (who have learnt somewhat about the management of an organ) how the organist could produce such wonderful variety, while playing alone and with the ordinary number of 10 fingers and 2 feet, so I went into the organ loft with him to learn his way of getting over what appeared almost impossibilities. The organ is one of the finest I have ever seen; it has 4 rows of keys, of which the 2nd can move back or forwards so as to play upon as many pipes as 3 rows of keys when drawn forward, and to be rid of these when pushed back. It has then 2 octaves of pedals, and above 40 stops, but I forget the exact number. As far as I could make out there was no swell, and it wanted the beautiful invention, in English organs, of composition pedals. However, as a whole, it struck me nothing could possibly be wanted finer than this organ is, in variety, sweetness or power.

[Parry's journal ends on Thursday 15 September 1836.]

Thursday 15. Today, as we passed through country which possessed features neither of beauty, curiosity or interest, we had beautiful weather, and enjoyed the drive to Constance very much, seeing as much of the lake as possible by taking a road that went straight down to the lake, instead of that one generally taken which traverses the country, as the crow flies, from St. Gallen to Constanz. The lake is…

[More than a year later he turned once more to that final, unfinished page.]

Amen! and so much for perseverance! Oh virtue of Philosophers! Oh spirit of reality – I do not altogether possess ye; though many give me credit for much. 'The lake is...' what? but there I stopped on Thursday the 15th of some month or other, just about this time last year – it is now 1837 – September has passed away, like a boat through the calm sea. It made a little, and very little impression upon me; it was but a moment to eternity, gone for ever, and now has sunk to nothing.

Lacking in perseverance? Hardly. Parry's modesty was appropriately becoming, but it scarcely reflected the energetic spirit of enquiry which led him to seek out Sir John Goss (1800-1880), organist of St Paul's Cathedral from 1838, to enrol with him as a student of counterpoint and harmony; or which took him to the door of the celebrated landscape painter Peter de Wint (1784-1849) for lessons in water-colour drawing. There was far more to Parry's enthusiasms than the passing fancies of a wealthy man seeking to while away endless hours of leisure. He remained convinced to the end of his days that fine art could and should act as a beneficial power for all of society: a very Ruskinesque notion. As he put it in an address to the Social Science Congress at Cheltenham in 1878:

Our people have more than hands to employ and mouths to fill. They have senses and sympathies which listen to appeal. They have needs of heart-relief no less than rest of muscle, souls to respond to an awakened imagination no less than minds to be trained to healthy reason. They need all the cheering elements that can be got for them out of this world's state; and fine art is just that gift of God for the solace of mankind which is best fitted to fill the void in the cold mechanical routine of life which poverty or necessity may have forced upon them.[8]

He wanted to be of use; to play his part in bringing the healing balm of beauty to the poor and underprivileged through education in, and experience of, fine art, or:

...the gradual influence of educating beauty falling on ground capable of receiving it. That influence, the educating influence of *experience*, must be the basis of all that we can hope to do, to undermine the degradation and disgrace around us, and by the narrow edge of better things to introduce with patience the materials of a higher and happier life.[9]

Fine art, he firmly believed, was not a superfluity in human life; 'a mere thing of luxury, a thing impossible for the poor, undesirable as a national interest for the lower classes, and destructive of a vigorous spirit; a mere toy for weaker minds and wearied humanity to play with'. No,

Fine Art is the mirror of ourselves. Collectively it tells to futurity facts and truths which the present little thinks of. Individually it represents its producer. Art is an *alter ego*.

---

[8] Thomas Gambier Parry, *The Relation of Fine Art to Social Science* (An address delivered at the Social Science Congress, Cheltenham, Oct 1878) (London, 1879).
[9] *Ibid.*

Practically it is a thing of compound nature in three parts – science, skill, and poetry. Thus it is like ourselves, a thing of bodily parts and aptitudes, and a spiritual nature. Science is its bone and muscle, skill its enlivening spirit, and poetry its soul. It has that about it which is visible, and that *within* it which is invisible. It is because it so intimately represents ourselves, because it rises with our emotions, so burns with our passions, and so bends to our sympathies that we love it. The source and fountain of Fine Art is in the human soul.[10]

Fine art without a spiritual dimension was therefore impossible; but equally, nothing could be achieved in art without a strict application to the scientific and technical principles upon which all skill is dependent. Parry told his son, Ernest, how Peter de Wint 'used always to ask the reason for everything done with colours, and give a reason himself... When one had nearly finished a drawing and it all looked very pretty, de Wint would come along, and say – "Don't you see that light and this shadow are so & so, & so & so?" – and down would come a wet sponge and blot the whole out'.[11] And Parry's fascination with the organ at Fribourg was more than idle curiosity, too. He was intent on discovering exactly *how* so glorious a sound was made. As he expressed it in another lecture: 'Unless an artist is a mechanic too, he is only half an artist... There is no degradation of art's poetry by descending to its mechanism'.[12]

Tom Parry ended the year 1837 with his philosophy of life already substantially established; with his university days at an end; and, having reached the age of twenty-one, the possession of a great fortune. The huge sums left to him in trust by his father and grandfather were now his to do with as he wished.

---

[10] *Ibid.*

[11] GPM p 157.

[12] Thomas Gambier Parry, *The Adornment of Sacred Buildings*. A paper read at the Annual Meeting of the Associated Architectural Societies, held in the County Assembly Rooms, Lincoln, 17 June 1868; Lincoln Diocesan Architectural Society published as *Reports and Papers read at The Meetings of the Architectural Societies of the Diocese of Lincoln....during the year MDCCCLXVIII* (Lincoln, 1868), pp 141/53.

IV

Highnam Court

Isabella Lear, wife of the Reverend Francis Lear, Vicar of Chilmark, Wiltshire, had gone up to London for a few days in the summer of 1839; but instead of spending Sunday 22 June in the capital, she determined to pay a short, unexpected visit to her sister, Katherine Fynes-Clinton, at Welwyn in Hertfordshire. The Fynes-Clintons had only recently returned from a trip to France; the house was in considerable disorder; and the arrival of Mrs Lear's carriage at the front door caught her sister absolutely by surprise. None the less, Isabella, whose visit had not been quite so impromptu as she pretended, was given an affectionate welcome.

Two hours after Mrs Lear's appearance at Welwyn, another carriage bringing travellers from London arrived at the door. It contained Katherine's husband, Henry Fynes-Clinton, MP, a descendant of the Earls of Lincoln (afterwards Dukes of Newcastle), Henry's friend William Webber, and the Fynes-Clinton's second daughter, Anna Maria Isabella, who, while the family were on holiday in France the previous winter, had met a young man in Tours to whom she was now engaged to be married. The next morning, whilst the Fynes-Clintons and Mrs. Lear were at church, the object of twenty-three year-old Isabella's affections, Tom Parry, paid his first visit to Welwyn and, as Mrs Lear noted in her diary, 'most affectionately was he addressed by the whole family'.[1] The young man's future father-in-law was a dry old scholar in the Casaubon mould:

> Originally intended for the Church, like his father, Henry Fynes Clinton was diverted from his calling by a small fortune left him by a benefactor who especially desired that he should not take orders. His aristocratic Newcastle relations pressed him to accept a seat in parliament, and he sat as Member for Aldborough from 1806 to 1826. In those days the duties of a private Member were not rigorous. Parliamentary life was foreign to his tastes. He was a scholar with a passion for chronology, and spent most of his life at Welwyn, reading the Greek and Latin authors, and compiling the *Fasti Hellenici* and *Fasti Romani* which gained him no little repute for his scholarship and research. Of the

---

[1] Mrs Lear's diaries, copied by Dorothea Ponsonby. Shulbrede Priory archives.

beauties of what he read he apparently took little heed. But he recounts with obvious satisfaction the number of verses and the total number of pages they filled: *e.g.* 'At Oxford I went through about 69,322 verses making altogether an amount of 5223 pages'.[2]

With Mrs Lear's curiosity well satisfied, and the Fynes-Clintons determined to make a good impression on their future son-in-law, the family and their guest settled down to dinner, only to face the acute embarrassment of 'a new cook sending up the worst dinner I ever saw on a gentleman's table'.[3] Katherine Fynes-Clinton's mortification turned to intense anger when she later found the cook:

> in the most shameful state of drunkenness. Next morning she beat off nobody knows where, and shortly afterwards her unfortunate body was found drowned about twelve miles off. How dreadful to think of the state of her soul. I was grieved to see in Church a thin and apparently inattentive congregation morning and evening. Mr. Clinton gave me up his share of my dear [sister's] bed, and slept at his opposite neighbour Mr. Grey's.[4]

Mrs Lear appears to have grieved rather more over the sparseness of the Welwyn congregation than about the drowning of the hapless cook; and what, one wonders, was in Henry Fynes-Clinton's mind as he left his own home for the night? Tom Parry, however, seems not to have been deterred by the alarms and excursions around him. Less than two months remained before his marriage to Isabella; but in Mrs Lear's mind there were serious doubts about her niece's suitability for the match. As early as 1832 she had confided to her diary that:

> As for my god-daughter Isabella, I was grieved and disgusted with the hauteur and 'inferiors' manner she has towards everybody; the consequence is she destroys her beauty and makes everybody in the house dislike her.[5]

Now, seven years later, her dislike of her niece seems, if anything, to have intensified:

> Isabel struck me as less handsome than when I saw her last, and I feel that her disposition is not calculated to contribute to Mr. Parry's happiness, who appears one of the most pleasing and superior young men I ever saw. Cannot help from my private observation entertaining some fears respecting the result of the engagement'.[6]

And the next day:

> I was grieved and pained to observe Isabel was far from being as good humoured and gracious in her manners as she ought to be to Tom Parry who is only too good for her,

---

[2] Charles L Graves, *Hubert Parry* (London, 1926), Vol I, pp 6/7.
[3] As Note 1.
[4] *Ibid.*
[5] *Ibid.*
[6] *Ibid.*

and my fear is that she will drive him from her in despair of future happiness. This I know is also a cause of anxiety to my dear Siss.[7]

But her fears were groundless. The young couple clearly adored each other. On 12 August, 1839, Mrs Lear was back to stay at Welwyn for their wedding on the following day. Her fellow guests were the bridegroom and his uncle, Henry Parry, whom she thought 'an odd, amusing but [I] suspected not a very reputable man'. Of her niece she was at last able to write: 'Isabel looked very lovely'; and of the wedding day itself:

> A most lovely day, and after breakfast the company began to assemble – consisting chiefly of different members of Tom Parry's family – namely his nice old grandmother Mrs Gambier with her two daughters and two sons, Charles and Fred… Without exception, Tom Parry does certainly appear to be one of the most delightful, superior young men possible, with a fortune of £10,000 a year, while she has not a penny.[8]

Mrs Lear was one of the thirteen children of the Right Reverend Henry William Majendie (1754-1830), the Bishop of Bangor, sometime Bishop of Chester, previously Canon of Windsor, and of St Paul's Cathedral, and erstwhile tutor to William IV when a boy. Unsurprisingly, she had married a churchman, but Francis Lear's career had proved less successful than that of her father. Although his friends assured him that preferment would be bound to come, Lear had, in 1839, reached the age of fifty and was still parish priest of Chilmark, where he had held the living for fifteen years. [*When George Augustus Herbert, 11th Earl of Pembroke, died in 1827, his younger son, Sidney Herbert, left Harrow School and went to board with the Rev Francis Lear at Chilmark, not far from the Pembroke family home at Wilton near Salisbury. Lear, with his brother-in-law and curate, George Majendie, undertook the young man's tuition. In 1843 Lear was given the living of Bishopstone, closer still to Wilton. Three years later he was appointed Dean of Salisbury, but died of cancer in 1850.*]

Mrs Lear had been impressed by Tom Parry's charm, winning manners and agreeable personality at least as much as by his wealth. Although not tall, he was a handsome young man. His intelligence was clearly outstanding, and he possessed what to her was the paramount virtue: he was a devout Christian. Her opinion of him was only strengthened when she visited the Parrys at their new home, Highnam Court in Gloucestershire, where Tom proved to be the perfect host, even amusing the company after dinner with his skill as a conjuror. He had learned a great many card tricks and other feats of sleight-of-hand, and as a *pièce de résistance*, enjoyed baffling his audience by cutting up Isabella's handkerchief and then producing it whole![9]

Throughout Tom Parry's minority, all of the money left to him by his grandfather and father had been allowed to accumulate. It was his grandfather's wish that he should settle in the country and found a home and a family. Old

---

7 *Ibid.*
8 *Ibid.*
9 GPM p 205.

Thomas Parry left directions that when his grandson came of age a place was to be found for him, and pictures and descriptions of suitable properties had begun to arrive even before Tom was twenty-one.[10]

Drawn at first to buying a house at Sharpham in Devonshire, close to the Dartington Hall home of his old Eton and Cambridge friend, Champernowne, Tom finally rejected rural isolation in favour of Highnam Court, a seventeenth-century house with extensive grounds, woodland, river wharf, water grist mill and six farms, set in a total of some 1,800 acres only two miles to the west of Gloucester. Here he would be close enough to the city to enter fully into its civic life, and to realise his aim of putting his wealth and skills to social and charitable use. He was, at last, coming into his own, and in recognition both of his new-found independence and of his gratitude to the family which had brought him up, Tom added their name to his own. From now on, although still spoken of by many as 'Mr Parry', he signed himself 'Thomas Gambier Parry'.

Highnam Court had been built by Colonel William Cooke in the mid-seventeenth century; one of the very few examples of such houses erected during the Commonwealth period in the years following the death of Inigo Jones, whose influence it clearly reflects. It replaced an earlier house which had been a grange of the abbots of Gloucester, to whom the Highnam estate had belonged for over five hundred years before the Dissolution. Sir Robert Cooke, the owner of the house at the time of the Civil War, was a receiver at the Court of Wards, Member of Parliament for Gloucester, and a man of great wealth and influence both in Gloucestershire and London. He had married the widow of George Herbert, the metaphysical poet; and he was also a Roundhead. Hounded at Highnam by Royalist troops, Sir Robert was forced to leave the house and to take up residence with his wife and family in Gloucester. In February 1643, a Royalist army of 1,500 foot and 500 horse, raised in South Wales, encamped at Highnam under the command of Sir John Brett, threw up trenches, and menaced the Parliament garrison in Gloucester for over three weeks. On 23 March Massey, the governor of Gloucester, made a frontal attack on the house, while Waller, who had crossed the Severn at Framilode and marched through Huntley, mounted an assault on the rear. Brett's troops were completely routed; 1,600 of them were taken prisoner and locked in Gloucester's St. Mary de Lode Church for ten days where, crowded to suffocation, they were fed on nothing more than turnips and cabbage leaves. The house at Highnam was set on fire – and with it perished the precious manuscripts of George Herbert which Lady Cooke had left behind. Sir Robert Cooke died soon afterwards, 'and his widow petitioned 'to be exonerated from rates and taxes and asked for payment of her husband's arrears'. These requests were refused and she was obliged to vacate the house in Gloucester and live in want until her eldest son – a known Royalist [William] – changed sides and paid a fine to recover the estate'.[11]

---

[10] Notes by Hubert Parry, copied by Dorothea Ponsonby. Shulbrede archive.
[11] Joan Johnson, *The Gloucestershire Gentry* (Alan Sutton, 1989), p 82.

Colonel William Cooke was succeeded by his younger son, Edward, whose younger son, Dennis, succeeded him but died without issue in 1747, leaving two sisters, Anne and Mary, as co-heirs. Mary Cooke married Henry Guise, of Upton St Leonards, the younger son of the ancient Gloucestershire family, the Guises of Elmore. Their son, John, purchased the moiety of the Highnam estate when he reached the age of twenty-one in 1755 and embarked upon a major redecoration of the interior of the house. When Sir William Guise, 5th baronet of Elmore, died without issue in 1783, his baronetcy became extinct, but was revived in favour of his Highnam cousin; and Elmore and other Gloucestershire properties were added to the Highnam estate.

Sir John Guise's seat as it was in the late 1770s is depicted in a water-colour by T Bonner, the original of an engraving reproduced in Rudder's county history.[12] It shows an old chapel standing a few yards south-west of the house; but this had been demolished by the time that Tom Parry rented Highnam from the Guise family in 1837, purchasing the property in the following year. The house to which, two years later, he brought Isabella was of red brick with stone quoins and window dressings, with two storeys below the cornice, and with a hipped roof. It had been planned as a half H with the wings coming forward on the south front, the central and most distinctive of the original features of which was, and is, the doorcase, with swan-necked pediment and characteristic Mannerist details. But Isabella had taken no part in the choice of her married home and was never entirely happy there. Perhaps it was with her persuasion that Gambier Parry set about making additions to the north front about 1840, and at the same time placing pedimented dormer features with chimneys in the centre of the south front, thus stamping a personal imprint upon the property. The entrance to the house was set into the new north front, whilst the original south-facing entrance hall was turned into a library, but a library in which books were to play a subordinate role to paintings: the two end walls were left free for the display of pictures.

In time, Highnam Court was to become the showcase for a great collection, the disposition within the house of which was unchanged when Arthur Oswald visited Highnam in 1950 for the magazine *Country Life*.[13] Oswald noted that the style of the interior decoration suggested a date in the seventeen-sixties, ie, under the patronage of Sir John Guise:

> For although the stucco compositions are of an elaborate Rococo character, the door-cases and some of the ceilings (that of the music room, for instance) reflect the new Adam fashions. This music room occupies the north-east corner of the main pile, but when about 1840 the new entrance hall with its portico was added on this side of the house, the north wall of the room was broken through and it now forms a sort of inner hall. On the walls are very elaborate stucco decorations built up on wire and given a deep projection. The trophies of musical instruments are masterpieces of virtuosity. On the side-walls are four of these ornaments framed in tall panels with shaped and scrolled heads. The lyre in the group over the fireplace is surmounted by an Apollo's head, with emanating rays recalling the use of this feature in the decoration of some of the rooms at

---

[12] Water-colour of Highnam by T Bonner (late 1770s). Highnam archive.
[13] Arthur Oswald, *Highnam Court, Gloucestershire*. Published in *Country Life*, 12 May 1950, pp 1376/80.

Old Norfolk House. One is reminded of the similar trophies of musical instruments on the walls of the saloon at Hagley, where one of the plasterers was the Italian Vassali. He, or compatriots of his, may have worked at Highnam both in this room and on the ceiling of the drawing-room...But what is highly unusual is to find this Rococo plasterwork in conjunction with the chaste Adamesque designs in the doorcases, frieze and ceiling. The stucco workers were given, or took, *carte blanche*...

At first glance [the ironwork of the balustrade of the main staircase] might be assigned to the first years of the 18th century, but the design may be compared with that of the staircase at Staunton Harold, which...may be dated to the seventeen-fifties by its likeness to other wrought-iron balustrades of that decade.

In the north-west corner of the house there remains an original oak staircase. It has been thought that this is a survival from an earlier house, because it bears traces of having been damaged by fire, but its turned balusters, moulded handrail and the acorn-like finials of the newel posts all accord with a date during the Commonwealth...

Opening right off the library is the Gold Drawing-room with windows looking east and south. Although the fireplace was introduced by Thomas Gambier Parry and the gold wall-paper to display the pictures was his choice, the doorcases, the frieze and the ceiling date from the seventeen-sixties. The ceiling displays the same elaborate Rococo plasterwork as appears on the walls of the adjoining music room. In the outer border of decoration at the four corners of the room are a dolphin, eagle, lion and wyvern, fashioned in high relief; the inner border, which is in the form of an oval, introduces flowers and fruit, and there is a central rosette, also in high relief. This exuberant kind of plasterwork, often exhibiting, as here, a very high standard of technical ability, was doomed in the seventeen-sixties to give way to the chaste elegance of the Adam brothers. At Highnam, where Adamesque designs already occur in doorcases and friezes, Rococo stucco-work must make one of its last appearances.

Not only did Isabella find it difficult to settle at Highnam but she discouraged her husband from entertaining there or from exercising much hospitality. Indeed, very little of the first year or so of their married life was actually spent in their new home. Touring in the continent, travelling in their own carriage and hiring post-horses *en route*, the couple visited Milan and Bologna in 1839 and, between March and June 1840, Geneva, Rome, Genoa, Leghorn, Florence, Carrara and Naples. Thomas and Isabella made many acquaintances on their journeyings, including Robert Browning, whose appearance so resembled his own that when in London Gambier Parry was often mistaken for him. It was on these travels that Gambier Parry's first great burst of collecting began, and under the heading *Squanderings on the Continent 1839-1840*, he listed his new treasures, along with the places where they were purchased and the prices paid.[14]

In his last year as a bachelor, Parry had travelled extensively throughout the British Isles and Normandy, making water-colour-sketches of natural and architectural features which interested him. These studies, accurately drawn and showing a confident if restrained use of water-colour, reflect the influence of William Evans of Eton. The warmth and brightness of Italy, on the other hand,

[14] Thomas Gambier Parry, *Squanderings on the Continent, 1839-1840* (manuscript). Highnam archive.

elicited a more vivid and colourful response from the young man in love and no longer alone: a more brilliant light contrasts with deeper shade.

On their return to England, Isabella was six months pregnant, and on 16 September 1840 gave birth to a son, Charles Clinton Parry. Foreign travel was abandoned the following summer in favour of a sketching holiday in North Wales; and in December 1841 the couple were visiting Isabella's sister Anna and her husband William Baker at their Bayfordbury home when their second child, Lucy Anna, was born. In 1843 and 1844 the Parrys were once again off on their travels, touring extensively in Italy, and, whilst in Rome, commissioning sculptor W Tweed to make a bust of Isabella.

On 25 March 1843, a baby boy, Francis Gambier, was born to Isabella at Naples and baptised there on Easter Eve, 15 April, but failed to thrive; Francis died at Messina in Sicily, where Parry left instructions with the British Consul for a tombstone bearing the simple inscription:

Francis Gambier Parry

dear child

Messina June 9th 1843

aged 10 weeks

Isabella was to suffer the loss of both of her next two babies. Edward Clement Hervey was born in London on 19 November 1844, died at Highnam on 8 July 1845, and, because Highnam had no church of its own, was buried at nearby Churcham. Another son, Henry, was born at Bayfordbury in 1846, but lived for only a few hours; and although Parry did not yet realise it, Isabella herself was by this time terminally ill. The villagers of Highnam had grown fond of the Squire's lady. They saw her pass by on her cream-coloured pony on her way into Gloucester, and watched as she rode across the fields in the evening, Mr Parry walking by her side, on their way to nearby Lassington for the weekly practice of the choir which she had started there. 'She were very kind', one had said, 'and gave the poor folks blankets in the winter, which they went to the Court and fetched about Christmas time'.[15]

By the end of 1847 Isabella was not only in the final stages of tuberculosis, she was once again heavily pregnant. On medical advice, Parry took her down to Bournemouth, hoping beyond hope that the fresh sea air would halt the destruction of her lungs. On Sunday 27 February, summoning her remaining strength, Isabella gave birth to a son, Charles Hubert Hastings Parry. Thomas's uncle, Frederick Gambier, journeyed to Bournemouth to find his distraught nephew reciting the opening sentences of the Litany at his wife's bedside, but there was nothing which he could do to help. On 11 March, twelve days after Hubert's birth, Isabella died; she was thirty-one. Parry knelt at her grave as the

15 GPM pp 147/8.

service was said in the churchyard of the not yet completed church of St Peter's, and on 20 March returned there for little Hubert's baptism. Although of no significance at the time, it is an odd coincidence that the entry immediately preceding that of Hubert Parry in the baptismal register, that for a baby girl, records her surname as one shared with another great figure in English music. She was the daughter of a Bournemouth tailor called Elgar! Three more years were to pass before Thomas Gambier Parry was able to write about his loss. On 27 February 1851 he recorded in his journal that he had once again travelled by train to Bournemouth:

> This is my little Hubert's birthday. This day three years ago he was born in this place. This is a very sweet place. There is a wild nature about the surrounding heathy plains studded here and there with the dark groves of Pinasters, which is quite different to anything I know in England. The high cliffs commanding an immensely wide sea view are not bare and barren like most other cliffs, but are clothed with ling and heather. As the evening grew dusky I wandered upon the open heath above the house where I last looked upon the beloved form of my incomparable Isabel. It was a beautiful evening, warm as June and bright with stars. Long and deep were the prayers I made on that wide open heath for my three children and myself. I called to my recollection that too happy day, just at this period of the year in 1839 (twelve years ago), when I first made the acquaintance of my loved and now lost wife. How miserably ungrateful man's blindness and infirmities make him, me in particular.
>
> The house we had, No. 2 Richmond Terrace, is occupied. I looked long at that window – that room where I last nursed and watched that beloved being. As it grew dark I went to the churchyard. All was silence – not a breath of air stirred the dark pine wood around that sacred spot. By the bright starlight I read and reread the inscription on her grave. I need not write more – I want no memoranda of what is indelible in memory. Some kind hand has planted crocuses and snowdrops and other flowers about her grave… I sent a snowdrop from that sacred place to dear Lucy, and to dear Mrs. Clinton… The charm of this place is its simplicity. There is no attempt at cultivation; no fine shops. It is as yet undefiled – about fifteen or sixteen little detached villas, a baker, a chemist and a post office, and two moderate sized hotels form the whole settlement. I wandered about the walks trodden by dear feet – and returned late to the hotel.[16]

---

[16] Thomas Gambier Parry, *Journal 1851*. Highnam archive.

V

The Answer

Thomas Gambier Parry had taken Highnam Court with an avowed determination to refound his family; it was to be his Banstead. A man of quite remarkable energy, he had thrown himself into the restoration of the long-neglected house and the creation of an imaginative terraced garden scheme; but rarely content to sit idly by whilst other hands carried out his bidding, he often chose to roll up his sleeves and get down to digging and delving himself. Remembered as one who 'habitually vaulted over gates instead of opening them' and who 'used not uncommonly to come down stairs three steps at a time'[1], the squire of Highnam was always busy. He and his brother-in-law, William Baker, shared an interest in conifers, and in 1844 Parry had begun planting a *pinetum* at Highnam, one of the earliest in the country. He studied his subject thoroughly and spared neither effort nor expense in determining which specimens were best suited to the local climate and soil. Baker also set about creating his own *pinetum* at Bayfordbury in Hertfordshire, and the two men exchanged plants and ideas at a time when little was known in England about conifers and when specimens were extremely difficult to obtain.

On 29 April 1848, Gambier Parry stood again in his *pinetum*, a widower of six weeks. He was not alone. Two of Isabella's sisters, Emma Fynes Clinton, who was unmarried, and Agnes, with her husband, the Honourable and Reverend Godolphin Hastings, rector of nearby Lassington, were there, as were two of Parry's little children, seven-year-old Clinton and his sister Lucy, who was six. Lucy, Clinton, Emma and Hastings all planted young conifers of different varieties, one tree each for Isabella and her three lost children. The occasion was recorded by Parry in the small, gilt-edged notebook in which he recorded all such plantings: his *Pinetum Highnamense*; but an even longer-lasting memorial was already in his mind.

Parry had long felt the need of a church, a resident clergyman and a school at Highnam. He had often discussed his ideas with Isabella, and together they had chosen a site close to the centre of the parish. For several years he had

---

[1] GPM p 205.

granted an allowance and the use of a house to Godolphin Hastings for the maintenance of his ministry at Lassington, whilst tithes on the Highnam estate were paid to the vicar of Churcham, forming a large proportion of his stipend. On 7 October 1848 he wrote to the Bishop of Gloucester setting out his proposal to 'build a school with a mistress's house attached, and to secure the means for its continual maintenance'. The education of Highnam's children would be 'founded on the Catholic doctrines and practice of the church' and therefore the continual supervision of a clergyman would be absolutely necessary. Also, the school 'ought to be near the church, where the minister who overlooks the daily order of the children should receive, teach and catechise them on Sunday' and, in consequence, he proposed 'to erect a district church close to [the school], capable of holding upwards of 200 people, including the schoolchildren, and to endow it with £120 a year, with the provision of a residence for the incumbent, free of rent; to supply also a fitting space for churchyard, a playground for the children, and a school garden. And if it please God that I am allowed to carry out the whole of my design, I hope, in years to come, to erect a small almshouse in the immediate neighbourhood, so that the aged and infirm may join with the young in the daily ministration of our holy Church'.[2] This was an offer which the bishop could hardly refuse. The church would be dedicated to the Holy Innocents in memory of the children he and Isabella had lost; and the whole grand plan, along with continuing work on the *pinetum* and gardens at Highnam Court, would absorb much of Thomas Gambier Parry's abundant energy for the next three years, diverting his mind from grief.

The Gambiers, whose ancestors were Huguenots, had taught Parry the devoutly Protestant convictions which were to inform his thinking throughout life. He remained, in his own word, a 'miso-papist' but by the late 1830s had become convinced of the rightness of Tractarianism, which , under the impetus of the Oxford Movement, was re-awakening the catholic spirit within the *Ecclesia Anglicana*. In 1839 he had become a founder member of the Cambridge Camden Society, known from 1845 as the Ecclesiological Society, one of the most influential bodies to have existed in the nineteenth century. The group, composed largely of romantic young idealists like himself, were convinced of the need to revive the full glory of historically authentic Anglican worship and ceremonial. They were passionate about the restoration of medieval churches, and the supervision of the building of new churches in accordance with the deeply-held tenets of the Society. Gambier Parry set down an impassioned defence of the Gothic style in his journal following a visit in 1851 to the eleventh-century church of Santi Apostoli in Florence, the church from which Brunelleschi is said to have derived his first ideas of resuscitating classical architecture :

> The constant action and activity of pointed architecture with its broken curves and jagged foliations, its towering thinness and dangerous equilibrium... is essentially

---

[2] Ernest Gambier-Parry, *Highnam Memoranda* (manuscript, 1902). Property of Mr TJ Fenton, Highnam archive. Abbreviated hereafter to 'HM'), pp 110/112.

Christian. It flies up from the earth. It acknowledges the necessity of active exertion in religion. Its seeming perilous height and long drawn upward flowing lines imply a sense of sure foundation on a goodly rock, and a nature yielding to the sun of Light which draws up the delicate stem and expands the arching leaf, curls up the quickly growing tendril and ripens the crisp forms in an endless and harmonious variety. Such is the principle of Christian architecture miscalled Gothic. Such was it in the days of circular as well as of pointed architecture – both plants of nature, of Christian nature, different in outline but natives of the same soil, built upon the same Rock, rising to the same Heaven, and animated by a kindred soul. The pagan worshipped the creature of his own invention. That which was about him he knew, and traced out cause and effect in regular routine. His most exalted imagination and the unsurpassed ideal beauty with which it endued the creatures of his fancy expressing a most exceeding loveliness, and claiming our sympathy in every sentiment of human passion, still never knew that higher, keener, purer light which first shone upon mankind from the heavenly glory which dazzled the Israelitish shepherds and the bright star which stayed its course over the manger of Nazareth.

The pagan built his temple to suit the form of his worship. The imagination which created the temple had first created the creed. It was the very obverse of ours. Where was the awe combined with the confidence, the fear and love joined hand in hand? Where the hope and consequent heaven-turned eye of the Christian? Where the common love of the external forms of nature, of landscape, of leaves and tendrils and of everything great and small which were the works of Him whose works we also are? The pagan took not external nature into his ideas as we have. Christian architecture abounds in direct adaptation of simple forms drawn fresh from the fount of all beauty, idealized indeed, so that from a type you can recognise the very species and race. But in Pagan work where do you find any natural type idealised in the volutes, orders, cymas, bases and capitals – lovely forms, beautiful conceptions, all borrowed and chosen with insurpassable perception of abstract beauty from the natural objects and combinations but still banishing nature in its actuality and therefore claiming a stronger right to art as *art* contradistinguished from nature, but not therefore higher in beauty?

Thus and on such principles Gothic architecture is more fitted for temples which are for the ministry of that sanctuary, that true tabernacle which the Lord pitched and not man. Nature is the boundless inexhaustible source of all variety. Variety is the very principle of Gothic or Christian architecture… while the architecture called Classic variety is the very enemy. One leaf of a Corinthian capital, one volute above it, one inch of an evolo, one outline of the curved profile of a column, and you have all the executed forms that could be found in a temple which might enclose London. The rest would only be endless, infinite repetitions of the same, precisely the same, leaves, volutes, ovolos and profiles. Not so in nature. A forest is a lovely assemblage, but no two trees, no two sprigs are alike.

The classic temple is indeed a most beautiful creation and abstract creation of man's invention. I pity him whose feelings are so warped that his very enthusiasm would not warm at so fine a thing. Keep it by all means. Let every building fitted for great works of science, museums, halls, triumphal stately edifices for the decoration of wealthy cities, courts of law, mansions for commercial companies, offices for departments of government, galleries for exhibition of art be classic, if you will, and many a grand and glorious thing you will have… But pray keep Gothic and its sister forms for the sanctity of the cloister and the church, the Bishop's Palace, the country school, the humble parsonage and the college court.

When, in 1841, the Ecclesiologists announced a scheme for the erection of a Model Church on a grand scale in London, they insisted that it must be in the Gothic style of the late thirteenth and early fourteenth century; it must be honestly built of solid materials; its ornament should decorate its construction;

its artist should be 'a single, pious and laborious artist alone, pondering deeply over his duty to do his best for the service of God's Holy Religion'; above all the church must be built so that the 'Rubricks and Canons of the Church of England may be Consistently observed, and the Sacraments rubrically and decently administered'. The result, All Saints, Margaret Street, is a triumph of Victorian church art. Its architect, William Butterfield, drew his first designs in 1849; and by May of that year, the drawings and plans for Parry's own new church at Highnam were on their way to the diocesan registrar.

The architect chosen by Parry was his friend Henry Woodyer of Guildford. Tenders were called for from two firms of builders, Wingate of Gloucester and Myers of Lambeth, and Myers were awarded the contract. The sandstone used for the church came from a quarry at Hartpury, a few miles from Highnam, whilst the dressings are of hard Bath stone thought to be from the old Combe Down beds. Building began in the early part of the summer of 1849, the foundation stone being laid at a ceremony recorded in a booklet of 11 pages on the cover of which Parry wrote: 'Used on the occasion of laying the foundation stone of the new church at Highnam by my dear son Charles Clinton Parry. July 12, 1849'[3]. The sight of so fine an edifice rising in their midst gave the villagers of Highnam cause for wonder and, as they passed by, they 'looked up and thought of the trouble of the young squire, and muttered – "The Answer" '.[4]

> Henry Woodyer was born the same year as his client, and was educated at Eton and Oxford. He was a distinguished-looking man, tall, rather spare, always attired in an easy-fitting blue serge suit, loose shirt collar, and crimson silk tie. His soft black hat, rather wide in the brim, bore a small steel brooch in front. During inclement weather a long dark Inverness cloak was worn. A most picturesque bearded figure often smoking an extremely fragrant cigar, he lived the life of a country gentleman in Surrey, and had an intense dislike of anything which savoured of professionalism. The style adopted for Highnam was described as middle pointed of the fourteenth century; but Parry had a lot to do with the plans himself.[5]

Work proceeded so rapidly that by May 1850 the roof was already in place. Parry noted that:

> At about this time Woodyer and I were conversing about the way in which we could improve the turrets at the corners of the tower. The design was lying on the carpenter's bench in the temporary workshop on the south side of the church. I took a clumsy pencil and sketched a spire at a careless venture without the least intending to realise it. It became, however, so evidently the right and only thing to do. Woodyer was charmed with the opportunity of exercising his taste and skill. Not long after this he completed the design for it. Myers estimated it at £1700. This was exceedingly cheap for such work, for it is as lofty as that at Cheadle, which… cost £4000, inclusive of the tower, and was built by Myers from a design by Pugin.[6]

[3] HM p 118. Original in Highnam archive.
[4] GPM p 147.
[5] David Verey, *The Building of Highnam Church*. Published in *Country Life,* 13 May 1971, pp 1160/62.
[6] HM p 120. Original in Highnam archive.

Augustus Welby Northmore Pugin (1812-1856), the driving spirit behind the Victorian Gothic revival, published his *True Principles of Pointed or Christian Architecture* in 1841. In it, he lashed out against Classical architecture and sang rapturously in fervent advocacy of pointed arches, stained glass and encaustic tiles. One of his very finest buildings, the Roman Catholic church of St Giles, Cheadle, in Staffordshire, had opened in 1846. The epitome of the Ecclesiologists' ideal, 'a single, pious and laborious artist alone', Pugin was antiquarian, decorator and furniture designer as well as architect; and the man, his philosophy and his buildings alike were inspiration to Parry in all but one important particular. Pugin had converted to Roman Catholicism at the age of nineteen, believing it to be the only faith in which he could be true to his medieval style. Parry's allegiance remained zealously faithful to the Church of England, and the altitude of his chosen layer of anglicanism is beyond doubt. After visiting Wells Street in March 1851 he wrote, 'some quibblers have attacked the proceedings of the services at this chapel and spitefully but in vain brought the matter of complaint, viz. the chanting, before the House of Commons'. Later in the same year he refers to himself and his fellow Tractarians as 'we Anglo-Catholics', and whilst in Nîmes on the following Christmas Day asks:

> Are we English Catholics most allied to the Roman Catholicity or to French Protestantism? If I knew more what the latter was I could answer more easily: *if* it be Genevan Calvinism, I think we must repudiate the faintest idea of any connexion. Their fixed decrees of Predestination and Reprobation – and total rejection of the doctrine of the Sacraments, including that of orders, reduce Christianity to the very threshold of Mahomedanism.[7]

The tower at Highnam was finished by the end of June 1850; the masons then returned to the interior of the church to finish off the mouldings and leave all in readiness for the plasterers, carvers and glaziers. Only the finest and most costly materials were used throughout the church: a Minton tile floor; carving of the highest quality on font, pulpit and capitals; south aisle windows glazed by Hardman from designs by Pugin, and those in the north aisle by William Wailes. Parry was especially intent on achieving an ideal effect with the stained glass; such a window should not resemble a 'pretty transparency' but should look like 'an encrustation of Gothic gems'.[8] He was dissatisfied with the original east window at Highnam, and Clayton and Bell were later employed to replace it; but in dividing the south and north aisle windows between Hardman and Wailes, deliberately pitting 'one against the other that they may do their very best'[9], he astutely achieved work of jewel-like perfection. Hardman was also engaged to make hanging lights, single candles in the chancel, and magnificent radiator covers. The organ was made by Nicholson of Worcester. The church plate designed by William Butterfield, was made by John Keith and Son, the

---

[7] Thomas Gambier Parry (hereafter 'TGP'), *Journal 1851*. Highnam archive.
[8] *Ibid.*
[9] HM p 123.

Tilly Kettle: Captain Richard Kempenfelt, Thomas Parry and Admiral Samuel Cornish on board HMS *Norfolk* at the Battle of Manila, 1762. (*Highnam archive*)

Bishop Henry Parry (1561-1616). (*Courtesy the Bishop of Worcester*)

Sir William Beechey: Thomas Parry (1732-1816). (*Highnam archive*)

Mason Chamberlin:
Richard Oakes (1750-1779).

Sir Thomas Lawrence:
Mary Parry, née Gambier
(1787-1821).
(Highnam archive)

Watercolour by T Bonnor showing Highnam, c1778. (*Highnam archive*)

India House, Sale Room. *(By permission of the British Library) (Ref. P.699)*

Fort William. *(By permission of the British Library) (Ref. P.50)*

Fort Marlborough. *(By permission of the British Library) (Ref. P.329)*

Manu Lal: An inhabitant of the Poggy Islands. *(Richard Parry Collection, by permission of the British Library) (Ref. K.90321)*

Above left: Thomas Gambier Parry
(1816-1888). A painting by Mrs
Carpenter when he left Eton.
(Highnam archive)

Above right: Bust of Isabella Parry
(1816-1848) by Tweed. *(Church of
the Holy Innocents, Highnam)*

Right: Thomas Gambier Parry,
Florence 1861. *(Shulbrede archive)*

James Sant: Ethelinda Parry (1826-1896). *(Highnam archive)*

Highnam Court: Commonwealth detail in the centre of the south front, originally the entrance front. *(Country Life Picture Library)*

Highnam Court: The main staircase, c1760. *(Country Life Picture Library)*

Highnam Court: A group of Italian paintings in the Library. In the centre is the *Coronation of the Virgin* attributed to Lorenzo Monaco and below it *The Creation* by Mariotto Albertinelli and a 15th-century Florentine cassone. The centre painting to the left of this group is the *Virgin and Child* attributed to Andrea Del Verrocchio, beneath which are two predella panels: *The Visitation* and *The Adoration of the Kings* by Lorenzo Monaco. *(Country Life Picture Library)*

Highnam Court: The Gold Drawing Room. *(Country Life Picture Library)*

Highnam Court: The Morning Room. *(Country Life Picture Library)*

Highnam Court: The east wall of the Library. *(Above)* A 15th-century *Annunciation* between two *tondi*; *(below)* a North Italian cassone panel, *The Triumph of Chastity,* between two reliefs by Mino da Fiesole.
(Country Life Picture Library)

'The Master of SS Julitta and Quiricus': *S Quiricus slaps the Judge* c1430s.
(Courtauld Institute Galleries)

Richard Buckner: Clinton and Lucy Parry as children with their dog. *(Highnam archive)*

Hubert Parry in 1861. *(Highnam archive)*

Hubert Parry as a young man
(Shulbrede archive)

Clinton Parry. *(Shulbrede archive)*

Clinton Parry photographed by Julia Margaret Cameron in 1867. *(Shulbrede archive)*

Parry family photograph, 1869. Standing from left to right: Hubert, Clinton with Owen, Linda, Thomas Gambier Parry; seated from left to right, Beatrice with Noel, Florence with Isabel ('Bluebell'), Ethelinda with Hilda; seated on grass from left to right, Ernest, Sidney, Geraldine. (*Shulbrede archive*)

Hubert Parry, Lady Maude, Dorothea ('Dolly') and Gwendolen at Highnam Court.
(Shulbrede archive)

Thomas Gambier Parry.
(Highnam archive)

William Blake Richmond:
Lady Maude Parry (1888).
(Shulbrede archive)

silversmith favoured by the Ecclesiological Society, and given to the church by Parry's grandmother, Jane Gambier; the only item not paid for by Parry himself.

Whenever asked, as he frequently was, what the church had cost him, Parry always made the same reply: 'My dear friend, I took the very greatest possible care *not* to know, and I tore up every bill as I paid it. The only thing I do know the cost of was the bells, for that came in one sum'.[10] The three bells, weighing over 2 tons 4 cwt, cast by Mears of Whitechapel, cost rather more than £400, and by reference to Parry's bank book it is clear that the entire cost of building and endowing the church was little short of £16,000. Only once did Parry draw back from any part of his original intentions, but not on the grounds of cost. He had planned to fill the thirteen niches of the exquisitely-carved stone reredos with figures, but decided that this would be regarded by some as 'going altogether too far'.

Whilst work was continuing on the church, Parry was by no means isolated from other aspects of Gloucestershire life. For nineteen years he served as an officer in the Royal Gloucestershire Hussars, and was never happier than when drilling his troop or taking part in the annual tournament at Hardwicke. He was remembered as looking magnificent on ceremonial occasions, mounted on his beautiful black charger, 'Prince', and wearing the costly full dress uniform of his corps: a jacket of 'visible' blue, very heavily laced with gold; a slung pelisse, also of blue and heavily laced; pantaloons, also blue with gold; and for head-dress a busby with a plume of scarlet and white.

In 1850 Parry was appointed High Sheriff of the County. It was the custom then for sheriffs to ride out in great state to meet Her Majesty's Judges at the Assizes. Parry was escorted by twenty javelin men, or running footmen, dressed in his livery; his tenantry and several friends, mounted; and also by his troop of Yeomanry. His carriage was drawn by four grays, the postilions in his livery; and this whole cavalcade, as it crossed the River Severn at the Over bridge on the way into Gloucester, was considered to be a sight to go and see!

     *   *   *   *   *   *   *

Highnam Church was to be consecrated on Tuesday 29 April 1851. Parry and Woodyer had been busy on the previous day, painting the small alabaster pillars at the foot of the font blue because they looked too light – no detail was too trivial to be overlooked – and in the evening nineteen guests in addition to the children and their governess, Miss Cooper, sat down to dinner. Among those who stayed at Highnam Court that night were Francis Lear, the Rector of Bishopstone, and his wife Eda; Henry Fynes Clinton; Godolphin and Agnes Hastings; William and Anna Baker; the Revd Sir Lionel and Lady Darrell (Darrell had built a small Gothic church at Fretherne, Gloucestershire, where he was the vicar); Charles Gambier and his wife; Emma Clinton, who played her part as

---

[10] HM p 106.

mistress of the house for the occasion; and Henry Parry, who, at age seventy-two, was Thomas Gambier Parry's sole surviving paternal uncle.

Later that night, when all his guests had at last gone to bed, 'and the new church stood gaunt and silent under the moon', Parry made his way there alone. 'He carried in his arms the bust of her who had talked over and planned with him all that he had now achieved'.[11] He had instructed Woodyer to prepare a niche in the wall of the chapel on the south side of the chancel, and into this he now placed the bust of Isabella, made in Rome by Tweed in 1844.

> *At the mid hour of night, when stars are weeping, I fly*
> *To the lone vale we loved, when life shone warm in thine eye;*
> *And I think oft, if spirits can steal from the regions of air*
> *To revisit past scenes of delight, thou wilt come to me there,*
> *And tell me our love is remember'd even in the sky.*

(Thomas Moore (1779-1852) *At the mid hour of night)*

'The next morning', Parry wrote in his journal, 'was one of anxiety to me':

I was early at the church with Woodyer; all was got ready and the doors locked by 9 o'clock… The great tent had been brought from London and was erected on the lawn in front of the library windows, with long tables and seats arranged for more than 200 people. I could not wait to receive the many invited guests, having too much to organise.

By 10.30am all the invited guests had arrived. The laity had gone to take their seats in the church. The clergy were robing in the drawing room. On the bishop's arrival the clergy went in procession to the church [where] I presented the petition to the bishop in the porch.

The great service was soon over. The work so long the constant subject of my attention was given over and consecrated to the service of God and the benefit of his poor. All blessing be to Him. *Non nobis Domine, sed Nomini Tuo, etc.*

Little Hubert was taken to church for the first time in his life (since his baptism at Bournemouth) on this morning. May he have a great share in the blessings of this consecration! Cliny and Lucy too! The first lesson for the evening (not a selected chapter) happened to be the fifth of the First Book of Kings – a singular and most apt coincidence.

And, behold, I purpose to build an house unto the name of the Lord my God.

After that came the dinner for the poor, which they seemed to enjoy – plenty of beef and plum pudding. The church looked very beautiful for the evening service which took place at about 5.45pm.[12]

Henry Fynes Clinton, crusty chronologer as ever, made a characteristic entry in his diary: 'April 29, 1851. At Highnam. Consecration of Church. Tower, 97 ft., Spire, 85 ft., Vane, 15 ft. Total 197 ft.'.[13]

---

[11] HM p 133.
[12] TGP, *Journal 1851.*
[13] Charles L Graves, *op cit,* p 7.

'The greatest day of my life is over', wrote Parry:

> The day for which I have been at work for the past two years, and have been anticipating
> for a longer time. There on the spot over which I have often walked with my once
> treasured Isabel, and have talked of it as the place where some day we hoped to have a
> church built – there it stands – complete – and consecrated. But she is no longer by my
> side. Her bust is in the monumental niche in that church for which she chose the spot
> where now I have been permitted to raise it.[14]

*   *   *   *   *   *   *   *

Up to the time of the dedication of the church at Highnam, Parry left no
suggestion in his journal that any new love had entered his life. Early in May 1851
he and Clinton had gone up to London, where they visited the Great Exhibition
with Uncle Henry Parry: 'all wonder!... a vague overpowering impression of
astonishment – half doubting of the result of this wonderful accomplishment'.[15]
Clinton was sent off to his school at Feltham on 8 May, and Parry, who had been
appointed Justice of the Peace in 1847, returned home to attend Gloucester Petty
Sessions two days later. On the following Sunday he attended church with Lucy:
'the church crammed at evening service. I always feel Cliny's absence very much
when Lucy comes alone';[16] and two days later he was off to London again for a
stay of six weeks. Parry visited his elderly grandmother at her home, 69 Eccleston
Square; called at Taylor's the coachmaker in Brook Street to inspect a new
carriage which they were building for him; attended a recital given at the
Beethoven Quartet Society; went to see Mr Rashleigh, a Cornish friend of
William Baker's, with whom Parry was considering the preparation of a large
illustrated work on conifers (which failed to materialise); dined at his club with
William Webber and went with him to a lecture on mesmerism given by an
American, Dr Darling, who 'made some people look very foolish... he acted on
[them] by magnetism while they remain in a wakeful state... and he obtains great
command over them, although they resist in mind and muscle';[17] another visit to
the Great Exhibition – the Duke of Wellington was there, rather tottery in his
eighty-third year. Parry's movements, actions and thoughts from 17 May and
throughout the whole of June and July remain a mystery. The eight pages
covering that time have been cut from his journal. But on the date at which the
journal resumes, Tuesday 5 August 1851, Thomas Gambier Parry married
Ethelinda, the youngest daughter of the Very Reverend Francis Lear.

When did Parry's love for Ethelinda begin? Undoubtedly, he would have
been present at her father's funeral in the previous year. Lear had been appointed
Dean of Salisbury in 1846 and died on 23 March 1850; but had romance

---

[14] TGP, *Journal 1851*.
[15] *Ibid.*
[16] *Ibid.*
[17] *Ibid.*

blossomed soon after that, then surely Parry would have hinted at it in his personal journal. Although Lear's son, the Revd Francis Lear, rector of Bishopstone, had been present at the dedication of Highnam Church, there is no record that his mother or sister Ethelinda had been with him. Can it be that the widowed Mrs Isabella Lear, who had been so impressed by Parry and his fortune at the time of his marriage to her niece twelve years earlier, had re-visited the eligible widower in London, and with her daughter on her arm?

The wedding took place at Bishopstone, the Rt Revd Edward Denison, Bishop of Salisbury, officiating. W Kerr Hamilton, future Bishop of Salisbury and husband of Ethelinda's sister Isabel, and Sidney Herbert of Wilton House signed the register as witnesses. What thoughts were in the mind of Ethelinda's mother? She and the mother of Parry's first wife were sisters, both daughters of Bishop Henry William Majendie; the children of the two marriages would be not only half-brothers and sisters, but cousins too.

After the wedding, the couple travelled by coach to Bath, a journey of four hours. Parry had booked a hotel and ordered a dinner of roast mutton and apple tart to be ready on their arrival. The next morning, Ethelinda announced that 'she knew Bath and had no wish to stay there', and so they moved on to Taunton: 'disappointed at the far-famed church; bad talk in plenty; ill from some horrid poisonous coffee; posted to Dunster – pretty but nothing worth staying for. Walked about for some time, dined, and came on to Lynton... it was a long drive, tremendously hilly'. In Lynton they set out to explore the locality, Ethelinda riding a donkey, Parry walking and trying to sketch but 'quite out of practise' and unable to 'draw a bit, returned to the Castle Hotel to a late dinner very hot and tired'. An excursion to Edensmouth was an equal letdown; after a 'wild drive across the open and up and down lanes', they thought it 'not worth going to – it is merely a point for an expedition and to pay well to donkey men'. Ilfracombe was 'disappointingly bare'.

After only five days away, Parry sent his servant, Frederick, to Highnam 'to fetch dear Cliny'. The eleven-year-old arrived at Ilfracombe by steamer from Bristol on Thursday 14 August, and on the following Saturday the little party set off for Clovelly via Bideford. Night fell before they had reached their destination. Suddenly, the horses stopped in the middle of the road and the palboy announced that it was impossible for him to take them any nearer to Clovelly. All around was inky blackness and no nearby habitation was to be seen:

> Luckily, a man passed by with a lantern. We went down to the village and got assistance to unpack and carry down what luggage we wanted. It was damp and slippery. We three, Ethel, Cliny and I each carrying what we could, started off by the light of a candle held in a man's fingers, and descended this steep path leading to Clovelly... [It] was very slippery, being roughly paved, and so steep, that it was cut into long steps. On the way down, slipped I. Ethel's desk was in my hand – down went the desk and many things went out into the mud! There was a trial of temper and humour. She only laughed. There are few out of whose lips some slight expression of annoyance at least would not have escaped.[18]

18 *Ibid.*

This was the last trial of a speedily improvised and hitherto strained honeymoon. The next day brought sunshine and happiness. 'I never saw such a county as this in England' wrote Parry, 'Clovelly Bay is a recess in the Bristol Channel; ever calm and lonely; oaks growing to the edge of the tide; fine rocks, wooded cliffs and sparkling villages giving feature and variety to the coast'.[19] At ease with himself and with his family, Parry was again able to relax with pencil and tablet, and spent the whole morning of their last day at Clovelly sketching.

Back at Highnam, Parry delighted in introducing Ethelinda to her new home, but they were soon off on their travels again. On 8 September they kissed Clinton, Hubert and Lucy goodbye in London, and set out for Dover to catch the night mail packet to Calais:

> It was a great grief to me to part from my precious children. Sweet Cliny felt it excessively, but kept himself up to the last by saying, 'well I shall see you soon again'. I hope to indeed. I need to be grateful indeed for such sweet affection as exists between my dear children and myself, and how much more grateful now that it has pleased God to allow me to afford them the tender care and affection of dear Ethel. They are already devoted to her, beyond my expectation. Their loss is great indeed! But how blessed are they to have such a friend as Ethel, the only person in my acquaintance who could be for them what I wanted for them. I need not write here what she is also to myself![20]

Even so, apart from a visit of under two weeks at the end of November and the beginning of December 1851, during which Ethelinda stayed in Paris with her mother, Parry and his wife remained out of England, touring on the continent until the summer of 1852. By the time of their return, his watercolour technique had much improved; his interest in fourteenth-century painting had been awakened; his collection was greatly enlarged; and he had purchased his first *trecento* painting.

---

[19] *Ibid.*
[20] *Ibid.*

VI

The Best Brand of Amateur

Thomas Gambier Parry's detailed study of the history of art began at the same moment that Highnam Court came into his possession. When he and Isabella set off on their tour of Italy in 1839, Parry had with him a copy of Gould's *Dictionary of Eminent Artists*, and whilst in Florence began to make formal notes on the schools of painting, using Gould as a guide and source of quotation. Unsurprisingly, his attention was drawn to the achievements of the sixteenth and seventeenth centuries; to classical landscape; to the French, German, Flemish, Dutch and English schools; to the Florentine, Roman, Venetian and Lombard schools; to the works of the Carracci and their Bologna school; and to the legacy of Sir Joshua Reynolds. Admittedly, Gould had considered Cimabue (c.1240?-1302?) worthy of mention as the reviver of painting 'which had languished since the fall of the Roman Empire', but only as an introduction to the later glories of the Florentine school: Verocchio, Leonardo da Vinci and Michelangelo. Italian painters of the *trecento* and *quattrocento*, the 'primitives', would continue to be undervalued for a while longer; their paintings thought to be crude and beneath consideration. Sir Robert Peel was expressing a conventional view when, in 1836, he opposed the acquisition of works by the early Italian masters for the National Gallery: 'I think', he said, 'we should not collect curiosities'.

A change in attitude in the 1840s and 1850s, a willingness to view European art in a comprehensive historical perspective, was advanced as much by the lead of the Prince Consort as by any home-grown initiative. Albert, who as a youth had learnt to paint, and had travelled to Italy with his brother Ernest to study art and music, was the first to propose a chronological list of works to the National Gallery; and his own appreciation of the early Italian masters was clearly demonstrated by purchases of paintings for the Royal Collection, including a triptych by Duccio (c1255/60-1318/9) and a Madonna by 'a close follower of Fra Angelico (c1400-1455)'.

It was decided in 1843 that the new Houses of Parliament, designed by Pugin and Sir Charles Barry, should, when completed, be decorated with frescoes in the early Italian style. Johann Friedrich Overbeck, who had been a leading member of the Nazarenes, a group of German artists devoted to the revival of religious art and inspired by the late medieval masters, was approached but refused to participate. However, Ford Madox Brown and William Dyce, enthusiastic admirers of the Nazarenes and amongst the several British artists influenced by them, agreed to join the *frescanti* at Westminster. Dyce, who had been interested in the Italian primitives for some time, visited Italy in 1845 to study their art at first hand. He sought to emulate the brilliance of colour and pure luminosity of their work by painting on a white, rather than a toned, ground; and his magnificent fresco above the high altar at All Saints, Margaret Street, serving as both medieval reredos and (in the absence of space for glazing) east window, was inspired by fifteenth-century Italian work.

The year 1848, marked in Europe by the revolutionary movements which swept through France, Italy, the Austrian empire and the Germanies, also saw the birth of the most controversial and influential movement in the history of English art: the founding by Dante Gabriel Rossetti, William Holman Hunt and John Everett Millais of the Pre-Raphaelite Brotherhood: the 'PRB'. One of the prime aims of the PRB, like that of the Nazarenes in Germany before them, was to revitalize religious art. Indebted to Dyce for his technique, and marching in step with the critic John Ruskin, they sought to rescue art from the degeneracy into which they believed it to have fallen; to escape from the 'dim religious light' tradition of painting: the 'slosh' of dark, funereal colours combined with the loose handling of paint so beloved of Sir Charles Eastlake and others of their contemporaries who followed in the tradition of the first President of the Royal Academy, Sir Joshua ('Sloshua') Reynolds. They were convinced that this decline had begun with Raphael (1483-1520) and the High Renaissance, and sought to halt it by constructing a bridge between their own art and that which predated Raphael; to return to the styles and techniques of painters of the early Italian Renaissance: to the primitives. As Ruskin expressed it in a letter to *The Times* of 13 May 1851 in response to a critical attack upon Millais and Hunt:

> These Pre-Raphaelites (I cannot compliment them on a *nom de guerre*) do *not* desire nor pretend in any way to imitate antique paintings as such. They know very little of ancient paintings who suppose the works of these young artists to resemble them. As far as I can judge of their aim – for… I do not know the men themselves – the Pre-Raphaelites intend to surrender no advantage which the knowledge or inventions of the present time can afford to their art. They intend to return to early days in this one point only – that, as far as in them lies, they will draw either what they see, or what they suppose might have been the actual facts of the scene they desire to represent, irrespective of any conventional rules of picture-making; and they have chosen their unfortunate though not inaccurate name because all artists did this before Raphael's time, and after Raphael's time did *not* this, but sought to paint fair pictures, rather than represent stern facts; of which the consequence has been that, from Raphael's time to this day, historical art has been in acknowledged decadence.

Although by no means all the work of the Pre-Raphaelites was confined to religious subjects, they rapidly became associated in the critical mind with the Tractarian movement. Holman Hunt was a devout Anglo-Catholic, and it was he who suggested that Millais's *Christ in the Carpenter's Shop* was prompted by a sermon given in 1849 by a member of the Oxford Movement. Evangelicals condemned them for being too 'Romish'; and Ruskin, a Low Church man, lamented in his *Notes on the construction of sheepfolds* (1851) that 'the schism between the so-called Evangelical and High Church Parties in Britain [was] enough to shake men's faith in the truth or existence of Religion at all'. None the less, he championed the Pre-Raphaelites, whose aim of restoring art to the sincerity and true values of former times he shared. 'In early times art was employed for the display of religious facts,' he wrote, 'now, religious facts were employed for the display of art'.[1]

It is therefore perhaps significant that whilst *en route* for Italy with Ethelinda in September 1851, Gambier Parry made a special point of stopping off in Munich to examine the work of two leading Nazarenes. Julius Schnorr von Carolsfeld's frescoes for Ludwig I of Bavaria in the Royal Palace failed to please him:

> The many encaustics by Schnorr are to be admired for their variety of composition and huge size. There is much power of drawing too, but he had such a vast quantity to do in covering huge surfaces, and such a number of them, that one need only look for what one finds to one's satisfaction. But the rapidity and coarseness of the work give such a crude wall-paper look to many of these large paintings, the lightness of the colouring and only half-worked expression in the countenances make one so much regret that a painter with his evident knowledge of his art had not had less to do and more time to do that less in, that I received more pain than pleasure in looking at them.[2]

But Peter von Cornelius' frescoes in the Ludwigskirche were quite a different matter:

> I greatly admire Cornelius's frescoes – *The Last Judgement* all by his own hand, covering the entire eastern wall of the Choir – there is depth and vigour of colour in many parts of his work and that of his pupils on the vaulting which does the greatest credit to the Munich School. These Germans are endeavouring to establish a phase of art as the basis of a new school, which shall combine the abstracted contemplative expression of the early Pre-Raphaelite painters, with the full forms, richly massed colouring and dramatic character of more fully developed art. They draw very well and often design very finely. I think that the mellowing influence of a few years will smooth down lines and colours so that the expressiveness of the countenances and impressiveness of their groups will be very much indeed increased.[3]

Always with Gambier Parry, artistic judgements were inextricably linked to a profound sense of spiritual certainty; to matching inner convictions with a pure and uncluttered external expression in paint, stone and glass. Stopping at Bamberg he was moved to write of the cathedral:

> A glorious Romanesque pile! There is here a western and an eastern apse. I hope to remember it all and describe it and all it conveyed to me of that deep contemplating religious feeling which was the fostering spirit of the art of the 11th century...

---

[1] J Ruskin, *Modern Painters*, Vol 3, (2nd edition in small form)(George Allen, 1898), p 55.
[2] TGP, *Journal 1851*.
[3] *Ibid.*

"GREAT" is the only word which at once embodies in one sentiment of the glorious design of this temple.[4]

Whilst visiting the churches of St Sebald and St Lawrence in Nuremberg he was relieved to find that, 'at the Reformation the Protestant religion was quietly embraced without any church demolition. The Protestants allow all the old Catholic arrangements to remain as before the Reformation';[5] but if the town of Hans Sachs and Sixtus Beckmesser had been spared the worst excesses of the iconoclasm which so ravaged the pre-Reformation religious art of England, much of what remained suffered, in Gambier Parry's view, from 'prettiness and fancifulness and littleness':

> The designs, whether for Adam Kraft's famous *Sacramenthaus* at St. Lawrence's Church or for the painted glass or for wood-carving or for metal, had but little separate characteristic identity. Stone is cut into twirligig patterns; pinnacles twist about as if they were made of whalebone; and the spirit of art is degraded into ingenuity and whim. All repose is lost. All intellectuality is balked by what seems to have been the public demand for novel combinations. For abstract beauty, German art has not very much to boast of – any more than Dutch pictures. I speak of the high ideal such as speaks in the early art south of the Alps in the work of Masaccio, Gentile da Fabriano, Fra Beato [Angelico] and so on; in Guido da Siena as early as 1221. Van Eyck sometimes approaches to great beauty, as for instance in one or two of the small pictures in the cabinets at the Pinacotek [*sic*] at Munich. But in spite of all the unmistakeable ugliness in A. Dürer's works, in L. van Leyden's and others of the early German school, I feel the greatest interest in them. They speak to me and excite a sentiment which I cannot put into words – as music in the same way is unwordable – *art* begins where language ends.[6]

In the last week of September 1851 Thomas and Ethelinda sailed down the Danube from Linz to Vienna, where they spent a few days inspecting the pictures in the Belvedere and Esterhazy Galleries together, and Parry spent a morning 'going about several people's houses' where he heard of paintings for sale and 'found nothing but rubbish'. On Sunday, as usual, they read their own service, including one of the sermons which Christopher Wordsworth had preached in Westminster Abbey, 'exposing Calvinistic errors', and which were greatly admired by Parry , and went to the Prater:

> a flat ugly uninteresting field… There were horse races, a sort of sham affair got up by a 'circus' company, and fireworks. How exceedingly painful it is to see the way in which Roman Catholics universally go counter to the real object of their church in the abuse of Sunday. We stayed in the Prater only for a short drive, and returned home in time for the Cathedral Vespers [at St. Stephen's].[7]

Their attempt to enter Hungary was thwarted by the police, who refused to sign Parry's passport. Hungary's bid for complete independence from Austria

---

[4] *Ibid.*
[5] *Ibid.*
[6] *Ibid.*
[7] *Ibid.*

had been defeated by the intervention of Tsar Nicholas I of Russia with 100,000 troops in the summer of 1849, and now:

> No stranger *except a Russian* is allowed to go into Hungary... Several other English have been refused within the last few days. One might get leave perhaps by pressing and by assailing the English chargé d'affairs, but we rather fancy a longer time south of the Alps, and willingly give up our Hungarian tour.[8]

Pressing on to the south via Graz and Laibach [now Ljubljana], they reached Trieste by 1 October, but were advised by the British consul against a Dalmatian tour; 'the country was almost inaccessible – and entirely so for ladies'. Consequently, before moving on to Italy, they spent the following two weeks touring in Istria, finding, then as now, a beautiful country beset by political upheaval,

> The Croatians are in great discontent. They were faithful to the Emperor in the Revolution of 1848-9. In return for spilling their blood, their system of government is altered and their taxation greatly increased. The liberty to pay a small annual fine to relieve a private house of the obligatory reception of soldiers, is taken away. Salt and tobacco are monopolized as they were not before 1848... and an universal poll tax is imposed even down to a beggar of 16 years old!!... At Fiume [*which previously had belonged to Hungary*] the Croatian language is being forced on the people against their will.[9]

Gambier Parry, who was rarely troubled by illness, suffered badly from a gastro-intestinal upset whilst in Istria and was still feeling far from well on the short voyage across the Adriatic to Venice. In spite of this – and harassment on their arrival by the police, who, in obedience to Austrian censorship orders, confiscated several of his books – Venice soon wove its magic charms. Aided by an Italian doctor's prescription for a bottle of magnesia, he was soon 'lionizing' enthusiastically with Ethelinda, and much of what he saw brought inspiration to Parry the artist:

> Saturday October 25th.

> A glorious day. Spent the morning in the Ducal Palace. Endless fine things to fill a mine for the exultation of memory! To write about all the lions of this glorious old palace, deposited as it has been, burnt, gutted, robbed and modernized, yet full of great and glorious productions would take up more time than I could well write in these short notes.
> In the afternoon we went in a gondola for me to put in the colour of S. Giorgio Maggiore. [*At sunset their gondolier steered into the open lagune towards the Lido*] The effect of the sunset, and of the sky long after sunset with its deep orange and melting green-blue with the beautiful outline of Venice and its many domes and towers relieved against those glowing hues and reflected in long wavy lines in the gently undulating water was such as few or no pencils could describe. Turner would indicate and idealize it. Danby might nearly produce its effect. But who could give all beside!
> The moving boats, the gliding gondolas, the chorus of bells chiming for the *Ave Maria*, the fresh evening air, the feeling that it was Venice before us and around us...

---

[8] *Ibid.*
[9] *Ibid.*

Left our gondola at the piazzetta of St. Mark's, and walked home to the Europa [Hotel]. The Piazza St. Mark's and the Palace lit up with gas in full blaze is a most brilliant and animated scene not easily forgotten.[10]

Overwhelmed by all about him, Gambier Parry rose to the challenge of Venice in a series of watercolour drawings exceeding in quality anything which he had achieved before. In particular, he perfected the difficult technique of making water appear truly 'wet'; so wet that we, the viewers of his art, can easily sense the rocking motion of the gondola in which we are his imagined companions, anticipate the approach of noble buildings towards which we float, trance-like and unaided, and persuade ourselves that we need only to stretch out a hand to feel the cool canal water wetting our fingertips.

Gambier Parry and Ethelinda had, by happy chance, found themselves among 'a large art-pursuing party of compatriots'; a party which included the topographical painter, David Roberts, RA, the architects George Gilbert Scott and Benjamin Ferrey, and the artist EW Cooke, RA, with whom Gambier Parry spent some time:

> looking at his charming studies and sketches. His adopted name "Lagunetto" from these lagunes is clever in apposition with "Canaletto". Cooke has *adopted* Venice and paints here every year.[11]

Perhaps it was the example of Cooke's work more than that of any other of the 'compatriots' which exercised so strong an influence on Parry's watercolour technique; but there was in Venice a critic of art and society whose influence, enormous on his own age, is still powerfully felt today. 'Mr. Ruskin is here', wrote Parry, 'very busy about his book' [the second volume of *The Stones of Venice*]. Ruskin had married Euphemia Chalmers Gray ('Effie') in 1848, and the pair had set out for Venice the following year. In 1851, the year of the Parrys' visit, Ruskin had made the acquaintance of the Pre-Raphaelites and completed the first volume of *The Stones of Venice*; and in that same year an artist admired by Parry and revered by Ruskin, J M W Turner, had died.

Parry was an enthusiastic collector of Turner's *Liber Studiorum: illustrative of Landscape compositions, viz. Historical, Mountainous, Pastoral, Marine, and Architectural* over many years, parting with his extensive collection towards the end of his life only because the condition of several items had begun to deteriorate. The series, issued in fourteen parts between 1807 and 1816, has been described as the greatest serial work of our greatest English landscape painter; and when the Burlington Fine Arts Club mounted an exhibition illustrative of the *Liber Studiorum* in 1872, Gambier Parry was one of nine contributors of proofs, etchings and first published state plates for display. Ruskin had written a pamphlet defending Turner from his critics as early as 1836, but at the artist's request had not published it. In 1842 he began work on the first volume of *Modern Painters* in response to further savage attacks on Turner's work by reviewers of the annual Royal Academy exhibition, and had hailed Turner as the

---

[10] *Ibid.*
[11] *Ibid.*

master of diffused light, on a level with Michelangelo, the master of form. Ruskin may well have found Gambier Parry's Tractarianism indigestible, but he certainly approved of his new acquaintance's watercolour technique, and the mutual interest of the two men in Turner was bound to lead to their continued contact. After he and his wife returned to England in July 1852, Ruskin wrote to Gambier Parry in response to an invitation to visit Highnam Court:

> I found your kind note yesterday… and hasten to assure you how much pleasure it would give me to come and see you and talk over the many things which we should both have so much pleasure in discussing. But at present I cannot, for we have workmen in a new house in which I have to establish myself and all my goods and chattels [*at Herne Hill, next door to his old family home*]; and besides this to unpack half a shipload of things from Venice, and when this is done I want to get my notes at Venice into form as fast as possible, and to be done with them, and then to devote myself altogether to Turner. I shall then have to make an erratic tour over England in search of his scattered works – and *then* I shall ask permission to avail myself of your kind invitation: but for the present I am fastened like a rock limpet after my eleven months of exile.
>
> Thank you also for your enquiries touching our health. We enjoyed the warm weather at Venice far more than any other period of our stay, and I think Mrs. Ruskin never was so well as she is now!… After looking at the noble study of colour which you made from the Ducal Palace, how provoked you must have been with Mr. Roberts' 'academical' view of the same – with (NB) the gondoliers all rowing on the wrong side of the gondolas.
>
> If it would not be too much troublesome to you, I should be exceedingly obliged if you could let me know the subjects and (roughly) the sizes of the Turner drawings still in your possession, as I am engaged in making a chronological catalogue of his works and am desirous of knowing where each of them is placed.
>
> Mrs. Ruskin joins me in sincere regards to Mrs. Parry and yourself.
>
> Believe me, most faithfully yours,
>
> J. Ruskin [12]

After spending an evening with the Ruskins in Venice, Gambier Parry had described Effie Ruskin as 'very pretty – very Scotch and peculiar'.[13] Eighteen months later, in London, Ruskin introduced Parry to William Dyce, Holman Hunt and John Everett Millais. A friendship between Ruskin and Parry had clearly been developing as, for instance, when the two men visited Turner's house together. Parry dined at Millais's home several times and found him, like Effie, strangely 'peculiar';[14] what he could not have been able to predict was that within a few months, Effie would leave Ruskin, that their marriage would be annulled on the grounds of non-consummation, and that Effie would later marry Millais. After this, Parry's invitation to Ruskin to visit Highnam does not seem to have been renewed.

*   *   *   *   *   *   *

---

[12] GPM p 155/60.
[13] TGP, *Journal 1851.*
[14] *Ibid.*

The first phase of the Gambier Parrys' tour of 1851/2 was coming to an end. At each of their destinations, Thomas's first priority had been to collect his forwarded mail and to read eagerly of any news concerning his children: the 'bedoes' as he affectionately called them. So acutely was he missing Clinton, Lucy and Hubert that he was prepared to travel back from Italy to England overland in the winter of 1851 to see them. But even on this hurried diversion no opportunity for 'lionizing' was wasted; and one overnight stop on the railway journey westward from Venice through northern Italy to Simplon provided far more than mere rest and refreshment.

At Padua, Gambier Parry stood in the Arena Chapel, built in 1303 by Enrico Scrovegni, possibly to atone for the life of his father, a usurer who appeared in Hell in Dante's *Divine Comedy*, and recognised, as had Dante himself, that Giotto (c1267-1337), the painter of the magnificent series of frescoes which covered every surface, had, by his innovative genius, obscured the fame of Cimabue. 'His was a wondrous stride', wrote Parry, 'Giotto was certainly the father of Italian painting', but then added:

> ...this arena chapel impressed me particularly with this idea, that in a building painting must be subservient to architecture...never was it seen to be so true as in this chapel, which is meagre in its effect; even painfully so for want of light and shade and form: the walls flat, the ceiling coved, and all and each cut up into little squares divided only by a line of paint and covered with subjects of similar tints and proportions[15]

Which was rather to miss the essential point. This modest, barrel-vaulted rectangle of no more than 67 feet long, 28 feet wide and 42 feet high was planned specifically for painting; those 'little squares', sixteen of them on the south wall, eighteen on the north wall, as well as the additional images on the east and west walls, encapsulate the whole story of man's Redemption and final Judgement; and Giotto's style, 'imperfectly dramatic' in Parry's view, presents an unclouded narrative of peculiar intensity. Giotto's architectural scheme *was* painted.

The next day, the last day of October, Parry and Ethelinda visited the Baptistery and the Oratory of S. Giorgio, both renowned for their wonderful fourteenth-century frescoes; those in the Baptistery by Giusto de' Menabuoi, and those in S. Giorgio by Altichiero. Presumably, lack of time prevented a visit to the Chapel of S. Felice, that other great Paduan monument to Altichiero's genius:

> Spent much time on the Baptistery examining the interesting Giottesque frescoes AD 1380 with which the whole walls and ceiling or dome are covered... They are not equal to those in the Arena Chapel, having more of the Characteristic features of Byzantine art apparent in the blackish shadows and smaller pleats and folds of drapery than Giotto. There is much very original in composition and rich in colour. Some of the heads in the cupoletta of the sanctuary (over the altar) are worthy of an early Raphael, and the first gloried head to the right of our Lord's figure in the marriage of Cana on one of the sidewalls is worthy of a Michaelangelo, or any one of the greatest students of ancient classical forms.

---

[15] *Ibid.*

The frescoes in the S. Giorgio... are glorious [and] vastly superior to those of Giotto in the development of dramatic action and composition, rich in colour and strikingly beautiful in much arrangement of the light and shade. We were much hurried, being obliged to get to Verona today so that we may reach Milan by Saturday night or Sunday morning. We wished for hours in this most fascinating series of paintings.[16]

But hours to spare there were none. Gambier Parry's priority now was to get back to England to see his children. He had already decided that both Clinton and Lucy would accompany him and Ethelinda on the next stage of their continental travels, but ahead of them now lay the Alps, and the Simplon Tunnel had not yet been built! The Parrys spent the night of 5 November at Domodassola, breakfasted the next morning at 5.30am, and set out to cross the Simplon in their carriage:

The day was brilliant as it dawned over the mountain tops and put the little stars to shame. As we rose higher and higher the cold increased. People warned us and said that there was much snow, but all looked so bright that it was hard to believe those reports. Gradually, towards the middle of the day, the scene became more bare and bleak. The wind blew very cold from the north. On issuing from a ravine of towering precipices we came suddenly upon winter. Snow drifted by the strong eddies of wind warned us what we should find higher up the pass. I was amused at the hardihood of a peasant woman whom I passed leaning against the railing by the roadside. There was a piercing wind blowing down the pass; the road was slippery with frozen snow; and as I had found it very freezing work to sit in the carriage and blow my fingers in vain, I was walking fast up the hill to warm myself. Seeing this poor woman stopping to rest herself, and as she stood her clothes flickering and shivering in the sharp breeze, I said in Italian that it was rather cold here. To this she shook her head. She said, with a broad pronunciation in her broad German, 'Ah! Nai! – frishe gar nick', by which I understood her to mean that it was not a bit cold...

The village of Simplon was half buried in snow. The premature winter has set in. A little hot coffee was a most revivifying allopathic remedy for what we had been suffering... It was a wild scene all around this wind-blown, icebound village. All was white with snow, except where a strong breeze had drifted it away from some little pieces of pasture ground. To mount the rest of the pass, and to descend it on wheels, was declared impossible. So the carriage was lowered down upon a sledge, and the wheels packed on a second, smaller sledge drawn by one horse. Four horses were then harnessed to the carriage in a single file. Four men also attended us beside the post boys. Thus we started. At every turn in the road the snow became deeper. The whole landscape was one vast ocean of snow and ice. The air condensed about the highest peaks and drifted down upon us in flakes of frozen cloud. It was the very kingdom of Winter; we were penetrating his inmost realms where all things owned him supreme.

Our attendants were very useful in digging a road through the snow at intervals, and occasionally righting the nearly capsized sledge which ploughed the road beneath us. The summit was at last attained. As we broke upon the first open valley in the descent, the vast range of the Alps and their deep chasms covered with the white sheet of winter, the rocks by the roadside coated with transparent ice, from the projecting sides and brows of which hung innumerable icicles measuring more than six or seven feet as they hung suspended like stalactites of glass, altogether presented a view such as I had never seen before – and shall not soon forget. To dear Ethel, who had never before seen an Alp, nor any further development of winter than the milder character of

---

16 *Ibid.*

such as covers with its white sheet the gentler undulations of an English landscape, this savage scene was surprising indeed.

As we descended from the high plain among the mountain tops, and skirted the sides of the precipitous valleys, the road became entirely blocked with snow… It was an awful sense of immediate danger which seized one as the sledge on which we slipped along on the hardened surface of the snow swung on one side within an inch or two of the yawning gulf of hundreds of feet depth which opened below us. The stones which had been placed for safety along the roadside to mark the brink of the precipice were entirely hidden by snow. Our sledge often passed over these, so near were we to that awful brink. Nothing saved us but the untiring exertions of our mountaineer attendants. I thank God with all my heart that these means were successfully employed. It was hard to bear it as we felt a sudden swerve to the left, and looked over into space, where the air was all between us and the bottom of the chasm over which we leant. At last, we could sit still no more. We got out of the carriage and walked.[17]

Ethelinda had arranged to remain in Paris whilst her husband was in England, and very late in the evening of 19 November her mother and Sidney Lear arrived to join her at the Hotel Mirabeau. Gambier Parry left the next day, crossed from Boulogne to Folkestone, and travelled by train to Brighton, the home of James Gambier, where he was reunited with his two youngest children:

I found my precious Lucy and Hubert very well… the sea air has made them very bonny. I am to have a room at my Uncle Butler's while I remain in Brighton. I have had a correspondence with Miss Cooper about her leaving my children. I must wind up matters by having a talk with her tomorrow.[18]

The talk took place: 'I have had a final conversation with Miss Cooper about her going away, the good reasons for which she sees very reasonably'. What could those 'good reasons' have been? Had Miss Cooper committed some indiscretion? Three days later Parry was off to Feltham where Clinton was at school:

Found *dear Cliny* looking very well. Mr. Westmacott and I had some conversation about Cliny's work for the next four months on the continent. He is a schoolmaster after my own heart and sets store on French and History, instead of only those old models of Homer and Virgil which, glorious as they are, are certainly not the sole object of an education fitted for the world as it is, as schoolmasters in my first schooldays used to think. Modern languages, history and science are worth more to 9 men out of 10 now than all the Latin and Greek of the world of the classics.[19]

Leaving Clinton to complete his autumn term, a matter of a few days, Parry returned to London and took the evening express back to Highnam, where he inspected the now completed church and schoolroom, and the work which Myers the builders were doing on the rectory. Henry Woodyer came over, and during dinner the two men 'chatted architecture and many other things', including 'the method of building a church at Aden on the Red Sea, which was

[17] *Ibid.*
[18] *Ibid.*
[19] *Ibid.*

to have no direct light from any window and not to have a stick of wood in it'! Something of Gambier Parry's amazing energy is revealed in his journal entries for the following three days of November 1851:

> Thursday 27. A morning's work vainly attempting to plan out the siding of the railway at Over [*The Gloucester and Dean Forest Railway purchased land at Highnam and Over in 1849. The line was under construction until 1856*]. Afternoon busy writing letters. An evening spent over accounts.
> Friday 28. Church. Timber marking, etc. Giving directions to Barclay and Wells. Farming. Gardening.
> Saturday 29. All sorts of work indoors and out. Wound up by a couple of hours with Spring: shot 3 pheasants and a hare. Went to dine at Hardwicke [*the home of the Lloyd-Bakers*]. Two Miss Fenwicks were there and Mr. Le Merchant.

Back to the capital by the early train on Monday; over to Vauxhall Station to meet Clinton; and across London to the home of friends, where Miss Cooper had been instructed to fetch Lucy and where Gambier Parry now 'settled matters' with her about her leaving his children. Little Hubert, it seems, had been left in Brighton; Miss Cooper was gone – and he would not see his father again until the summer of the following year.

On the evening before he returned to France with Clinton and Lucy, Gambier Parry dined with his uncle, Henry Parry, at his club. The old gentleman, now 72 , was feeling low, worried that he might not see his nephew again; but the two men 'spent a most agreeable evening' together, Gambier Parry's recollections of which hint at the reasons why his grandfather, Thomas Parry, had disowned his youngest son all those years ago:

> What a wonderfully strange constitution of mind [Uncle Henry] has! After all the *fastness* of his early and mature life, and the many things which with other men destroy all fine feeling, his heart is as fresh as a child's. His has been a fine disposition ill-managed by those who in his youth should have trained it. His strong feelings led him away; but his better judgement was transgressed, not destroyed, his naturally fine disposition violated by want of moral force and training. He is still as affectionate as a child.[20]

As Gambier Parry and his uncle were quietly dining, news was reaching London of rioting that had broken out in Paris, and of a *coup d'état* by the French president, Louis Napoleon, who had forcibly dissolved the government following its attempt to abolish universal suffrage. On arriving by steamer at Boulogne with Clinton and Lucy on 5 December, Parry was 'somewhat terrified' by reports of widespread violence in the country, including a rumour that mobs had torn up sections of the railway track. Leaving the 'dear bedoes' at Boulogne for safety, on the following morning Parry took the earliest train to Paris, where he was hugely relieved to find that the track was still intact and that Ethelinda, her mother and Sidney were unhurt. But France was in chaos; hundreds were being executed without trial; and news from the provinces made it impossible to travel south as planned. Returning to Boulogne for the children, Parry took them to

---

[20] *Ibid.*

Amiens, where he and Ethelinda had arranged to spend a last evening with Mrs Lear and Sidney. After a further frustrating week, stranded in Paris, Parry 'determined to start on Monday [15 December], go as far as Lyons and find out the real state of things by being so much nearer to the scene of the action'. Whereas most parents might have been tempted to return to the safety of home, the Parrys were determined to proceed in the opposite direction, even though they knew that their road would take them through the department of the Basse Alpes, the scene of some of the worst disturbances. Setting out from Paris they were caught up in a general exodus from the city:

> We reached Châlons by railroad; arrived late. The hotel was a glorious scene of confusion; crowds of people rushing in from the railroad, at the same moment scrambling for rooms! The next morning we got on board the dirty steamer very early, and through a dense fog worked our way as far as Bourges. It wanted but another two hours paddling to reach Lyons. The fog was so dense that we could not possibly proceed.
>
> There were many people on board. No other English but ourselves. We took a walk after dinner, by way of passing the time; and then came in to spend the evening as we could. Reading, writing, dominoes and chess were our means of amusement. The French people all of middling class – probably merchants – some officers, and one or two persons, whom I suppose I must call ladies, amused themselves very differently. They commenced by a late dinner about 6pm that was succeeded by at least two hours of incessant jabbering. Then came a woman with a guitar and sang not badly but accompanying herself discordantly to the agony of our ears, but apparently to the delight of the French. They then began to sing songs. Oh! such songs! and pay fines if they missed a song when their turn came. This caused deafening bursts of laughter... Two men, sitting at the end of our table, having taken a fancy to Cliny, got him between them and made him drink beer!
>
> Now came the difficulty! What were we to do for beds? The large first-class sitting room cabin was full of people. We had taken up our quarters from the first in the *salle à manger* cabin. What to be done with the dear children was no easy matter. It was out of the question for them to bear the intense frost and cold fog on deck by sleeping in the carriage (*à caléche* with curtains), so Ethel and I determined to do that, and to make the bedoes as comfortable as we could in their cloaks on the hard, narrow seat in the cabin. They are lying there, but sleep will be impossible as yet; for the French have redoubled their noise over a bowl of punch
>
> Wednesday 17th. Ethel and I were nearly perished. We suffered extremely from the intensity of the frost during the night. Such was its rigour that I found my shaving brush turned to a hard mass in my carpet bag, although it was packed among woollen things in a thick bag, and under cover of quantities of other luggage all covered with a strong tarpaulin.
>
> We managed to sleep a little. At 5 in the morning I woke with my feet and legs dead with cold. So, getting out of the carriage, I went in the dark to the cabin to look after the dear children. I could hardly believe my eyes: the French party were actually going on just as I had left them. What on earth could they have found to talk about! for their conversation was nothing but pleasantry and laugh. The dear bedoes had at last fallen asleep in the midst of the row.
>
> Two steamers were nearly sunk yesterday by coming into most violent collision in the fog. The shattered hulk of one of them floated down the stream and anchored close by us.

Fog worse than ever. All the passengers dispersed. We got our carriage off the steamer, and sent to Villefranche for horses; and after a freezing drive of three hours reached Lyons at about 4 o'clock. [21]

As 1851 drew to a close, the Parrys passed eastward through the department of Var where a fortnight before there had been scenes 'of the most frightful atrocities of socialism'. They stopped for a meal at Brignoles, where, in the town's prison, 'there were upwards of 200 of the late *émeutiers* [rioters]; many had already been sent to the hulks of Toulon'; and as they drove on in their carriage they passed many more, trudging the hopeless road with an escort of soldiers and gendarmes.

At year's end, safely arrived in Nice, Gambier Parry was both grateful and entranced:

> All nature smiles here. Nettles, brambles, thistles and other signals of the curse pronounced on earth seem to have no place here. Olive yards, orange groves, cypress, cactus, aloe and palm cover and ornament the valley and mountain sides which sparkle with sunny white walls of villas, cottages and church towers in all directions. Today was such a day as August can hardly bless us with in dear old England.
>
> The past year has marked the beginning to a new era in my life. Few men have had such blessings as I have. So great and so many as to baffle the powers of memory to review them all. In the year that has now only one more hour to run, I and my precious children have received blessing beyond all price in this dear woman who is now, indeed, all that their own most precious mother could be to them, in care, tenderness and confiding affection. May that gracious Father of Mercies bless her to them, and them to her, and lead us all to peace along the steps of Time marked by the passing years, with increasing conviction, sincerity and wisdom.[22]

*　　*　　*　　*　　*　　*　　*

'Oh! what a country is this Italy!' wrote Gambier Parry, 'every scene is famed in history; every town of one's path opens fresh beauties with new impressions charming eye and mind'.[23] The Parrys reached Florence on 14 January 1852 and remained for over a month. William Baker, his wife, Anna, and their son, Willy, were already there, as were their mutual friends the Ellisons, and the three families joined together to share in the pleasures of 'lionizing'; but pleasures were not all. A daily governess was engaged for Lucy; and, as well as the lessons which Gambier Parry himself gave to his eldest son, Clinton was sent each day to Willy Baker's tutor. A singing master, Signor Campana, and a French mistress were engaged for Ethelinda; and Parry spent an hour each morning with an Italian master, Signor Guerini. Nor were the evenings wasted. Parry was reading, amongst other things, Sir Charles Eastlake's *Schools of Painting in Italy*, and Giorgio Vasari's massive *Lives of the Artists*, first published in 1550, including the *Lives* of some hundred and sixty painters, sculptors and architects. Although Gambier Parry was taking lessons to improve his Italian, it is unlikely that he was reading Vasari in the original language, but more probable that he had purchased the first

[21] *Ibid.*
[22] *Ibid.*
[23] *Ibid.*

complete translation in English, by Mrs Jonathan Foster, which had been published in 1850.

Vasari's great literary accomplishment, the history of Tuscan art from Cimabue and Giotto to the crowning achievements of Michelangelo's genius, still commands enormous respect from art historians; but like many other scholars, Gambier Parry was careful to filter Vasari's attributions and descriptions of works through the fine mesh of his own critical judgement. First and foremost, he was searching, as Dennis Farr has pointed out, 'for an unforced spiritual content' in the paintings which he examined and, later, in those which he purchased, 'that was not conveyed by the elaborate exuberance of much seventeenth century art'.[24] Gazing out over Florence from the green slope of Fiesole whilst on a sketching walk with William Baker, Parry's thoughts turned on the enigma of beauty born alongside man's black fratricide:

> Were it not for the horrors of crime which have blackened the records of the past days of Florence, the associations of genius, of beauty, of nobleness and grandly striding intellect, which characterised the development of Christian art in this most interesting neighbourhood, would be almost too great a temptation, and make the real world and its doomed labour and sorrow disappear from one's recollection, and lead on the dreamy thoughts of better things in a charmed train and moody contemplation of an imaginary state of things; which, if too much indulged, would lead the mind to the precisely opposite point to that which the Christian artists directed their labours, *viz.* the expression of suffering in all mundane affairs, and of purity and glory as alone found in Realms above.[25]

Parry's unforced spiritual ideal in art became ever more difficult to satisfy as his taste matured. Of a fresco by Andrea del Sarto (1486-1531) in the convent of S. Salvi he wrote: 'I seldom see much religion in his paintings... I feel that I am looking at a picture; I realize nothing else'; but on visiting the Chiostro Verde of S. Maria Novella a few days later, the frescoes by Paulo Uccello (1397-1475) illustrating the story of *Genesis* prompted him to write:

> The abstract simplicity of the early painters has a peculiar charm, which can be better felt than described. Their pictures seem at least to have this advantage over more advanced art, that they tell their story plainly and without interruption, while their followers embarrassed their simple meaning by scientific accessories – making most perfect pictures but not embracing a tenth part of the story of the older artists.[26]

Crossing to the south of the Arno, Parry was deeply impressed by the frescoes in the Brancacci Chapel of Santa Maria del Carmine, commissioned in 1425 from Masolino da Panicale, who chose the great master of the renewal of Tuscan painting, Masaccio, to work with him on the chapel. When Masolino was called to the court of Hungary in the following year, Masaccio continued in his place, but did not finish the work, which was completed by Filippino Lippi between 1481 and 1485:

---

[24] Dennis Farr, *Thomas Gambier Parry as a collector,* an essay published in *Thomas Gambier Parry (1816-1888) as artist and collector* (Courtauld Institute Galleries, University of London, 1993), p 35.

[25] TGP, *Journal 1851.*

[26] *Ibid.*

Filippino Lippi, his father [Fra Filippo Lippi], Masolino da Panicale, and Masaccio are assuredly great men for their day. They are in many ways superior to Giotto and the Gaddis but I cannot grant them superiority over Aldighieri [Altichiero] and Giacope di Avanzi [Jacopo Avanzo] in the San Giorgio at Padua, in *expression*. In drawing there is a superiority, and greater naturalness, also in grouping, but there is no greater advance than might have been expected.[27]

In making passing reference to 'the Gaddis' – Giotto's pupil and assistant Taddeo Gaddi, and the most important of his three painter sons, Agnolo – Gambier Parry was unwittingly anticipating his first acquisition of a major painting on the tour of 1851/2, and his first purchase of a work of the *trecento*. Throughout his travels, Parry was constantly seeking out items of quality for his growing collection. Whilst in Germany on this tour he had already made several purchases, including a thirteenth-century Limoges pyx, four early eighteenth-century ivory reliefs, and a sixteenth-century Flemish triptych of an *Ecce Homo with Saints and Donors,* which he placed in Highnam Church, where it is still to be seen; but he had so far seen little of particular interest for sale in Italy. Then, on 18 February, he and Ethelinda arranged for a young English governess to look after their children whilst they went off by train to Pisa for a few days.

Everything they saw in their 'lionizing' delighted them, and Parry was particularly thrilled by Nicola Pisano's magnificent pulpit in the Baptistery. On their second day in Pisa, Parry records that they 'went to a dealer in engravings, and I bought some indifferent old tempera paintings of him'. He makes no mention of any significant purchase, and yet, in his own handwritten catalogue of the Highnam collection, compiled for insurance purposes in 1863 , he lists a painting 'bought at Pisa, 1851: Angelo Gaddi [*sic.* Agnolo Gaddi] – a repetition of a subject attributed to Giotto, but this is a fine example in admirable condition – Virgin and Child, and adoring angels', setting against it the low insurance value of £8. The Parrys visited Pisa only twice on their 1851/2 tour: this excursion of February 1852, and again on their way home in the following May, when no purchases are mentioned in Gambier Parry's journal; and so it seems very likely that the Gaddi work was among the job lot of 'indifferent old tempera paintings'; the first jewel in a *trecento* collection which was to become his lasting delight.[28]

Ethelinda and Thomas were glowing with happiness. They returned to Florence, via Lucca, arriving in time for his birthday on 22 February:

> The dear children greeted me with many kisses and good wishes. Lucy gave me a charming little basket to collect ferns in. Cliny gave me a little head of Dante in alabaster on a green marble pedestal. Dear Ethel gave me a very pretty set of tourquoise studs. This day I number 36 years – I cannot write my musings.[29]

Two days later the couple spent a long morning in the church of Santa Croce, where the Chapel of the High Altar and the Castellani Chapel are frescoed by Agnolo Gaddi; the Baroncelli Chapel is frescoed by Taddeo Gaddi; and both

[27] *Ibid.*
[28] TGP, 1863 List, *sv* No 68. Highnam archive.
[29] TGP, *Journal 1851.*

the Peruzzi and Bardi Chapels contain frescoes by Giotto, the latter cycle, illustrating *Stories of St. Francis* (c1325), being amongst the painter's finest achievements. 'I love more and more the old masters – Giotto, Gaddi and their schools' wrote Parry, 'Santa Croce is full of their masterpieces. It would take all the rest of this book to write all I think about them'; and Ethelinda's news soon afterwards would give him much more to think about. Her baby was due exactly nine months after that happy excursion to Pisa.

Although Gambier Parry made several more extensive tours in the continent, none was more important in cementing his artistic taste than that which he made with Ethelinda in 1851/2. Leaving Florence, they had sailed from Leghorn (Livorno) to Rome, arriving there on 13 March and staying for two months. At Easter, Ethelinda had 'overtired herself and very nearly produced what ladies call a mishap'. She was well enough to travel by 14 May (Clinton had been sent back to England four weeks earlier), but rather than heading straight for home, they completed a month-long circular tour of Assisi, Arezzo, Siena, Florence and Pisa in their carriage, before heading north to Genoa and Turin on their way out of Italy. 'Eth bears the travelling famously' wrote Parry, 'by the help of a spring cushion, which makes a sort of bed for her in the carriage'.[30]

Back at Highnam, Gambier Parry gazed at the walls of his newly-completed church and pondered afresh a problem which had already been on his mind for at least two years: how to achieve ideal results in fresco? Some wall decoration had been completed in the church by Crace and Company in 1851, but it fell far short of Parry's vision, stimulated as he was by recollections of the work of the Nazarenes and of the great Tuscan masters of the *trecento* and *quattrocento*. John Gregory Crace, the head of a decorating firm founded in 1760, had formed a partnership with Pugin in 1844 to decorate country houses in the Gothic style. One of their most successful collaborations was Eastnor Castle in Herefordshire, the home of Earl Somers, only ten miles from Highnam, where Crace completed the decoration of the magnificent Gothic Drawing Room in 1850. Parry almost certainly would have visited Eastnor, and could hardly have failed but to be impressed by the richness of the decorative scheme. Crace's superb chancel ceiling at Highnam, gold stars set in a deep blue ground, still survives; but Parry wanted more.

In Giotto's time, and for at least two centuries after him, the paint in wall decoration was applied directly on to fresh plaster; hence the term fresco, meaning 'fresh'. The powdered pigments were mixed with water and united chemically with the lime of the plaster, but it was essential that they were applied before the plaster was dry. In the warmth of Italy there was no difficulty in plaster drying rapidly, the colours drying lighter than they appeared when wet. But in the cold and damp of the English climate plaster dries very slowly, the colours soon fade, and the paintings are prone to be spoiled by discolouration, staining and microbiological growth.

---

[30] *Ibid.*

In an effort to overcome this problem, William Dyce had made *secco* additions to his frescoes at the Palace of Westminster, *ie*, by adding paint in a starch medium after the plaster had set; but his work rapidly deteriorated. The fresco work in what became known as 'The Jolly Campaign of 1857', so great was the fun enjoyed by all who took part, was also an unfortunate failure. Dante Gabriel Rossetti had drawn together a group of Pre-Raphaelite friends to decorate the Debating Hall (now the Union Library) at Oxford University. The group, which included William Morris and Edward Burne-Jones, decided upon a scheme of ten paintings illustrating subjects taken from Malory's *Morte d'Arthur*. The walls of the newly-built hall still had damp plaster on them when the artists, none of whom knew anything about fresco technique, set to work; and by the following year the paintings had all but faded away. The revival of fresco painting in England was impeded for lack of an adequate native technique.

Parry knew all of this well, and determined to find a solution. No stranger to experiments with chemicals, he had enjoyed making fireworks with William Baker and entertaining their two families with exciting displays. Now he turned his attention to the creation of a fresco medium which would be effective in a damp climate, and his experiments were every bit as dangerous as those with fireworks! His search for a lasting and workable medium ended in 1859 with the discovery of a technique which he termed 'spirit fresco', and in that year he set to work to paint a blazing *Doom* over the chancel arch at Highnam. Parry had much to celebrate. In the six years following their tour of 1851/2, he and Ethelinda had been blessed by the births of five healthy children: Linda, Ernest, Beatrice, Geraldine and Sidney. But two shadows darkened his happiness: Clinton, who on leaving his preparatory school at Feltham had gone on to Eton and, in 1859, to Christ Church College, Oxford, was displaying increasingly erratic behaviour; and in that same year Parry could only watch helplessly as the bloom of good health which had shone in Lucy's face slowly faded away.

In a hand-written work of extraordinary resolve, contained in two leather-bound volumes, each of three-inch thickness, Ernest Gambier Parry, in the years between 1900 and 1914, set down a detailed record of his family history and of his father's achievements: *Gambier Parry Family Memoranda* and *Highnam Memoranda*.[31] In these, Ernest recalled how his father took infinite pains both to prepare a wall-surface for painting and in the manufacture of his spirit fresco medium:

> He did it all himself, and great and glorious was the fun when father had a brew in hand of spirit fresco medium. He used to make it out of doors, on the upper or lower terrace, or on the big flagstones outside the garden door near the billiard room. There was risk of the various highly inflammable materials catching light, and only charcoal was used so that there might be no flame. But even then the mixture caught sometimes while he stirred with a long spoon, and then father used to call out – 'Mind your eye!' and in fits of laughter himself beat it out with what he called 'swabs or swags of carpet' which were part of the paraphernalia kept handy.[32]

---

[31] Both volumes are in the possession of Mr T J Fenton. Highnam archive.
[32] GPM p 162.

The spirit fresco medium, used not only for binding the ground and the paint layer, but also for priming the wall, comprised a mixture of resins, oil and wax. As Tracy Manning has explained, Parry was emphatic that it was an overall process:

> The medium was mixed with $1\frac{1}{2}$ parts of turpentine, and then heated, and applied to the dry wall until it was saturated. The wall would be left for a few days, and the ground then painted quickly over the surface in two layers. This consisted of the medium (slightly diluted with turpentine) mixed with equal quantities of white lead and gilder's whitening (a fine white chalk).[33]

In an account of the process, published in 1880, revealing his recipe and technique, Parry explained that his wall preparation, when dry

> for which two or three weeks may be required, produces a perfect surface – so white that colours upon it have all the internal light of *Buon Fresco* [true fresco] and the transparency of pure water colours – and it is so absorbent that their attachment is complete.[34]

Ernest remembered clearly his father's work on the *Doom* over the chancel arch at Highnam. The scene represents the Judgement, with Christ in Majesty as the central figure; the two subjects right and left over the first two arches of the nave represent the expulsion of Adam and Eve, and the Annunciation. The Parrys' fifth child, Sidney, was baptised in the church on 20 February 1859, and in the following month:

> A considerable scaffolding was erected enclosing the upper part of the chancel arch and the bays right and left, and to give sufficient light to work by, tiles were removed from the roof and replaced by glass. The present dormer windows were put in subsequently when the work was finished [*to light the Doom*]...Father had one or two assistants who did the lettering and the diaper patterns as well as the gilding...He ground and mixed all his colours himself, and nothing was put on the walls, even the most insignificant portion of groundwork or filling in, that he did not do a part of it himself first...
>
> The work extended over a period of practically three years. Three years or less would be no wide margin to allow for such an undertaking, especially when we consider that the work from first to last was, in this case, the achievement of one man. But indeed father took nothing of the kind. He was always a very rapid worker – very rapid in all that he did: he was none the less so even in such a new enterprise as this. Apart from his various labours and interests in Gloucester, there were the social duties and claims upon his time at Highnam and the consequent incessant interruptions. And there was something more. Lucy had shown signs of the complaint that was then regarded as simply a death warrant – consumption; and every effort had to be made for her. In the autumn of 1859 two months or more were spent at Brighton, and during the whole of the winter of 1860/61 we were all at Mentone. Thus, these short three years were very considerably curtailed, and a degree of mental anxiety which wore father down, and

[33] Tracy Manning, *The 'Spirit Fresco' Technique and its historical context,*an essay published in *Thomas Gambier Parry (1816-1888) as artist and collector* (Courtauld Institute Galleries, University of London, 1993), pp 47/8.
[34] TGP, *Spirit Fresco Painting, An Account of the Process* (London, 1880), p 4.

subsequently ended in the only illness he ever had, was added to his difficulties'.[35]

The *Doom* was the first and most important element in Gambier Parry's work of comprehensive internal polychromy at Highnam, which continued for several more years, and he enjoyed recounting how, when working in his overalls in the church, visitors would come up to him, imagining that he was a hired workman, and say knowingly, 'Now we can see it is not true that Mr Gambier Parry does all the painting himself'! The entire scheme was not finished until around 1880, the frieze scene, running the whole length of the north aisle and depicting a procession of New Testament people who were 'followers of God as dear children' (Eph. 5 v.1), being the last feature to be completed:

> In preparing his cartoons for this, and indeed all his other work, he habitually drew from models. The pose or action of the figure, the grouping and general composition, were roughed out first, and in not a few cases the heads were actually finished; but when possible he made a study of a head from life, not making a portrait, but following the main lines and characteristics, and idealising them. Hands and feet, especially hands, he almost always drew from life, several of us being his regular models. Hair, too, he always liked to paint from life, and he would ask perhaps a man, a woman or a girl he might meet anywhere to come and sit to him. I remember one was a girl from Huntley who he happened to notice as he drove into Gloucester.[36]

Thomas Gambier Parry's work at Highnam, described by Professor H-R Hitchcock as 'the most important Anglican example of painted internal polychromy, rivalling Pugin's St. Giles, Cheadle', was both a labour of love and an act of unshakeable faith; it was, said Goodhart-Rendel, 'the fulfilment of the Pugin ideal'.

Parry published the results of his experiments in spirit fresco in the *Ecclesiologist* in 1862, but by then both Ford Madox Brown and Frederic Leighton had taken the trouble to learn details of the technique from Parry's own lips. Ernest remembered how Leighton had visited Highnam; how he and his father had gone over to the church; and how Leighton had painted a large head on the vestry wall (Ernest used to stare at this head when as a small boy he was busy blowing the organ for Hubert). Leighton, already a close friend, wrote to Parry in September 1862 to report how delighted he was with his own results in spirit fresco: 'You can wash, you can load, you can model, you can glaze and all in a wonderfully short space of time. The result, too, seems to me as satisfactory as any substitute for fresco can be'.[37] Sixteen years later, Leighton began work on his two grand frescoes in the South Kensington Museum, now the V & A, *The Arts of Industry as Applied to War* (1878-80) and *The Arts of Industry as Applied to Peace* (1884-6) – and he selected Gambier Parry's spirit fresco technique for the task.

* \quad * \quad * \quad * \quad * \quad * \quad *

---

[35] HM pp 147/8.
[36] HM p 151.
[37] Leighton to TGP (September 1862). Highnam archive.

From time to time, in the years when he was perfecting his spirit fresco technique, Gambier Parry had made attempts at painting in oils. His first lessons in the medium, taken in Rome in 1852 with a poverty-stricken expatriate English artist called Mason, came to nothing. Between April and July 1855 Parry and Ethelinda had attended their first London season. Highnam Court was being extended to accommodate a new billiard room and other facilities, and whilst in the capital Parry renewed his search for a good teacher of oil painting. On 21 May he recorded in his journal: 'Went in the morning to Hulme and Gilbert to engage one or the other of them to give me lessons in oil painting – not successful', but even so, seven days later he was able to write that he 'went early to Mr. Gilbert for my first lesson in oil painting',[38]presumably referring to Sir John Gilbert (1817-97). In the same season, Parry also sought out lessons in figure drawing from an artist he refers to simply as 'Warren'. In his watercolour drawings up to this time Parry had generally avoided painting figures as his main subject, and in the few examples which do survive there is a noticeable lack of anatomical proportion. Henry Warren (1794-1879), President of the New Watercolour Society, had published his *Artistic Anatomy* in 1852 and would have been a natural choice of teacher; within days, Parry found himself working 'from the model – an African!' [39]

Although his lessons in figure drawing with Warren were of great value to Parry, notably in preparation for his work on the Highnam frescoes, he seems not to have persevered with oil painting further than in the considerable skill with which he restored several of the pictures which he purchased. But the London season of 1855 was worthwhile and enjoyable in other ways too. There were visits to Charles Dickens's private 'theatricals'; to the opera at Covent Garden, where Ney, Viardot and Graziani were singing in Verdi's *Il Trovatore* only four weeks after its first performance in England; to a concert at the Philharmonic conducted by Richard Wagner, whose 'new music' Parry failed utterly to understand; to lectures on anatomy, art and design; to the studios of John Everett Millais and Frederic Leighton; and to several dinner parties, including one at the home of Sir Charles Eastlake, where the Parrys 'met many notorieties, among them Landseer, Thackeray, etc).[40] Within a few weeks, Parry was invited to see Eastlake's collection of paintings, and found among them two pictures, one by Giovanni Bellini (c1430-1516), which he had very nearly purchased himself when last in Venice. A few days later, Parry spent the afternoon at the home of 'Mr. Rogers (the old poet) looking at pictures', amongst them works by Poussin, Raphael, and Tintoretto.

Samuel Rogers (1763-1855), the son of a banker, succeeded to his father's fortune and became head of the firm in 1793, thus gaining the opportunity to collect great works of art and to indulge his fancy for writing poetry. He had commissioned Turner to illustrate an edition of his *Italy* (1822-28); and on the

---

[38] TGP, *Journal 1851.*
[39] *Ibid.* Henry Warren was first identified by Dr. Dennis Farr as the artist under whom TGP studied. See Farr, *op cit*, p 31.
[40] *Ibid.*

death of Wordsworth in 1850 had even been offered the laureateship, which he refused. Rogers died only a few months after Gambier Parry's visit, and today he is almost forgotten; but it seems likely that he agreed to sell one of his pictures to Parry, who, on the following morning, arranged with an agent, Mr. Bayley of Cheltenham, 'to purchase the Corregio'.

If this painting was indeed a work by Antonio Allegri da Correggio (1489?-1534), it was undoubtedly the unfinished picture of *The Baptism of Christ*, listed at No. 72 in Parry's catalogue of 1863 as 'an unfinished picture by Correggio...bought in England', which, at an insurance value of £150, was the fifth most valuable painting in his collection at that time; a grandly expensive acquisition, and perhaps a compensation for his failure to secure the Bellini purchased by Sir Charles Eastlake.

Although Parry had been a collector for twenty years, the rate at which he acquired art treasures accelerated from 1855, and by 1863 he had purchased all of the most important items in his collection. The paintings by sixteenth-century Italian artists which Parry already owned by 1855 included a magnificent *Creation and Fall* by Mariotto Albertinelli (1474-1515), and the delightful *Holy Family with St. John and St. Elizabeth* by Garofalo (c1481-1559), both purchased in 1849. The Garofalo has the additional interest of having belonged to Charles I and has his cipher on the back of the panel. But after 1851, following Parry's discovery of the primitives, and the purchase in Pisa of *The Madonna of Humility with Adoring Angels*, attributed to Agnolo Gaddi (d 1396), his interest in later Italian painting gradually waned. 'He had in a high degree', wrote Anthony Blunt, 'the essential qualities of the collector: keen enthusiasm, independence of judgement, and a fine sense of quality'.[41] That independence of judgement was clearly demonstrated by Parry's energetic study of the work of the primitives, a taste shared by few of his contemporaries; and certainly the greatest rarities as well as the greatest masterpieces are to be found among the paintings of the fourteenth and fifteenth centuries which account for about half of his collection of seventy-five paintings.

When Roger Fry visited Highnam Court in 1902, works of the *trecento* were still not generally estimated at their real value. Fry was moved to observe that the collection, then barely known to the art world at large, showed that as a connoisseur, Parry 'was as original, as independent of the fashions of his day, and of as fine a taste as in his other capacities. For, at the time when the Highnam collection was made it was not yet a title to social distinction to have one's walls decorated with Italian primitives'.[42] Taking the works in chronological order, Fry began with a *Nativity and the Adoration of the Magi* which, in a list drawn up in 1860, Parry had attributed to 'Giotto or Giottino', later replacing the first name by that of Cimabue. Fry considered this picture to be, in its way, unique:

[41] Anthony Blunt, Introduction to *The Gambier Parry Collection* (Provisional Catalogue, Courtauld Institute of Art, 1967), p v.
[42] Roger Fry, *Pictures in the Collection of Sir Hubert Parry, at Highnam Court, near Gloucester* (*The Burlington Magazine*, July 1903), p 117.

The singularity of this is that we have here a panel painted in tempera, belonging at the latest to the early years of the fourteenth century, which is not only untouched, but in complete preservation, and which for brilliance and intensity of colour and the perfection of its enamel-like smalto can scarcely be surpassed by works of the succeeding century… We have here no Giottesque work in the ordinary sense of the word, which might be more appropriately termed Gaddesque, but a work executed by Giotto himself, or more probably by some contemporaneous artist who was elaborating at the same time with him the new idea; or if by a pupil, one who came under his influence at a very early date, before Giotto's own style was fully matured. Certainly this work has none of the academic qualities of the followers who, like Taddeo Gaddi, accepted the formulae of Giotto's later style; it has in it, like Giotto's own work, the spring and vitality which come with the germination of a new and fruitful conception. And among the works of this fascinating period of Italian painting, we know of none which surpass this in the polished perfection of the technique nor in the marvellous preservation of its surface.[43]

Inevitably, modern scholarship has resulted in the modification of several of Gambier Parry's attributions, and this *Nativity and Adoration of the Magi* is only one picture in his collection the provenance and authorship of which has been disputed over time, in this case varying from the School of Rome to that of Rimini, and from the followers of Cavallini to those of Giotto and Cimabue. In 1916 Sirén proposed the name of the Riminese painter Giovanni Baronzio. Bernard Berenson was the only critic actually to accept Baronzio himself as the author, but, as with many of his attributions, this was later questioned, and the work is now attributed to 'The Master of the Gambier Parry Nativity', believed to be Riminese from the first half of the fourteenth century. Not in doubt are the exquisite quality of the work and Parry's unerring discernment in choosing to purchase it.

Among other superb paintings of the *trecento* in the collection, none is finer than the great *Coronation of the Virgin* by Lorenzo Monaco (c1370-1425), one of the ten pictures, seven of them *trecento,* which Parry purchased at the Davenport Bromley sale of one hundred and seventy-four lots in June 1863. The Reverend Walter Davenport Bromley (1787-1863) of Wootton, near Ashbourne in Derbyshire, had, between 1841 and 1845, bought over forty paintings from the collection which belonged to Cardinal Fesch, the uncle of Napoleon I, one of which was the *Coronation of the Virgin*, listed in the Davenport Bromley sale catalogue at Lot 148 as by Giotto, with the added assurance: ' "This work agrees in every respect with Giotto's well-known picture in Sta Croce, Florence." – *Waagen*, vol. iii. p.137.'

Parry was not entirely convinced, noting in his catalogue that: 'No. 148 is either truly by Giotto – or by some first rate pupil working on Giotto's design, but there is so much of Giotto's own handling, style, colour and feeling that it is quite justifyable [*sic*] to put his name as the painter of it';[44] and he was sufficiently confident of the superlative quality of the work to pay £204. 15s. for it, the highest price which he paid at the sale. Again, his judgement proved to be absolutely right. Although subsequent scholars demoted the painting to the rank

---

[43] *Ibid*, pp 117/125.
[44] Catalogue of the Davenport Bromley Sale, 12 and 13 June 1863, annotated by TGP. Highnam archive.

of 'Florentine School, late fourteenth century', Roger Fry later ascribed it to Agnolo Gaddi; Langton Douglas, to Andrea Orcagna; Sirén, to Mariotto di Nardo under the close influence of Lorenzo Monaco; and Berenson, to Lorenzo di Niccolo. But in 1950 'Hans Gronau proposed an attribution to the young Lorenzo Monaco and identified the picture as the top panel of the High Altar of S. Gaggio, Florence'.[45] Two small predella pieces, *The Visitation* and *The Adoration of the Kings*, bought by Parry at the sale as by Giottino, were recognised by Roger Fry as also 'not only among the most charming pieces of the collection, but… among the best works of an artist whose sense of beauty was almost of the highest order – Lorenzo Monaco';[46]but there were many works in the Davenport Bromley sale which Parry, equally wisely, avoided, noting pithily in his catalogue:

> Of this collection many pictures attributed to painters of great name were ugly and uninteresting, and therefore sold for very little. Some were excessively restored, and some improperly attributed to great painters – 2 or 3 were inconveniently large for ordinary purchasers… Hence the remarkably small prices. Those which I bought are in a remarkably fine condition.[47]

Another *trecento* masterpiece from the Davenport Bromley sale, bought by Webb, who sold it immediately to Gambier Parry, is, in Roger Fry's words, 'one of the most magnificent of the many noble altarpieces which have come down to us from the fourteenth century'. This is the large polyptych in five parts, *Crucifixion with Saints*, signed by Bernardo Daddi (active 1312-1348). 'Even in Florence itself', wrote Fry, 'it would be hard to find an altarpiece in which the religious sentiment of the time is expressed in more imposing forms, or in which the decoration is more sumptuous and the execution more refined'.[48]

Of especial interest among the fifteenth-century works purchased at the Davenport Bromley sale is a series of beautiful small roundels, representing *The 'Imago Pietatis' flanked by Saints*, which is thought to have formed the complete predella to an altarpiece, purchased as by Starnina but now widely regarded as by Fra Angelico (c1429).[49] Gambier Parry must have gained quiet satisfaction not only from the number of superb works which he was able to purchase at the sale, but also from having taken possession of an important part of the coveted collection of Walter Davenport Bromley, a man of whom he had some experience. Whilst in Venice in 1858, Parry bought a superb painting by Bartolommeo Montagna, *The Holy Family*, inscribed and dated 1497, for which he paid 200 napoleons (about £160); entering the work in his 1863 list he noted:

> Bought at Venice. In very pure condition. One of the finest specimens of the master. The Virgin and Child quite beautiful, the other figures very grave and reposeful. Mr

---

[45] Anthony Blunt, *op cit*, pp 35/6.
[46] Roger Fry, *op cit*, p 126.
[47] As for Note 44.
[48] Roger Fry, *op cit*, p 125.
[49] Joanne Cannon in Farr, Dennis (ed), *100 Masterpieces from the Courtauld Collections* (1987), pp 20/21. See also Dennis Farr, *op cit,* (as Note 24 above), p 39.

Davenport Bromley who was rather too fond of abusing other people's pictures and running down what he did not possess, said to me 'well that picture is worthy of a good place in any gallery in Europe'. He asked me to sell it to him – and saw that it was worth very much more than I had given for it.[50]

Naturally, Parry did not sell! Other purchases made in Italy in 1858 from W B Spence, a dealer operating in Florence and London, included two of the three enigmatic, beautiful and disturbing panels illustrating *The Story of St Quiricus and St Julitta*; and Spence obtained the third, smaller, panel for Parry in the following year. They were bought with an attribution to Masaccio, but Spence added a note that they were perhaps by Masolino da Panicale. Berenson attributed them to an artist 'between Masaccio, Uccello and Castagno'; but Longhi created a 'Master of St Quiricus and St Julitta' (Tuscan, first half of the fifteenth century) which still holds. The story of St Quiricus and St Julitta is an unusual and cruel one:

> Quiricus and his mother Julitta were accused of embracing Christianity. The judge took Quiricus on his knee to persuade him to apostasize and the child slapped his face, whereupon mother and child were both martyred. This story is very rarely found in Christian art, and the legend was officially condemned as unacceptable in the *Decretum Gelasianum* (a Latin document, probably of the fourth to sixth centuries, which defined the canon of the bible and of legends of the Saints). In spite of this ban, however, it was depicted in a cycle of frescoes in the church of S. Maria Antiqua in Rome, painted during the Pontificate of Zacharias (741-2). Later, however, the story seems to have been almost completely forgotten, and the Highnam panels appear to be among the very few representations of it in the art of the Italian Renaissance.[51]

Spence was also the source of a small diptych of *The Annunciation*, originally attributed to Fra Filippo Lippi, but now accepted as an exquisite work by Lippi's close follower, Francesco Pesellino, one of the most refined Florentine artists of the mid-fifteenth century. 'You may challenge all England to produce its equal', Spence wrote to Parry in 1859, and asked for first refusal should his customer not wish to buy it;[52] but it *was* bought – as a gift from Ethelinda to her husband.

In 1860 and 1861 Parry bought several works of art, including sixteen paintings, nine of which were purchased in Florence. One of these, and one of the most important items in the entire collection, is the *Madonna and Child*, catalogued by Parry in his 1863 list as by Antonio Pollaiuolo (c1432-98), for which he paid 500 scudi (£112. 10s.), knowing that he had acquired both the work of a master and a bargain. He noted in his list:

> Bought in Florence – 1861. March. It is by the same hand as one in the National Gallery called D: Ghirlandajo. Sir C. Eastlake confesses *that* wrongly named – & believes in the name I give it [*i.e. Pollaiuolo*]. I believe it worth double what I gave for it – frame included.[53]

[50] TGP, 1863 List, *sv* No 40.
[51] Anthony Blunt, *op cit*, p 33.
[52] W B Spence letters to TGP, 1858/9. Highnam archive.
[53] TGP, 1863 List, *sv* No 27.

Worth at least double it most certainly was. Writing in *The Burlington Magazine* in 1967, John Shearman asserted unequivocally that this *Madonna and Child* was the outstanding fifteenth-century painting in the Gambier Parry collection. 'I believe', he wrote:

> it was the experience of everyone who saw the *Madonna* at Highnam that he stood before a masterpiece, and the work of a major artist; the lucidity of thought in its design is as remarkable as the subtle lateral counterpoise of its parts, the beauty of its forms as refined as its technique, the quiet concordance of its colour as distinctive as the delicacy of its emotion. We are not looking, it seems to me, for the Master of This or That, but for one of the great names of the Quattrocento.[54]

Berenson had attributed the *Madonna* to 'Florentine unknown... between Pollaiuolo and Leonardo'. However general, Shearman believed that this localization made perfect sense, that it pointed to one artist only, Andrea del Verrocchio (c1435-88), the teacher of Leonardo da Vinci, and tentatively proposed his name as the author of the painting. In more recent years, the name of Pietro Perugino (c1445/50-1523) has also been proposed.[55] Perugino, who taught Raphael, had himself probably been working in Verrocchio's studio at about the time that Leonardo was there, and the *Madonna* in the Gambier Parry collection shares the undisturbed serenity and softly diffused light so typical of his work. In any event, the *Madonna* is a painting of the very first rank.

The same sure judgement and fine taste which influenced his choice of paintings were employed in Parry's selection of *objets d'art*. His love of the Italian Renaissance is reflected in superb collections of German and Italian glass, maiolica, and marble, including a beautiful bas-relief *Madonna and Child with four Angels* signed by Mino da Fiesole, bought by Parry in Venice in 1875. His collection of Islamic metalwork, stunning in the beauty of its craftsmanship, includes a brass with silver and gold inlay 'wallet' of the mid-thirteenth century, described by B W Robinson as:

> by far the most important object in this part of the collection, and is, indeed, one of the most remarkable examples of its kind in existence. To begin with, its form is unique. It is clearly intended to represent that of a leather wallet, such as might be used to carry a prince's documents and seals, and this may well have been its purpose.[56]

Of no less interest is a group of medieval ivories and Limoges enamels, including an extremely important Limoges Champlevé book-cover of c1190-1200 representing *Christ in Majesty, with the Symbols of the Evangelists.*

In his search for works of quality, many of Gambier Parry's important purchases were found abroad, but he also made equal use of the London market, and, as notes in his catalogues show, obviously enjoyed the thrill of the chase when set on acquiring a certain piece:

---

[54] John Shearman, *A Suggestion for the Early Style of Verrochio,* (The Burlington Magazine, March 1967), p 121.
[55] See Dennis Farr, *op cit,* p 39. Pietro Scarpellino, *Perugino* (1984). pp 70/1, No 7, publishes it as Perugino, and rehearses the evidence for this attribution.
[56] B W Robinson, *Oriental Metalwork in the Gambier Parry Collection* (The Burlington Magazine, March 1967), p 169.

Of a group of three pictures:
In March 1861, I found this in a *cottage* at Castellano some miles from Florence. It belonged to a carpenter. It had been in his family for *many generations*. It had originally belonged to a monk of Val Ombrosa. It was extremely dirty and almost black when I bought it of him. He was obliged to pay his brother-in-law money – hence the necessity for sale. I paid 50 napoleons for the picture. I gave 5 to the man in Florence who told me of it (after my telling him he was a humbug after taking me about for a whole day showing me rubbish *fit for Inglesi*!!). It cost me several journeys to persuade the family to part with it. I gave 5 scudi to the woman of the family. I found it in such wonderful condition on cleaning it in England. I am in great doubt about the painter. Some of my friends best able to judge say that the *centre* is a most perfect bit of Filippo Lippi. The 2 side figures, S. Peter and S. Paul, have a resemblance to the early style of F. Bartolomeo. *Is it not altogether an early* religious picture by F. Bartolomeo? [57]

Of an ivory tryptich with Virgin and Child:
This is Early French 14th century or end of 13th century work. I got it in a village among the mountains of the Friuli… I was sketching in the neighbourhood, and on a wet day I went about to see if any works of art were to be found in that wild and unfrequented district. A poor woman sold it to me for 13 napoleons.[58]

Thomas Gambier Parry used freely the fortune made by his grandfather, father and uncles in the East India Company to fund his passion for collecting. His taste was impeccable, but to support such a passion required considerable wealth, and the collection of fine art and travels abroad were not the only drains on his finances; nor were the large sums which he had spent on the building and decoration of Highnam Church, the village school and rectory; nor even the continuing cost of maintaining the Highnam estate, the restoration and extension of the house, the establishment of the gardens and pinetum, and the support of both indoor and outdoor staff. His generosity to those less fortunate than himself was also boundless.

Benedict Nicolson, writing in *The Burlington Magazine* in 1967, described Parry as 'a character straight out of the pages of Trollope, the best brand of amateur, a country gentleman of means willing to spend his money in the public service… He left behind him three foundations in his county town: the Schools of Science and Art, of which he was first president from its foundation in 1859 until his death; a free Hospital for children, and a Home for the poor – the last two created in the face of fierce opposition, but by persistence he won the day. Almost the whole cost was borne by himself'.[59]

Even the deepest purse has a bottom, and whilst still working on the *Doom* Parry was aware that his expenditure had, for some time, been exceeding income; it was exactly then that he was asked to accept the largest and most important undertaking of his life and, inevitably, yet again, to bear the cost of it himself.

---

[57] TGP List 1863, *sv* No 66. Attributed by Berenson to Antoniazzo Romano (active 1460-1508; Umbrian School).
[58] TGP List 1875, *sv* No 12.
[59] Editorial, *The Burlington Magazine,* March 1967, p 111.

VII

Brothers

If Gambier Parry's life was centred on the pursuit of a spritual ideal and its expression in fine art, it left him little time for simple family pleasures. Hubert, whose brother Clinton was eight and sister Lucy seven years older than himself, had known the loneliness of a childhood without companions of his own age, without a mother of his own, and with a father who was preoccupied. When, on Sunday afternoons, Gambier Parry did gather his children about him, the pattern was both serious and unchanging. 'The hour and more talking about sacred things, reading and saying hymns', he wrote, 'is among the brightest moments of one's life'.[1] Brightest for him perhaps, but for the children?

For want of a living companion, as he once told his daughter Dorothea, Hubert created an imaginary friend with whom he could talk and play, and music entered into that dream world as both charm and consolation. Ernest's first recollection of his half-brother, when Hubert was about eight years old, 'was his appearing in a dark cloth kind of blouse with rather a broad leather belt fastening with a buckle, and with short trousers'.[2] It was a Sunday morning. Ernest had climbed the stairs to the top of the house and made his way into one of the attic bedrooms. He found Hubert, a solitary little boy, standing by the window, gazing out across the rooftop of Highnam Court.

Gambier Parry had worried about Hubert's apparent slowness in his lessons. Miss Cooper's successor, Mlle. Foertsch, had tried to teach him to read, but so troublesome was Hubert to his governess that in 1854 Ethelinda decided to take on the task of his tuition personally. Years later, she acknowledged to Ernest that of all the children she had tried to teach to read 'Hubert was the most difficult – so difficult... as to approach the impossible'.[3] Clearly, a different approach had to be tried, and on 7 January 1856, boarding the Ledbury coach which passed Highnam daily, Gambier Parry travelled to Malvern to inspect a

---

[1] TGP, *Journal 1856*. Highnam archive.
[2] GPM p 211.
[3] Charles Graves, *Hubert Parry* (London, 1926), Vol I, p 12.

(Right) Thomas Gambier Parry:
*Study of Cypress Trees, Villa d'Este,
Tivoli 1844*. Pencil and watercolour,
36.3 × 26.

(Below) Thomas Gambier Parry:
The Ponte Vecchio, Florence 1844.
Pencil and watercolour, 28.7 × 45.9.

Thomas Gambier Parry: *The Doge's Palace, Venice 1851*. Pencil and watercolour, 28.9 × 46.3.

Thomas Gambier Parry: *Torcello 1851*. Pencil and watercolour, 28.5 × 39.4.

Thomas Gambier Parry:
San Michele in Isola, Venice c1875.
Pencil, pen and watercolour,
29.3 x 46.1.

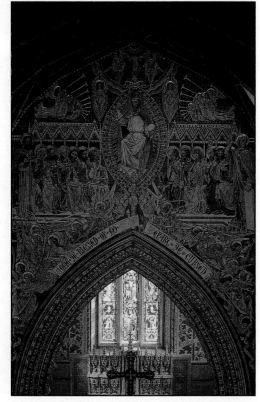

Thomas Gambier Parry: *Doom,*
Chancel Arch, Church of the Holy
Innocents, Highnam 1859-61.
(Photograph Jack Farley)

The Nave, Ely Cathedral.
(Pitkin Guides Ltd)

Thomas Gambier Parry: The
Nave Ceiling, Ely Cathedral
(detail), 1862-64. (*Pitkin
Guides Ltd*)

preparatory school run there by a Mr. Taylor, noting in his journal that he 'saw a curious meteor in the sky due south at a little before I set out'.[4] He was 'much pleased' with the school, and twelve days later delivered Hubert to Mr. Taylor: 'He went in the highest spirits', he wrote, 'anticipating great pleasure at having so many boy companions to play with. I felt parting with him very much'.[5]

Hubert's arrival was not made easier by the laughter of the other boys at his appearance: he had been sent to school wearing a ridiculous frill around his neck. But he settled down, made good progress, and at weekends was back at home displaying a new-found self-confidence. In September 1858 he left Mr. Taylor to take up a place at another preparatory school, at Twyford in Berkshire, where the principal, the Revd. George William Kitchin, later to become successively Dean of Winchester and Durham, took an immediate liking to Hubert, and recognised and encouraged his musical gifts. At the end of his first term at Twyford, Hubert proudly carried home a good conduct prize: *The Wonders of the World*, two volumes bound in blue morocco; and master and pupil remained firm friends until Kitchin's death in 1912.

Gambier Parry was an accomplished musician, and a mutual love of music formed a delightful part of his life with Isabella. Surviving books of music manuscript written out by him include a small number of *Lieder*, such as a setting of *Kennst du das Land wo die Zitronen blühn...* inscribed 'Song composed for Isabel at Naples March 1843 T.G. Parry', and others which might be by him also, including the *Abschied von Athen*. There are also piano duets which Thomas and Isabella no doubt played together, and part-songs and glees which might have been sung at family gatherings. Gambier Parry also ran the Highnam Choral Society for many years, was president of the Gloucester Choral Society from its inception, and served on the committee of the Three Choirs Festival. Unsurprisingly, he had a particular interest in church music; he published a collection of *Hymn Tunes and Chants* (undated) 'dedicated to the Highnam choir', and a Gregorian Psalm Tune composed for 'Easter Week. 1845', written out in his hand, also survives.[6] But although Ethelinda took lessons in singing and piano, music seems not to have been so strong a source of mutual delight in Gambier Parry's second marriage as in his first – and no songs were composed for Ethelinda. Nor did he encourage the obvious musical abilities of his two eldest sons, Clinton and Hubert; rather the reverse. But, happily, there was one at Highnam who did.

Hubert remembered the organist at Highnam, Edward Brind, as 'the best organist we ever had. He gave me lessons on the pianoforte when I was a boy, almost the only ones I ever had'. Thanks to Brind, not only was Hubert taught both piano and organ, but he 'played and took services before his feet could reach the pedals'.[7] Brind introduced Hubert to the elements of counterpoint and harmony, and by the age of seven he had already completed his earliest

---

[4] TGP, *Journal 1856.*
[5] *Ibid.*
[6] Highnam archive.
[7] Graves, *op cit,* p 14.

compositions: chants and hymn tunes. It was also Brind who took Hubert to his first Three Choirs Festival, at Hereford in 1861. As Ernest recalled:

> Hubert from his earliest days was always for music… He took the organist's place at times in the church, but he was still quite a little boy when he did so first, and I believe little more than 9.
>
> He had come to trousers when the following happened. He was to take the service the next day and had therefore to take the choir practice. We walked across to the school together. The choir in those days was a large and very good one, and the vicar, Mansfield, was always present and sung tenor. The organist, Brind, kept order with a cane – the weapon being laid on the top of the piano when the practice began, and being by no means infrequently used amongst the boys. On the occasion in question there seemed no reason to anticipate any breach of the peace, much less a case of open mutiny; the cane was in the cupboard, the organist being absent, and the psalms were got through without incident. But when it came to the hymns, and the dear, nervous, kind-hearted vicar gave out the first, Hubert, at the piano, set his face and flatly refused to play it…Possibly the one selected at this peaceful choir practice was the worst of the whole bunch; but however this was, it moved Hubert, a boy then of about 13 or 14, to the most dire wrath. There was very little said; indeed, a silence fell upon the room, and I know I, aged between 9 and 10, felt cold all over. Then there were a few words, and the choir practice came to a sudden and painful conclusion. Hubert got up and left the school, and I went with him.
>
> It was a peaceful summer evening; and we two boys walked back along the church path without uttering one word, while behind us at a distance of some 40 yards came the vicar. He was on his way to interview father: the next day was Sunday: there was no organist! As to what followed, my mind is a blank, for I was sent to bed; but this I know, Hubert did take the organ the next day, and I am inclined to believe that the obnoxious hymn was *not* played.[8]

Ernest, Mansfield and the choir had, for the first time, seen three facets of Hubert's character which were never to be relinquished: obstinacy, a quick temper, and the absolute courage of his convictions.

Such time as Gambier Parry was able to spare for his family decreased as, encouraged by Ethelinda, he accepted ever more civic and charitable commitments. Although few detailed records of his many activities in Gloucester survive, something of the pressure on him shows through in journal entries, such as that for the first week of January 1856 in which he records that he is 'constantly occupied with gaol, infirmary and lunatic asylum'. In the following April he is again in Gloucester 'about my scheme of refuge for destitute prisoners, buying crockery, furniture, etc', and visits a prisoner named Butterworth, 'who is to be the first experimented upon [*i.e. to be helped by Parry's relief scheme*]. His age is 19. he has been 11 times in prison. I have got him some work promised on the road, stonebreaking'.[9]

'None of us know the whole of father's work in Gloucester', wrote Ernest, 'and it is safe to say that *nobody* does or, indeed, did':

---

[8] GPM pp 212/3.
[9] TGP, *Journal 1856*.

92

Its channels were innumerable, and it took him into byways, only a few of which we have heard of, and by accident, since. The number of people of *all* classes that sought his counsel and his aid were at all times very great, they were to be found among the rich and the poor, the young and the old, among men of entirely different tastes, pursuits and opinions to himself, among men whose lives were before the public, among the clergy, the men of business, the smaller shopkeepers, the artizan and the labourer, among the criminals, the drunkards, and the fallen...He never believed in posthumous charity. He did not consider that charity at all, and he called it 'defrauding your heirs'...[On] five days out of six he was in Gloucester for either the whole or part of the day. Until the last few years of his life he habitually rode there, and he had a line of gates [opened] that he might get a gallop over the grass going and coming. No weather – not even the worst – ever stopped him, and even in his last few years, when he drove in an open pony-trap, he was in and out of the town early and late, often returning after seven o'clock at night in winter, drenched through or half numbed with cold, but always treating it as the greatest possible of jokes, and never apparently in the least hurry to change his clothes.[10]

No mere committee man, Gambier Parry became actively involved with the many causes in which he had a concern. Besides the routine of a magistrate's duty, visiting the prison and the lunatic asylums, attending the Bench and the Board of Guardians, he was energetically supportive of the local archeological society; the choral society; the photographic society; the Three Choirs Festival; diocesan conferences; meetings of antiquarians, ecclesiologists, supporters of technical education and free libraries, and even of the Root, Fruit and Grain Society. The list was seemingly endless, and Ernest recalled that to be in Gloucester with his father was for their progress along a street to be 'limited to perhaps a hundred yards at a time owing to the number of persons who wished to speak to him'. But closest to Parry's heart were those charitable institutions established entirely as the result of his own generosity and compassion. At a time before the welfare state was even a distant dream, he saw, as he entered the town through the area then known as 'the Island', the appalling condition of Gloucester's poor, and resolved that something must be done, a personal initiative, to alleviate such suffering:

> Squalor, dirt and vice reigned supreme: drunken men and women reeled along the filthy street; half-dressed, unwashed children with bare feet and legs crowded in the gutters and made driving difficult in the narrow roadway: the babel of sound was hideous: brawny amazons, whose physical strength was scarcely inferior to that of the bargees forming a large part of the local male population, fought with one another and tore each other's hair and clothes; others, their faces aflame with drink, appeared to be half murdering their children who, emulating their elders, fought and swore together almost like animals. The language was of the foulest; the noise often deafening... while a local tallow factory exhaled the most nauseating odours. To pass through the Island after sundown in winter was to pass through a perfect pandemonium. The population... supplemented now by a number of hawkers yelling their cheap fish, while their flares served only to make more hideous the general scene, thronged the muddy road and made this entrance to Glevum [*the Roman name for Gloucester*] – the beautiful city! – little better than a hell on earth.

---

[10] GPM pp 185/6.

The well-nigh uncivilized condition of the general mass in the Island filled him with horror; but it was the pitiable state of the children that awoke his pity and made him determined to try and do something for those that were sick in body, if he could not reach their minds or their souls.[11]

As Gambier Parry worked high on the scaffolding to complete the *Doom* at Highnam, his thoughts must often have turned on the desperate plight of Gloucester's poor, to the brutish many who would never share his artistic vision or come to accept the truth, as he understood it, of its message. As the months crept by, a scheme formed in his mind which was at once philanthropic and far-reaching: he would found a hospital and home to care for the children of the destitute poor, and ensure that they were brought to the Christian faith by appointing a clergyman as warden. But such a plan would require a huge investment of time as well as money, and not only was every available hour not spent on other commitments devoted to the *Doom*, but his mind was also deeply troubled by Lucy's declining health and by increasing fears for Clinton's moral and physical well-being.

As a young boy Clinton had endured loneliness even more acute than that of his younger brother. Like Hubert, his musical gifts were highly developed from an early age but discouraged by his father as being unworthy of anything more than a hobby. The notion, in those days, that the son of a gentleman could be a musician was considered absurd; art and architecture were accepted as fitting professions for men of rank, but not the stage or music, the status of which occupied a similar position on the social scale to that of the grocer. That which meant more to him than any other human endeavour and to which he longed to devote his life was dismissed as a triviality. Clinton's Eton years were miserable; and the faith, which to his father was the cornerstone of life, failed to bring comfort. When, at age twenty-five, he came to reflect in his diary on his early life, it was to remember a boyhood filled with 'hours alone'. Of Eton, he wrote:

> Life became more unhappy for two reasons: on account of my very strong religious feelings, and on account of my acutely sensitive and highly-strung nature. Always alone and could not tolerate the company of any of my fellow pupils. At 18 began to doubt my Saviour was any longer ever-present to my sorrows and trials.[12]

Adrift, lonely and desperate for affection, Clinton sought solace in ever increasing amounts of alcohol. A Highnam friend, Joe Ollivant, seems to have exerted a pernicious influence, and by the time of his admission to Christ Church College, Oxford, Clinton was unable to break free from the even stronger clutches of opium addiction. His diaries for the next several years, pathetic barometers of emotional turmoil, record a desperate struggle between determination and weakness. In September 1859, in love with a girl called Cecilia Summerhayes, he wrote poetry, composed a grand sonata, and determined to 'live well'. In the following weeks he played his cello at the Deanery before the

---

[11] GPM pp 196/7.
[12] Clinton Parry (hereafter 'CP') diaries. Shulbrede archive.

Prince of Wales, was involved in a 'Town and Gown' fight, played at a concert attended by an audience of two hundred, and then promptly slumped into deep distress – Cecilia is mentioned no more. After taking opium on 7 December he imagined that he saw spots of blood on the strings of his cello as he was playing. On Christmas Day he attended Eucharist but felt only 'indifference in heart, though not in manner', and that night remained alone in his room, reading John Henry Newman's *The Soul*.

From New Year's Day 1860, when he was feeling unwell from the effects of too much opium, Clinton embarked upon several months of drifting and drunkeness, arriving at his twentieth birthday on 16 September filled with remorse and, again, a determination to do well. Five days later he travelled down to Exmouth, from where he wrote to his father that he would not be returning to Oxford. Gambier Parry, known affectionately to his children as 'Possie', warned in his reply how very difficult it would be to get back into Oxford having once left and begged him to come home to Highnam. Clinton obeyed, arriving home on 9 October. Gambier Parry, obviously shocked by his eldest son's condition, set aside his work on the *Doom* and prepared to take his family to Italy for a six-month sea-side holiday at Mentone, clearly hoping that the break would cure Clinton of his opium and alcohol addiction; but he was also desperately worried about Lucy. A pale transparency of her former happy self, perhaps she too would benefit from the fresh Mediterranean air.

Four weeks before Christmas the Parrys set out for Italy, and on Christmas Eve Clinton confided to his diary:

> I find I cannot be happy unless I practice a virtuous mode of life. I have vastly improved since I have been here in application, abstraction and power of reason, and in music and in temper, but not in virtuous thoughts. I most heartily pray God, to give me some portion of his glorious perfection. I will this week read *The Soul*.[13]

But on 16 January he has to confess to yet another relapse; to what he calls 'one of my bad paroxysms'. The next day he 'walked with Possie to Roccabruna'. His mood lightened. It was, he wrote, a 'lovely day. The pleasure of a walk in lovely country with a pleasant little damsel is one. The pleasure of a walk in a beautiful country with an older and noble mind is another'. For ten more days he steered an even course, sure that he was making real progress and able to put the past behind him. At last he was able to claim that he could 'now review with great pleasure the enormous improvement in myself morally, mentally and physically, contrasted with the vacillations, weaknesses and degradation of Oxford days'. Such optimism was not to last. Exactly one week later he was plunged once more into despair: 'O Virtue, thou hast a stern sister – Self-control', and in the remaining months of the holiday sighed again and again at his 'Sysiphean labour'.[14]

Back in England in June 1861 Gambier Parry resumed work on the *Doom*, Lucy's health continued to decline, and Clinton, who had returned to Oxford,

---

[13] *Ibid.*
[14] *Ibid.*

was back at Highnam after yet another spell of debauchery and wildness, vainly promising himself to work hard and practice self-command. His good intentions began in an effort to help Ernest, who received his first violin lesson on 20 July 1861 under the expert guidance of his eldest half-brother, and who always remembered Clinton with undimmed admiration and love:

> I have known clever men, men who were made in Nature's finest mould and who by reason of their physical perfection were a delight to look upon; men who were linguists and widely-read in more than their own language; men who were musicians, who excelled in all manly pursuits, who feared nothing on earth, who were first rate across a country on an awkward horse, and who were the keenest sportsmen with the gun. I have known men who possessed one, two, even three of these qualities; but… I have never known one who combined in himself each and all of these characteristics save dear Clin. I remember a man once saying to me, in answer to my inquiry as to whether he recollected Clin – 'my dear fellow; to have seen Clinton Parry once was to remember him always'.
>
> Clinton was singularly handsome [*according to Hubert, his brother Clinton bore a strong resemblance to Richard Oakes*], and his physical strength was prodigious. He was well versed in Greek, Latin, German, French, and his books are scribbled over with quotations in these and other languages, including Welsh. He had a considerable knowledge of geology. He was a first-rate shot, and he and I shot together many hundreds of times; he was a thorough sportsman, and a first-rate rider. As a musician he at one time played the cello, and he gave me my first violin lessons when I was seven years old. But it was as a pianist that he was at his best. His touch was simply divine, and neither I nor others in the family have known his equal here, our father coming nearest, I think. Clin never studied music deeply as an art; but I was talking to someone who knew him well, a short while ago, and he told me that when at Highnam many many years back, Hubert pointed to Clinton and said – 'You see that man: he has more music in his little finger than I have in my whole body'.[15]

Even allowing for the hero-worship of one who idolised him, it is clear that Clinton was an exceptional man, brilliant to the outside world but deeply scarred within. On the same day that Ernest received his first violin lesson, his 'big brother' was wrestling hopelessly to give meaning to his life:

> Though I am weak… I still humbly put my trust in God my Creator, for what else can I do? Has he not supplied my every want. Nor is this all. He has not only granted me the necessities of life but has super-added a hundred superfluous delights, as music, poetry, [and] taste in paintings.
>
> O that I could love Him more and live more to Him. Alas, alas how swiftly time flies. It seems but yesterday that I was here a year ago. That all my time abroad was but a bright dream of one night, and now I have just awakened and found myself in the same place which I left before going abroad. What a mysterious power it is that impels us ever onward, and how often I have compared our life to a meteor that catches fire upon entering our atmosphere. For what else is it but this – from obscurity we are born into day, but only to pass into obscurity again…
>
> The aged ones tell me that life seems shorter and quicker as we grow older. Can time be quicker, can life seem more fleeting than it is to me now? I am hurried towards the hereafter. I cling to each day. Yet an invisible power impels me onward. And life: what is it? Why should I be fond of it…

15 GPM pp 149/150.

I wish to be good and I cannot. I wish to pray and something holds me back. I wish to *die* and I fear death. I wish to love and hope: and love and hope come not near.[16]

Gambier Parry's labours on the *Doom* in Highnam Church were coming to an end. There is nothing equivocal about the message of this great work. Christ sits in judgement. Waves of angels crowd both sides of the chancel arch: those to the left, bearing palms and crowns, greet the chosen with a welcoming scroll: 'Come ye Blessed of My Father'; those to the right wield flaming swords, ready to strike down the damned: 'Depart ye cursed', reads their scroll; and throughout, angels are sounding the last trump.

Alone in his room Clinton longed for his father's certainty of faith as much as for his tenderness, but could neither accept the one nor, precisely because of that, expect the other:

I wish to make the most of life for I know not what is beyond the grave. To me it is all dark and mysterious – and whoever has come back to tell us what the great secret is? My now dead mother loved me, and why has she not appeared to me and told me of the hereafter: O fearful thought. Shall I never behold her again. Shall I never see my three dead brothers again – dead, dying, death: fearful words if they imply annihilation.[17]

Clinton returned to Oxford at Michaelmas in 1861, and at the same time Hubert entered Evans's House at Eton. On 9 November the scaffolding was finally cleared away in Highnam Church: the *Doom* was finished – and on the very next day Lucy died.

The two brothers were recalled. Both were heartbroken. 'I was summoned from Oxford on that sad Sunday', wrote Clinton, 'but unhappily came too late ever to see her again alive or hear her dear voice'. Drawn together in their grief, Clinton spent the Christmas vacation 'with dear Possie at No.1 Hesketh Crescent' [Torquay]; but on New Year's Eve, at 3 o'clock in the morning, he recorded the death to him of any remaining vestiges of faith:

...last year I believed God heard me when I prayed to him and praised him. Now all is a blank. No God hears me. I steer into the dark unknown without a living God. Alas, alas would it were not so![18]

A few more months of determination fractured by failure culminated on 27 May 1862 with Clinton's deciding, yet again, to quit his studies: it was, he wrote, 'my last day in Oxford as an undergraduate... I have formally shut up my Homer, Cicero, Lexicons, etc... and laid aside my academic costume'. Gambier Parry was forced once more to plead with his son and with the university, and by July Clinton was back at Oxford. His steady application to work was not to be expected, and reports of Clinton's inconstancy, added to the sorrow of Lucy's death, placed Gambier Parry under such stress that, for the first time in his life,

---

16 CP diaries. Shulbrede archive.
17 *Ibid.*
18 *Ibid.*

his health began to suffer. There were other stresses too. One of Gambier Parry's oldest friends, Edward Hawkins; a soul-mate who had shared his interest in art and had accompanied him on a sketching tour of Dalmatia in 1856, had met a ghastly death, garrotted in the street in London. And another close friend, since their days together at Eton, Henry Styleman Le Strange of Hunstanton in Norfolk, died suddenly on 27 July 1862.

Gambier Parry was Le Strange's executor. The two friends had kept in close touch over the years, drawn together by a mutual interest in church painting, about which both had contributed articles to *The Ecclesiologist* and elsewhere. Le Strange was also on good terms with the clergy at Ely Cathedral, who seem to have turned to him for advice on artistic matters. During the restoration of the cathedral by Sir George Gilbert Scott in the 1850s, Dean George Peacock had a boarded ceiling constructed in the nave, following the contours of the A-frames and scissor braces to produce a five-sided half-barrel shape. In 1853 Peacock had invited Le Strange to paint the ceiling of the west tower, a task which was completed in 1855, and in July of the following year Le Strange agreed to Peacock's suggestion that he also paint the new nave ceiling.

Le Strange started work in 1858, breaking off at the end of 1861 'to work upon cartoons for wallpaintings proposed to be executed at the East end of St Alban's Church, Holborn. Before these cartoons were finished he died'.[19] The Dean and Chapter, as Ernest recorded,

> looked round to find, if possible, someone to carry on the work, and also, it may be said, to do much besides. It may well have appeared to them hopeless. The circumstances and conditions were peculiar. Even had there been professional artists at once capable and willing to undertake so vast a work, their employment would have been impossible, for if the work was to be done at all it could only be as a labour of love – there were no funds at the disposal of the Chapter for the payment of an artist: all that could be done was a grant in aid.[20]

Gambier Parry was the obvious choice, and the Ely Dean and Chapter wrote to him seeking his help in completing the project – at his own expense! In a letter to the publisher John Murray, dated 8 October, Parry explained that he had 'just returned from Ely':

> Le Strange has only just finished the 6 west bays of the nave roof – the remaining *half* (6 more bays) are committed to me by the Dean & Chapter. My dear old friend Le Strange died in July last. I am his executor. He has left no designs for the work committed to me, except a few slight scraps of small pencil sketches. The Eastern half of the nave roof must therefore be mine both in design and execution. It is a tremendous undertaking.[21]

Le Strange had, as Parry explained,

> desired to harmonise his work with the Architecture, and had therefore followed rigidly a peculiar form of Norman Art of about 1180 [*the present cathedral at Ely was built between*

[19] TGP, letter to the editor of *The Builder*, 6 May 1865.
[20] GPM pp 165/6.
[21] TGP, letter to John Murray, 8 October, 1862. Shulbrede archive.

1083 and 1189]... He proposed to divide the ceiling into Bays...and to cover them with paintings expressive of Our Blessed Lord's connexion with Mankind...The arrangement of subjects kindred to these in one of the painted windows of Chartres Cathedral had suggested to him the general laying out of his work. The early papers at Hildesheim had suggested to him the method of connecting the genealogy of our Lord, (as detailed in St. Luke's Gospel) with the rest of the work [*there are similarities between the ceilings at Ely and the Michaelskirche at Hildesheim in Germany*]; and MSS of the twelfth century, especially a Psalter in the British Museum (in Nero, C.4.) gave him the characteristics of the Art contemporary with the Architecture of the Cathedral.[22]

The six bays completed by Le Strange depict The Creation of Man; The Fall of Man; Noah and the Flood; Abraham and Isaac; Jacob's Dream; and The Marriage of Ruth. The 'scraps of small pencil sketches' which he left behind were for a Tree of Jesse and a Christ in Majesty; Parry borrowed 'two or three forms' from Le Strange's Jesse, and used this commonest of late medieval symbols as the first of his six subjects, following it with images of King David and attendant musicians; The Annunciation; The Nativity; The Adoration of the Shepherds and the Magi; and Christ in Glory, seated in judgement, with apostles and angels.

'Father began studying at once', wrote Ernest, ' "I drew Norman", I have often heard him say – "I drew everything Norman that I could lay my hands on; I literally thought Norman; I believe I could have talked Norman"...

Each bay was the subject of a separate cartoon drawn by father in charcoal and in pencil to the scale, I think, 6 inches to the foot. Father worked for the most part from models, with draperies arranged on full-size lay figures. Heads, hands, feet were generally drawn, or partially finished, in pencil; other parts of the body that might be showing, and draperies, in charcoal. When completed they were set by steam... The steaming was done with a kettle devised for the purpose... the lower part contained a spirit-lamp with two wicks; the upper part held the water; the steam issued from a neck about 18 inches long; and the form of the kettle was oval, being perhaps 7 or 8 inches high.

When a cartoon was finished it was enlarged in outline to full size, by assistants, on huge drawing boards and many sheets of paper which were afterwards cut up for tracing onto the ceiling of the nave of the cathedral. To carry out this part of the work a very large and high room was required, the figures alone, at their full size, being 9 to 10 feet high. Such a room and such a house was found in London at 41 Portman Square. At the back of this house was a small room in which father used to draw all day, and where several of us, especially myself, in the holidays, stood as a model... This small room led into a large ball-room, very high, and lighted from the top.

At Ely father stayed always at The Lamb, close by the cathedral, mother often spending some weeks at a time with him there... He rose early, breakfasting I think at 8 – a boiled egg, some toast and coffee, much what it was all his life. Many men were employed on the scaffolding and in mechanical work on the ceiling, and these, with father, had a special service each morning in a side chapel, conducted by a minor canon. Then they all went up the ladders, father to paint lying on his back slung in a chair nigh 90 feet above the pavement of the nave, tackling these great heads and figures and scrolling as best he might, without a chance of judging the effect from below until the maze of scaffolding was ultimately removed.[23]

---

[22] As 21.
[23] GPM pp 167/8.

Because Gambier Parry was painting on wood, as opposed to stone or plaster, he did not use his spirit fresco medium at Ely, adopting instead a medium made up of pale drying oil, strong copal varnish, japanner's gold size, and turpentine. 'The recipe for this medium is one part, *in bulk*, of each of the two first, and two parts of the two second; the colours, in powder, to be rubbed up with it and put into tubes. It is called "the Ely medium".'[24] Gambier Parry found by experimentation that paintings executed in this medium 'dry perfectly dead and as hard as iron'; and when, in 1988, conservators cleaned away the discoloration from the nave ceiling, caused by a century of smoke from coke-fired Gurney stoves, they confirmed that his medium was 'a tough mixture of oils and natural resins' which had deteriorated much less than Le Strange's work.[25] Not only were Parry's paintings more durable than those of his old school friend, they are also infinitely more satisfactory in design. As Peter Burman has pointed out

> His compositions are more balanced, his draperies finer and his human figures and especially their heads much more sharply drawn, moreover Le Strange's colours are, by comparison, rather muddy – Gambier Parry's sing out, with his characteristic strong reds, blues and a good deal of gold, and a gentle green as the general background.[26]

Gambier Parry spent two years in the completion of his work on the nave roof at Ely, leaving it as a memorial to his old friend Le Strange. 'It was', he wrote, 'a very awkward work to execute, lying on one's back, in a painfully bad light, impeded by the scaffolding, and without the possibility of getting a clear view of it at a fair distance to judge of it in the various stages of its progress'.[27] But at the end of each day, at least, he was able to recapture something of that freedom which, long before, as a youth riding his pony along Cambridgeshire lanes in search of churches to sketch, had given him joy:

> When the last 'Amen' of the Evensong had echoed up to the artist and his men, and the notes of the organ rolled along the old Norman roof and died away, father cleaned up, took off the white painter's smock in which he worked, and mounted his horse that was waiting for him at the door. Those evening rides on 'Tipperary', accompanied by his Scotch deer-hound 'Tana', father always spoke of with delight; and one can picture him now galloping over the grass of flat Cambridgeshire in the evening light, 'going for a good – a downright good stretch', as he always called it, till the towers of the great Cathedral stood grey-blue against the gold sky, and it was time to return to the evening meal, the inevitable letters and correspondence, – and bed.[28]

Amongst those letters were yet more worrying reports of Clinton. Throughout 1863 Gambier Parry was under constant strain on account of his

---

[24] GPM p 165.
[25] *Friends of Ely Cathedral Year Book* (1988), p 16. See also Peter Burman, *Thomas Gambier Parry. An Introduction*. An essay published in *Thomas Gambier Parry (1816-1888) as artist and collector* (Courtauld Institute Galleries, University of London, 1993), p 23.
[26] Burman, *op cit*, p 22.
[27] As 21.
[28] GPM pp 168/9.

eldest son's behaviour at Oxford. Twice, in both January and March, Clinton had been rusticated, and twice, as a result of his father's intercession, reinstated; but in June he was yet again at Highnam, 'plucked as a natural consequence of not working'.[29] Having already been six years at Oxford and his degree still not completed, he was now sent by his father to spend the summer at a language school in Paris to improve his French. Clinton was well aware of the shame that he had brought upon his highly respected family, but was incapable of freezing his personality into a chosen shape; instability was his destiny, deepened as it had been by a lonely childhood, the loss of his mother and the inaccessibility of his father. Superficially, he seems to have been enjoying himself: 'saw the charmer of charmers in Paris', he wrote in his diary; but the dreaming was soon to end.

There was better news from Eton. During a school holiday in 1864, the first year in which he began to keep a regular diary, Hubert visited Gambier Parry at Ely. 'Nervous at first' on finding his father at the top of the huge scaffolding, he went on to explore every corner of the 'enormous and glorious' cathedral, finding it especially inspiring in the deep silence of night. He played the organ and described its every feature; and sat as a model to his father for one of the heads in the genealogy of the family of Christ which feature in roundels, framing the entire decorative scheme. Father and son rode out twice to explore the Fens, and spent a day together in Cambridge, where, apart from sightseeing, they inspected the manuscript collection in the Trinity Library, the Handel manuscripts in the Fitzwilliam and the German glass in the Peterhouse Chapel.

Although Gambier Parry had chosen a man totally unsympathetic to music, Russell Day, to be his son's tutor at Eton, two of Hubert's greatest friends there and in later life, his cousin Edward Hamilton, the son of the Bishop of Salisbury, and Spencer Lyttelton, shared his enthusiasm, and Hubert was one of the first boys at Eton to have a piano in his room. Another contemporary, Sir George Greenwood, noted that Hubert 'combined *res olim dissociabiles* – music and football, or at any rate became wonderfully proficient in both. As a musician, Hubert stood higher than any schoolboy before or since at Eton, or probably at any other public school'.[30]

Along with Lyttleton and Hamilton, Hubert was one of the key members of the Eton Musical Society, the life of which flourished marvellously as a result of their energetic and skilful musicianship. In his last two years at the school Hubert took part in no fewer than six concerts, appearing as composer, singer, pianist and organist, and at his last concert introduced his half-brother Ernest, who played a violin solo and one of Hubert's own compositions, a duet for violin and piano – his 'Op. 1'. Hubert remembered the Musical Society with affection in a letter written to Ernest some years later:

> There were a lot of boys who liked music heartily, and masters like Cornish and Browning and Snow (afterwards Kynaston) encouraged them. My diary shows that

---

[29] CP diaries.
[30] Graves, *op cit*, p 22.

there was a lot of it going on, and boys used to come and sit in my room for me to play to them, and really preferred Bach and Handel and Mendelssohn and such. The Musical Society was a singularly casual sort of affair at first. The members were allowed to meet in some room or other under the supervision of a master, but it consisted in little more than spending an evening in an irregular manner. Some boys played the pianoforte and sang, and we had a try at a simple part-song or two. Then by some one's advice, 'Johnnie' Foster, as we used to call him [*the singing master, an alto singer and one of the lay clerks at Westminster Abbey and the Chapel Royal, and in later years conductor of the Choral Class at the Royal College of Music*] was appointed to get things into some sort of order, but the order didn't amount to much. I find an entry in my diary for February 16, 1864: 'Foster came down in the afternoon, and played the organ in the New School. I blew for him and he afterwards blew for me. In the evening – the Musical Society's meeting – only four boys came at 6, and Foster didn't come till 7. So we set up a grand steeplechase, and put up chairs and tables and forms in the Music-room to jump over. We afterwards sang Handel's *My heart is inditing*'. However, by degrees, the Society got plenty of members, and we worked away at part-songs and madrigals and Handel choruses and Mendelssohn's Psalms, and gave concerts, which we looked upon as great larks, and in which most of the things were encored... I and Eddie Hamilton used to play duets, and at my last concert you played the fiddle and were vociferously encored.[31]

Until the end of 1862 Hubert continued to take composition lessons with Edward Brind at Highnam during the school holidays, but these, as was to be expected, were limited in scope. Hubert very much needed to advance his studies. The college organist at Eton, whose incompetence had already gained Hubert's contempt, was totally unsuited to the task; but the right man was only a short walk away. Hubert Parry began lessons with Dr. George Elvey, the organist of St George's Chapel, Windsor, in 1863. Elvey's methods were conservative but sound; his pupil both brilliant and eager for work; and very soon a number of anthems, an Evening Service in A, and a madrigal setting of Shakespeare's *Tell me where is fancy bred* were added to the growing list of Hubert's compositions.

Hubert's other preoccupation whilst at Eton, football, also satisfied in part his irrepressible love of excitement and danger, a tendency which remained with him throughout life. Spencer Lyttelton's brother, Robert, remembered that:

> The athletic side of Hubert's character was mainly on the side of football, of which there are two sorts at Eton, the Field and the Wall; the first being a game most emphatically of motion and rapidity, the second of pushing and scrummaging, to borrow the Rugby phrase, and though Hubert was good at both the field was by far his more favourite form of amusement. His nature delighted in the concentrated essence of excitement found at the highest in Eton football as played in the Field, and I can see him now rushing all over the ground, rash and therefore always injuring himself, shouting to his side and bubbling over with joy at the rush and tumble.[32]

Hubert's spirited athleticism flew in the face of physical ills, including a heart condition and assorted other ailments which frequently troubled him. His

[31]Ernest Gambier-Parry, *Annals of an Eton House* (London, 1907), pp 166/7.
[32] Graves, *op cit*, p 21.

daughter, Dorothea, placed a love of danger, and of mastering and overcoming difficulties both physical and moral, at the very top of a list of her father's strong characteristics; and certainly Hubert went all out to win when playing competitive sports, in spite of his less than robust constitution. So much so, that his time at Eton was regularly punctuated by accidents; one collision in football in 1865 being so violent that he had to be carried from the field on a sheep-hurdle in a state of collapse, unable to speak and subsequently laid up for a week.

Hubert had, for some time, been more than happy to join in numerous drunken parties, both at local pubs and within the Houses at Eton; and although he continued to fling himself into sports with a disregard for personal safety bordering on the reckless, he was, by contrast, far more careful in controlling his consumption of alcohol after the summer of 1864. This change, due in part to the dictates of his own conscience, also coincided with a deeper understanding of the hurt caused to his family by his elder brother's waywardness.

On his return from France, Clinton had taken lodgings at Dawlish on the south Devonshire coast. Whilst there he had made the acquaintance of John Hinde, an officer in the merchant service, and was invited by him to visit his mother and three sisters at their home, Eastdon Cottage, in the nearby village of Starcross. One of the two elder sisters was engaged to be married – and before very long Clinton had lost his heart to the other.

Clinton spent the first few weeks of 1864 with his new-found sweetheart, Florence Hinde, in a small inn at Calbourne on the Isle of Wight. 'There are two people I am determined to devote my life to: Flo and Possie', he wrote, 'She is devoted to me and I to her, and Possie is most glorious in so many ways'. One of those ways was, of course, in providing him with his allowance, but on returning to Highnam, Clinton was puzzled by Gambier Parry's reaction to his ever-open palm: 'Possie seemed to let out tonight that he was rather hard up. Can he, so careful a man, be so?'[33] Well yes, he could; he had just lost £6,000 in an ill-advised investment in iron and coal, and he might also have been reluctant to fuel a habit which was rapidly reaching the extent of 'three quarters of a bottle of spirits *per diem* besides beer, wine, etc.'[34] Unpleasant scenes were to follow.

On 6 June Clinton wrote to his mother, his beloved 'Muzzie', asking for cash, giving a glowing account of his new friends the Hindes and their respectable standing, and telling her that he wished to marry Florence. Five days later, summoned to London, Clinton had a 'most painful interview with Possie and Muzzie... He agreed to pay my debts and let me do as I like about Flo'.[35] Gambier Parry bristled at having been *told* of Clinton's intentions, rather than having been asked; advised his eldest son that he had no intention of maintaining him in idleness; warned him that he could consider marriage only after he had

---

[33] CP diaries.
[34] *Ibid.*
[35] *Ibid.*

taken his degree and settled into a profession; and returned to his work at Ely in a state of considerable agitation.

In the meantime, Ethelinda lost no time in mobilising the family network to discover all she could about the Hindes. At the suggestion of Lady Devon, an acquaintance of the Majendies, Lady Anna Maria Courtenay was contacted. Her response to William Majendie was immediate and damning:

> I received your letter this morning and will give you all information I can respecting Mrs. Hinde and her family. I have had two daughters of hers in my family as Governesses from 1853 to this year. The eldest was a most superior ladylike person and she died of consumption. When she left me from illness I took the second one and only parted with her as I did not require a Governess any longer, and she is about to be married to an excellent young man who is the son of a clergyman.
>
> The third daughter has also been educated for a Governess and has been in two situations and is at present at home – there is a younger one of 14 – and three sons – the eldest is a Clerk in a Lawyer's office in London. The second is in the Merchant Service as Mate, and the third doing very well as a Tutor in a school in Essex, I think.
>
> Mrs. Hinde was one of a good family in affluent circumstances and married very young, the son of the Duke of Norfolk's Steward. They met with great reverses and Mr. Hinde met with a sad accident when head of a Brewery in the North, which brought on paralysis, and they struggled hard for years before we knew them. A sister of Mr. Hinde's married André the Hatter in Bond St. Mr. Hinde was a well educated, talented man and died after much suffering in 1859. They are a serious family, what is called high church, but they are in *great* poverty. Mrs. Hinde has spoken freely to us of all her affairs, particularly since her husband's death, and therefore we are aware of an engagement between her third daughter and Mr. Parry, the son of Mr. Gambier Parry, which I think is what you allude to in your letter.
>
> Mr. Parry became acquainted with the sailor brother and after coming to Mrs. Hinde's house for some time and shewing marked attention to her third daughter, Mrs. Hinde was at last obliged to say to him, that she could not allow him to come to her house any longer, unless he wrote to ask his father's consent… We have never seen the young man, but from what we hear, I do not think he behaved honourably about this matter and I fear altogether he has given his father cause for uneasiness before this and I do not think the girl has a happy prospect if the marriage ever comes about.
>
> You ask what their social position is, from their great poverty they see no one but the Clergyman of their Parish and his family and ourselves. Mrs. Hinde takes lodgers and that is all she has to look to, except what her family can make by their own exertions.[36]

Given an opportunity to exercise love and understanding, Gambier Parry chose instead to adopt the stern and unfeeling dogmaticism of class-based bigotry. The possibility that Clinton might actually find real happiness with Florence Hinde seemed to him not to have been remotely possible. In a harsh letter, he accused Clinton of having deceived him for years past and of having given him an entirely false description of the Hinde family:

> I must most strongly protest against this wretched alliance. Miss Hinde may herself be a ladylike and good person, but that will be no sufficient reason for your rashness. You cannot be such a fool as to believe in the theory of love in a cottage. Trust me, the realities of life soon close in upon a man, and all the tinsel of foolery in youthful ideas

[36] Lady Anna Maria Courtenay, letter to William Majendie, 9 July 1864. Highnam archive

soon falls off. And if there is any rope round a man's neck which weighs him down, and works him and wears him out it is a mésalliance.

Is this all your boasted care and caution? Is this the fruit of your self-sufficient wisdom… this! a family of a Yorkshire Brewer! the son of a Steward! the allies of a Bond Street Hatter! a family of Governesses! Merchantmen Sailors and Lawyers Clerks! Is this the family that is not to compromise you!!

Alas! my poor family and home. Poor old Highnam and ourselves, that I had striven by gentlemanly associations, friends and habits to raise in the County estimation for my children's sake – and you, my future representative, are to bring us down to this![37]

Even worse, Gambier Parry wrote to Mrs. Hinde by the same post protesting against the marriage. Both she and Clinton replied; he in the deepest distress:

My dearest father,

After your awful letter I have been so broken down that I can scarcely think of anything. That your letter is a misconception of the respectability of this family I will soon show you. I wish first to lay before you the circumstances in which your letter found us, and if you have a heart I am sure you will feel a little compassion. I will colour nothing; *and as I did in my last letter, will tell you the whole truth*, of all I know and all I hear and see. Jevon Perry who is engaged to Miss Hinde, has been worn down with anxiety on account of a chancery suit. This sorrow and trouble is not sufficient for him, for last week his intended has evinced some very dangerous symptoms; there is no doubt, I believe, that she is in a consumption: the anxiety of all, myself included of course, was immensely augmented.

When I saw her (that is Emma, Jevon's intended) the little bride, the wife that is to be in a fortnight, was lying pale and exhausted on a sofa, propped up by pillows, her anxious and affectionate mother was going about with all the little dainties she could afford, pressing her to eat, with smiles on her face and agony in her heart, with difficulty repressing tears. All this sorrow and wretchedness is not sufficient; that very morning your awful letter came. She had but a short time to answer it by return of post, as she was going up to Exeter to get Dr. Knighton to come and see Emma. She did answer it however and if her letter is not coherent, don't wonder at it, since she had but half an hour, and that with so many sorrows about her.[38]

Clinton attempted to justify his belief in the respectability of his intended in-laws. 'If poverty has forced them to take professions', he wrote, 'I am very sorry for it… Flo's heart is given to me. Please, I entreat you, forgive us. I throw myself on your pity'.[39] In her sad little letter, Mrs. Elizabeth Hinde tried to soften Gambier Parry's heart, outlined the details of her own birth and standing, and assured him that since Clinton's arrival in Dawlish his habits and conduct had been exemplary:

In Dawlish he is spoke of in the *highest* terms. I have never called at his lodgings at various times without finding him at work for his examination. I need not tell you of his fascinating and affectionate manner; no one can be with him without feeling the power. His *determination* is to take his degree. He intends trying for a Government appointment – something in the House of Lords, or the House of Commons, and at the same time

[37] TGP, letter to Clinton Parry, 14 July 1864. Highnam archive.
[38] CP, letter to Thomas Gambier Parry, July 1864. Highnam archive.
[39] *Ibid.*

to study for a profession; he is certainly in earnest. My child's *whole soul* is given up to him…[40]

Gambier Parry had heard it all before. His love for Clinton was unchanged, but he could no longer trust him to tell the truth, nor begin to understand, or even wish to understand, the Hinde's predicament. They would get no sympathy from him; but when he came home on 22 July to find Clinton at Highnam he was still prepared to show affection to his eldest son, who, even then, was playing the old game of self-deceit:

> I am just going to have a glass of beer before going to bed (which is a wonder for me now), but I must not and will not *touch beer or spirits till after I am married* – except perhaps at *dinner* I will have some *very very* weak brandy and water, as an assistance to my digestion, but not more than is *absolutely necessary.*[41]

It required only a few days for Gambier Parry to realise that Clinton was deceiving not only himself. On 27 July there was an 'awful scene with Possie and Muzzie'. Clinton was told that he could no longer consider Highnam as his home. His marriage to Florence, at Sutton Courteney in Berkshire (now Oxfordshire), had been arranged for 14 August; but there was no joyful parting as Clinton set out from Highnam on 6 August: 'My last day a most blessed day, yet very sad. I have had a long talk with darling Muzzie and a good cry. Hubert and I cried together'.[42]

*   *   *   *   *   *   *

Alienated from his eldest son, Gambier Parry's attitude towards Hubert seems to have been refreshed by a new-found intimacy; a realisation that the child who had seemed to be so slow to learn had grown to share many of his own tastes, was possessed of a first-rate intellect, and was, furthermore, an excellent companion. Although Hubert spent much of the summer of 1865 in the enjoyment of sports, dances, picnics and local excursions with his young friends, he was equally happy to wander further afield with his father to see the recently restored cathedral at Llandaff, where Dante Gabriel Rossetti had recently completed his magnificent altar-piece, a triptych, entitled *The Seed of David*. On all of his excursions to places of interest, Hubert made copious notes about details of architecture or archeology, taking particular care to make full descriptions of the organs in the many churches and cathedrals which he visited. The organ of St Mary Redcliffe, Bristol, made a particular impression:

> The most interesting instrument I ever played on. It was originally built for the Temple Church, by Harris and Byfield. It is almost entirely in its original condition. There are no separate pedal pipes, but the Great goes to CCC with 16 foot metal diapasons. The Trumpet also goes throughout. The Cremona on the Swell and the Bassoon on the Choir are most beautiful stops. The most remarkable part of the organ is the Diapasons, which are far the finest I ever heard. The keys are remarkably short, little

---

[40] Mrs Elizabeth Hinde, letter to Thomas Gambier Parry, 17 July 1864. Highnam archive.
[41] CP diaries.
[42] *Ibid.*

over 1½ inch or 2 inches; the naturals black, and sharps white. There are two or three 5 rank stops on the organ. 29 or 30 stops in all with most tremendous power.[43]

At the beginning of September Highnam Court was filling with guests for the Three Choirs Festival in Gloucester, the first under the direction of Samuel Sebastian Wesley, who, like Elvey at Windsor, was fighting against the indifference of the Anglican clergy to raise choral standards in the English Church. Wesley had visited Highnam in the previous March, when he and Clinton had practiced together, and Hubert had become a staunch admirer of the great man. The staple fare at the Three Choirs Festival, *Elijah* and *Messiah*, confirmed both Hubert's devotion to the music of Mendelssohn and his conviction that Handel's masterpiece was 'the grandest music ever conceived'. He was also deeply impressed by Wesley's *Ascribe unto the Lord*, in a concert on the second morning which also included Mendelssohn's *Hymn of Praise* and Beethoven's *Mount of Olives*; by Wesley's playing , in the same concert, of the *St Ann Fugue* 'in the true Bach spirit'; and especially by the superb improvised fugue which he played as a concluding voluntary on the Sunday which followed the Festival:

> He began the accompaniment in crotchets alone, and then gradually worked into quavers, then triplets and lastly semiquavers. It was quite marvellous. The powerful old subject came stalking in right and left with the running accompaniment wonderfully entwined with it – all in the style of old Bach.[44]

The Festival ended with a ball. Hubert danced all night, and was 'quite knocked up by the fatigue and excitement of the week'; but not sufficiently so to prevent him spending a few days with his cousin Eddie Hamilton at Salisbury, where, amongst other things, he played cricket and enjoyed the distinction of hearing one of his own anthems sung in the cathedral – Hubert was already a published composer. From Salisbury he was off to nearby Wilton for several carefree days of croquet, billiards, beagling and, best of all, riding and driving with young Maude Herbert. He had first met Maude, the second daughter of Sidney, First Baron Herbert of Lea, seven years earlier when, as a little child, she had gone over to Bishopstone with Lady Dunmore and her two daughters to see the Parrys, who were visiting their cousins the Lears. Sidney Herbert, remembered as the Secretary at War who took the initiative of inviting Florence Nightingale to go out to the Crimea in charge of a body of nurses in 1854, had died in 1861. Now, four years later, Maude, at fourteen, was already much in Hubert's thoughts; and, walking side by side in the moonlight or sitting on the Palladian bridge at Wilton, their friendship inevitably blossomed into a deeper affection. But a potential problem was waiting in the wings. Maude's mother, Lady Elizabeth Herbert, described by the biographer of the Herberts of Wilton as a woman 'prone to act emotionally and incalculably, to be easily swept into indiscretions', was not only possessed of a mercurial temperament, but was also

---

[43] CHHP, *Diary 1865*. Shulbrede archive.
[44] *Ibid.*

'blinded by religious fervour… [She]did not become a Roman Catholic in her husband's lifetime, [but] was received into the Roman Church after his death';[45] the seeds of turbulence, as yet undetected, had already been sown.

An incident which occurred a few days after Hubert's return to Gloucestershire gave him cause for much more immediate alarm. Riding home on his pony 'Bob' after spending a pleasant evening with friends at the riverside village of Frampton-on-Severn, he met a mysterious and silent horseman, ghostlike in the moonlight, on the straight, deserted stretch of road between Whitminster and Hardwicke. Hubert's curiosity sharpened to apprehension as the stranger turned his horse and, still silently, began to follow him. Suddenly, the blackness of night was turned to dazzling brilliance: a meteor shot across the sky illuminating the entire landscape; 'Bob' started up in fright; and, with pulse racing, Hubert, all thought of the now-vanished stranger forgotten, continued speedily homeward.

Hubert's work at composition continued apace, and at Eton in 1865 he completed several more pieces , including an Overture in B minor, a madrigal setting of Herrick's *Fair Daffodils*, and an anthem, *Why boastest thou*.

Song-setting had long been important to him, prompted by a love of sixteenth and seventeenth-century English verse; and from 1865 by his increasing attraction to nineteenth-century poetry, an interest reflected in his setting of Thomas Moore's *Why does azure deck the sky*, written for his friend Cecil Ricardo.

When Elvey decided that his star pupil should be entered for an Oxford B Mus degree in the following year, increasing amounts of time had to be set aside for extra lessons and, in spite of the constant din of the school around him, for his own compositions. Nor was Hubert spared any of the usual round of schoolwork and games; and if this was not enough, on 18 May 1866 he went up to Oxford to attempt an Exhibition at New College in response to a suggestion made by his cousin Lewis Majendie and approved by his father and Eton tutor. The attempt was not successful, but the time at Oxford, crammed with music and the company of old friends, was not wasted: at Magdalen he heard Stainer play 'the last three movements of the Sonata in B flat (Mendelssohn)… most gloriously';[46] he also tried the Magdalen organ himself, and Stainer, whom Hubert had met briefly at the Gloucester Three Choirs Festival in the previous year, 'was very kind and told me also about my musical degree and how I am to take it. And what I am to write'.[47]

Returning to Highnam for the summer holiday Hubert found that his father had accepted an invitation from a Mr. Thomas Marling of Gloucester to restore the St Andrew's Chapel in Gloucester Cathedral (the east chapel in the south transept) as a memorial to his late wife. Gambier Parry's work in the cathedral, begun in 1866, was not completed until 1868; and although Marling had given £400 towards the project, the total cost, including the pay of gilders

---

[45] Tresham Lever, *The Herberts of Wilton* (London,1967), p 217.
[46] CHHP, *Diary 1866*. Shulbrede archive.
[47] *Ibid.*

and other craftsmen, was far in excess of that. Once again, Parry found himself digging into his own pocket to complete a labour of love.

All the decoration in the chapel, except for details such as lettering and the diapers, was completed by Gambier Parry's own hand. Every surface, including the buttress which slices across the western arch into the chapel, is smothered in polychromy. Amongst his main themes, Parry intended the two figures at each side of the altar to illustrate the verses in the *Te Deum*, ie, Elijah (Prophets); St Paul (Apostles); St Alban (Martyrs); and a female figure representing the Holy Church. On the south wall the principal subject is the Crucifixion of St Andrew, above which are Christ in Judgement with angels, seraphim and the legend 'I will give thee a crown of life'. On the north wall St John the Baptist acknowledges Christ as the Lamb of God; Christ, accompanied by a delightful lamb, beckons to Saints Andrew and Peter above a legend in Greek which translates into 'the first called'. The whole scene is set in a stony landscape softened by trees; and in a recess to the east the figure of an angel hovers, with scrolls saying 'Blessed is the man that endureth' and 'Thou faithful unto death'. But Gambier Parry's time between 1866 and 1868 was not devoted solely to the decoration of the St Andrew's Chapel. These were the years in which he was at last able to advance his scheme to alleviate the suffering of Gloucester's poorest children – but even he can hardly have anticipated the biting opposition which lay ahead.

Gambier Parry had already purchased a house and several acres of ground at Kingsholm in Gloucester (the site is now a residential area: Gambier Parry Gardens) where he established a home for nursing sisters, and which, in memory of his daughter Lucy, he called St Lucy's Home. The vicar of the nearby St Mark's Church was appointed as Warden of the Home. Parry devised a uniform for the sisters, the bonnet of brown straw, the dress and cloak of dark blue serge; and thus dressed, the nursing sisters of St Lucy's Home went out and about in the back-streets and alleys of the city, and especially in the Island, bringing some small degree of comfort to the sick:

> Yet in spite of the good work that was being done, the movement was not popular. Feeling about it and about the Sisters ran very high, and even the Sisters themselves on their errands of mercy did not escape ridicule sometimes in the streets.[48]

When, in 1865, Gambier Parry proposed that nursing in the woefully inefficient Gloucester Infirmary should also be undertaken by trained nurses belonging to one of the religious sisterhoods, such as those at St Lucy's Home, his idea was received with an outcry:

> It was voted 'the rankest Tractarianism'; the local press teemed with letters against the movement; a pamphlet was circulated with the following title – 'The Owlet's Home, or out of what <u>Cage</u> did the <u>Owlet</u> fly that is seeking its Roost in the Gloucester Infirmary?'; and finally a public indignation meeting was held at the Old Tolsey... To read the 15 closely printed pages of the pamphlet is to gather some idea of the feelings

---

[48] GPM p 198.

that were then rife… Referring to the Nursing Sisters and their organisation with a sneer, the writer remarks – 'a partial examination of the heresy referred to will I believe satisfy you that it is <u>Tractarianism</u>, that <u>speckled owlet</u> which has been hatched by <u>Antichrist</u>'. *The Spectator* issued an article supporting the Nurses; but the low church party, headed by a poor creature who was then Dean [Henry Law], opposed it tooth and nail, together with and assisted by many influential people in the neighbourhood.[49]

Gambier Parry withdrew his proposal – but the opposition only served to strengthen his resolve. He determined to found a Children's Hospital in conjunction with the Home, to be worked by the St Lucy's Sisters. The foundation stone was laid in the grounds at Kingsholm on 7 March 1866, and on the next day, most auspiciously, Ethelinda gave birth to the Parrys' sixth and last child, a daughter, Hilda. By 19 September, when there was already accommodation for thirty patients in the partially-completed building, the hospital was formally opened. In the following fifteen months 1,798 children were treated, including 158 in-patients. The initial cost of the hospital to Gambier Parry was £4,000. It was to be, he insisted, a free hospital for children of the poor, placing the following at the head of its charter: 'No orders or recommendations are necessary. The poverty of the parents and the suffering of the child are the title to admission'.

[*The demands upon space at the Children's Hospital were so great that it was soon necessary to build an extension. In 1872, following a further extension, the hospital at Kingsholm was taken over by the Sisters of the House of Mercy, Clewer. Gambier Parry then started what was practically a new foundation. He bought a house in Hare Lane, close to Gloucester Cathedral, making considerable alterations and additions to it for use as St Lucy's Home, the old Home at Kingsholm being converted to the Warden's residence. Further Clewer Sisters arrived at Hare Lane in 1874, devoting their time to the care of orphans and incurable female patients*].

*   *   *   *   *   *   *

Hubert's holiday at Highnam in the summer of 1866 was enlivened by the presence there of his brother Clinton, his wife and their baby girl, Isabel, born on 15 June. For some months, Clinton and Florence had been living in lodgings at 11 Tennis Court Road, Cambridge, eking out a small allowance in order that Clinton might continue his French studies. The tension between Clinton and his father having eased a little, the visit to Highnam seems to have been successful. Isabel, affectionately nicknamed 'Bluebell' by the family, was baptised with water from the Jordan on 12 August, and two days later Clinton and Florence celebrated the first anniversary of their marriage – an occasion which very nearly ended in catastrophe. Whilst out driving with Hubert, a pony frightened their horse, Griselda. She bolted, ran half a mile up the road, and came to a halt only when she was stopped by a quick-thinking boy whose action prevented serious injury to them all.

---

[49] *Ibid.*

In the following weeks Hubert continued to enjoy the social round, visited the Three Choirs Festival at Worcester, where he met Spencer Lyttelton, worked hard at his exercise for the Oxford degree, and returned to Eton *via* Bayfordbury and London. Ernest, who entered Evans's House at Eton at the beginning of that Michaelmas term, remembered well the pressures of the time on Hubert:

> I realized nothing of it then, but have often wondered since how he got through that half. He was Keeper of the Field, in other words, captain of the School football eleven; he was Second Keeper of the Wall, no one being allowed to hold the captaincy of both; he was captain of my Dame's school eleven; he was of course in 'Pop' [*the debating society*]; and there was besides his work to be done. Added to this, he was working with Elvey in preparation for the examination for the Bachelor's degree in music at Oxford, and he was writing his exercise for this – 'O Lord, Thou hast cast us out'. His room was always thronged with friends, and the piano there was always to be heard.[50]

By a strange irony, it seems that only more of the accidents to which he was so often prone were instrumental in providing Hubert with the time to complete his composition exercise:

> At the first game in the Field he got shinned, strained his ankle badly, being unable to put a boot on for a whole week, on top of which he caught a violent cold and scalded his hand. But his staying out enabled him to get on 'flowingly' with his cantata and other compositions, in which Elvey was most kind and helpful.[51]

The cantata, *O Lord, Thou hast cast us out*, was completed on 22 October, checked by Elvey, and a fair copy dispatched to Oxford on 30 October. 'It is all copied and looks immense.' Parry wrote in his diary, 'I gave it a last touch and sent it off in the evening for its awful inspection'.[52]

More football followed; more 'shinning, effusion of blood and cutting open of heads';[53] once again the ankle collapsed; and then, at the end of November, Hubert was confined to his room with a fever diagnosed by the school doctor as erysipelas. Less than a week later, on 5 December, he obtained leave to travel to Oxford for his written examinations On the evening of his arrival he was pleased to be asked to attend a musical party at the home of Professor W F Donkin, Savilian Professor of Astronomy. Stainer and James Taylor, organist of New College, were amongst the guests, as was the Revd Sir Frederick Gore Ouseley, by whose initiative formal examinations for the degrees of Mus B and Mus D had been instituted at Oxford. Ouseley, wrote Hubert, 'extemporized marvellously'.

The next morning Hubert reported to the *Schola Musicae*, along with two other candidates who were attempting the Mus D. All went well in the written examinations, and when he was only a quarter through the miscellaneous and last

---

[50] Ernest Gambier-Parry, *op cit*, p 136.

[51] Graves, *op cit*, p 66.

[52] CHHP, *Diary 1866*.

[53] Graves, *op cit*, p 66.

paper, 'they told me I need not do any more and let me go. Sir Frederick was very kind and when they came out about a quarter of an hour afterwards I heard that the other two fellows had "muffed" and I had got my *testamur*. Glorious! Sir Frederick Ouseley asked me to come and stay with him at Tenbury'.[54]

Ouseley had founded St. Michael's College at Tenbury in 1854, a music school where the emphasis was very much on church music; but even if Hubert had shown an interest in Ouseley's invitation there is little doubt that Gambier Parry would have refused him permission to accept it.

Hubert Parry's cantata was performed at Eton on Saturday, 8 December 1866 under its young composer's own direction. It was, reported the *Eton College Chronicle* for 24 January 1867, a performance which everybody thoroughly enjoyed.

> We must also tender our best thanks to Mr. C.H. Parry himself, for the great honour he has conferred upon the School by obtaining his Musical Degree; and it is with the deepest regret that we have to announce his departure from the School, and the loss the Musical Society has sustained in being deprived of so able and energetic a President.

Hubert had fulfilled the promise so aptly recognised by one of his Eton contemporaries who, years before in a written satire, representing him as 'Young Amphion', asked the question:

> Who rashly dares to him to hold a candle –
> This young Beethoven, this our youthful Handel? [55]

---

[54] CHHP, *Diary 1866.*
[55] Graves, *op cit*, p 25.

VIII

Golden Afternoons

Hubert Parry left Eton on 14 December 1866. His travelling companion on the train to London, George, 13th Earl of Pembroke, 10th Earl of Montgomery, 2nd Baron Herbert of Lea, was also the eldest brother of Hubert's young sweetheart, Maude Herbert. 'I watched the old place from the train until I could not see it any more', wrote Hubert, 'and so now I have done with the happiness of school life. I don't at all comprehend it, and I think it's a good thing I don't'.[1]

Many years later Hubert was to tell his daughter, Dorothea, that he 'was well up in Latin and Greek when he left Twyford for Eton' and that he thought 'he might have done a good deal in this line, but lost it at Eton. He looked back with great affection on the School – but did not believe in it educationally... By the time he was 17 he had read and thoroughly absorbed most of Shakespeare and Milton, and had a profound knowledge of the bible... Milton seems to have entered into his soul'.[2]

In London, Hubert stayed with his cousin Lewis Majendie in Albany Street, and found a partial antidote to wistfulness in a performance of *Black-Eyed Susan* at the New Royalty before the two young men set off for a short break at Majendie's home, Hedingham Castle in Essex. The Castle was built c1140 by the powerful de Veres, Earls of Oxford. Its four-storey keep with square turrets; its massive walls; its moat and fifteenth-century bridge all fascinated Hubert, and Hedingham became a favourite stopping-place for the rest of his life.

During his five-day stay with Lewis Majendie, Hubert examined the keep at Hedingham and the churches in surrounding villages with a thoroughness and appreciation for art and architecture to be expected of his father's son; and what he saw he described in vivid detail. But his impressions, not simply a record of styles and dimensions, reveal a deeply romantic spirit beneath the technical expertise, as when, on a lovely night, standing in 'the glorious upper room in the castle – spanned by an enormous Norman arch – in the moonlight, with mist and

---

[1] CHHP, *Diary 1866*. Shulbrede archive.
[2] Dorothea Ponsonby, *Notes on C H H Parry* (manuscript).

rime on gates and trees down to the lake', the view from one of the windows was transfigured in his mind:

> I never saw anything so lovely... looking through the ilex, whose leaves glittered in the moon, and through the old walnuts and down the hill to the water, whose calm surface reflected softly the trees all round it, and looked inconceivably lovely with a very slight veil of mist; and the frost on the grass, and an awful silence in the air, and not a breath to stir the sleeping mist, or move the glittering leaves.
>
> The appearance of the big room from the gallery was very magnificent. The moon streamed in through the windows, and made the room look twice its real size. The great arch in the middle seemed stupendous. And the whole thing with its wonderful gloom, and contrast of lovely moonlight in the window recesses, looked (as Lewis said) rather like a lovely scene in a play when you expect to see some wonderful apparition, or a man in armour standing in a halo in the middle of the room, without any previous notice.[3]

Still hobbling on his as yet not fully healed ankle, Hubert returned to Highnam for a wet, windy and dark Christmas. The weather matched Gambier Parry's mood of recent weeks: Clinton had quit Cambridge and been deeply upset by his father's long, critical and 'dreadful' letters; and then, back at Highnam in mid-October, there had been an angry scene in which Gambier Parry had again been 'very savage'.[4] Clinton packed up his remaining belongings at Highnam, went down to Exeter to collect Florence and Isabel, who had been staying with Mrs. Hinde at Starcross, and two days later the family were on their way to Lyndhurst in the New Forest, meaning to stay there until the following spring. As Hubert was exploring the delights and interests of Castle Hedingham, Clinton lay ill with a gastric fever: no doubt withdrawal symptoms resulting from a real attempt to break his alcohol addiction. On 9 December he wrote : 'Oh if only I could make £10 by my two songs. I shall defer my working at French for some time and devote myself this month to authorship'.[5]

Why had Clinton chosen to stay in Lyndhurst for his attempt to dry out? It might well have been Thomas Gambier Parry who, once again, had made the arrangements. The church at Lyndhust (St Michael and All Angels) was built in 1860-61. During the summers of 1863 and 1864, Frederic Leighton was at work there on the fresco *The Wise and Foolish Virgins*, which he painted beneath the east window (mainly the work of Edward Burne-Jones) and behind the altar. It was probably Leighton's discovery of Gambier Parry's spirit fresco medium which encouraged him to undertake this work, which he painted free of charge. Whilst in Lyndhurst Leighton lived at Forest Bank with a friend, Captain Hamilton Aidé, the writer, artist and ecclesiologist who, in 1861, had stayed with the Parrys at Highnam; and it was Aidé who found a cottage in Lyndhurst for Clinton and Florence. Certainly, whilst at Lyndhurst Clinton was much in the company of Aidé, and the two men were often accompanied by the Irish poet and essayist William Allingham, who lived nearby at Lymington.

Shulbrede archive.
[3] CHHP, *Diary 1866.*
[4] CP diaries. Shulbrede archive.
[5] *Ibid.*

These new associations, linked to a period of partial sobriety, began to bear beneficial fruit. Clinton's health continued to improve, and in January 1867 he enjoyed a walk in the snow-covered forest with Allingham and Aidé. With their encouragement, he began to write an essay, *A Curious Man*, and to turn once again to music. Clinton had decided to compose under the pseudonym 'Carl Hirsch' – an adaptation into German of his own first name, Charles, and his wife's surname, Hinde – a step which seems to corroborate the English musical inferiority complex of the times. On 3 February, full of optimism, he writes that he 'worked hard and got my Carl Hirsch op 1 finished – for I do not know what else to call it'.[6] This was probably the piano piece which he later entitled *Remembrance*, but which is now lost. At this time Clinton also wrote 'a little song for which Aidé wrote words, beginning: "Peaceful Holy thoughts come o'er us"'.[7] Another song to words by Aidé, *I Ride Upon the Golden Sand*, a gentle ballad, is the only piece by Clinton still retained in the music collection of the British Library.

When his father visited Lyndhurst on 15 February, Clinton was hugely encouraged, writing that 'he had not known me so clear and healthy-looking for years'.[8] In the following weeks Clinton finished a paper on 'music and painting', visited his mother's grave in Bournemouth, and 'began an experiment. A great one'.[9] What was the experiment? He did not explain; but if it was an attempt at tee-totalism, it failed. Clinton and his family left Lyndhurst soon afterwards, and yet again his life began to spiral out of control.

Hubert, in contrast, started 1867 at Highnam in busy preparation for his Oxford matriculation attempt. During the first three weeks of the new year time was spent each day with Mr. Washbourne, a local clergyman, working at the set books: the *Bacchae*, the *Hippolytus* and the *Georgics*; but there was also music and leisure aplenty, including a day of skating in the company of Dr. Charles John Ellicott, the Bishop of Bristol and Gloucester, a man so unmusical that in 1865, two years after his appointment to the united see, rather than attend the Three Choirs Festival selected to spend that week on skis, crossing from Lauterbrunnen over the Tschingel glacier to Kanderstag. But he was, as might be supposed, an excellent skater, and Hubert learned 'all sorts of dodges' from him.

Unlike many of his friends and his own elder brother, Hubert was not destined for Christ Church, a college which enjoyed traditional links with Eton. Perhaps the shameful way in which Clinton had behaved there had persuaded Gambier Parry that an alternative should be found. Hubert's Eton friend Robert Bridges, the future poet laureate, suggested Corpus Christi; but the Majendie family had ties with Exeter – and so Exeter was chosen.

Hubert arrived at Oxford on 24 January and immediately made it his business to introduce himself to F. Scotson Clark, the Exeter chapel organist. Two days later he matriculated, chose his rooms – and set off back to Highnam,

---

6 *Ibid.*
7 *Ibid.*
8 *Ibid.*
9 *Ibid.*

where he found that Sir Samuel Baker was the principal guest at a large house party. Hubert, with a love of adventure inherited from his grandfather and great-grandfather, was enthralled by Sir Samuel's tales of the ancient kings of Ceylon and their great cities: of Anuradhapura, Polonnaruwa and Kandy; and of the peoples and animals of Central Africa. Unlike Clinton and Ernest, Hubert was never a keen shot, but he took part in the last day of pheasant shooting at Highnam and, much to his delight and surprise, contributed a fair share to the bag and thoroughly enjoyed himself.

On 2 February 1867 Hubert made the rounds of well-loved Highnam things and places, the familiar anchorages of childhood, bade them all farewell, and returned to university to begin his studies in law and history; to the 'strange and novel position of an Oxford Freshman'.[10]

If Hubert's rooms at Exeter College were 'most awful holes',[11] he could at least take satisfaction in spending as little time in them as possible. As at Eton, he threw himself with zest into sports of all kinds, regardless of injury or exhaustion and, in addition, his social engagements flowed in a seemingly endless stream. He was already amongst old friends from Eton, several of whom, including Eddie Hamilton (known by all as 'Flab'!), were at Christ Church; he dined often with Robert Bridges at Corpus Christi; and Scott Holland, a frequent companion, was at Balliol. In his first fortnight he breakfasted by himself only once, and the pace of his college life can easily be supposed from just two of several similar diary entries:

> 29 March. Played tennis for an hour and a half in the morning with Moffat. Lunched with him without changing and then went to the gymnasium, where we boxed and fenced and single-sticked and gymnaticized for another $1\frac{1}{2}$ hour and then went and played rackets for yet another $1\frac{1}{2}$ hour. Dined with Moffat.

> 30 March. Breakfast with Lucas. Played tennis for three hours in the morning. Lunched and spent most of the afternoon with Flab. Dined with Moffat.[12]

Apart from the lively fellowship of his contemporaries, Hubert was often in the company of the Revd. George Kitchin, his old master at Twyford, now living in Oxford; he was a frequent and most welcome guest at the home of Dr. Leighton, the Warden of All Souls, whose young daughter was then 'a jolly little girl with delightful hair' to whom he waggishly gave the nickname 'Miss Wig' and 'took a great fancy… with my usual absurd predilection for kids'; and throughout his Oxford days there was no recital or entertainment at the Christ Church Deanery to which he was not invited – and , as well as music and conversation, feminine charms were to be found there too.

Alice, the second of the three daughters of the Dean of Christ Church, Henry George Liddell, had been immortalised by Lewis Carroll in *Alice's Adventures in Wonderland*, published in 1865. When Hubert arrived in Oxford Alice was already fifteen years old and Lewis Carroll (Charles Dodgson) had not yet

---

[10] CHHP, *Diary 1867*. Shulbrede archive.
[11] *Ibid.*
[12] *Ibid.*

begun work on *Through the Looking-Glass*. Neither the shy Dean nor the even more shy author of the *Alice* books feature in Hubert's diaries – but the three girls certainly attracted his attention, and especially the eldest, Ina (short for Lorina), the 'Imperious Prima' of the third stanza of the poem with which Lewis Carroll prefixed *Alice in Wonderland*:

> Imperious Prima flashes forth
> Her edict "to begin it" –
> In gentler tone Secunda hopes
> "There will be nonsense in it!" –
> While Tertia interrupts the tale
> Not *more* than once a minute.

Hubert's steps turned with increasing frequency towards the Deanery. By the end of 1867 he had become a constant visitor, and his Christmas gift to Ina was a song written especially for her; but even so, Maude Herbert's place in his affections appears not to have been displaced by the most senior of Lewis Carroll's boating companions of an earlier 'golden afternoon'.

The artist William Blake Richmond, six years Hubert's senior, had been commissioned by Henry Liddell in 1864 to paint his three daughters, and the result, a conversation piece, *The Sisters*, was highly acclaimed when exhibited at the British Institution in the following year; it is, arguably, the finest of all Richmond's many portraits. Hubert met Richmond at Oxford in 1869, probably at the Christ Church Deanery, and the two soon forged a lifelong friendship.

The burning of nervous energy in strenuous sports; dinner-dances and balls; lunches and teas; croquet parties with the Leightons in the large quad at All Souls; conducting the Glee Club at the Liddells; singing and playing at the College Musical Society in Exeter and the University Philharmonic Society – these were idyllic years for Hubert. But lectures were not ignored, and he was as successful in examinations as in the pursuit of pastime and pleasure. Nor was Sunday a time for amusement. Hubert had joined the College choir immediately upon his arrival at Oxford, attended up to four chapel services every Sunday, and, in addition, made a point of going to St. Mary's to hear the sermons – but within a year or so a faint voice of doubt would grow ever louder in his ear. His daughter Dorothea recalled that:

> Up to the time he went to Oxford [he] was very devout. When he employs a cypher in his early diaries it is usually about religion. He was genuinely moved and helped by religious services and sermons. It was never possible for him to observe anything as a form or custom, therefore religion was something very real to him and he applied it to life. But it was impossible for so thoughtful and sincere a mind not to discover the Pharisaical attitude of many churchmen. By the time he was 21 he realized that a narrow sectarianism such as his parents' high church position was not truth, and that dogmatic theology was not religion. He was exasperated by his step-mother's talk: "We of course are not in communion with them", referring to some other sect. He burst out to Eddie Hamilton his cousin on this subject and found that Eddie, the son of the Bishop of Salisbury, was going through the same experience. [13]

---

[13] Dorothea Ponsonby, *op cit.*

To entertain such misgivings at such a time was to face more than intellectual debate. Religion, the Christian religion, permeated every aspect of nineteenth-century life in England: political, educational, social, artistic and scientific. In choosing to swim against the doctrinal stream a self-confessed doubter faced powerful currents; and the very last person to whom Hubert would be able to reveal his thoughts was his own father. But the still waters had not yet been ruffled, and when they were, apart from that single confession to Eddie Hamilton, he chose to remain silent – at least for a little while.

Unconventional and disturbing as were his thoughts to become, Hubert's actions were oftentimes filled with very real danger; his struggles against the tide not merely metaphorical.

A keen swimmer, Hubert enjoyed bathing at Sandford Lasher whilst he was up at Oxford. Soon after his dip on 10 June 1867 a fellow undergraduate was drowned at the same place. But two days later Hubert was quite undeterred from bathing there as usual, even though the river was still being dragged for the victim's body. On 15 June he narrowly avoided drowning himself, 'being regularly sucked under by an undercurrent when I went in, and when I tried to come up to the top; so I had to dive again and wait for a more convenient opportunity for coming up. I must say it was an unpleasant experience'.[14] Another adventure, equally typical of Hubert's lack of regard for his personal safety, and even more dangerous, threatened to rob Hubert and his half-brother of their lives and England of her musical renaissance. Ernest Gambier-Parry remembered it vividly:

> I suppose if there is one river more treacherous than another it is the Severn. That was accordingly the scene of our exploit. With a supreme contempt for 'wet-bobs' at Eton, I had nevertheless brought home with me a cheap canoe one summer holidays. It was a long, exceedingly narrow craft, and so crank that to sit in it at all without capsizing was by no means easy… On Hubert returning from Oxford he at once decided to start a canoe too; bought one in Gloucester accordingly, of wider beam and more roomy; and brought it out in triumph in a cart.
>
> Needless to say that paddling about the big water at home soon palled on us, and we cast our eyes towards the Severn. Hubert was the ringleader of course, he being then 20 and I not yet 16. The plan was soon made – we would go 'down the Severn'. I don't know that we had any clear idea of what we meant or where we meant to go, though of one thing I am quite sure, that we had no idea there was any risk of our going down to the bottom of the Severn and being no more heard of. I suppose going *up* the Severn – a much more suitable course with such canoes as ours – appeared too tame: it was to be *down*, and down it was.
>
> We furnished ourselves with no map or chart; we made no provision for the expedition beyond a spare shirt and a toothbrush; and we did not trouble ourselves about tides. True, we might meet the Bore [*the great tidal wave which washes up the Severn*]; and as the thought struck us we both repeated – "the Bore"! When Powell who kept 'The Dog' at Over [*an inn close to the bridge which crosses the Severn at Over*] heard what was afoot, he was for coming up to see the Squire. He had owned vessels in the Bristol Channel and knew the Severn well, also the dangers to be run, and he certainly said he would pray for us when Sunday came.

---

14 CHHP, *Diary 1867*.

The canoes had been taken to the bridge at Over and there we found them. We were under way about 3pm, and no-one came to see us off. Our objective before night was Newnham. We knew it to be between 10 and 12 miles distant by road: whether it was 20 or 40 by river was no concern of ours. Well, on we went down stream past Minsterworth. It took us a long time we thought to get as far as that, but then we knew nothing about the great bend at Corn ham. As the river grew wider the work grew more exciting, especially when we reached the first great variable sand, called Dumball, below Bollow pool and opposite Longney. This open stretch of water was received with a 'Hullo, what's this?'; but we skimmed over the shallows in high glee, and just then I remember the sun set and we passed Framilode passage. Here the river widens out considerably. The tide was out, and as it was growing dark the various sounds and shallows puzzled us, and when we tried to get a footing we found the sands were quick sands. There are some two miles or more of shifting sands at this part of the river, the main channel being known as The Lake.

It seemed odd that we had not seen Westbury Cliff yet; but no matter; it was all odd, and it was quite dark; but we must of necessity reach Westbury, and ultimately Newnham, if we kept on in spite of all the sands and shallows and the curious currents.

We were at this time hugging the left bank – not from choice, for Westbury is on the right, but because a wide sandy mud flat separated us from the other shore. At this time, in the dark, we heard someone walking on the bank and hailed him. 'How far from Westbury?'… 'Why, a mile or more'… 'How can we get across?' More questions followed. The man knew the river; lived on it all his life; if we were for Westbury, there was no way across here at low water, we must come on down a mile: he was going that way and would show us. So he called from the bank to us in the dark, and the swift black stream carried us along without much work with the paddles. Then at last the man called, 'Now then, look ye: ye must strike straight athwart the stream to them lights; and when you be across you be under the Cliff'. We wished him 'good night' and did as we were bid.

The voyage across that stretch of a mile seemed an eternity: there was the black water close to one's fingers as one dipped the paddle, and there was the black sky above. There were neither stars nor moon, and one could see nothing of either shore, moreover it was no longer possible to keep together. There was no wind, but there was the sound of rippling water, and now and then the cry of a gull. Then, of a sudden, there came another sound, the sound of a church clock striking, a long way off – it was the voice of Westbury Church – and it struck eleven!

We had been afloat full eight hours, and our two frail craft were swirling along now in the darkness, close under Westbury Cliff, Newnham lying a mile and a half or more below. Hubert was some way ahead; and now something occurred that puzzled me greatly. I knew nothing of the pace we were going as the shore was invisible; but now and then I was conscious that something in the water passed me going up stream. I could see something black rise out of the water with a splashing sound and only a foot away: then it disappeared and passed into the darkness up stream, – they were very big things and black, and there were several of them. I did not know it at the time, but these black things were rocks covered with sea-weed, and the swiftness of the current alone saved me from being capsized – it took me past them, while I fancied they passed me.

To add to the trepidation of the moment, Hubert's voice came to me over the flood, shouting – Look out, good heavens! – here's the Bore coming! He had stopped, and I drifted up to him. We listened. Yes, sure enough, there was the roar in the darkness – the Bore was coming. To meet a ten-foot wave in the dark at midnight, and in the crankest of canoes, simply spelt drowning. The sound came nearer and nearer and we were sucked towards it. But even at that moment, when it was apparently just upon us, our canoes struck and struck again, and in a moment we were out of them on a ledge of mud and rocks – it was the reef just above Newnham, and the sound we had heard was the water pouring over it.

We had long before taken off our boots and socks and rolled our trousers up, so now all we had to do was to carry our canoes to the mainland. The Severn is a muddy river, but you want to be actually in its mud to know what it means. When we had laid our canoes down above high water, we stood out in the road, our paddles in one hand, our few things in the other, and our legs plastered with black mud from the knees down.[15]

A servant at a nearby house gave Hubert and Ernest a bucket of water to wash their legs; they reached Newnham on foot at about midnight; spent the night at an inn; and the following morning paddled on in their canoes to Sharpness, and then to Frampton where they ate a supper of eight fried eggs and bacon before tumbling into the solitary bed available at the inn. The next day they paddled back up river to Gloucester. On their return to Highnam Court nobody expressed the least surprise or concern about their adventure; but then, as Ernest recalled, nobody ever *was* surprised about their youthful scrapes. 'Danger', wrote Hubert's first biographer 'all through his life was an incentive rather than a deterrent'.[16]

*   *   *   *   *   *   *

Although discouraged by his father from considering music as anything more than a diversion, Hubert's creative impulse was never likely to be stilled. In the first months of 1867 he had continued to work on the composition of various pieces for voice, on an assortment of anthems and a Morning Service in D; but his interest in writing music for the church was diminishing in favour of the secular. Chamber music was enjoying a revival of popularity at Oxford. Recitals were given at the homes of Professor W F Donkin and James Taylor, and Hubert's rooms at Exeter College became a focus for less formal music-making. Soon, Hubert was at work on his own first Quartet in G minor, the first two movements of which were tried out in the Christ Church rooms of Martin Le Marchant Gosselin, a friend from Eton days who had been a fellow member of the Musical Society there. Gosselin, a fine pianist, was, like Eddie Hamilton, also a leading player in the Christ Church Philharmonic. Hubert recognised the deficiencies in his own keyboard technique and decided to seek James Taylor's help. He had discovered the music of Beethoven and begun to explore the piano sonatas, and with Taylor's guidance was soon scaling the peaks of the *Appassionata*; but only after the ending of the Trinity term would the full impact of Beethoven's genius take him like a flood.

Changing his mind about going down before the summer balls, Hubert stayed on to attend four of them, including acting as a steward at the Exeter ball where his 'most perfect' partners were Ina Liddell and her cousin Minnie Fellowes, and had 'about the happiest time of my life'. He had another cause for happiness: S S Wesley had suggested that Hubert would benefit from lessons in instrumentation, and his father had agreed that he might spend the vacation in Stuttgart studying music with the expatriate British composer Henry Hugo

---

[15] GPM pp 216/22.
[16] Graves, *op cit*, p 80.

Pierson. Hubert was to have travelled immediately to Paris to meet Pierson and then to have continued to Stuttgart with him; but Pierson was obliged to delay his departure by two weeks and so Hubert was able to spend the interval at Highnam, looking 'beyond measure lovely', and Bayfordbury, and in London, where he attended the University cricket match at Lord's in the company of the Liddells and Minnie Fellowes. On the same evening, at a Philharmonic Society concert, he heard for the first time a performance of Beethoven's Fifth Symphony :

> Words cannot express the hopeless gloriousness of this old ruffian! Such a whacker! So tremendously massive! Rubinstein played a Concerto of his own. Some of the music was rather rot, but I thought his playing wonderful... We also had Wagner's *Tannhäuser* Overture. I couldn't understand the *reason* of a great deal of it. Some of it was very fine; somewhat giving the sensation of Chaos with Creation and Form beginning to be perceptible. Sterndale Bennett's Symphony in G minor was pretty, Mendelssohnian and well written. I wasn't very fit to listen to it after old Beethoven.[17]

He set out for the continent on 8 July; was disappointed that the channel crossing was 'not rough enough'; and was met the next day at the Gard du Nord by the 'exceedingly kind and most wonderfully jolly' Pierson, who had lived in Germany for twenty years, was 'German in appearance, with long dark hair, greyish eyes, tallish and slightly Beethovenish altogether. Not quite what I expected I must say'.[18] Thomas Gambier Parry had first met Henry Hugh Pearson, as he was then known, when the two were students at Trinity College, Cambridge, and where Pearson was reading medicine. They had continued to meet from time to time when Gambier Parry visited Salisbury, where, in 1846, his father-in-law, Francis Lear succeeded Pearson's father, Hugh Nicholas Pearson, as Dean. In spite of strong parental opposition Pearson had abandoned medicine for music in 1839, living and studying in Germany and touring Europe. He had returned to Britain in 1844 on being elected Reid Professor of Music at Edinburgh but, detesting the bias in British musical academia in favour of sacred music, resigned after only a few months, returned to Germany, and changed his name to Henry Hugo Pierson. Although forgotten now, Pierson enjoyed considerable celebrity in Germany during his lifetime, especially as a composer of opera and songs. 'His ideal was artistically far higher than that of most of his contemporary countrymen', wrote Ernest Walker, 'had he known what to do with his ideas, he would have been one of the really remarkable English composers; as it is, he remains an isolated figure of ineffectual revolt'.[19]

With a day to kill before their evening train to Stuttgart, Hubert and Pierson set out to visit the sights of Paris, including the 'glorious Louvre and Tuileries'. In spite of the difference in their ages a rapport was rapidly established. Pierson was a 'wonderfully well-read man' and for two months their conversations were to be filled not only with music but with poetry and art as

---

[17] CHHP, *Diary, 1867.*
[18] *Ibid.*
[19] Ernest Walker, *History of Music in England* (Oxford, 1928), pp 270/1

well. There were to be 'tremendous arguments' too, but all in a most amiable spirit. Pierson lived with his German wife and their children in a villa set apart on high ground amidst vineyards. Except during lessons, 'if lessons they can be called', only German was spoken in the house – and so, by osmosis, Hubert's German steadily improved. Pierson's two student sons became good companions to Hubert, and the three of them walked, talked and bathed together, and drank the local beer with gusto. 'I couldn't help thinking', wrote Hubert, 'of the rum position. The German student and the English 'Varsity man: Oxford and Würzburg fraternizing on sofas with beer and smoke'. There was plenty of smoke during Hubert's lessons with the boys' father too. 'We sit with weeds in our mouths while Dr Pierson descants on the peculiarities of different instruments for nearly two hours before luncheon. After luncheon we smoke and have coffee. Then I practise, and after that we go for a walk'.[20]

Enveloped in a blue haze, master and student worked with diligent intensity at the only lessons in orchestration which Hubert Parry ever received. Within a fortnight of his arrival Hubert was set to work 'instrumenting' his own song-setting of Thomas Hood's 'Autumn', and this was followed by pieces as diverse as Rossini's *William Tell*, the Entr'acte from Beethoven's *Egmont*, the March from Pierson's incidental music to Goethe's *Faust* – for many years a popular favourite with the German public – and Weber's Overture to *Der Freischütz*. Other compositions of his own which Parry orchestrated under Pierson's guidance included the Overture to his cantata *O Lord, Thou hast cast us out*, and his *Intermezzo Religioso* (which was performed at the Gloucester Three Choirs Festival in the following year). In the limited time available Hubert also received some instruction in composition from Pierson and was able to complete the first movement of a Piano Trio in D minor and an Entr'acte for *As You Like It* – a reflection of Pierson's interest in drama and incidental music which also prompted Hubert to read Goethe's *Faust* in English, as well as *Hamlet*, *King Lear* and Shelley's *The Cenci* – a blood-soaked tragedy which does not succeed in the theatre and which Hubert found 'very horrible'. Hubert, an enthusiastic devourer of books, had been reading Shelley with his Christ Church friend Brooke Deedes during the previous term at Oxford and, in addition to *The Cenci*, continued his study whilst in Stuttgart by reading *The Revolt of Islam* and *Queen Mab*. In complete contrast, he also read Wilkie Collins's *Hide and Seek* and Dickens's *The Old Curiosity Shop* there, believing the latter to be the most touching of the already very many books which he had read. He was even able to find time for viola lessons with a local musician named Huhn; to play the organ in the English Church; and to do a great deal of sight-seeing.

Robert Schumann (1810-1859) had reviewed Pierson's songs most favourably in *Neue Zeitschrift*. Not surprisingly, Pierson inclined towards the school of Schumann; and Hubert's own admiration for the master, one of the eleven to be included in his *Studies of Great Composers* (1887), never dimmed. 'Robert Schumann was', he wrote,

---

[20] CHHP, *Diary 1867*.

the first composer who illustrated several thoroughly modern traits of character in his life and work. He was the first composer of dignified instrumental music in whom certain romantic and mystic influences came to a head; the first who combined singular gifts of appreciative criticism and a capacity for analysing the inner meaning and purport of music with a power of original musical production; and the first of great mark in whom the modern tendency to luxuriate in warm and rich colouring in every department of art became decidedly pronounced.[21]

Hubert left Stuttgart on 11 September. On his return journey he visited Heidelberg, where Schumann, a reluctant student of law, had completed his education. He also spent an evening in Cologne Cathedral where, on 12 November 1850, while at work on the *Rhenish* Symphony, Schumann had been present when Archbishop Geissel was enthroned as a Cardinal, the grandeur of the scene creating so overwhelming an impression on him, so mystic an influence, as to find artistic expression in the glorious central *Maestoso* of the symphony. Hubert explored the still uncompleted cathedral and was moved, not by any grand ceremony, but 'by the Vespers celebrated in a little side-chapel, clouded with the smoke of incense, while the rest of the huge building was only lit by a few lamps. The voices of the choristers chanting, with an occasional booming chord from the organ, rolling out into the dim stillness, and the scent of incense all combined to make the scene solemn and memorable'.[22]

He returned to Highnam, where he was alarmed to find that burglars had broken into the house a few days earlier, stealing £100 worth of silver, including an inscribed silver plate which they had ripped from a wooden casket presented to his father by the Dean and Chapter of Ely in grateful recognition of his work on the nave roof frescoes. Clinton and Florence were there, along with other family friends, the Morants; and Hubert's father was busily occupied with his work in the St. Andrew's Chapel at Gloucester Cathedral. The atmosphere in his own home must have contrasted markedly with the stimulation and easygoing friendship in the Pierson household. Hubert's daughter, Dorothea, recorded her father's memories of Highnam Court life at that time:

> In the '60s and '70s the family lived in a certain amount of old-fashioned state. They had a large staff of servants – a butler, two footmen in maroon coloured liveries, two ladies' maids, a great fat cook with her satellites, and the celebrated Rebecca Gibbs, the housemaid, who came to Highnam when my father was 18 and died in harness when he was 68 and she over 70. Great cans of hot water would be carried up the steep oak stairs to the attics where the young gentlemen slept and where they would have baths after hunting. 'Granny', Mrs Gambier Parry [Ethelinda] would drive out nearly every afternoon with one of her daughters in a very large landau and a pair of horses, and call upon her neighbours.
>
> They moved exclusively in county circles and in the clerical circle of the [Cathedral] Close. Bishop Ellicott was an intimate friend of my grandfather's, and his wife and daughter ardent admirers of C.H.H.P. There was always a great deal of churchgoing, and all the Festivals of the Church were made a great deal of. The descriptions in C.H.H.P.'s diaries of the New Year's Eve services have something mediæval and romantic about them which is appealing.

[21] CHHP, *Studies of Great Composers* (George Routledge & Sons Ltd., 1887), p 292.
[22] Graves, *op cit*, pp 87/8.

My grandfather worked very hard. He was always busy. He had fitted up an ugly room as a studio and there he would paint all the morning. My sister and I would sit to him for the heads of angels – or rather, stand until we dropped. My sister fainted one day. But my grandfather was so absorbed, he never noticed – and illness or weakness was never mentioned to him. He would spend hours on a ladder painting the walls of his own church, and attend all county gatherings and church meetings. He also wrote music – there is a charming hymn by him in Hymns Ancient and Modern [*up to 1909 – excluded from recent editions*]. It must be said that he made Highnam a home. C.H.H.P.'s roots were there and no man could have loved a place more.[23]

But there were tensions at Highnam Court when Hubert arrived back from Germany – and Clinton was at the centre of them. On leaving Lyndhurst he had been quite unable to earn any money, and was still entirely dependent upon the allowance of £500 per year which he received from his father. A neighbour, Mr. de Salis, had said he thought it very possible for him to get some employment at £200 a year in London. 'How I wish I could', wrote Clinton, 'I should then have £700 per annum besides what else I might make! I am now determined to work at arithmetic, and French writing and grammar every day'.[24] Clinton's dreams and drink were still his masters; his failure, Gambier Parry's pain.

Perhaps to dispel the gloom, Hubert suggested a day's outing in the Cotswolds to his brother and his sister-in-law, and they duly set off through Upton St. Leonards to the Black Horse, perched high above the woods at Cranham:

> The view from the sort of platform in front of the inn was quite magnificent. It stands almost on the edge of a sort of precipice which looks over the tops of the trees of the Cotswold woods, and the enormous expanse of the Severn vale, stretching to the right so far that the distance seemed to melt into the sky, and in another direction ending in the Malverns and May Hill; the view to the left being cut off by the side of a rough hill covered with glorious beechwoods. It had the effect of a great sea (as it once was) whose shores are the abrupt sides of the Malverns and May Hill, and reminded me of the land that Faust redeemed from the ocean – so rich, so homely, and so happy. Exquisite curls of blue smoke rose here and there in the still air; and the sun blazed in all its glory over the whole expanse, which was to my eyes infinitely more lovely than anything I have seen abroad… After we had satiated ourselves with the glorious view we rode through the Wolds, splendidly wild country full of stunted trees, wild juniper and low underwood, with occasional glimpses of the vale below, to Painswick Beacon, round it and so home. It is very extraordinary that I have never been there before, as it is one of the most lovely rides I have seen in Gloucestershire, where lovely rides are by no means scarce.[25]

For Clinton, the happiness of the day, as ever, did not last long. On Sunday 29 September he confided in his diary:

> I had a great many things to do early, before breakfast in Gloucester. I am sorry to say that I had two glasses of brandy and soda water: I also had a flask filled with brandy, and I grieve to say was imbibing all day. So far from being happy, I was miserable. I felt

[23] Dorothea Ponsonby, *op cit.*
[24] CP diaries.
[25] CHHP, *Diary 1867.*

incapable of exertion; incapable of thinking connectedly. In the evening I was like a *perverse brute.* I contradicted people, quarrelled with darling Flo, was utterly without self-control or management, and utterly miserable and dissatisfied with myself. It brought out that hateful red spot on my forehead which always seems an index to the amount I may have imbibed.[26]

Yet again, Clinton was ordered out of Highnam Court by his father. He and his heavily pregnant wife made their way forlornly down to Freshwater on the Isle of White, where they lodged with a Mrs. Rice at Hooke Hill Farm, and where, on 7 October, a dejected Clinton sat down to write a 'Lay of an outcast'. Ten days later he received another 'dreadful letter from Highnam. Flo glorious and brave. Happy in our love for one another. A new era begins – of poverty?'[27]

For a while at least, Clinton abstained 'from anything stronger than water', and by the end of October had 'written several things in music, and written nearly two things for magazines'. In the following month he revisited an old friend in Lyndhurst, the writer 'Dolores' Caroline Dickson, and soon afterwards resolved that 'all work gives way to literary work, and writing for the press'. Then, on 4 December, his diary records that 'today the Tennysons called'.

Alfred Tennyson, Poet Laureate, aged fifty-nine and at the height of his powers, had been living at Farringford, close to Freshwater on the Isle of Wight, with his wife Emily since 1853. Almost certainly the Tennysons had been told about the Parrys' arrival on the island by their mutual friend William Allingham, who, since first meeting his idol at Twickenham in 1851, had venerated Tennyson almost as a god. Allingham's own poetry, barely remembered now beyond *The Fairies* ('Up the airy mountain, Down the rushy glen'), is of little worth; but his diary, meticulously maintained, is one of the most absorbing source-books of Victorian literary life. Born in Ballyshannon, Co. Donegal, in 1824, Allingham had worked his way up from bank clerk to Customs Officer, and when, in 1863, he was transferred to the Custom-House at Lymington in Hampshire, he found himself only a ferry crossing away from his deity. And surely it was Allingham who suggested to Clinton that he too should bask in the rays of that empyreal light!

On the day of that first visit to the Parrys, the Tennysons found Florence laid up with a painful toothache and expecting, within a matter of a few weeks, the birth of her second child. Clinton was working hard at a translation of Hoffman's letters to Hippel as well as an article entitled 'The Furnaces'; but the visit seems to have passed off well enough, and Clinton was invited to Farringford on the next day to play in a football match against some of the army officers stationed on the island. It was to be the first of several visits which he and Florence made to the home of the Tennysons in the following months, entering a circle which included the pioneering photographer Mrs Julia Margaret Cameron, who, with her elderly husband, had moved to Freshwater in 1860 and

---

[26] CP diaries.
[27] *Ibid.*

bought two cottages adjacent to Farringford House in order to be near the Tennysons. These she linked together with a Gothic tower, naming her new home *Dimbula Lodge* after the tea estates owned by her family in Ceylon, and settled down 'to rule the place as a charitable despot'.[28]

Allingham himself arrived on 24 December to spend Christmas on the island, and was met from the steamer by Clinton:

> We walk by muddy path and copse to Hook Hill: his wife and baby (3 days old), both well; luncheon. Take up my quarters with Mrs. Curry at Myrtle Cottage, then to Farringford with Parry. I introduce him to Mrs. Tennyson. [*Presumably, Clinton had not mentioned the earlier visit of the Tennysons to Hooke Hill Farm*]. He soon retires.[29]

And the next day:

> *Wednesday, December 25.* – Parry's; walk with him to sea-side, black rocks, breakers ghostly white, light at sea. Back with him, tea. His childhood, etc. We walk along the dark road to Albion Hotel, Mr. and Mrs. Murrow [*the publican and his wife*] personal acquaintances of C.P. P. tells of his tribulations when his wife was confined. No bed, lay down by a fire and went to sleep, wakened by woman putting on pots and kettles; went into another room and fell asleep by the fire, wakened by some one putting on pots and kettles there; went out, nearly asleep, and lay down in a passage, wakened by Doctor wiping his boots upon him, at which Murrows laugh. Walking back P. explains to me that Murrow (a Welshman) is a 'high Freemason' – 'He doesn't call me "Sir" when we're alone. If you're a Mason your Servant may be a higher Mason than you. Garibaldi head of Italian Masons, which added greatly to his power. L. Napoleon a High Mason, etc'.[30]

On hearing news that his second grandchild, Owen, had been born on 21 December, Gambier Parry sent a gift of £50, bringing the total amount of money which Clinton possessed to little more than £165. At the end of the year he had almost finished his first full-length novel, *John Halifax*, 'a book', he wrote, 'likely to make a difference in my life'; it did not. Mrs Cameron was about to leave England *en route* to Ceylon, but before her departure made two portrait studies of Clinton,[31]capturing, with her extraordinary gift, the 'overpowering weariness' by which he was oppressed. Even Allingham, in spite of an acquaintance of years, was never able to consider his relationship with Tennyson as one of equal terms; his welcome at Farringford never quite assured:

> Allingham from Ireland upsets the wine. 'I spilt some port on the cloth, and T.,' – always T., and not Alfred, even in the seclusion of his diary – 'with his usual imperturbability spread salt on it, remarking as he did so "I believe it never comes out".' Tennyson corrects his mis-pronunciation, the way he pronounces 'dew': 'There's no *Jew* on the grass!' The poor man forwardly remarks that a large tangled fig-tree in the garden at Farringford is like a breaking wave. 'Not in the least,' says he. And Allingham at once continues in his diary 'Such contradictions *from him*, are in no way disagreeable'.[32]

---

[28] Robert Bernard Martin, *Tennyson – The Unquiet Heart* (Oxford, 1980), p 429.

[29] Geoffrey Grigson (ed.), *William Allingham's Diary* (Centaur Press, 1967), p 167.

[30] Grigson, *op cit*, pp 167/8.

[31] One of Julia Margaret Cameron's photographs of Clinton Parry is in the National Portrait Gallery, London; the other is in the Shulbrede archive.

[32] Grigson, *op cit*, p viii.

When Hubert visited Tennyson in 1892, a few months before the poet's death, he found an equally outspoken and combative conversationalist; but the great man was 'quite amiable' when Hubert played his superb setting of *The Lotos-Eaters* to him. It is unlikely that Clinton found much encouragement for *his* writing in the company of Tennyson. At the beginning of March 1868 he wrote to his father, again asking about a loan, and to Hubert, enclosing a snowdrop picked at the Farringford House on Owen's baptismal day, 24 February. His hopes of literary success had failed and the time had come to face harsh reality:

> I feel that in writing English literature… it does not come easily to me. I feel such a difficulty in composition, *les idées ne me manquent pas.* I am not wanting in ideas, but in the *façon* of speaking them; in arranging and expressing them – and how can it be otherwise? Until last year when I went to Lyndhurst, I had never dreamt of writing fiction. I had never studied how it was done by others.
>
> In music my ideas do not come sluggishly. It is true that I had heard but very little music from others. At home we never or scarcely ever heard music; but this I consider rather an advantage, and the fact that I never had but about 15 music lessons in my life, and those not till about 18 years of age, I consider also an advantage.[33]

He had grown to adulthood in the shadow of his father's abundant artistic talents, but had never been encouraged or understood by him, and, like Hubert, was discouraged by him in terms of the most determined opposition from ever considering music as a career. At Lyndhurst he had enjoyed the friendship of writers, Hamilton Aidé, William Allingham and Caroline Dickson, all of whom had urged him to develop his literary talents. Now, for the first time, in the company of Tennyson's genius, the cold waters of reality washed over the shifting sands of his self-delusion. 'I have', he wrote, 'an unfortunate overwhelming sense of inferiority added to my natural indolence'. He would never be able to earn a living by his pen.

*   *   *   *   *   *   *

As 1867 gave way to a new year, life seemed to hold a very different prospect for Hubert. If unable to entertain the idea of a life in music, at least his B Mus degree had opened doors at Oxford. His election to the committee of the Exeter College Musical Society, for which he acted as repetiteur, brought with it opportunities to compose part-songs for the Society's choir and valuable experience with one of the first names in English music, the Society's conductor, John Stainer. Although, like Clinton, Hubert was prone to mood-swings, depression often following spells of elation and *joie de vivre*, his work, unlike that of his elder brother, was unimpeded by slavery to the brandy flask. The sparkle of Hubert's social life was balanced by hard study and solid scholarship; and his musical horizons had been considerably expanded by those all too few weeks in Stuttgart with Pierson. Mendelssohn still dominated his compositional style but was no longer his idol.

---

[33] CP diaries.

At the end of February, in London to be treated for eye trouble, Hubert attended a 'gorgeous' concert at the Crystal Palace: Wagner's *Tannhäuser* Overture; Schubert's Symphony No. 4, the *Tragic*, which he had not heard before but thought 'magnificent'; and Beethoven's Overture to *Egmont*. In the following month, whilst Clinton pondered his future in melancholy, Hubert, still wearing blue spectacles to protect his eyes from the light, attended another Crystal Palace concert. The main work, Schumann's Symphony No. 2, came as a revelation to him:

> [It] surpassed everything *almost* I have heard lately. The Scherzo was wildly glorious. The slow movement was very fine, and contains a most wonderful bit of modulation, in which the chief feature is a very long passage in shakes for the Ist violins, which had the most delicious effect. I'll never go to hear anything of Mendelssohn's in preference to Schumann's C major symphony if I can help it. Madame Schumann played Mendelssohn's Concerto in D magnificently, but it fell very flat after Schumann's Symphony...[34]

Disappointment soon clouded his mood. He had submitted a song, *The Banks of Doon*, and his Morning Service in D to the publishers Lamborn Cock. Their response arrived on the eve of his departure for Highnam. It was, he wrote, an 'unfortunate day':

> Missed the Liddels in the morning: bad news from Lamborn Cock: won't publish my music. Everything drunk or mad. Got home in the evening.[35]

But this was only a temporary setback. There were several other pieces in his manuscript book, including sketches for the opening of a setting of his revered Milton's *At a Solemn Musick*, one of the most sublime short poems in English.

> Blest pair of Sirens, pledges of heav'n's joy,
> Sphere-born harmonious sisters, Voice and Verse...

And that would wait for twenty more years before seeing the light of day!

---

[34] CHHP, *Diary 1868*. Shulbrede archive.
[35] *Ibid.*

IX

An Ever-fixèd Mark

In the metrical artistry of Milton, Hubert Parry discovered a careful attention to the musical value of vowel and consonant which, after Pope and Gray, remained unsurpassed until Tennyson. And at Oxford in the autumn of 1868, the same season in which his brother Clinton had made the close acquaintance of the great poet, he turned to Tennyson's *Idylls of the King* and read, not for the first time, 'Vivien'. Only four of the nine *Idylls* had thus far been published, and these were issued separately in 1867 and 1868. Tennyson's verse spoke directly to Hubert, as to countless others of his generation, in the very accent of his day, and his response was to contemplate the composition of an overture based upon the legend of Vivien, the wily sorceress who charmed a besotted Merlin and, using one of his own spells, imprisoned him. This was exactly the type of melodrama which Pierson would have favoured as a source of inspiration for orchestral treatment; Hubert completed the initial sketch of the work over two October days – and then set it aside for five more years. He too had been charmed, and was now deeply in love.

In the previous summer Hubert had spent ten idyllic days at Wilton; days during which his diary was temporarily abandoned because he was 'afraid to sit down and commemorate a time which was too enjoyable to be described'; days when he was 'intensely happy' in the company of his 'dear and only love', Maude Herbert. Had Thomas Gambier Parry agreed to finance it, Hubert would actually have chosen to spend the whole of that summer holiday with Pierson in Germany once more. Pierson certainly wished his young friend to come, and had written to 'my best Uberto' some weeks earlier to ask if it would be possible:

> Now just send me a line *prestissimo.* there's a dear boy, and tell me what are your plans and wishes. Wilshere (quoting some passages from a letter of your father's, not complimentary to the musical vocation) said he did not know whether you are coming to me or no.[1]

---

[1] Hugo Pierson, letter to Hubert Parry, 16 June 1868. Shulbrede archive.

But Hubert's plans and hopes had been dashed by his father, effectively halting his development as a composer for five years. It was with a heavy heart that he had arrived at Wilton on 24 August, but submerged his disappointment in the company of Maude, no longer an elfin child but now, at age 17, a dark-eyed and precocious young girl, due to 'come out' in the following year. The days were passed in riding and rowing; in 'the most delightful little dinner parties conceivable'; and, one night, in watching a magical fireworks display which lighted up the Palladian bridge with red and blue lights:

> Wilton is quite the same as it used to be when I was there last, only the people are more kind, more affectionate, and more delightful than ever… Maudie and I were like brother and sister, always together. I should never be tired of being with her. Both she and Mary [her sister] are the most wonderfully well read, and informed girls you could find anywhere. Sidney and Reggie [Maude's younger brothers] are a perfect pair of little boys and Lady Herbert is as fascinating and impulsive as ever… Sandie [Lady Alexandrina Murray, sister of the 7th Earl of Dunmore and a cousin of the Herberts] and Maudie and I were photographed to cement the bond of unity between us.[2]

Hubert gave Lady Murray the nickname Una 'because she used to trot along with us out riding on a little white pony, and was the very image of Spenser's character', and Maude, the object of his closest affections, was herself his 'little Faerie Queene'. All was enchantment and delight – at least on the surface – but it was not possible for him to sense the carefully concealed irrationality and corrosive turmoil which seethed beneath the 'fascinating and impulsive' nature of Maude's mother, Lady Elizabeth Herbert.

Widowed for seven years, Lady Herbert, had noticed with alarm the closeness developing between Maude and her young suitor, a closeness further promoted by Gambier Parry's stubborn refusal to allow Hubert to rejoin Pierson for the summer. Lady Herbert, the daughter of General Charles Ashe A'Court Repington, had, as a child, fallen for the good looks and charming personality of Sidney Herbert, 'and had solemnly declared to her family that she would never marry any boy but him. She had her way. On 12th August, 1846, Sidney Herbert and Liz A'Court became man and wife'.[3] She had married into the aristocracy, and having done so had no intention of allowing the family pedigree to be diluted by marriage outside of that exclusive caste. Hubert's origins were no more humble than her own, and as the son of a member of the landed gentry he was welcomed as a guest at Wilton, but that was as far as she was prepared to allow his association with her noble family to go. And there was another difficulty which must have weighed on Lady Herbert's mind. After her husband's death she had embraced Roman Catholicism with all of the single-minded religious fervour reserved for a convert to the faith – and Hubert's father was, she well knew, a miso-papist!

Outwardly smiling, Lady Herbert longed for Hubert's departure, and was relieved when on 3 September he set off back to Highnam in time for the

---

[2] CHHP, *Diary 1868.* Shulbrede archive.
[3] Tresham Lever, *The Herberts of Wilton* (London, 1967), p 212.

Gloucester Three Choirs Festival, in which his *Intermezzo Religioso*, orchestrated during his stay with Pierson, was to be performed. If he had been in low spirits on arriving at Wilton, his return home was marked by a much more profound melancholy. 'Here I am again', he confided to his diary, 'too seedy to work, too depressed to think, and too dull to do anything reasonable'.[4] Clinton and his family had arrived at Highnam two days earlier but left again before the Festival began. With financial assistance from his father, Clinton had purchased a house, 'Springfield', in Shirley near Southampton, but his health had begun to deteriorate seriously. At Highnam, and for several weeks later, he was very unwell, passing a great deal of blood, weak and often in pain. All of this can only have added to Hubert's distress, but the gloom was lifted when the house began to fill with old friends, including Eddie Hamilton and Spencer Lyttelton, down for the Festival.

Thomas Gambier Parry was for many years a member of the Three Choirs Festival Committee at Gloucester, and this position, in addition to his exceptionally close connections with the cathedral clergy and the organist, S.S. Wesley, clearly helped to pave the way for one of Hubert's compositions to be heard at the most prestigious and longest-lived (and still flourishing) of the many festivals which were so much a feature of musical life in Victorian England. The Festival of 1868 began on 8 September with, as usual, an Opening Service in the cathedral. The performances in the nave began at half-past one with selections from Haydn's *Creation*, followed by Hubert's short orchestral *Intermezzo Religioso*, and continued with a selection from S S Wesley's 111th Psalm. Beethoven's Mass in C came next, exposing Wesley's serious shortcomings as a conductor:

> An unfortunate breakdown at the commencement of the *Kyrie*, owing to the uncertainty of the tempo adopted, created an uneasy feeling that more disasters were in store, and by the time Miss Edith Wynne came in with her solo hopeless confusion reigned supreme, so that the movement came to a sudden collapse, and was recommenced.[5]

Hubert's piece was well enough played, but the occasion was hardly an auspicious one for his Festival debut. The critics were lukewarm, and one in particular, whom Wesley claimed had a grudge against the Festival, was positively hostile. But there were compensations during the following days, including the superb singing of Therese Tietjens, John Sims Reeves, and Charles Santley, who 'created quite a sensation in Lord Byron's translation from Anacreon *I wish to tune my quiv'ring lyre*, set to music by Mr Arthur Sullivan, who conducted his own composition'.[6] Sullivan's collaboration with W S Gilbert was still three years in the future, but his *Contrabandista*, to a libretto by Burnand, had been produced in London in 1867. Hubert, who enjoyed it greatly, had been to hear the operetta twice, and was delighted when the composer was introduced to him at Gloucester by Sir Herbert Oakeley. In the previous year Sullivan had visited Vienna with George Grove in a successful search for the missing items of

4 CHHP, *Diary 1868*.
5 Rev Daniel Lysons, John Amott, C Lee Williams and H Godwin Chance, *Origin and Progress of the Meeting of the Three Choirs of Gloucester, Hereford and Worcester* (Gloucester, 1895), p 239.
6 *Ibid*, p 242.

Schubert's incidental music to *Rosamunde*, and the two were together in Gloucester for the Festival. Sullivan introduced Hubert to Grove – thus opening the door to their long association – and Grove congratulated Hubert 'on having been abused by the critics, which he thought was a good sign'.[7]

With the Festival excitement over and his friends gone, Hubert was left feeling 'as dull as lead' once more; but the muted formalities of the Highnam breakfast table lost their stifling tension for him on 17 September with the unexpected arrival of a letter from Maude. His reply was sent off on the very same day:

> My dear little Faerie Queene,
>
> Thank you so very much for your most delightful letter; I can't tell you how delighted I was when it came. I never thought before that little Maudie cared for me enough to write me such a glorious letter. You may be sure I shall always keep it as a great treasure in a very safe place, and I hope some day I may have another like it. I waited some time for the dream of St. Gerontius thinking I had better not write till it came, but I am sorry to say that at last instead of the little book there came the intelligence that it is out of print, and cannot be had for any trouble. I may find it for you some day, and then I shall send it. I am very glad you have got a Keats, though I don't expect you really to like it for some time. You must read the Ode to the Nightingale and those sort of things many times before you get accustomed to the style, and to his peculiarities of expression which sometimes are rather difficult.
>
> …And when are the other photos coming; I have been longing for them day after day, as they are such pleasant remembrance of that delightful time. I do hope still that such a time may yet come again, though chances seem so against it. I don't think "coming out" will much change the little Faerie Queene, and if the spies don't put on too much pressure, the little brother and sister may still gallop on the downs together again.
>
> Do you think I may be allowed to write to you sometimes, to tell you if ever I come across… anything you should read? I should like to very much, and it would serve to remind you of me sometimes…
>
> Ever your most affectionate
> C. Hubert H. Parry.[8]

The brotherly tone, the hopeful literary guidance and the formal subscription cannot disguise the apprehension which Maude's letter had obviously aroused in Hubert's eager mind. Lady Herbert had begun to secure the locks against him. A week later another letter arrived from Maude to tell him of her mother's insistence that their friendship must end. Again, his reply was immediate:

> I was so glad to get your letter this morning, as I have been thinking of you very much, and quite longed for some pretext for writing to you… Don't say that Lady Herbert will never let us be together again; I can't believe she would be so cruel; we must meet at all events sometimes, and in the interim, we can keep our minds together by the medium of letters.[9]

---

[7] CHHP, *Diary 1868*.
[8] CHHP, letter to Lady Maude Herbert, 17 September, 1868. Shulbrede archive.
[9] CHHP, letter to Lady Maude Herbert, [?] September, 1868. Shulbrede archive.

But the news from Wilton could not have been worse. Hubert was forbidden to visit the house or to attempt ever to see Maude. Faced with the apparent hopelessness of his position, he threw himself into composition, turning again to the sketches for a symphony begun during his stay with Pierson (and which was never completed); the String Quartet in C; the Overture *Vivien*; and, turning again to Milton for both inspiration and for consolation, the second of two sets of *Lieder ohne Wörte*, three piano pieces – *Resignation*, *L'Allegro*, and *Il Penseroso*, the dedication of which, 'In Memoriam, Sept. 1868', speaks volumes of his sense of loss:

> Hence loathèd Melancholy
> Of Cerberus and blackest midnight born,
> In Stygian Cave forlorn
> 'Mongst horrid shapes, and shreiks, and sights unholy.

And then a sunbeam pierced the gloom. A letter from Maude's sister arrived on the evening of 9 October.

> "*O diem laetum, notandum mihi candidissimo calculo.*" In the morning I finished my C major Quartet. In the afternoon I finished the second set of *Lieder ohne Wörte*, and in the evening I had such a letter from Mary. Hope first dawned upon me, and an object in life which I never felt before.[10]

Mary Herbert sympathised with their predicament, knew the heaviness of separation which afflicted her sister, and offered to act as a go-between. In further letters she exhorted Hubert not to give up, but to adopt patient diplomacy in his treatment of Lady Herbert, and assured him that Maude's feelings towards him were genuine and unchanged. Saddling up his horse 'Bob', Hubert rode out of Highnam, breathed deeply of the sweet-smelling air, sought out high ground, and gazed down upon the Severn Vale:

> [It] looked like the garden of Eden, seemingly separated from the rest of the world by a belt of distant hills, watered by as fair a river as that which flowed through the ancient garden, and altogether as blessed a place to all appearance as the eye of a man might wish to rest upon.[11]

In his reply to Mary's second letter Hubert abandoned all restraint:

Dear Mary,

I really don't know how to thank you for your two intensely kind letters. I am perfectly wild with happiness after reading the one which made its appearance last night... It is no use concealing what you know already that Maudie is to me more than all the world besides, and that I love Wilton more than home, and for some inconceivable reason everyone connected with it more than brothers and sisters (which sounds a humiliating confession, but it is not really). But with all this I never felt that I had any right to expect a return, much less in the way you spoke of, for though I confess the fulfilment of my

[10] CHHP, *Diary 1868*.
[11] *Ibid.*

affection had often taken the form of a happy but quickly fading dream, it never took the form of a hope till your letter came and then for a moment it was like the long subdued fire bursting into a brilliant flame... My happiness however soon trembled a little when I thought how soon Maudie might find somebody worthier of her, or someone of the young fashionables she will meet in such multitudes when she comes out next year whom she may like better... I promise to act up to your advice if I am allowed to come to Wilton again, and be very careful and be as civil to Maudie as a Town mouse when anybody is watching us. Do let me keep your letter. It is very precious. I will keep it tight locked up where nobody can possibly get at it but myself. It will be such a talisman to me, greater than the power of a very Savonarola... You are the only created being in the whole world who knows my whole heart.[12]

Not surprisingly, Hubert was in unsettled mood when Oxford beckoned him back for the Michaelmas term. 'I don't usually care whether I am at Highnam or Oxford, but this time somehow it was different'.[13] The pace of Oxford life proved to be hardly any different from before, with the 'Mods' exams added to the usual breathtaking round of sports, dinners, dances and music-making; but the meetings of the Adelphi wine-club, of which he was the enthusiastic President, were 'tremendously rowdy', and Hubert allowed himself, unworthily, to lose self-control:

> One dinner at the Randolph being followed by considerable damage to public property, a running fight with the police, an interview with the Senior Proctor, and the payment of £16 in fines... Hubert's departure from Oxford at the end of term was delayed for two days by "conferences" with the Senior Proctor, at which, on his own showing, he behaved with a most unseemly levity, in view of the seriousness of the offence. The Proctor was in two minds – whether to report the matter to the Vice-Chancellor, or fine the culprits. In the end he took the milder course, and Hubert (quite impenitent) turned his detention to convivial account by attending another meeting of the 'Adelphi' and dining at the 'Cross' with Frank Pownall and 'Poppy' Wyld.[14]

When, at last, he was able to get away from Oxford, Hubert made straight for the restorative comfort of Hedingham to spend the first week of the Christmas holiday with Lewis Majendie before joining his family at Highnam. In Shirley, Clinton's illness was steadily becoming worse, and whilst he was struggling to write a novel, *Aglaja*, drinking, taking opium for his pain, and burdened by self-disgust, Florence was in the final stages of a complicated pregnancy. 'Why am I permitted to live who am so bad and selfish', he wrote in his diary; and then, on 23 December:

> Another little unit ! A little son is born to me. His entry into the world was retarded by his catching his umbilical cord round his neck and thigh.[15]

Not a word about Florence's condition, even though the baby, Noel Francis, had narrowly escaped death by asphyxiation.

---

[12] CHHP, letter to Lady Maude Herbert, [?] October, 1868. Shulbrede archive.
[13] CHHP, *Diary 1868*.
[14] Charles Graves, *Hubert Parry* (London, 1926), Vol I, pp 107/8.
[15] CP, *Diary 1868*. Shulbrede archive.

Hubert's problems, meanwhile, were deepening in direct proportion to the increasing intensity of his feelings for Maude. Lady Herbert had detected the unmistakeable signs, and Maude had felt obliged to write to him that there must be no more letters. His response was to write again in even more passionate terms than before:

> I have just come back from our midnight celebration which we always have here at the birth of the New Year, and I cannot resist the temptation to disobey your wish, that I should not write to you any more, and write my first letter in the year to my little Faerie Queene... Wilton and you made 1868 a sacred year in my life... I am as in earnest as ever mortal was; and if I wish you a happy new year, it will not be as the common compliment every man pays to his friend, but rather an earnest prayer such as can only be made by those who know all the intensity of a pure love... You must not be angry with me for writing to you again. I have been obedient so long – so long without a word to you or from you... Goodbye my most dear little Faerie Queene (Do you still put an interminable veto on my writing to you? Must I be silent again for months?).

> Your loving Hubert.[16]

But the Herberts were not always at Wilton. They were frequently to be found in their Chesham Place residence in London, and soon Hubert and Maude had arranged to meet secretly when he was up in town. These meetings, however brief, served to confirm him in his love, and when, on 11 January, he wrote up his diary, his thoughts flowed out in verse which, inevitably, he later set to music:

> Brightest dreams shall be forgotten,
>   Fade from out the heart;
> Love by earthly thoughts engendered
>   Faints when lovers part.
> Dearest hopes may be despaired of,
>   Beauty lose her art:
> They are earthborn and must fade
> In Lethe, with the bliss they made.
>
> Hopes that are in Heaven sealed,
>   These shall perish never;
> Love that springs from souls' divineness
>   Floweth on for ever.
> Purer spirits, knit by loving,
>   Naught on earth shall sever,
> Till together, as they roam,
> They reach their everlasting Home.[17]

At the end of January, Maude, a willing accomplice in their secret stratagem, wrote to Hubert, 'Do you think we shall see each other again on your way back from Oxford? I daresay we shall be in London then';[18] after which,

---

[16] CHHP, letter to Lady Maude Herbert, 1 January 1869. Shulbrede archive.
[17] CHHP, *Diary 1869*. Shulbrede archive.
[18] Lady Maude Herbert, letter to Hubert Parry, 28 January, 1869. Shulbrede archive.

frightened by her boldness and not knowing whether to obey her mother or her heart, tried again to dissuade Hubert from seeing her. No doubt at Lady Herbert's insistence, Maude imposed a limit on their correspondence, proposing an exchange of letters only at Christmas, New Year, Easter, Whit Sunday and on their birthdays. Deeply perplexed, Hubert wondered at the totally different tone of the letter which he had received from Maude for Christmas, in which her love 'seemed as if it would never desert me', and 'the withering birthday letter' which he received on 28 February. He refused to believe that Maude's seeming coldness was a genuine reflection of her own desire. 'I do not agree with you… that we are bound to write to each other as mere friends', he replied,

> You are a very wise little lady, Maudie, but what made you think that you could cure any human being of his misery by telling him to forget the only thing that could give him happiness; and that is indeed what you did; and you did more – you taught me, that you being my only physician, had trained yourself to forget the only remedy that existed, by hardening the kindness of your words; I think you will see that your advice did not admit of much examination. But I am too bitter for wisdom; and *will* not see that my earnestness has any need to be restrained…
>
> I am very glad that you are happy now, even though it be by forgetting, or almost forgetting me. It is very wise and just you should do so. Yet there are words of consolation, – little bits of kindness here and there in your second letter, which seem yet like a little reflection of the happy past; and as if you did not wish to forget me yet… Since I may not think of the hope of a consummation of worldly love, I ask that one prayer may always be each others, that our love, though we may be obliged to be silent from henceforward may not die, and that we may be divided without forgetting each other, because our spirits shall always be together.
>
> Please write to me on Easter day because it will be no use my writing again till I know whether you are angry with me for writing so madly… While we were together I never said one word to you about my love; I thought you far too much above me to be ever nearer than a good angel. But the world with its formalities and fooleries of etiquette drove me to write more than my greatest impudence could ever have said…
>
> Forgive me Maudie, for my violence, and believe me when I tell you that your writing to me does me no earthly harm; but what made me write like this was that change from your Christmas letter to your birthday letter so verified the change of your way of signing yourself that my only hope was to write you one last earnest letter; the last I mean in which I will speak my entire heart, and will hereafter learn resignation, or at least obey your command to fight against my sadness of heart; on condition that you keep your promise to write to me as you suggest, on Easter, Xmas, New Year's day, our birthdays, *and* Whit Sunday…
>
> I am afraid that you must be wearied as well as angry with this long letter. The peculiarity of the emergency called it out of my thoughts. I cannot write any commonplace now; but when I answer your promised Easter letter, it shall be all correct, proper and matter of fact, unless you permit me one word of what I feel.
>
> Goodbye dear Maudie. I will never write again like this. It seemed so much like the last word of earnestness I might write, that I could not help speaking out. Do forgive me,
>
> > your ever loving,
> >
> > Hubert.[19]

The last vestiges of Maude's resistance were broken down, and it was she who now proposed that they could at least try to resume their occasional

---

[19] CHHP, letter to Lady Maude Herbert, undated 1869. Shulbrede archive.

meetings in London. Opportunities were few and circumstances far from ideal: fleeting moments outside Westminster Abbey and St. Paul's, Knightsbridge, as Maude and her sister were filing in with the worshippers, fearful lest they be seen by spies. Bolder still, the three of them took short walks in Constitution Hill, which, for Hubert, became 'an enchanted place – It was sad to part with them; it may be so long before we meet again, while these miserable formalities of the world separate us so hopelessly'.[20]

After a few days at Highnam, Hubert returned to London on 7 April for a choral concert conducted by Stainer in Willis's Rooms which included two of his own compositions, a part-song, and an Anacreontic Ode in which his friend Frank Pownall was the soloist. Mary Herbert, as kindly and caring as ever, introduced him to her close friend Mary Gladstone (Mrs. Drew) at the concert, and Hubert was invited to visit the Gladstones on the following morning. The Liberal Party, under the leadership of William Ewart Gladstone, in the first of his four administrations as Prime Minister, had swept to power in the previous year, commanding the first clear-cut majority in the House of Commons since 1841. Hubert's visit, at which he met Mrs Gladstone and Miss Agnes Gladstone, was the first of many. It was, he wrote, 'such a morning as I shall never forget'. He played to the admiring ladies; and Mary Gladstone, herself an enthusiastic amateur pianist, quickly became an ally and confidant, sharing the secret of his feelings for Maude, encouraging him not to give up hope, and being 'more unutterably kind to me than any one was ever before in my life'.[21] She and Eddie Hamilton, both privy to Lady Herbert's thoughts, were well-placed to report back to Hubert on her determination to thwart any idea of his becoming engaged to Maude – and determined she most certainly was!

During the summer holiday Hubert and Maude snatched whatever opportunity they could to see each other, including visits to the opera in company with Mary Herbert; and best of all, Maude's brother, George, Lord Pembroke, invited Hubert to spend three days yachting with his family on the schooner *Gem*. Since Lady Herbert was to be of the company, Hubert wisely decided to take Eddie Hamilton down to Cowes with him, and to his considerable relief the break proved to be not only 'too delightful to be particularised', but even Lady Herbert 'was more at ease on a certain subject'.[22]

These all too few treasured days were followed by many less romantic weeks far away from Maude. Thomas Gambier Parry had arranged for Hubert to spend July and August in Belgium in the Liège home of an old friend, Monsieur Pradez, a Protestant pastor, with a view to improving his French in preparation for a business career; and, in spite of many irritating distractions, including the piano practice and vocal scales of near neighbours, Hubert worked diligently under the stern eye of his tutor. Writing to Maude for her birthday on 30 July, he complains that:

[20] CHHP, *Diary 1869*.
[21] *Ibid.*
[22] *Ibid.*

I am dragging on a very weary existence, which I make endurable by working and reading all day long. My chief sufferings arise from the daughters of the old Pasteur, who weary my life out. One of them "rubs me up the wrong way" so much that I can hardly endure being in the room with her. She intends to be very kind, so I do my best to like her, but my endeavours are not very successful.[23]

But perhaps his reproaches were aimed more at reassuring Maude of his fidelity than in any genuine feeling against Mlle. Pradez. After all, it was she who introduced him to the poetry of Hugo, Chénier and de Musset, for which he must have been grateful, even if unable to warm to verse constrained by the straight-jacket of the French metrical system. And perhaps he was able to identify with the de Musset of *Espoir en Dieu*, which he greatly admired; it was, he wrote, 'a wonderful sort of moan of a man troubled with waverings of faith and yet wishing to believe'.[24]

Spiritual soul-searching was, of course, not the only concern on Hubert's mind. Apart from the emotional stress engendered by the obstacles thrown across the path of his personal happiness, and the parental pressures driving him towards an unchosen career, his conscience was disturbed by an increasing awareness of social injustice and the plight of the working poor. Earlier in the year, at, of all things, the London Orphanage Dinner, he had felt genuine disgust at finding himself surrounded by wealthy do-gooders 'guzzling violently'. In the previous October, at the annual Mop Fair in Gloucester, he had been saddened by the sight of labouring men queuing to be taken on as farm servants – and by despair in the faces of those turned away. At Highnam, privilege was taken for granted; at Wilton it was treated as a God-given right. In Liège, amongst much else, he read Victor Hugo's *Les Miserables* and found it totally absorbing, 'an immense poem on the philosophy of suffering'.[25] Later in the same year he tackled John Stuart Mill's *On Liberty*, and also his *Principles of Political Economy*, first published in 1848, to which, in the 1865 edition, Mill had added a section on 'The Probable Future of the Labouring Classes', advocating the self-dependence of workers and their right to relate to their employers on the basis of equality. Hardly the stuff of casual conversation at Thomas Gambier Parry's table. But Hubert was beginning to pull away from the political and spiritual orthodoxies of his father; and when his reading came to encompass John Locke he undoubtedly found an ideal in one whose views, influenced equally by religious toleration, a belief in parliamentary democracy and *laissez-faire* economics, braced his confidence to think entirely for himself.

Inevitably, if his livelihood was not to be made by music, Hubert was obliged to consider the alternatives open to him, and they were few for a young man of his background. Given his increasing sense of religious uncertainty, the idea of a life in the Church, which, he told Maude, had clung to him for years, seemed ever less of an option:

---

[23] *Ibid.*
[24] CHHP, *Diary 1869.*
[25] *Ibid.*

It begins to take the dimensions of impossibility nowadays, and I am very glad you guessed right as I know all your feelings on the subject. As to the Army, I know that would suit me even worse. The species 'army man' is utterly distasteful to me. The idiotic contempt for intellectual pursuits which generally characterises the younger officers and their selfish sporting tendencies always disgust me.[26]

The weeks in Liège provided little opportunity for music, but Hubert made the acquaintance of at least one musical friend, a German pianist by the name of Kayser, who invited him to attend one of his concerts in the nearby factory-filled town of Seraing, a Belgian 'Coketown' founded by an Englishman, John Cockerill. Passing through Seraing at night, Hubert could only wonder at 'the fierce blaze of infernal-looking fires... The regular strokes of the immense iron hammer sounded like the beating of the Fire demon, and the hissing of the huge steam engines like his breath... The turmoil has no end; the fires are not quenched. The power of man... has an immensity which belongs not to the earth, and a restlessness that belongs not to heaven... It looks and sounds, at such an hour of the night, like a vision of the fearful magnificence of Inferno'.[27]

Kayser shared Hubert's love for the music of Schumann, and it was probably at his prompting that Hubert was emboldened to attempt the composition of a piano concerto in G, and by 21 August he had completed copying the first movement. The work was never completed, and all that remains are eight pages of full score and the incomplete remainder of the movement as a sketched short score, showing Hubert to have been still firmly tethered to his Mendelssohnian moorings.[28]

Returning home from Liège, Hubert travelled first to Hedingham; then to Bayfordbury, and to see his elderly and much loved maternal grandmother, Mrs. Clinton, at Park Gate. Back at Highnam Court the house was filled with relations, including Clinton, whose visibly deteriorating condition was as alarming as ever; but a blessed 'summons' from Maude to him and Eddie Hamilton to join her family at Cowes once again filled Hubert with joy. For one blissful week he was 'gloriously happy', in company with Maude, her elder brother and sister, in gentle strolls on the Isle of Wight, and in cruises on the *Gem*; but on returning to Oxford he soon became alarmed at the tension evident in Maude's few letters. Her brother, George Pembroke, concerned at the growing number of their friends who knew about Maude and Hubert's secret assignations, believed that betrayal was a very real danger.

An invitation from Mary Gladstone for Hubert to spend a few days at Hawarden, where Lady Herbert and her daughters Mary and Maude were to be amongst the many guests, gave him a kindly-meant opportunity to be close to his sweetheart – but a passionate glance might also have set tongues wagging. Some weeks later, Lady Herbert announced her intention of spending part of the winter abroad, giving Hubert and Maude precious chances to see each other in London rather more often. Then came the crash.

[26] CHHP, letter to Lady Maude Herbert, 27 July 1869. Shulbrede archive.
[27] CHHP, *Diary 1869*.
[28] See Jeremy Dibble, *C. Hubert H. Parry – His Life and Music* (Oxford, 1992), pp 70/2.

Knowing that their secret could not be kept for long, they decided to get engaged in the spring of 1870 but to make no public announcement for as long as possible. George Pembroke was infuriated by this and insisted that Maude tell her mother of her plans, and threatened to take sides against her and Hubert if she refused. 'We must make up our minds for a row, but I hope we have both courage enough to see it out', Maude wrote to Hubert, 'Opposition can make no *earthly* difference to me... It will all come right some day, though the clouds are very heavy just at present... '[29] Hubert, on the eve of his Oxford finals, received news that their secret was out: '[A] great evil came upon me... correspondence and loving converse were stopped, and for a short time all was black. But the people concerned were still kind, and my sorrow was soon dispelled by the assurance of a faithful heart yet left to me in all the changings of fortune'.[30] A few days after obtaining a Second Class degree Hubert received a letter from Lady Herbert; it could not have been more dreadful:

38, Chesham Place S.W.

My dear Hubert,

I am very much grieved to have to write to you on the subject of Maude. But you have left me no alternative but to write or speak – and I prefer the former.

I am sure you will do me the justice to say that I have never for one single moment led you to suppose that I could sanction an engagement between you which would result in utter ruin and misery to both. From the very first moment when gossip coupled your names together and I saw there was a danger that your boy and girl friendship would ripen into Love I spoke to Eddie and forbid [*sic*] your meeting. When you were invited to Cowes it was done by Pembroke without my knowledge. And when I remonstrated with him, he positively assured me that there was nothing between you but brother and sister feelings such as the girls have for Eddie, and he added that the way to create the sentiments I dreaded was to separate you entirely. I foolishly yielded and did not take Maude away when you arrived, which now I feel I ought to have done. When you met at Hawarden, I was extremely annoyed and told Mrs. Gladstone that had I known you were to be there, I should not have brought Maude at all. She was vexed and said she 'quite saw it all – but it had been managed by the "two Marys" and she knew nothing of it'.

I go over all this to show you that I have never varied in my opposition to your wishes. And now for a practical businesslike view of the case. Owing to Lord Herbert's having given his name to the Duke of Newcastle for a newspaper speculation some years ago, which failed, I became liable after his death to the whole debt and had to pay £130,000. That took away the whole of my younger children's fortunes as well as my own, so that Maude will have next to nothing. Pembroke himself will never have more than £40,000 a year from the heavy charges on his estate. Supposing that he gives his sister £20,000 which is more than he could well afford in justice to the others, that would give her £600 a year. How is it possible that she could live on that? Your father says that first and last you can never have more than £10,000 and after his death. That would give you £300 a year. So that your joint income would be £900 a year. Now I ask you plainly if you think it *possible* for Maude to live on that, educated as she has been and brought up in every luxury and comfort? Can you love her and wish to expose her to such utter misery? And should children come, would you like to see yourself unable to bring them up as gentlemen or send them to school or college? I put it to you so plainly because you seem to have got a most marvellous misconception of

---

[29] Lady Maude Herbert, letter to Hubert Parry, 25 May 1870. Shulbrede archive.
[30] CHHP, *Diary 1870*. Shulbrede archive.

the state of things. Pembroke himself wrote to me to say 'he had never undertaken to provide you with the means of marrying'. But what he, in his boyish ignorance, does *not* know, is that *he has not the means of doing so*, even if he would!! I cannot understand any honourable man either, liking to be dependent on the charity of a Brother-in-law, and the chance kindness of any future wife he may have. My Brother-in-law, Lord Clanwilliam, wrote to me on this wretched business a fortnight ago and said "Before many months have rolled over his head, I will answer for it that Pembroke will see the utter madness of such a proposal as strongly as we do. The thing is so thoroughly inadmissable that I hope you will make your 'no' so emphatic that there shall be no loophole for future hope. Turn it which way you will, there is nothing but misery in store for poor Maude in such an alliance to which no parent or guardian of hers could *ever* give consent.

I confess I am lost in astonishment when I think how you could have the courage to entangle Maude into an engagement when you have no home to offer her nor any prospect of one. I cannot but feel that you took advantage of George's inexperience and of my widowhood; for if her father lived you would never have ventured to take so cruel a course. I say *cruel* deliberately, for you have brought terrible suffering on Maude and on me. It breaks my heart to be the cause of making her so unhappy; but I feel I must be firm now to save her from an amount of future misery which I really cannot contemplate.

I must also say that I think your corresponding with her as you have done without my knowledge and knowing what my feelings were on the subject, is utterly unjustifiable. I am very sorry to speak so harshly; but when I see how my darling Maude's life is wrecked for the time, you cannot expect me to be patient with the cause of all this misery. What I want you to understand clearly is, that the thing must be altogether at an end; that I can allow *no* correspondence between you, and that you must release Maude from any engagement implied or otherwise. She told me herself that she 'considered herself so completely bound to you that she could no more receive the attentions of others than if she were married.' – Now, as an honourable man, I must charge you to release her from this tacit engagement. *It can never be.*

So that to ruin all prospects of her being well settled and having a happy home by a folly of this sort is sheer madness on your part. You cannot wish to drag her down to misery and ruin if you care for her, and yet you have selfishly engaged her affections to such an extent as altogether to compromise her future! She will not give you up. Therefore I can only hope you will have sufficient right feeling to give her up yourself and tell her that you have done so. I know it will cost you both a great deal. But if you will once believe that the thing is *utterly hopeless*, you will, I am sure, be generous enough to help her to give it up. – Dear Hubert. If I have written severely it is not that I do not care for you, but that for both your sakes, I feel and see the utter madness of such a marriage to an extent of which you can have no idea. After all, Maude and you would never get on if you had even the means of living. She hates music except for your sake, and you have a passion for it, and she is thoroughly unbusinesslike and would make the worst poor man's wife in the world! Then, as Clanwilliam says, 'not one woman in 10 marries her first love, and certainly not one man in a thousand!'

So, for the love of God and of Maude, dearest Hubert, be generous and honourable in this matter and try for once to see it and judge it fairly. I will not say all the pain this letter has cost me to write. But I love Maude dearer than my life and I feel that she will thank me hereafter for having been what she and you may think hard and cruel now.

yours affectionately,

M.E. Herbert[31]

---

[31] Lady M. Elizabeth Herbert, letter to Hubert Parry, 20 June 1870. Shulbrede archive.

Wounded as he must have been by Lady Herbert's rapier thrusts, the most hurtful and subtly perceptive of which might well have been the insinuation that Maude and music were incompatible, Hubert remained resolute, refused to abandon the young woman he loved, and determined to come to terms with relinquishing any idea of music as a profession. Assuring his future mother-in-law that he was about to take up a fitting occupation to enable him to keep Maude in an appropriate manner, Hubert readily fell in with a suggestion made by both Lewis Majendie and Thomas Gambier Parry: that he should enter a career in insurance at Lloyd's Register of Shipping. Gambier Parry put up the necessary £5,000 guarantee, and Hubert went over to Hedingham, where his cousin had arranged for him to meet a prospective business partner, Ranald McDonnell. Several days were spent relaxing with Majendie, attending the reopening of the chancel of the church at Hedingham, restored by Henry Woodyer, visiting the churches at Lavenham, Thaxted, Samford and Barfield, and Gainsborough's birthplace at Sudbury. In the middle of October McDonnell visited Hubert at Highnam to discuss final arrangements for the partnership. The two young men got on well enough, but neither could be sure of the ability of the other – and Hubert, totally lacking in business experience, was decidedly apprehensive about taking up his responsibilities at Lloyd's in the middle of November.

Clinton, too, had abandoned any thought of a career in the arts and embarked, literally, on a new venture. The arrival of a third child seems to have stiffened his resolve, and in the early weeks of 1870 he and Florence had made plans for a completely new beginning far away from England. Lists of essentials were made, trunks packed and, soon after Florence's birthday on 7 May, they were ready to leave. Equipped with a manual of farming and estate management, Clinton and his family set sail for South Africa, their sea passages and their new home at Norwood Farm, close to Pietermaritzburg, the inland capital of the British colony of Natal, paid for by Thomas Gambier Parry. Before leaving, Clinton entered a few last words in his diary: 'Strong and stout. Body and mind, and resolute for action'.[32]

---

[32] CP, *Diary 1870*. Shulbrede archive.

X

Not a Spark of the Amateur

In the autumn of 1870 Hubert Parry, in sombre and reflective mood, faced without enthusiasm the prospect of forsaking Highnam for London. It was a mood deepened by ghastly reports of the Franco-Prussian war. Napoleon III had been swept from power, and a republic proclaimed in Paris:

> There, near at hand, are thousands upon thousands suffering and dying in the terrible war between France and Germany. Napoleon taken; Toul making a noble resistance; Strasbourg and its noble cathedral suffering the horror of bombardment; Paris invested and France suffering once again the horrors of spoilation; death and living miseries. What are we, in the midst of these painstricken, sorrowing millions, that we should consider our own trivial discomforts? Yet so it is, and yet again all is vanity and vexation of spirit, and now the end of the home life of peace is come. This is my last night at home with Possie. I cannot but be sad. London is to receive me that I may try the hateful occupation of money-making.[1]

Before leaving home for any length of time, Hubert unfailingly visited his favourite and well-loved places in and around Highnam, settings for his silent thoughts since childhood. But this time there was a deeper sense of parting; an infinitely greater reluctance to tear himself away. 'Bob' was saddled up for the long ride to May Hill, viewpoint for the whole of Gloucestershire and the surrounding counties, returning by Bulley and Rodway Hill through quiet woods, and on to pay a farewell visit to the *pinetum*, every tree of which was precious to him. And surely the trees represented to Hubert more than a beautiful manifestation of nature in a cherished place? They were no less than a living link with the mother he had never known; she whose absence had planted an aching void deeply within him which no other human relationship would ever be able to fill.

In the shadow of Highnam Church were the graves of dear old Uncle Henry Parry, who had died full of years in 1860, and of Hubert's beloved sister Lucy, taken from him in the following year when she was nineteen and he only twelve. Lucy it was who had tried so hard to fill her mother's shoes; who, in her

---

[1] CHHP, *Diary 1870*. Shulbrede archive.

letters to him at Eton[2], had affectionately exhorted him to do his best and, touchingly, to improve his posture; and who, as Hubert told Maude, was 'my only sister – the only person in the world whose loss I still regret.'[3] Then there was the church itself, its organ and its splendid bells:

> ...for Hubert had a personal affection for bells as well as trees. He played a last concluding voluntary at the evening service, and ended his last home Sunday sitting 'in my dear little study, with Uncle Henry's old clock ticking away comfortably and composedly, my music paper and books lying all over the place and my long pipe breathing out comfort'.[4]

A short visit to Bayfordbury, and then, on 22 November, it was time to take up his London lodgings at 5 Chapel Street, off Grosvenor Place. Everybody, it seemed, was pleased. Thomas Gambier Parry, increasingly concerned about his dwindling fortune, was comforted by the thought of a financially independent son. Lady Herbert dreamt of a son-in-law able to keep Maude in an acceptable level of comfort. Maude's brother, George Pembroke, saw a clear way out of social embarrassment: 'If you can only earn enough to support a wife', he wrote to Hubert, 'no-one can or will stand in your way.'[5] Hubert, on the other hand, was unable to find anything encouraging to communicate to his diary about the fascination or profitability of insurance. Composition came to a virtual halt; and even the diary itself was often neglected between 1870 and the middle of 1873. By far his greatest joy was the wealth of music to be heard at the Crystal Palace, the 'Pops', and the opera; and his circle of friends steadily grew to include many of the most eminent names in musical society.

A near neighbour, Walter Broadwood, a partner in the family firm of piano builders and an old friend of Thomas Gambier Parry, invited Hubert to musical soirées at his Queen's Gate Gardens home, where regular guests included the great violinist Joseph Joachim, the equally celebrated baritone, Julius Stockhausen, and Clara Schumann and her daughters, who, Hubert wrote, 'I revere hugely as the wife and children of one of the highest of my ideal composers.'[6] Hubert first met Clara Schumann at a reception given by Lady Goldschmidt (the soprano Jenny Lind), and it was from her, Joachim and Stockhausen that he learned about a composer who was destined to become one of his heroes, Johannes Brahms. The music of Brahms was barely known in musically-conservative England, but another of Broadwood's regular guests, the Dutch pianist William Coenen, determined to swim against the popular stream by presenting a series of three 'Chamber Concerts of Modern Music' at the Hanover Square Rooms in the 1871 London season. It was at one of these that Hubert heard 'a [Brahms] Quintet, frightfully difficult and some of it rather crude at a first hearing. But wonderfully vigorous and bold in treatment.'[7]

---

[2] Letters from Lucy Parry to CHHP, Shulbrede archive.
[3] CHHP, letter to Lady Maude Herbert, 12 June 1870. Shulbrede archive.
[4] Graves, *op cit*, p 125.
[5] Letter from George Pembroke to CHHP, 6 December, 1870, Shulbrede archive.
[6] CHHP, *Diary 1871*. Shulbrede archive.
[7] *Ibid.*

Another friend, made whilst visiting Broadwood, the pianist Lubeck, was dismissive of Brahms, the most classically inspired of all romantic composers. Brahms belonged to a school, Lubeck said, which had 'developed and worked out the crudities and irregularities or "crackedness" of their high priest Schumann, but had omitted to take due notice of his beauties'[8] – and this was three years after the first performance of *Ein Deutches Requiem*! But Hubert took eight extremely valuable piano lessons from Lubeck and was greatly saddened when his tutor returned to Germany, as 'a few more lessons might have enabled me to attain a certain degree of excellence, which I altogether despair of without help.'[9]

At the beginning of 1871 Hubert had spent a few idyllic days at Wilton, silent and beautiful under a thick blanket of snow, a highlight of which was 'a gorgeous drive in the Woronzoff[10]sledge, with bells and all, Maude and I tucked in under a pile of rugs in front, with Sidney behind. I drove and both ponies were very fresh, much excited by the jangling of the bells, and went like the wind'.[11] Hubert's happiness, blissful beyond description, was reinforced by the thaw in Lady Herbert's attitude towards him. He was now positively encouraged to visit her London home in Chesham Place and, although she failed to tell Hubert first, Lady Herbert at last felt confident enough of Maude's future happiness to reveal to family friends news of her engagement. On 20 June 1871 Hubert was invited to a ball at the home of Lady Crawford, who, much to his amazement, congratulated him as he was saying 'How d'ye do'. 'It was to be no more a secret', he wrote, 'Oh! the fever of happiness when the cloud was cleared away'.[12]

Thomas Gambier Parry and Ethelinda were in London for two months, and Hubert, who stayed with them for this time, was much relieved when, after a brief meeting, his father and Lady Herbert discovered that they quite liked each other. In July a proud Hubert took Maude down to Highnam for the first time, and with her by his side drove out to explore the Forest of Dean, Chepstow and Tintern. It is unlikely that either was aware of the ancient links between their families, or of the significance of Tintern to the House of Pembroke, but the liaison between Hubert and Maude was about to restore a four-hundred-year-old bond.

Two of Hubert's ancestors, the sons of Griffith ap Harry of Newcourt in Herefordshire's Golden Vale, Henry and Thomas, served the well-intentioned but inadequate King Henry VI in the dynastic blood-letting labelled by Sir Walter Scott the 'Wars of the Roses'. In 1461 the two brothers had joined a Welsh army led by Jasper Tudor which, having linked with an invasion force commanded by the Earl of Wiltshire, marched towards the English border to face the Yorkists. They met at Mortimer's Cross, close to Leominster, where the Welsh were routed by Edward, the Earl of March, and Henry ap Griffith Parry lost his life.

---

[8] *Ibid.*
[9] *Ibid.*
[10] Lady Maude Herbert's grandmother, the second wife of George Augustus Herbert, 11th Earl of Pembroke and 8th Earl of Montgomery, was Catherine, daughter of Simon Romanovitch, 3rd Count Woronzoff.
[11] CHHP, *Diary 1871.*
[12] *Ibid.*

Amongst the great nobles ranged on each side in the Wars of the Roses, none enjoyed more power than William Herbert, Earl of Pembroke (of the first creation), Edward IV's chief counsellor from 1461 and virtually viceroy of Wales. It is a measure of the social position of the Parrys in the fifteenth century that Milo Parry of Newcourt, eldest son of Henry ap Griffith, married Jane, daughter of the extremely influential Sir Harry Stradling of St. Donat's, Glamorganshire, whose wife was the Earl of Pembroke's sister, Elizabeth – an alliance which seems to have prompted a shift in the Parry family allegiance away from the Lancastrian side.

Milo Parry prospered, counting amongst his close relations not only the Earl of Pembroke but also the Earl of Northumberland, Lord Greystock, Lord Lisle, the Earl of Powys, and the Earl of Kent. But these were savage times for men of power, and Pembroke's shining hour was all too short. Even though his loyalty to Edward IV had never been in question, he was doomed by his failure to gain victory for the royal forces at the Battle of Edgecote in 1469. Pembroke and his half-brother, Roger Vaughan, were both sons of Gwladys, the daughter of David Gam [*the hero of Agincourt whose death is reported to Henry V in Act 4, Scene 8 of Shakespeare's play*]. At Mortimer's Cross they had played a major role in defeating the Lancastrian forces; but at Edgecote the Yorkists were outnumbered and overwhelmed.

Pembroke and his brother, Sir Richard Herbert, fought desperately but were decisively beaten. When both were captured, Pembroke declared his willingness to die but pleaded for the life of his young brother. On 27 July he made his will, appointing Thomas Parry of Wormbridge, a nephew of Milo Parry, as his executor, giving directions for his funeral, making bequests to Tintern Abbey and other religious foundations, and providing almshouses for the relief of six poor men. The next day Pembroke and Sir Richard were taken to Northampton and beheaded. Pembroke was buried in Tintern Abbey, and Sir Richard in Abergavenny Church.

Perhaps Thomas Parry of Wormbridge had been with Pembroke at Edgecote, and it is may not be too fanciful to suppose that Thomas Parry's selection of the name William for his eldest son was a mark of his admiration for the great earl. But, in addition to his relationship to the Herberts through Milo Parry's mother-in-law, Thomas's sister had married a Vaughan. The Parrys, could, like the Herberts and Vaughans, claim an ancestor in David Gam, and several more marriages between Parrys and Vaughans in succeeding generations cemented the kinship of the families.

Thomas's son, William Parry of Wormbridge, a Commissioner of Augmentations in 1539, had four children, the eldest of which, Henry, was appointed a residentiary canon of Salisbury Cathedral in 1547, deprived under Mary in 1553, but restored on the accession of Queen Elizabeth and held the appointment of Chancellor from 1559; an appointment which perhaps owed more than a little to the influence of the powerful Herberts at nearby Wilton. Henry left three children by his wife Pascha: Jane, Vashter, and one son, also

Henry, who was born in Wiltshire about 20 December 1561. It was this younger Henry who, thirty years later, came to the notice of Elizabeth and became her chaplain, rising to become Bishop of Worcester under James I, who considered him one of the best preachers he ever heard.

Might Lady Herbert's attitude towards Hubert have been different from the outset had she known something of their shared ancestry? Probably not. As it was, she continued to blow hot and cold, even suggesting that Maude should spend four months in the Mediterranean with her before the wedding – an offer which Maude stoutly refused. Instead, Maude was required to spend the rest of July with her family at their Booterstown estate close to Dublin, while Hubert and his business partner McDonnell set off for a short continental holiday, visiting Le Havre, Caen, Lisieux and Rouen. August brought reunion and bliss at Wilton, and on Christmas Eve Lady Herbert, at last fully converted to his cause, wrote to Hubert at Highnam:

> God bless you, dear old boy and give you many, many happy Xmases. This is the last, please God, you will spend without her.
>
> You will have a good deal to do to fill up all the love she has had in her home, but I trust you to make her happy and not to let all the deep love evaporate (as I see in so many married people) after the first Xmas or two…
>
> My heart is full to the brim when I think this is the last Xmas she will be with us, so you must forgive all the fears which crop up in my mother's heart.
>
> God bless and keep you ever in His Holy Love.
>
> yours ever affectionately'
>
> M.E. Herbert. [13]

All seemed to be set fair – and yet a small doubt remained. A disturbing and, to Hubert, inexplicable remoteness began to chill the letters which he received from Maude. The forces which for so long had combined to tug them apart served only to strengthen the ties between Hubert and Maude. Now, with all restraint removed, free to fly to each other, Maude began, however slightly, to draw back. Unable or unwilling to accept that there was in this any presentiment of future trials, Hubert, filled with melancholy, sat in his room at Highnam on Christmas Day 1871 and wrote a letter, half admonishing and half pleading, to the girl whose image dominated his every thought:

> Though you are the biggest darling in the world my precious Maudie, I declare you are very funny. Your letters are so matter of fact that they very often act as a positive damper to the intensity of my affection… I looked forward with fierce eagerness for your letter, and when I got it there was such an amount of philosophical indifference displayed in it that I think the ordinary looker on would have thought… that the engagement was only a sort of mutual agreement which we had entered upon for some fancied convenience which the general public was incapable of appreciating. The signature being a matter of courtesy, and all that approached to affection in the letter being the sort of commonplace that a pair of French fiancées made for the sake of mutual social advantage, might enter upon. It makes me quite ashamed of the impulse I have to pour out the burning love I feel, which is so chilled by matter-of-factness. When I think of the difference between your Xmas letter and mine I can only wonder;

[13] Lady M Elizabeth Herbert, letter to CHHP, 24 Dec 1871. Shulbrede archive.

but I must confess to you Maudie that I should be utterly miserable if I felt it necessary to write to you as you do to me…

This is not a happy Xmas day. My love for my own family is only half real and full, for there is a vacant place of yearning love between me and them. Yesterday was positively hateful. Oh Maudie if there is anything disagreeable in this letter it is only the bitterness which pervades my mind for your absence. I couldn't love you so intensely if you were anything but what you are… Don't be shy, *please*.[14]

The gulf between the two was, as Lady Herbert had hinted, an intellectual one. Maude protested that she was unable adequately to express herself in writing, but surely she had already sensed that it would be impossible for her ever to compete on equal terms for Hubert's affections with her greatest rival, music; a rival from which Hubert was inseparable but for which Maude's own lack of appreciation or understanding could never be disguised. Nonetheless, Hubert convinced himself that Maude's reticence was no more than maidenly reserve, that her passion was the equal of his own, and that 'Hearts in equal love combined kindle never-dying fires'. On Tuesday 25 June 1872 Hubert and Maude were married at St Paul's Church, Knightsbridge. It was, wrote Hubert:

the supreme event of my life. I remember I was not a bit nervous at the marriage, only absorbed in utter happiness. It was rather like a dream. It was a showery morning, but cleared up sufficiently for Maud [*sic*] and me to have a ride over the windy downs when we got back to Wilton, where we spent our honeymoon. Such a place to honeymoon in in Summer! Next door to impossible to do anything else. I had all sorts of plans beforehand of what I would I would do with such a lot of time at my disposal, and it ended in absolutely nothing but being happy and leaving the rest alone. From Wilton we went to Highnam, where they got up a little greeting for us – triumphal arches and decorations, waving hats and cheering. We had a very happy time there, and then went to London to Chesham place for a little and finally to Bengeo where I began going up to the City as usual.[15]

'St Holme' at Bengeo in Hertfordshire, the Parrys' home until July 1873, was a short drive from William Baker's house at Bayfordbury, and was rented from one of Hubert's Gambier cousins.

The garden was a small paradise of roses, and the strawberry beds were marvellously productive; Hubert picked and ate strawberries to his heart's content. But the chief charm of the place was in the adjoining woods, which he and his wife scoured in 'glorious botanical walks', hunting for orchids and other wild flowers, roaming amid forests of foxgloves. Hubert Parry was more than a mere 'hedge-naturalist' and his careful observations on the peculiarities of the growth of yellow flowering nettles were only the first of a series of experiments which led him on to the use of the microscope, and his subsequent studies in mycology and algology. He joined in hunting snails with his gardener, not without feelings of compunction at their wholesale destruction, and the strange and inconsistent evidences of the maternal instincts in animals, as manifested by their own cats, did not escape an eye which never regarded facts in isolation but always in relation to other facts. Strenuous pastimes gave place at Bengeo to the milder recreation afforded by bowls and quoits, but at Bayfordbury, whither he

---

[14] CHHP, letter to Lady Maude Herbert, 25 December, 1871. Shulbrede archive.
[15] CHHP, *Diary 1873*. Shulbrede archive.

frequently drove over in his pony trap, he took a characteristic pleasure in sailing model boats on the pond and exploding squibs under water, torpedo-wise.[16]

Six thousand miles away in Natal the contrast to this 'sweet especial rural scene' could not have been greater.

*   *   *   *   *   *   *

Clinton Parry had no more idea about the existence of his cousins in South Africa, the descendants of his paternal grandfather's brother, William Parry, than had Hubert about his ancient connections with the Herberts. Eight years after William's daughter, Lucy Maria, had been taken to Cape Town by John de Wit in 1812, British conquest of the colony was consolidated by a large influx of settlers from England. Natal, a second focus of British political authority in Southern Africa, was formally annexed in 1843, and in the years 1849-51 five thousand men, women and children were drawn there by a scheme which offered transport to Natal and possession of twenty acres of land per head in return for a modest deposit. Many failed to make the grade as farmers, and returned home to England with empty pockets. Even so, by 1870, the year in which Clinton and his family arrived, there were eighteen thousand Whites in the colony. But this was still a small number in comparison to the African population, which was estimated to be fifteen times as many:

> …the Natal colonial government tried to place the Africans in reserves (which it called *locations*), leaving the rest of the colony available for white settlement. By 1864, there were forty-two locations, with an area of 2 million acres, and twenty-one mission reserves, with 175,000 acres, out of a total colonial area of 12.5 million acres. In terms of colonial law, the rest of the colony was either owned by Whites or held by the government as unassigned Crown lands. At least half of the African population, however, lived not in the reserves at all but on Crown lands or on land owned by Whites, to whom they paid rent. Until the 1870s the white landowners were making more money from 'Kaffir farming' than from their efforts to produce agricultural or pastoral products for the market.[17]

Clinton Parry, like every other white settler, depended upon African labour; but unlike most of his European neighbours in the Pietermaritzburg area, he soon proved to be incapable of managing a farm. The long voyage and change of lifestyle had done nothing to cure his thirst. In January 1872, Florence gave birth to a fourth child, Lilian, thus adding to her already considerable burden. Exchanging her fashionable Victorian clothes for light cotton dresses, she rolled up her sleeves and coped as best she might. Her husband, meanwhile, resumed his old ways of drunken uselessness. Already uprooted and resentful of white power, the African labourers who looked to the master of Norwood Farm for their orders and pay soon found neither – and left. Clinton, in whose life physical work had previously played no part, was reduced, with results which may be

---

[16] Graves, *op cit*, p 133.
[17] Leonard Thompson, *A History of South Africa*, (Yale University Press, 1995), p 97.

imagined, to wielding the spade and the plough for himself. Then, dreams again took hold.

In 1867 alluvial diamonds had been found to the west of Bloemfontein, 350 miles from Pietermaritzburg. By 1872, twenty thousand Whites and thirty thousand Blacks swarmed over the area in search of instant riches. The temptation was too much for Clinton; leaving Florence to fend for herself and her children, he set out for the west, only to return empty handed and even more booze-crazed than before. Florence facing a nightmare of drunken violence, poured out her predicament in a letter to her mother-in-law, the details of which Thomas Gambier Parry conveyed to Hubert:

> What is to be done about or for his [Clinton's] family I cannot conceive. He simply does nothing – or rather worse than nothing. He said at first that everything was so cheap that we were to advise all poor people to come there – £200 a year was a fortune – of course irrespective of capital to establish any business – but he has got through his £500 a year and two thirds of the *capital* sum of £5,000 which I placed at his disposal to establish his family for their future existence.
>
> I enclose a letter from poor little Florence. What on earth is to be done with Clinton if he comes home in this state? I have told you, as I felt my duty to his next brother, all that has occurred. If Natal is so injurious a climate, why not sell off – and try healthy New Zealand... I wrote in reply to Florence's first letter... saying what madness it would be to come to England, unless for some extraordinary reason it were *forced* on them.
>
> What on earth could Clinton do? – *Here*, he would simply drop into intensest idleness, diffuseness – if not worse – unless, if it may have pleased God, it is my only hope and incessant prayer, he be utterly and altogether a changed being. I wish in all that is done or proposed with respect to him and his to have your confidence – and counsel.[18]

Two months later Hubert received an even more alarming letter from his father.

Do not leave the enclosed about but return them

Dearest Hubert,

The letters which I enclose will show you how things stand with poor Clinton. Nothing can be worse. He is in a Hospital under the charge of men – because poor Florence can manage him no more. She has been a good and faithful wife to him – hiding all from us as much as possible. He is simply frantic from delerium tremens – with lucid quieter intervals... Florence's letter... says that he knows his state and desires to place himself under some control, for recovery, when he comes to England. – That is what he means – though, as usual, he does not say so in words. He may now be on his way home – and arrive any day. I lose no time to prepare for him. Dr. Wood is much interested in our family – and I have felt that it is absolutely necessary to *make a friend* of some one. So I have been for a long time this afternoon with Dr. Wood. He enters most kindly and interestedly into the whole case. Of course Fisherton, the place mentioned by Florence, as chosen by Clinton, would be undesirable – close to the Lears, Hamiltons and Herberts. Nor would Barnwood [*an asylum near Gloucester*] be desirable – because too

---

[18] TGP, letter to CHHP, 3 November 1872. Shulbrede archive.

near home. It would be desirable to keep the matter most private – and therefore at a distance. Dr. Wood recommended two places – and will think it all over and enquire and let me know…

But our conversation went far beyond all that. He says that as for Clinton's idea of a 'cruise' home – and back – it is worse than absurd. Finally he said that such cases were incurable – on my expression of anxious remonstrance, he replied 'When did you ever hear of such a case recovering? – He can never go back. It would take several years' discipline to produce any lasting effect – and as for that, suppose he were to return to Natal, he would be sure to go off again – for the only hope is entire tea totalism [*sic*] and that wants such resolution in those cases as you rarely find. The *craving* for alcohol is such as we have no idea of – it is a mania – and is tantamount to incurable.' – Such is the pith and, so far as memory serves, very much the words of what Dr. Wood said. He offered to do anything – indeed far more than I would hear of.

He will fully enquire and report – the object being to find a fit place for Clinton to go to immediately he sets foot in England. I have thought it right to let the dear children here read Clinton's letter. Ernest, Linda and B. [*Beatrice*] know much about his case. G. [*Geraldine*] knows nothing of course. I could not let them read Florence's letter. I write to her telling her all – suggesting the desirability of consulting persons on the spot as to remaining or coming home. The children must be brought up for [a] hard life. How? – The property acquired in Natal is very small. Are the children to be Colonists or Homebirds? – if the latter, who is to support them? It is a bad business – and [as] difficult as bad.

People collect here today and tomorrow – all love to you and dearest Maude.

Your most affectionate Padre

T.G.P.[19]

Even without the added burden of these gloomy tidings, Hubert's spirits were at a low ebb in the first year of his marriage. Separated from the restorative power of London concerts, wearied by the long daily train journey to and from the capital, and downcast by the tedium and lack of progress in his position in the city, his health began to suffer markedly. Financial problems pressed hard. Maude had her own allowance, as did Hubert, but his failure to realise the level of income for which he had hoped, and which would have been essential to maintain Maude in her former style, resulted in embarrassing debts. Hubert's father made it quite clear that he was in no position to help:

About your Lloyds affairs I am indeed sorry to hear. I had hoped better things, but I had always hoped that your association with city work would lead to other opportunities – and they may come e'er long. Our family means need replenishing. I cannot blame myself for what I have spent. I know that the establishment of our family in a way worthy of it, could best be done by all the means I have employed. They have been costly. The only misfortune was that I could not receive better advice when I was young – but I had no confidence in what little advice was given me, because I knew that it was not based on any real knowledge or personal experience in those who gave it. But indeed it amounted to next to none at all. No-one told me the awful expenses entailed by Landed property – no-one hinted to me that Highnam was simply a ruin. Every farm, every cottage was little better than a ruin – and young as I was, I knew more of

[19] TGP, letter to CHHP, 7 January 1873. Shulbrede archive.

farmhouses as things to sketch than things to build! – and when I had got deeply into mud here, it was too late to withdraw. So I had but one course – to go on, and to plant a family in good repute – and with some influence for good – the only end worth living or dying for.

As for the works of art here, they are not to be thought of in the expenditure – for £3,000 *spread over* all the purchases of a *long series* of years, would pay for them – and they have more *than repaid* themselves by the wide interest they have thrown around our home, and the *influence they* have insensibly produced on our family and very many people far beyond it. I have but little to regret of what the work of establishing a family, as I have been permitted to do, has cost me – but it has to a certain degree injured the resources of our family income.[20]

In the event, Hubert was obliged to accept a gift of £400 from his brother-in-law, George Pembroke; and in July 1873 the Parrys left Bengeo, their 'dear little snuggery', to stay with Lady Herbert at Chesham Place whilst their own house at 7 Cranley Place was being prepared – a procedure not assisted by the unwelcome interference of Lady Herbert!

*   *   *   *   *   *   *

In these early years of the 1870s, beset by worries about Clinton and the rapidly declining family fortune, Thomas Gambier Parry continued his work on the decoration of the north aisle at Highnam Church, maintained an undiminished interest in his many civic and social concerns, and even embarked upon a major project which was to occupy him on and off for the best part of a decade. This was the magnificent reredos, the subject of which, in ten panels, is that of the Crucifixion and its witnesses. It is one of Gambier Parry's finest achievements, and was painted 'with a view to pay off the mortgage of £1,000 on the property of St Lucy's House of Charity in Gloucester, which had been a great burden on the Sisters there'.[21] As Ernest remembered:

In no work that father undertook did he experience more difficulties… than when he was engaged upon his great Altar-piece. Here, a church was not the scene of his labours but a room here, a room there – in London, in Rome, at Highnam… He had many models for the different figures, and as an example of the care and trouble that he took, I know that he made a study from the nude for each of the figures in the central predella, the subject of which is the Last Supper. The whole work is on panel and it is painted in "Spirit Fresco".[22]

The oak frame in which the panels of the reredos are set is of superb quality and was designed by Ernest's younger brother, Sidney, who was to go on to gain distinction as an architect. A work of such beauty and value might have been expected to find a ready purchaser – but no. Ernest again:

Father had himself taken endless trouble to try and dispose of this work, but not long before his death the frame was taken to pieces and the whole thing packed up. About a

[20] TGP, letter to CHHP, 3 November, 1872.
[21] Extract from a memorandum left by TGP, and recorded in GPM, p.184. Highnam archive.
[22] GPM, p 184.

year after his death we asked the Dean of Gloucester to allow it to be set up in the Chapter House, as it was thought that in this way many people would see it and its existence become known. The Dean very kindly consented; there it remained for several years, though without a purchaser being found as was hoped.

When the restoration of the Lady Chapel was nearly completed I had a letter from the Dean asking whether we would present it to the Cathedral that it might be hung at the East end of the Lady Chapel.[23]

The reredos hung in the Lady Chapel at Gloucester for several years from 1897, and was then returned to the Chapter House, where it remained until the close of 1914. Over the years, Ernest received several requests for it to be presented to churches, and in December 1914 the Vicar of Tewkesbury wrote to him begging that the reredos be presented to the Abbey as either a gift or a loan. The mortgage at St. Lucy's having long since been cleared by other means, Ernest's family agreed that the reredos should be offered to Tewkesbury as a free gift. 'The Altar-piece', wrote Ernest proudly, 'was removed from the Chapter House on 19th December and by the 22nd had been erected behind the high altar in Tewkesbury Abbey, in its final and glorious home'.[24]

Although still at Tewkesbury, the Gambier Parry reredos is no longer to be seen (in 1998) in its originally chosen place. Relegated to languish in the Abbey shop, where eye, mind and expectation are drawn down to souvenir and gift, rather than upward to a work of art, the reredos has, sadly, become a mere backdrop, again waiting to be valued at its full worth.

*   *   *   *   *   *   *

Clinton and his family did not return from Natal in 1873 as Gambier Parry had feared; but in the latter part of the year, and at the end of her tether, Florence had abandoned Pietermaritzburg and was living at the Cape. Clinton seems to have remained under restraint, and was certainly not present when Florence wrote 'a very melancholy pair of letters' to Hubert, 'giving accounts of the dangers and difficulties of her position there with the children in considerable straitness of circumstances, with the Kaffirs in a very unquiet state and daily threatening to turn the country topsy-turvy'.[25] On one occasion, Florence told him, when a crowd of drunken Africans approached her lodgings, she had been obliged to pluck up her courage and go out alone to break them up, a revolver concealed under her dress. Her life, almost impossible for years, had turned into a nightmare. 'My position here, dear Muzzie', she wrote to Ethelinda, 'is becoming really unbearable. My being entirely alone is causing people to say the most cruel and untrue things of me'.[26]

That same year, so disastrous for Clinton, proved to be the turning point in Hubert's musical life. Never prepared to overestimate his own ability, considerable though it was, Hubert knew that real progress in his art would not

---

[23] *Ibid.*
[24] GPM, p 185.
[25] CHHP, *Diary 1874*. Shulbrede archive.
[26] *Ibid.*

come as long as he struggled in isolation, half pretending that it was, after all, merely a pastime. 'I work and work at my practising', he wrote, 'and yet my nervousness makes a bigger fool of me every time I play to anyone'.[27] A teacher of stature was essential, but who should it be? Would Brahms, whose music gave him increasing delight, take pupils? To whom could he turn for advice? Perhaps Edward Dannreuther (1844-1906), director of the new Wagner Society, whose concerts were making an immense impression on Hubert's mind, would give an opinion. But that same nervousness which increasingly stifled his ability to play before friends prevented his knocking at Dannreuther's door in Orme Square.

Dannreuther, a celebrated pianist, was born in Strasbourg and had settled in London after giving the first complete performance of Chopin's F minor Concerto there in 1863. His musical education had begun in Cincinnati at the age of 5, and from 1859 to 1863 he had studied at Leipzig under Moscheles and Hauptmann. He it was who, in the 1870s, brought the concertos of Grieg in A minor, Liszt in A, and Tchikovsky in B flat minor to English ears. But above all, he was a staunch champion of the music of his friend Richard Wagner, wrote several books on the music and theories of his idol, and founded the Wagner Society in London in 1872. He, surely, would be the ideal mentor for Hubert Parry – if only the boldness to approach him could be found.

In the event, it was Hubert's half-sisters, Beatrice and Linda, who grasped the initiative and called on Dannreuther in April, taking with them a copy of Hubert's charming, philosophical *Charakterbilder* (Character Pictures), seven Schumannesque piano pieces subtitled 'Seven Ages of Mind', and written for Susan Stephenson, a fine amateur pianist whom Hubert had befriended in London before his marriage. The titles of the individual pieces, omitted on publication by Augener in 1872, are revealed in Hubert's correspondence with Miss Stephenson as a prelude in G flat, 'Dreaming' (inspired by Tennyson's *Lotus Eaters*), 'Learning', 'Passion', 'Striving' (relating to intellectual freedom), '*Sehnsucht*' (longing), 'Triumphing' (of intellectual freedom), and a quiet finale, returning to G flat, which replaced a piece called 'Wondering and Waiting', described by Hubert as 'suspended judgement and trusting in God'!

Hubert was not left to wonder or to wait to discover Dannreuther's reaction to his pieces; Beatrice wrote to him without delay:

22 Mansfield Street

Here goes to tell you (that in my excitement) old boy what ought to please you much! – We have shown your 'Philosopher' as I call it to Dannreuther. The little man seated himself and looked quietly at the first page, whilst Linda and I almost stopped breathing – then he began. He *did* begin! and played the prelude quite through and then said 'that's good' – then he played the next thing (Linda swares [*sic*] his eyes glistened but I could not see his face) and said 'your brother must be a great pianist: these are very difficult' etc… When he came to 'Triumphing' he went at it in great excitement and said in the middle 'this is splendid!' The last thing we told him you had written long ago. When he

---

[27] CHHP, *Diary 1873*.

had played it he said 'very poetical'. I then ventured to tell him that you hope he will give you some lessons as you are coming to live in London: he said 'I could not teach a man who can write this.' He misunderstood me and thought I meant the science of music, but I informed him it was more playing you want. 'Yes I might help his fingers' said he: and then 'there is not a spark of the amateur in this. I shall certainly get them!' So you see how he pooh poohed them!

Love to Maudie.
From your affectionate and rejoicing sister,
M. Beatrice Parry[28]

An elated Hubert wrote back by return:

Sweet Little B.
– I was quite wild with delight over your letter. I never had such encouragement or any so worth having in my life before. I was quite crazy all day Saturday after it came. And what ducks you and Linda are to take such an interest in my music. It is so nice of you both to be so eager for a good opinion from Dannreuther. I hope he meant what he said and that you did not exaggerate through your dear willingness to make me happy. You need not have any qualms about learning any of them now, need you? after having such an opinion, and I hope you won't find them very hard… Was Possie pleased at Dannreuther's opinion?[29]

Dannreuther's good opinion of his work gave Hubert's self-confidence an incalculable boost. From that moment he began to see the world through the eyes of a professional, proud to declare his art. His father's opinion, whilst retaining great importance for him, no longer carried the weight to put a brake upon Hubert's chosen vocation. Now, too, the empty-headedness and insensitivity of so many of Maude's family and friends began to irritate him; far more so than previously when, unable to lay claim to any worthwhile calling of his own, his value to society had seemed little greater than theirs. At Wilton earlier in the year, Hubert met, for the first time, Lady Folkestone, later Helen Countess of Radnor, and in her found a lifelong friend who not only shared his passion for music but was a woman of great intelligence and a fine singer, 'better than any amateur I ever heard – French, Italian, English and Schubert all equally well… neither she nor her husband have any humbug or stuck-up-edness about them'. Back at Wilton in December 1873, Hubert again delighted in Lady Folkestone's company, but after her departure, surrounded by several 'sporting' people who were staying with Lady Herbert, his irritation spilled over into utter scorn:

The tone of indolence about the House is considerably increased. They despise anything intellectual and spend all their time in shooting, hunting, rabbiting, smoking and billiards. Music is naturally utterly contemned. The tone of their ideas is so inconceivably low as to be almost beyond belief. Though one is forced to be careful how

[28] Letter from Beatrice Parry to CHHP, 18 April 1873. Shulbrede archive.
[29] Letter from CHHP to Beatrice Parry, 21 April 1873. Shulbrede archive

one expresses one's surprise. They had a curious conversation at dinner about Bull fighting and Bull baiting, cock fighting, and prize fighting – on most of which topics they expressed their opinion that it was 'great rot' putting a stop to them, as they didn't see any harm in them. 'If cocks liked to fight why shouldn't they. As to bull fighting, the bulls got too excited to feel pain, and why should you stop two men who like to fight for a sum of money; it's their own affair, etc., etc.' And they were far too keen about it to entertain a contrary opinion for a moment. All aristocrats and specimens of the Upper Ten – Society's ornaments! It is enough to make a bitter democrat of one to be long in the company of people brought up in luxury and so utterly worthless as these are. They may do something good it is true, but it will be an accident if they do – For they are without aspiration of any kind; without ideas; without education of mind, and as uselessly ornamental and as injuriously bigoted about their 'rights' and 'position' as it is possible to be. The advance of morality, and the liberalization of thought and the enlargement of ideas are subjects unknown to them, or if known looked upon with contempt. All they live for is to enjoy the material prosperity which chance has put before them. And the pity of it is that they are not at all without wits. Far from it. But material prosperity has turned them into a useless direction, and they are wasted. I daresay the desire of praise or the inducements of ambition may lead both Sidney and George to distinguish themselves hereafter, but I am afraid they will never do anything for a lofty motive or for a disinterested one. Certainly, one of the primary conditions of a better constituted society must be a better and more equal distribution of the luxuries of life and the questionable advantages of wealth and opportunities of pleasure.[30]

Hubert had never been under any illusions about the true nature of Lady Herbert's personality, and she would test him severely over the coming years. During that visit to Wilton in December 1873 he found her deviousness pathetically amusing and her religious hypocrisy totally alien to his own revised creed, a creed born of the courage to think for himself:

A very amusing illustration of Lady Herbert's character occurred one evening when she made Bella Lewis play chess with her. Before the occasion Bella used to think her one of the saints of the earth, but after it she was perfectly bewildered to think how any educated person, as she said, could be so dishonest. Bella first of all noticed that when she took pieces if she happened to look away they suddenly reappeared on the board. This happened mysteriously several times – and finally she was just going to say 'Check Mate' when she happened to look down to do something to her shoe, and when she looked back the pieces were conveniently changed, and she had to go on with the game again. Maudie came in while the game was going on and caught her Ladyship putting back a knight and a pawn and called out, 'Now Mama, you're cheating' – whereupon her Ladyship with perfect composure removed the pieces again saying, 'Oh no my dear, I was only seeing how I might have played with those men on the board'. Bella Lewis was, of course, in a great state of excitement when the game was over, and thoroughly disgusted with her saint. For my part, I can't understand how her Ladyship can find any pleasure in a game which she doesn't play fairly. George says she does it for the mere pleasure of cheating. I daresay it is from mere force of habit, just like her lying, which she often does so stupidly that everyone must discover it. Sometimes she tells a lie about somebody before his face and in his hearing. She is a fine specimen of 'saintliness' and 'religiousness'. She makes enough fuss about religion and goes to church enough to do for a dozen people. And she points the old moral well that much church going, and

---

.[30] CHHP, *Diary 1873*.

being spotlessly 'faithful' (as theological people falsely call it), and attending Mass and making a fuss about religion does not make people good, nor ever indicate that they are likely to be so. I wish Possie and all the multitude of his High Church enthusiasts of the present day could take that maxim to heart. For my part, I think a man more likely to have a really high moral standard and to be less tainted with the meaner vices of the age if he doesn't go to church, or make a fuss about his religion. However, the said High Church enthusiasts are so saturated with religious sentimentalism, and the theory that nothing is worth doing though ever so heroic or unselfish an action if it is not done 'through Jesus Christ', (whatever that may mean) that they are impregnable to the most commonplace arguments.[31]

For some time, angered and saddened by Clinton's waywardness, Thomas Gambier Parry had let it be known that he no longer considered his eldest son to be fit to inherit Highnam Court; but his principal reason for this was less to do with Clinton's alcohol addiction than his declared rejection of orthodox Christianity. Hubert, appalled that he should benefit at his brother's expense, especially on the grounds of a religious principal which he could himself no longer accept, had felt obliged to explain fully and honestly his own position. Before setting out from London for Wilton he plucked up the courage to write at length to his father:

7 Cranley Place

Dec 15. 73

Dearest Possie

After considerable hesitation I have come to the conclusion that it is my duty to write you a letter which is very likely to give you pain, and likely also to make you angry. And though latterly I had had hardly any object more near at heart than that of pleasing you and doing all I can to avoid giving you pain I feel now constrained to run into the very jaws of that which I have so long avoided. One of my chiefest reasons for doing so is that you have made hints to me at times of intentions on your part which seemed to be governed by the feeling that you had no trust in Clin because he had thrown his religion overboard, and that you had more trust in me because you believed I was of a like mind with you in that matter. And I fear that without an explanation from me on the subject you might act upon your suppositions and thereby do Clin an injustice. There are other reasons which need not be mentioned. One of the least of them is my own feeling that it is better and healthier to be abused for what one really is than praised for what one is not.

You know very well, and I think there is none that will deny it, that as a boy I was of a very religious turn of mind, I say as a boy because I think that at that period my religion was of a kind to be more generally recognised, and not because I became less so in reality as I grew older. I think that even you yourself could hardly have wished me to be more High Church, more 'full of Faith', and more of a church goer than I was. I believed everything I was told, and was really very deeply impressed with the exercise of religion, and with all which I believed of my earnestness in this respect I could give you many proofs if it were not that they would make this letter inordinately long, and for the reason that I do not think you would require them of me as you can hardly fail

31 *Ibid.*

to do me the justice to allow what I say to be true. And in this matter I think Lewis [Majendie] would be a good judge, and would not deny what I say. However by accident I suppose (if it was by design it was the more honourable to those who educated me) a part of religious training which is now so generally impressed upon young minds in religious families was left out. I mean the indoctrination of the idea that in all points when reason proved one thing and revelation said another, the former was seen to be leading astray, and it would be wicked to doubt the so-called revelation. I consequently brought my reason to bear upon questions of faith very early, though at first only in a modified form and without any idea that my faith would thereby be in any degree changed: for I remember well thinking on the contrary that my faith would thereby be strengthened and made more worthy. It was in this manner and without any idea of heterodoxy that I ceased to believe in the theory that we are all punished for the sin of our first progenitors, as altogether contradictory to the theory that God was good and beautiful, as I conceived very early that no being called Good would punish other beings whom he himself brought into existence for sins they had nothing to do with. Along with this naturally went the idea of Hell – which I early thought an unfit conception for any rational being.

Of course it was natural that my unconscious heterodoxy should soon lead on to place the story of the Creation as told in Genesis, and Noah's Ark and flood, and the early History of Mankind, and such matters, among the poetical conceptions of a barbaric people in a very early stage of development. Interesting, no doubt, as poetry; but ridiculous if considered as petrified and unquestionable truth. I looked upon them much in the same light as the Scandinavian legends, and did not think I was thereby affecting my religion. I knew a little science, and what I knew of it, though elementary, was certain, and quite enough to justify my discarding the Creation legends.

You must acknowledge that all this while I had only been using the principle which Butler himself proposes in his analogy that Reason is indeed the only Faculty we have wherewith to judge confessing anything, even Revelation itself… And you must be kind enough to bear carefully in mind that I cannot justly be accused of changing my opinions through ignorance or negligence of the bible, as for 9 years (as far as my memory serves me) I missed but as many evenings when I did not read some chapters of the bible to myself before I went to bed. It was a long step with me from disclaiming the theory of Original Sin to finding and accepting the inference which it necessarily leads to.

It was not till I was reading history at Oxford and had done what logic was required...that I began to consider the value of modern dogmas and theology. I was struck first with the history of the mangling and fighting which went on in the earliest ages of the Church. The very unsaintly and acrimonious bitterness which the fathers used to one another in discussing dogmas. And the extraordinary and often questionable manner in which such dogmas were fixed, and how often they changed, and how much it seemed a matter of chance what we held now. I thought before that, what I was always taught by religious people I knew was of course true: *viz.* that all who disagreed with us were wicked, and that disagreement in religious matters was mainly a feature of depravity which was peculiar to our time. I suppose this new observation of mine on the quarrelling which has always gone on in the Church led me to appreciate the expression 'odium theologicum' in its true meaning, and to be conscious that it was not all on one side as I had been taught, and that those who taught me were not altogether so immaculate as I had supposed.

In order to show you that what I am writing is *bona fide* I will here quote to you a passage from my Diary of '69. From years ago – which will serve to convince you that my change has not been hasty, nor governed by the outward circumstances which some people will probably ascribe it. [*Quotation from Diary for October 1869, Hedingham, referring to 'High Church' people and the much talk and demonstration they used with regard to it*] That is quite enough to show you that what I thought of the religion and the worth of the opinions of those who had before been my teachers and guides, and you will readily appreciate that when my former respect for them was gone, and when those whom I looked upon as my Popes in matters of doctrine and trusted to for real religious truth, had lost their hold on me my belief was left face to face with my reason. It was by slow degrees they fought the battle out, and though I had no idea how the fight would end I never failed to be slow in judging and determining, patient in balancing, and always kept the object of finding what was the real earnest truth before my eyes. There is nothing in life which I have been so earnest about. And, dearest Possie, you will have no reason neither will it be just to question what I say when I tell you that I trusted the issue to God, and prayed as earnestly as ever I did in my boyhood that he would lead me to that truth at last.

There is little more to say, for a child could guess to what conclusion I came. And I do not wish to prolong the explanation further. (Though there is much more I could say on every point almost). I trusted the issue to God – Will you and those who think with you be of a mind to be distressed that that which you call faith has brought me to the belief I hold? Surely you will not be so unfaithful! No one can be the exclusive depository of infallible truth. There are thousands of form of dogma, and each form has believers who are convinced they only are right. No one can decide without examination – And those who are determined they are in the right without that examination simply in the dogmas because they happen to be the dogmas they hold, are, in my estimation indolent and blameworthy. Some there are who have been so brought up and are so constituted that they could not think otherwise than as they have been educated. I cannot blame them. Let them not blame me. I have done what I earnestly believe to be right and no one has either reason or even right to be unhappy that my conclusions are not the same as theirs. Here is the sum of them.

I believe in religion, but one so pure and simple that its chiefest maxim is 'Strive after virtue itself'. I believe that the theological part of Christianity and all dogmas connected with it are a mistake. I believe in Communion as one of the best formalities of religion possible – because it is the 'Eucharist' – that which reminds us of mutual dependence on one another and our mutual duties of love and affection to one another. And I think that if people had that idea when they went [to church] instead of some dogmatic theory or some extravagant feeling of sentiment there would be less sorrow and distress in the world. I believe in God, and I believe that he is good. And I think that is one form of 'faith' that will always stick to me. Beyond that I believe we can know nothing of him. I think that a general change in religious belief must come in time, but it would be a great mistake to suppose that such changes can be sudden or, if sudden, can be safe or substantial either in persons or communities. Those who have depended on theology and have fed upon what they call spiritual ideas all their lives and made them the the staple of their thoughts and the support of their piety could not possibly change. All I ask of them is that Charity of which St. Paul says 'it suffereth long and is kind – vaunteth not itself, is not puffed up. Beareth all things, believeth all things, hopeth all things, endureth all things'.

If you are faithful as you profess to be you ought not to be offended at that which a like faith has brought me to. It was not through negligence or carelessness that I became what I am, but rather through my great earnestness and interest in it. The faith I have chosen is a harder one to tread than the paths of those who live in the bosom of the Church, and think without reflection or examination the same as do most of those they love. Perhaps, too, it is easier to be good and virtuous in the Church than out of it, for ordinary mortals. I cannot help that. I cannot believe a thing because I should live easier for believing it. What is truth to me is truth for itself and for no other reason. No consequences can make it untrue or make me believe anything contrary to it. Do not suppose for instance that I am not fully conscious of the hard things which are likely to be said of me by Church people. I have lived too long among them to be ignorant of the things they say of people who think as I do, and am too sensitive to be callous to it. If you are just you will refrain from their unkindness.[32]

Hubert had joined the lengthening parade of mid- and late-Victorian intellectuals who found themselves struggling with a crisis of faith as religious certainty was increasingly challenged by science, historical scholarship and changing conceptions of morality. The mood of that struggle had been captured by Tennyson in 1850, nine years before the publication of Darwin's *Origin of Species*:

> There lives more faith in honest doubt
> Believe me, than in half the creeds.[33]

But for many, the doctrines of the Church remained non-negotiable; 'honest doubt' was, for them, incompatible with traditional Christian beliefs founded upon revelation, supernatural religion and miracle. Rationalism was, by definition, anti-Christian, and the only *honest* path was either to accept the teachings of the Church in their entirety or, alternatively, reject them, cease to be a Christian, and accept the social consequences. Thomas Gambier Parry was one of these.

The 'little science' which Hubert knew was self-taught. Science was still on the margins of the English educational system; it was not possible, for instance, to take a specialized science degree at Oxford University until 1886. Nonetheless, as Hubert's daughter Dorothea revealed, 'his reading during the years 1870 to 1875 was very rationalistic, philosophic and scientific'.[34] Amongst the writers whose work he particularly admired were T H Huxley, who, in 1860 had vanquished Samuel Wilberforce, the Bishop of Oxford, in a public debate about Darwin's evolutionary theory, and who invented the very word 'agnostic'; and Samuel Butler, another Darwin supporter, whose satires on the material foundation of Christianity hurled cannon shot into the torpidity of Victorian thought, and whose *Erewhon* and *The Fair Haven* Hubert had read soon after their publication in 1872 and 1873. Of *Erewhon* he wrote:

> I have scarcely ever liked a book better. I have always thought that it was on the principles of this book, *i.e.* analogy, that the fallacies of people's everyday beliefs and actions could be most tellingly brought home to them. And this book does it as well as anything could in my estimation – as searchingly, closely and truly.[35]

Hubert was also influenced by the writing of Matthew Arnold, particularly his *Literature and Dogma;* G H Lewes, remembered still for his liaison with George Eliot, herself an agnostic, and his influence upon her work (*Middlemarch* was Hubert's favourite novel); William Morris; and especially

---

32 CHHP, copy of letter to TGP, 15 December, 1873. Shulbrede archive.
33 Tennyson, *In Memoriam A.H.H.*
34 Dorothea Ponsonby, *op. cit.*
35 CHHP, *Diary 1873.*

Herbert Spencer, friend of both Eliot and Huxley, whose first statement of evolutionary philosophy, *Social Statics: or The Conditions Essential to Human Happiness Specified*, was published in 1851, predating Darwin by eight years.

One week before Christmas Day, 1873, Thomas Gambier Parry dispatched his response to Hubert's honest confession. It was a 'most melancholy letter':

My dear Hubert

I value the honesty of your letter – and your honourable intention in repudiating all claims, on any ground of religious principle, superior to those of your eldest brother, in respect to the future possession of property.

It has been a life's work for me to renew a family which had dwindled down to one survivor – myself. I should have been very glad to have lived more according to my tastes and natural character – but my duty was plain – I have tried to follow it – and probably with very many mistakes. The irksomeness of inaptitude for the sort of life I have been obliged to lead must have inevitably led to them.

I have had, throughout, one great object, *viz.* so to place and bring up my family as to obtain God's blessing and the respect of all around them – not by wealth or rank, but by what is incalculably nobler, high principles and blameless lives. My eldest son has from early days led a life too grievous to bear exposure. I know a great deal about it – and I know that there is more to know than I do know. His affectionateness gives him an element of personal endearment – but with his Christianity all basis of morality went long ago – as it inevitably must. I refrain from writing more about him. You may imagine that you know something of his life and conduct – but what you do know is comparatively nothing to what is known by me. I had therefore set my heart – and based my hopes on you. And now even *you* appear to fail me. It is too deep a grief – you, my loved Hubert, cast off the Lord who bought you! Him whose mercy will one day in some crash of sorrow, or in other way best known to Himself, draw you once again to know that He is the only Rock of life, the Wisdom of God and the power of God.

I have for some time past noticed in you with painful anxiety a growing pride of intellect and great impatience of any opinion contrary to your own. I offer no arguments and no answers to that long and vapid statement which you have written to me – they would be simply useless – or worse – in the present condition of your mind.

I am sure that on second thoughts you could not wish *me* (by the circulation of that painful letter) to be the instrument employed by you to publish to our relations and friends that my loved son Hubert is an Infidel! You can little conceive the bitterness and horror of such an idea to me.

I say no more – I leave you in higher Hands – one thing only. I ask – indeed with the awful responsibilities of a father I must demand it, that you avoid to the very utmost any influence, by expression of opinion or otherwise, on your brothers and sisters – to disturb those pure and holy principles of 'the Faith', which it has been the greatest object of my life – now nearly worn out – to sow in them. I must also hope and pray that your sweet and precious Maude may escape this deadliest Poison of the Pride of modern life.

You know not, indeed you may perhaps incline to despise the idea of that flood of sorrow that you are now laying up for yourself at some distant day. My loved Hubert, some distant echo of what I now write will one day ring in your ears. You will not then forget that it is your father, who tried to feed your young mind with what even under your present cloud is not altogether lost, that reminds you now, that no Prayers for guidance or for ought else can possibly reach the Throne of Grace but by 'one way'

– for the paramount law of our life is in those words of our most blessed Lord, that 'no man can come to Father but by me'.

May he recall and keep you!

Your most affectionate father

T. Gambier Parry[36]

No matter how deeply Hubert's honesty had wounded his father, or how irreconcilable their religious and political views had become, the relationship between the two, rather than being shattered, now drew closer than ever before. Throughout Hubert's childhood Gambier Parry, preoccupied by his second family and multiple concerns, had remained aloof from his two elder sons. The lack of mother and fatherly love had undoubtedly contributed to Clinton's moral collapse. Hubert, constantly teetering on the edge of instability, had managed to survive the bludgeonings of fate and, although he held steadfastly to his agnosticism, respected his father's demand that he refrain from expressing any views on matters of faith to Linda, Ernest, Beatrice, Geraldine or Sidney. All five remained firmly committed to their father's beliefs; Linda going so far as to compile a book on *The Inheritance of the Saints*, and, after the death of her mother and a close friend, to edit a book on angels, dedicating it 'To the Memory of E.G.P. and I.E.H. who in their Lives were Beautiful and Helpful as Angels and with the Angels now dwell in the Light'.[37] Ernest, who chose a military career, followed absolutely in his father's spiritual footsteps, continuing not only in the convictions and outward forms of faith which were such inseparable parts of Thomas Gambier Parry's life, but revering, almost mystically, the memory of his father, even to the point of naming both of his sons 'Thomas' (Thomas Robert and Thomas Mark) and, in 1911, adopting by hyphenation the surname 'Gambier-Parry'.

Running in parallel with his struggle for spiritual freedom, a new-found and bracing sense of artistic liberation was pointing the way to Hubert's future. His lessons with Dannreuther began in November 1873 and, although concentrated at first on keyboard technique, soon developed into the intellectual study of music, of the works of Beethoven, Schumann , Liszt and Brahms. In that same month, a month brimming with musical discoveries, he heard *Meistersinger* at a Wagner Society concert and succumbed completely to its magic. Wagner's art was no longer a mystery to him, as it had been half a dozen years earlier. This was music with which he was immediately able to identify; Richard Wagner spoke and Hubert Parry listened. And the impression gained from the very first bars of the *Meistersinger* Vorspiel remained with Hubert for the rest of his life, echoing still in 1916 in the inspired dignity of the opening bars of that best-known of all his works, *Jerusalem*.

---

[36] TGP to CHHP, 19 December, 1873. Shulbrede archive.
[37] Linda Gambier Parry (ed.), *A Book of Angels* (Longmans, Green, and Co., 1906).

It was in November 1873, too, that Dannreuther persuaded Augustus Manns to play through an orchestral work by his young protégé during a rehearsal at the Crystal Palace: Hubert's overture to *Vivien*, sketched five years previously and completed earlier in 1873. 'I was very nervous', wrote Hubert, 'lest my want of practice in writing for the orchestra should make me do something ridiculous, but was rather agreeably surprised at the effect of the orchestration'.[38]

By now music was more salvation than consolation. Maude, never blessed by robust good health, began to spend extended periods at Wilton, or with friends at other places in the country, to escape the cold and damp of London's winter. Back at Highnam for Christmas there were many of the old pleasures for Hubert to enjoy, none more so than the opportunity to play duets with Linda and Ernest – and his father said not a word about their vexed correspondence. But on returning to London in the new year Hubert was both lonely and depressed, not least because his business dealings at Lloyd's were showing no sign of improvement, his money and that of his partner Ranald McDonnell was 'at a very low ebb', and the great expense of living at 7 Cranley Place to the standard expected by Lady Herbert had all but exhausted Hubert's capital. These stresses brought a return of his heart condition, distressing palpitations, and by the spring of 1874 Hubert was obliged to seek once again the financial assistance of his father. Gambier Parry, in London to attend a meeting of the fabric committee of St. Paul's Cathedral, responded in terms near to desperation:

United University Club,
Pall Mall East, S.W.

Monday night
May 18, 1874

Dearest Hubert

...Your letter greatly distressed me. It is not for my own distress I care – but for your's. I am only glad that you write so frankly and fully about everything – as I hope you will always do. Trouble does people good – it makes them less selfish. Selfishness is the curse of many men's characters.

I am grieved at your heart trouble, in the family reflections on you and your position – I always, as soon as I first heard of your engagement, dreaded this as inevitable. Your most sweet and precious wife is true and unswerving. She made her resolve, and but girl as she was, she knew that she had resolved to abide by any circumstances, though the perfect luxury of life, ease, freedom, means, and all else that she was educated, or not educated in, little fitted her to realize the future – but the family is not Maude. Pembroke is a noble fellow – and has the making of a still nobler one – but he cannot realize your or our position. By plunging into such a family you have accepted great difficulties, humiliations, and great pains. They will and *must* come – I always felt it. I am greatly against such marriages as yours in general. The family is sure to be hard – vexed that one of its members should be brought into a sphere of anxieties to which she was not born... How you get on in that pet play thing baby house

[38] CHHP, *Diary 1873.*

of yours I cannot imagine. Things must cost money – and where yours comes from I know not. I have no more to give you. I have done with all the great expenses now – I have piled them up lately, feeling my life ebbing – and anxious to do what none would immediately do after me – but which I was sure that in *the end* they would be glad that I had done. So I am altogether on the wrong side of my accounts at present. Please God that I live till the end of next year. I feel confident all will be put square.

Your troubles are not my only ones. My Ely years are marked by troubles. It was in the last year there that Clinton came to that climax of vicious life that I was obliged to require him to leave us. He next contracted that marriage which gave me such pain – and caused such injury to our family. And now an Ely year begins again. Your trouble and pecuniary failure are terrible distresses – and this year has again been marked by a climax in Clinton's affairs.

I am in the utmost perplexity about him and his family. Poor broken down Florence writes in despair. She received him mad drunk. She ran away in terror. He got into some Hotel and was turned out to spend his first night in the street. His brother in law near Taunton [*Claude Hinde*] writes in great vexation on Florence's account – and adds that Clinton having been put under the care of a man, has escaped from him and has gone into his terrible passion again. A gentleman on board the ship [*presumably sailing from Durban, the nearest port to Pietermaritzburg, to the Cape*] appears to have been a sort of good Samaritan to him – and reported to Florence his having been in Delerium Tremens on board and having frightened people terribly – etc., etc. – and now I get a letter from Clinton himself written in the coolest way, ignoring it all and saying how he made the voyage and how utterly he has quitted his old habits, in short that among old friends in the colony it is 'an understood thing' that he is now going in for a totally different line of life – and much more to that effect – - !!

Florence can stand it and the colony no more – and is in despair about her children who are surrounded with all that is of low stamp of feeling and action. She will come home – and in her utter breakdown of health it is a necessity. Clinton confesses that the Colony has gone to the bad, and loving it and grieving over it, allows the necessity of leaving it. So they come home!! What to do, how to live I cannot conceive!

After the awful experiences with him and the terrible scandal to my household and people, and pain and grief to his brothers and sisters, I have given him to understand that as a most painful duty I cannot allow him to set foot in Highnam again except with a medical certificate of entire cure...[39]

When, at Easter in 1874, the steamship carrying him and his family from South Africa docked at Southampton, Clinton's first action on stepping ashore, before his sad little party could move on to temporary lodgings in Winchester, had been to get helplessly drunk. Gambier Parry, contemplating his return to Ely, was entirely preoccupied with worry over Clinton, who, wrote Hubert, 'having again been delerious from drink was removed to the Dumfries asylum... Poor Possie is broken-hearted about him'.[40]

At Whitsuntide Hubert and his partner McDonnell spent a short holiday in the Channel Islands, staying in Guernsey and visiting what for Hubert was always a very special place: Sark. The stress of life at Lloyd's was further relieved at the end of June by another musical revelation to lay alongside that of Hubert's new-found understanding of Wagner: a performance at the Phiharmonic of

---

[39] TGP, letter to CHHP, 18 May 1874. Shulbrede archive.
[40] CHHP, *Diary 1874*. Shulbrede archive.

Brahms's *Serenade*. 'I never was so delighted with anything at first hearing as at the Serenade'[41], he wrote, and underlined his enthusiasm by purchasing a score without delay and learning it thoroughly by making a detailed copy.

Hubert and Maude had been invited to spend the summer of 1874 with George Pembroke at his Irish seat, Mount Merrion, and whilst there Hubert received yet more news of Clinton from his father. The asylum at Dumfries had let Clinton go, and he and Florence were living at Tunbridge:

> Private Hotel
> 11, Harley Street
> London W
>
> Sunday eveng June 30

Dearest Hubert

I cannot tell you what a grief it has been to me that for the only fortnight I am likely to be in London you have been away – but I am doubly grieved at the cause, that dear Maude's health keeps you and her away. I have little flashes of happy memory of the sight of you in your short visit to us at poor old dull Highnam – and of the sounds we talked over with all their beauty and soul echo – but I grieve at missing your dear Maude too – and at the disappointment she must feel at being unable to bear the journey to Ireland and the risks when there.

We have had another terrible trouble about poor Clinton. He constantly asserted that his being kept from his family was the cause of his yielding to his terrible habit. Alas! Men like him always have an excellent reason and perfect excuse for what they do. He urged Florence to allow him to come home to that degree that she assented to it. It was allowed too soon – but he was free (for our wretched legislation on lunacy disallows confinement for drunkeness beyond the mere week or two of D.T. [*Delerium Tremens*]) – so there was nothing for it. He went home by agreement on Thursday last. He had spent two previous days with a friend at Oxford – and arrived in the morning at their cottage in Tunbridge in a state imminently bordering on Delerium Tremens – screaming and making disturbance [and] frightening all their neighbours. He drank all day, night and the following morning but was at last sent for and conveyed back to Dr. Fermè's[*the superintedent of a clinic at Stratton St. Margaret, Wiltshire*].

On his arrival in that state Florence telegraphed to me about it and begged that you should come. I telegraphed back that you were out of town – and that the *only capable* and proper assistants were a first-class medical man to whom such cases are, alas, common – and in case of violence a policeman. I should have gone – but *physically* I could do nothing – and all my *moral* influence has not only been long ago exhausted but would have been simply useless. In short I know so well by miserable experience how utterly powerless I am toward him, that I had begged Florence <u>before she left</u> Bitterne [*where, presumably, she had been staying whilst Clinton was in Dumfries*] to take immediate measures by taking the best medical man into *her confidence <u>immediately</u>* on her arrival at Tunbridge and to consult the best clergyman she could find (for a cleric's or magistrate's certificate is enough on a M.D.'s or F.R.C.S.'s authority for the confinement of 'dangerous lunatics') and to speak to the police – so as to have all ready for any emergency.

My presence would have only made bad worse – and you as a stranger could have been of no use. However, I suspect that she had not *fully* carried out my very carefully described precautions – so she telegraphed for her brother. He came and did what would have been done easily and at once if she had made the provisions I described. It

---

41 *Ibid.*

was a most painful episode. I dread the future. She can never receive him again. He is a terror to everybody. The Law disallows *forcible* detention – *open* detention like that at Dr. Fermè's is simply useless. He has no money but pawns his clothes and drinks. He is free *by law*! I dare not, I cannot house him. His wife dares not – cannot. He is free. What is to become of him? I have no power physically or morally. His greatest purpose is to blind me. No one is strong enough or cunning enough to master him – where is he to go? What is the future to be? The *cost* is no mean item. I see no way out of the trouble.

All here go home tomorrow but me. I wait for a committee on Wednesday and then go off to Ely.

God bless you and yours

Your affectionate father

T.G.P.[42]

Thus burdened, Thomas Gambier Parry set out once more for Ely, this time to decorate the timber vaulting of the magnificent fourteenth-century Octagon, 'one of the undoubted wonders of the western world'.[43]

---

[42] TGP, letter to CHHP, 30 June 1874. Shulbrede archive.
[43] Peter Burman, *Thomas Gambier Parry. An Introduction,* an essay published in *Thomas Gambier Parry (1816-1888) as artist and collector* (Courtauld Institute Galleries, University of London, 1993), p 24.

XI

Prometheus Unbound

The Norman crossing tower of Ely Cathedral, having collapsed in 1322, was, over the following six years rebuilt in octagon form; and between 1328 and 1342 a graceful octagonal coronet of timber construction was added. In 1874, following restoration of the fabric of the Octagon by Sir George Gilbert Scott, the Dean and Chapter of Ely invited Thomas Gambier Parry to undertake its decoration. As Peter Burman has suggested:

> In C.E. Keyser's authoritative *List of buildings in Great Britain and Ireland having mural and other painted decorations* (1883), it quite clearly states 'Vault of Octagon; original decoration and outline quite clear. Discovered in 1850'. It seems strange that Gambier Parry, who had such a profound respect for any surviving traces of medieval colour, should so cheerfully have painted over them (and there were those who criticised him at the time). But there can be little doubt that he was considering the aesthetic impact on the cathedral of the whole new scheme of painted decoration, embracing both nave and Octagon; and it has to be admitted that, taken together, nave ceiling and Octagon provide a triumphant vindication of the policy of reviving the use of colour on a big scale.
>
> In the Octagon the four central divisions of the vault in every bay have light backgrounds and *treillages* of flowers and foliage: the intermediate sections have a green ground – richer in tone than that in the nave – powdered with formalised flower patterns. Above, in the lantern, there are four figure paintings of musician angels in all eight bays; the two tiers of tracery are enriched with painting and gilding; the superb, intricate vault is lavishly gilded, there are seraphim towards the centre – gold on a green ground – and the central boss is a dynamic, boldly carved, figure of Christ (early fourteenth century work, but polychromed by Gambier Parry) emerging from stylised clouds, his right hand raised in benediction.[1]

Gambier Parry's work on this literally towering masterpiece, completed at a time when his emotions were stretched to breaking point, ranks, along with the nave ceiling at Ely, as the crowning achievement of his creative life. High in the

---

[1] Peter Burman, *op cit*, p 24.

Octagon his angels bear testimony to the life-enhancing glory of music – and to the irresistible bond between music and the spiritual self.

Meanwhile, in London, music hovered before Hubert as a tantalising possibility. Lessons with Dannreuther were giving him ever-increasing pleasure, but it was a pleasure offset by fruitless efforts to make money and, even more depressingly, the inescapable realisation that Maude's frequent illnesses were not to be the passing symptoms of a trivial ailment. At age twenty-three Maude was already setting the pattern of her life as a semi-invalid. Interest in microscopy, geology and astronomy provided Hubert with much-needed distractions. He became an active member of the Essay and Discussion Club held in the rooms of his friends Pepys Cockerell and W. Hamilton Hoare, and whose members also included Eddie Hamilton, Frank Pownall, Spencer Lyttelton, Robin Benson and occasionally George Pembroke. The group would dine together and read and discuss essays on various moral, philosophical or political subjects, Hubert being 'full of Herbert Spencer'; and it was Benson who reminded Hubert of how much he was missing by telling him of other British composers who were studying with eminent teachers abroad, including Charles Villiers Stanford – of whom Hubert had not previously heard. But there could be no escape from the anxiety and even fright which Maude's condition and frequent absences heaped upon him.

Hubert's sense of desolation was further emphasised when, on 4 February 1875, he went down to Southampton to see Ernest, now commissioned in the Royal Welch Fusiliers, embark to join his regiment in Gibraltar:

> Erny's ship the Indus was out about 3 miles down Southampton water. We went to her in a tug with all the then passengers. It was a lovely frosty morning and perfectly calm. Erny was very cheery about going, seeming quite to be looking forward to naval experience, and being thoroughly settled in the army in a first class regiment... Erny and I had a last shake of the hand over the side as the tug started. And I stood on the paddle box and watched him waving his hat till I couldn't distinguish him any more among the ropes and rigging of the bows. I am afraid it is a very big farewell. He is a great loss to me as I have more pleasure in his company than anybody elses in the world – and love him as thoroughly as he deserves to be loved – which is saying a good deal.[2]

A few days earlier George Pembroke had made it clear to Hubert that he considered him 'a pauper and dependent upon him. That I never took any trouble to make money and had deceived the family by the expectations I had raised before we were married... That I was indolent and lived upon Maude's money instead of making it as he said I ought'.[3] In Pembroke's eyes Hubert's work at Lloyd's was 'no work at all, and very dangerous – indeed mere gambling'.[4] His brother-in-law counted Hubert's exertions on composition as entirely worthless and extracted a promise from him that he would instead make an effort to realise an income from literature; and yet the will to succeed in his chosen art persisted.

---

[2] CHHP, *Diary 1875*, Shulbrede archive.
[3] *Ibid.*
[4] *Ibid.*

At Dannreuther's suggestion Hubert sent his three *Shakespeare Sonnets* to the composer George Macfarren for an opinion. Macfarren, a professor at the Royal Academy of Music, was not in sympathy with the work of two of Hubert's idols, Schumann and Wagner; his report brought disappointment: 'what distressed me very much', wrote Hubert, '[was] that Macfarren finds great fault with my 3 Shakespeare Sonnets on the score of unwarrantable progressions and unauthenticated treatment of form'.[5] In spite of, or maybe because of this, Hubert determined to beard the lion in his den, and on 7 March 1875 took his first composition lesson with Macfarren. Several stormy sessions lay ahead! The ratchet of nervous tension was steadily being advanced.

Believing that Maude's condition could be improved by cleaner air, and no doubt wishing to release himself from dependence on her family's money, Hubert naïvely wrote to his father seeking £5,000 to build a house well away from London. Gambier Parry's refusal, written a few days before setting out for Italy, was unequivocal; and for the first time he explained his financial position in something approaching detail:

> I do not see my way to assist you in any such scheme as you propose. I am indeed sorry to hear that dear Maude's health requires you seriously to think of leaving London – but as far as buying land and building a house, you write as one of a very far larger range of means than our family possesses. I have not £5,000 available for you – and indeed if I had, I should need to be very far better informed of the scheme before I could at all feel justified in aiding you toward it. Your plan has many sides to it. You only present the sunny one of a charming little Earthly Paradise. I wish you could – could have – got more into the acquaintance of some of the leading men in the city, with whom… through *your own abilities*, and other means, your introduction would most assuredly have opened ways to the improvement of your finances. All such work must be done while you are fairly young.
>
> As for me, I can assure you that our family finances require careful treatment. I am not happy at all about them. I do not feel that I have anything to blame myself for in regard to them – but there are some serious items which distress me. I have never had a chance of getting over the loss of £6,000 in the Iron and Coal mine, in which some of the cleverest and best informed businessmen lost everything… that was 10 years ago. I have felt about myself and my family that all great matters for their settlement and comfort must be done in my time – so I have brought all about this Estate in admirable order – but to do this I have been obliged to borrow £3,000 of my solicitor – and now to wind up everything before I go abroad (and that is *no joke*) I have to get advance of £2,000 from Ransom & Co. I also owe to [the] family capital account £1,000 – part of a mortgage paid off last year – but which part I was unable to do without, towards clearing things off for our leaving England. So there is *another* obligation of £6,000 at once to be got over by dint of saving somehow or other. I am distressing my income very much by insurances on my life – *viz.* £30,000 for my second family – *i.e.* £5,000 apiece… also £2,000 on my life to pay any outstanding debts at my death… and… a charge on the Farm buildings at Drings (Churcham) £1,000 which I pay off by interest and instalments in 20 years.
>
> I had hoped to go away and have no expenses going on at home – but that wretched Vulliamy [*Lewis Vulliamy, a builder engaged by Gambier Parry for many years*] had all

5 *Ibid.*

the outside work of the schoolroom, offices, *etc. etc.* done in cement which by succession of frosts has perished all round the cornices – so all that has to be done in weatherstone… I insure my life for £5,000 to secure an endowment of £200 a year for the Warden of St. Lucy's – and I pay off (by instalments) the cost of the Warden's Lodge… The greatest subject of anxiety is Clinton. I went to see him last week. As usual he protests that he is a totally changed person – Dr. Fermè does not in the least think so. He is kept without money – except a few shillings now and then for trifles… He protests that he will stay only another 3 months. Florence is quite broken down. her anxiety is *intense*. She dreads Clinton coming for her own sake, her children's and Clinton's. She desires to go abroad – it would be better – and education such as they require would be far less costly – but are they to go alone? – or unknown to Clinton? If he is with them he will end in breaking her heart – and ruining the children by example and all else. What is to be done – how he is to be provided for if he persists on leaving Dr. Fermè's, *etc. etc.*… endless eventualities which it is impossible to forecast – I cannot conceive.

It is the greatest grief to me and the deepest anxiety. Florence in her broken down condition is doing her utmost on her £300 a year. Clinton's expenses always exceed the remaining £200.

It is a good thing that we are going abroad – at least some expenses will be saved… Horses are all gone except old Iron Sides – no one remains but Slann who is careful and interested about the place. His family will live over the stables while I paint and paper his house, which needs repair terribly. We have a respectable old housemaid living in the house to take care of it – and a couple of labourers will have beds here by night. All others are discharged.

Muzzie and the girls are just gone. I leave early on Saturday.[6]

It is intriguing to contemplate the notion of foreign travel as an instrument of economic control, but clearly Gambier Parry was able to maintain himself, Ethelinda and the girls more cheaply abroad than was possible at Highnam with a large staff. The four of them visited the Italian Lakes from April to August 1875, and in the following year were travelling in Tuscany. Clinton was left in the care of Dr. Fermè at Stratton St Margaret, directed by his father to remain there for at least two years, whilst Hubert, unable to afford to build his dream home, let the house in Cranley Place and rented a house at Ottershaw from his friend Robert Oldham.

Hubert and Maude remained at Ottershaw from May to October. On days when Hubert could escape from the City, he and Maude enjoyed the beautiful spring weather, walking and driving in the Surrey countryside. Hubert busied himself in 'counterpointing, practising and collecting and setting microscopic specimens', and the house was alive with friends, among them Rhoda and Agnes Garrett. The Garretts, experts in interior decoration who had worked with Morris and de Morgan, were strong advocates of the movement for 'Women's Rights', a crusade close to Maude's heart. Hubert enjoyed their company, their conversation and their humour, and he too was soon converted to the cause, accompanying Maude to hear the Garretts addressing Women's Rights meetings. How much of Hubert's interest was generated by a desire to humour Maude is not clear, but when, thirty years later, women's suffrage became a major political issue, Maude's active involvement was to assume a much more

---

6 TGP, letter to CHHP, 1 April 1875, Shulbrede archive.

important element in his affairs: he was to be, by turns, pleased that Maude had found an active rôle for herself, and irritated by the constant comings and goings of meetings, protests and marches which began to dominate their lives. But he was delighted when, in 1917, *Jerusalem* was taken up by the Women's Movement as the Women Voters' hymn!

From Ottershaw Hubert went up to London with the Pownalls to hear *Lohengrin*. In spite of a less than ideal performance, he was deeply impressed by Wagner's achievement:

> I think Wagner is right in his idea of what an opera should be. Nothing can be more ridiculous than stereotyping human nature as it must be portrayed on the stage into a system of arias, recitatives, trios, etc., in fixed plan. No dramatic effect can come of it. And the best music can only serve as an excuse and save you from being insufferably bored with such trivial and unmeaning scenes. A great deal of the music is perfectly wonderful... the story and the situations are very dramatic and interesting, and leave a profound impression... Some people in the boxes seemed to think they were going to talk as usual when the Upper Ten has possession of the house, but we hissed them into silence.[7]

Whilst at Ottershaw, Hubert completed both a Violin Sonata in D minor and the first chapter of a novel, begun to fulfill his promise to George Pembroke that he would work at literature in an effort to make a little money, but it is doubtful if his heart was ever in the enterprise. He was, in any case, soon preoccupied by writing of another kind and also by concerns about his wife's condition. Maude was expecting the birth of her first child in January 1876. As the months at Ottershaw passed it became clear that the pregnancy was not to be an easy one, and towards the end of their stay Maude became seriously ill, cancelling out all the optimism of the beautiful spring and setting her again at the absolute centre of attention. Mrs. Alfred Morrison 'sent her housekeeper with dainty food, wine and ice for the invalid, and... Lady Maude's old and faithful governess... arrived laden with hampers from Lady Herbert'.[8] The prospects for a settled home life, independent of his noble in-laws, must have seemed ever more remote.

At the end of the previous July, Hubert had taken off for a week in the Channel Islands with Oldham, staying at the Yacht Hotel in St. Peter Port, Guernsey, visiting the still perfect island of Herm, and spending a day on his favourite island, Sark:

> The view from the Coupée – the most wonderful thing in the Channel Islands – was magnificent. Below our feet on all sides were wild cliffs and rocks, crevices and crags – the broad expanse of utterly blue sea – further off and still below the Île des Marchands, and across a further broad expanse of blue Herm and Jethou, and their wild rocks round them – then another expanse of blue and Guernsey, and blue sea even beyond that over the low-lying land to the north of that island. Then more to the right

[7] CHHP, *Diary 1875.*
[8] Graves, *op cit,* p 156.

rocks after rocks, – the Caskets shining white in the sun – and the cliffs of Alderney glowing through a slight haze.[9]

Oldham had intended to stay on in Guernsey for an extended holiday, but on the last day of their week together Hubert awoke with an extremely painful ear-ache. Although he tried to make light of it by 'playing boisterously with some children on the sands', the pain continued to intensify. On 29 July he collapsed, and that night Oldham, abandoning his holiday, brought his friend, ill and in great pain, back to Southampton. Hubert was about to receive a shock:

> On Wednesday morning the doctor and I were making an experiment with a tuning fork when I first discovered to my horror that my bad ear heard every note full a quarter of a tone sharper than my sound ear. If this were to be a lasting evil music would become impossible. The disaster that looms possible before me is so awful that I cannot even grasp it. I feel bewildered. This is Friday evening and there is not the slightest symptom of amelioration. I have tried the pianoforte. Every chord, every note produces an effect like an electric shock in the centre of my brain. To hear the notes is vague querulous uncertainty. Every note is out of tune with itself and the beats are produced not in the outer air, but in the very brain itself. A great indescribable throb. It is horrible. I shall try not to think about it.[10]

On the following Monday Hubert sped up to London to see a specialist who, he wrote, 'astonished me considerably by saying I ought to be thankful I wasn't dead. [He] said I had had a narrow escape of inflammation of the brain'.[11] Although this melodramatic diagnosis was probably worth at least another nought on the specialist's bill, there *were* undoubted dangers in that pre-antibiotic age if an ear infection was left untreated. Hubert suffered acutely for a few days and was not completely free of pain for several more weeks, but he did recover and was able to start work on a project which would prove to be of such significance as to change entirely the direction of his future life.

Since their first meeting at the Gloucester Three Choirs Festival in 1868 Hubert and George Grove had frequently been in each other's company at the Crystal Palace and at Dannreuther's home in Orme Square. Grove, who had trained as a civil engineer, had, in addition to constructing several railway stations, taken part in the building of the Crystal Palace, of which he was secretary from 1852 to 1873. After 1856 he had become increasingly involved in music, wrote programme notes for the Crystal Palace concerts for many years, and in 1873 had embarked upon the compilation of his massive *Grove's Dictionary of Music and Musicians*. He and Hubert shared a mutual friend in Mary Emilie von Glehn, whose house in Sydenham, Peak Hill Lodge, was close to Grove's home. Hubert was a frequent and welcome guest of the von Glehns and Grove was often among the company. 'Mini' von Glehn was an accomplished amateur pianist and having been greatly impressed by Hubert's *Shakespeare Sonnets* introduced them to her sister-in-law, Sophie Löwe, a professional singer who included the song *When*

---

[9] CHHP, *Diary, 1875.*
[10] *Ibid.*
[11] *Ibid.*

in disgrace in one of her Stuttgart concerts.[12] The friendship between Hubert and Grove drew closer from this time and, as editor of *Macmillan's Magazine*, Grove published six of Hubert's poems, *A Sequence of Analogies*, in the May 1875 edition. Two months later, on the eve of Hubert's short trip to the Channel Islands, Grove wrote inviting him to contribute an article to his *Dictionary of Music and Musicians*: 'the subject you are to write about is "Arrangement"…it is a jolly subject… I took Miss M.E. von Glehn into my counsel about it lately and she agreed that it was the very thing for you'.[13] So began a long and fruitful collaboration. Hubert completed the article in September, and in November, at Grove's invitation, agreed to join him as sub-editor of the *Dictionary*. It was, he wrote,

> a grand opportunity for me both to work and learn. It was very kind of him, and I soon had lots to do – reading all the articles through and correcting and cutting down those that were too long and adding to those that were incomplete, and, best of all, going to the British Museum to get up my own work which there will be plenty of.[14]

Work on *Grove's Dictionary* provided exactly the morale-boosting stimulus which Hubert needed – and he was to be paid for it! The prospect of quitting Lloyd's came into focus at last. In the following weeks he completed his Brahmsian *Großes Duo* in E minor for two pianos, a work which 'was to represent a crucial departure in his creative development',[15] and, having returned to Cranley Place, allowed himself the pleasure of joining the second basses in the Bach Choir, newly founded in London by Otto Goldschmidt.

The early days of 1876 brought the added and very separate pleasures of playing the *Großes Duo* with Susan Stephenson on two pianos at Erards, and submerging himself in checking the titles of 270 motets in Bodenschatz's collections in the British Museum. But the second week of the year introduced a very different mood: his first daughter, 'christened Dorothea, after our favourite character in *Middlemarch*', was born on 13 January:

> Maudie's sufferings were too horrible for description. To see a tender, delicate beautiful creature writhing in torments such as the most ingenious cruelty of man never yet devised is the most horrible thing I ever went through. For the time at least I lost all belief in the goodness and mercy attributed to God… Oh it was awful. And moreover Maudie did not go through the very worst pain consciously. For she was under chloroform for nearly 4 hours. I don't think she could have lived through them without it…
>
> I wrote to her Ladyship the same day. And never was her singular character more clearly displayed. Instead of being pleased at Maudie's being safe, she was miserable on hearing the news. Mary said she turned quite pale, and then burst into tears. She wrote to me and said she was horribly *mortified* at not having been present. Not because she loves Maudie or to sympathise with her, but because she loves the excitement of it, and delights in retailing the horrors with unlimited exaggeration to everyone she meets…

[12] See Jeremy Dibble, *C. Hubert H. Parry: His Life and Music* (Oxford, 1992) p 126.
[13] Letter from George Grove to CHHP, 14 July 1875. Shulbrede archive.
[14] CHHP, *Diary 1875*.
[15] Dibble, *op cit*, p 127.

She was furious with me and Dr. Black for not sending for her immediately, though Maudie had told her long ago that it would kill her to have her in the room during her confinement. And when she arrived on Friday she endeavoured to get up to Maudie's room before I could stop her, her dog with his jangling bells following her half-way up the stairs before I caught them and brought them down again. The many other exasperating things which she did would fill volumes if they were set down. And through them all alike runs a vein of blind egotism. I never saw so clearly before how every action she does, even her great charities and her profuse generosity, is prompted by the lowest vanity and egotism. She seems to me utterly without heart or sympathy, or truthfulness and honesty. A creature whom only the customs of society, which she worships as her real God, keeps from any conceivable enormity.[16]

Maintaining his stand against what to him was a meaningless ritual, and in the full knowledge of the outcry which his decision would cause in both families, Hubert refused to attend Dorothea's baptism.

Although 'the baby grew strong and healthy' it was several weeks before Maude was able to rise from her bed, and Hubert was much exercised in both looking after her and in deflecting Lady Herbert from repeatedly visiting. In spite of all, he was able to complete his Piano Sonata in A major in January 1876, the slow movement of which, warmly praised by Macfarren, sings softly of a melancholy which not even the joy of a first child could banish. It is hardly surprising that Hubert, so often alone, should have enjoyed the company of admiring women and, by modern standards at least, his self-control and unshakeable loyalty to Maude might appear baffling. Temptation inevitably crossed his path more than once, and the Piano Sonata in A major was itself inspired by an especially close confidante who brightened the long reaches of Hubert's solitude during Maude's continued sickness in the first quarter of 1876:

> I also had a very sweet little Idyll which cheered my somewhat dreary and sorrowful life a great deal; and this was the friendship which grew up between Tora Gordon and me. I got to frequent the Gordons' house a good deal and went to see Irving with them, as we sympathize strongly in our admiration for him. Then Tora got engaged to Victor Marshall and my excitement on this occasion being considerable I said partly in fun that I would write a Sonata in honour of it; but fun soon became earnest and as I began the sonata I began to idealize the object of it and to make a Romance out of it; and love grew till in my heart she was only second to Maudie.[17]

The nature of the relationship between Hubert and Maude was enigmatic. There is no doubt that she was well able to sparkle when surrounded by friends, was possessed of a mischievous sense of humour, and delighted in puncturing the occasional inflated ego with a practical joke. Unfortunately, she was also her mother's daughter, and there is no doubt that Hubert's constancy was repeatedly tested by her contrariness. The description of Maude left us by Dorothea's husband, Arthur Ponsonby [Lord Ponsonby of Shulbrede], albeit

---

[16] CHHP, *Diary 1876.*
[17] *Ibid.*

written by one who knew Maude only from her middle age, is an attempt to be fair to a particularly difficult mother-in-law:

> She had been most lovely in her youth and in spite of her utter carelessness with regard to her appearance she remained a very beautiful woman with exceptional and very aristocratic charm and a delightful sense of humour. They married young and he had loved her with such intensity that whatever transformations she might have undergone that wonderful memory enforced his loyalty to her and bound his affection to her forever. Only once or twice was he sharply angry with me and that was because, in my impatience I suppose, I had been inconsiderate to her. He always took her side to the extent of believing some of her extravagant fancies. But for himself deep down unseen by any mortal eye his disillusionment which followed the early brilliance must have been poignant and the constant effort to adapt himself, seldom very successfully, to her curious caprices and her perversity must have been terribly wearing...Difficult and trying as she was in many ways she had certain unique characteristics. Her charm was unfailing, her laugh was lovely and even in her old age someone described her as 'wondrously beautiful'. She was very amusing and at different times Jack Gordon (Stanmore), Louis Mallet, Sir Harry Johnstone, Francis of Teck, and others much appreciated her exceptional form of fun. No-one less snobbish has ever been created. In her car with the Dentist's wife, the cook and manservant and child and her latest young girlfriend she enjoyed herself more than with her sister Lady Ripon or any society people whom she loathed passionately. Her clothes were beyond belief torn and bedraggled but she drove in a Rolls Royce, she saved the coals on the fire and bought very expensive bits of furniture. She argued the Free Trade case well and was a keen suffragist but would talk absolute nonsense by the hour. She was quite unaccountable. Her likes and dislikes were extreme. We discovered a Russian ancestor of hers who seems to have had precisely the same characteristics down to the impossible clothes. She hated her mother Lady Herbert [but] she adored her brothers George Pembroke and Michael Herbert...The nearer you were to her, the more difficult, unreasonable and capricious she became. The degree this reached with her husband nobody will ever know.[18]

Perhaps the snapping of maternal and sisterly bonds had left in Hubert an emotional void so agonisingly empty that he would not allow the valency between himself and Maude ever to be broken, albeit that she often made him angry and unhappy. Perhaps Maude knew that her sicknesses would only intensify Hubert's need to be protective of her in a way that he had been powerless to protect his mother and Lucy. And perhaps, too, Hubert drew continued strength from the trust which Maude, more than anyone else in his life, had invested in him. But it would be quite wrong to assume that Maude's invalidism was the result of nothing more than artful pretence.

Soon after recovering from her confinement, Maude felt sufficiently well to be taken down to Hedingham and then, at Easter, to move on to her family home. Whilst at Wilton she was taken ill, first with diphtheria and then scarlet fever, with the result that she, Hubert and Dorothea were placed in strict quarantine within the house for several weeks. Hubert, as solicitous as ever, sat with his wife for the first fortnight, dissolving boredom by reading to her constantly. Although Maude recovered from what were then the potentially lethal

---

[18] Arthur Ponsonby, *Brief Glimpses: Hubert Parry* (MS, *c.*1938). Shulbrede archive.

effects of two serious infectious fevers, her urinary tract failed to function normally for some time, suggesting that she suffered from inflammation of the kidneys (nephritis), a known complication of scarlet fever. A continuing lung infection was another legacy, and it is also possible that Maude, never robust, might have inherited a heart condition from either disease.

'When one is in prison', lamented Hubert, 'I think one likes best to be able to hear some noises of the outer world, for all that they may remind one of the joys of freedom'. Quarantine seemed to have thwarted his hopes of joining with the Bach Choir in singing 'Bach's stupendous B minor Mass, which seems to me the most colossal choral work in the world. But alas I am not destined to take part in the performance though I have been passionately set on it'.[19] But by mid-May he was able to leave Maude in the devoted care of her old governess, Pre, and to get away to London at least to *hear* the *Mass in B minor* – and was then unable to resist joining the choir for the second part of the work. Hubert stayed for two weeks with the Garretts in Gower Street, where, he wrote, 'I was never so spoilt in my life. They seem to divine all one's wants before one has thought of them oneself'.[20] The charms of Bloomsbury soon seemed to transcend absolutely the disadvantages of Kensington – as he told Maude in a letter:

> I am quite out of love with Cranley Place since I have been in this part of the world. It seems so fresh and healthy up here, I feel quite different from what I ever do there. R[hoda] and A[gnes] think it is quite natural – That S. Kensington is not healthy for itself and the bad water and drainage there make it quite poisonous. The houses here are so fine and airy and they have such jolly gardens. If we lived in Russell Square for instance we should get a grand big house with lots of room for Dorothea to play about in, a garden to itself and the biggest and I should think the best kept square in London for *less* than we pay for Cranley Place; and we should be in the middle of everything except Society and that's just what you want to avoid.[21]

At the end of a fortnight with the Garretts it was a very reluctant Hubert who transferred to Chesham Place to stay with Lady Herbert to await Maude's arrival: 'no time to do anything reasonable, no practising possible, or work of any kind. Everlasting bustle, chatter, dressing and self admiration'.[22]

When Maude did arrive, pale, very thin and obviously unwell, it was the Garrettts who took the lead in extricating her from Lady Herbert's attentions. They suggested an 'old-fashioned farmhousy kind of Hotel near the beach', close to their own seaside home at Littlehampton in Sussex, and on 12 June Hubert and Maude moved in. Maude's spirits and condition appeared to be improving, and with them Hubert's morale. 'I never saw any place suit her so well', he wrote in his diary, and at last, as well as the restorative pleasures of swimming, rowing, walking and playing with the children on the beach, he was able to turn his mind to music once again.

[19] CHHP, *Diary 1876.*
[20] *Ibid.*
[21] CHHP, letter to Lady Maude Parry, 19 May 1876. Shulbrede archive.
[22] CHHP, *Diary 1876.*

Dannreuther had obtained free tickets for Hubert to attend the *Ring of the Nibelung* cycle which, in August 1876, twenty-eight years after its first conception, was to be given in its entirety for the first time in Wagner's newly-completed theatre at Bayreuth. Hubert was to attend the second of three complete cycles, from 20 to 23 August, and, eager to learn as much as possible about the work in advance, took the scores down to Littlehampton for detailed study:

> I worked at the great Trilogy. Playing it all through more than once (which was no inconsiderable labour and which I did not finish until after I had left Littlehampton) also working all through the German with a Dictionary and reading the music to myself, so that when I came to hear it I may miss nothing. I shortly began to understand Dannreuther's enthusiasm about it; the man has grown so enormously since his earlier works I have heard of his and I miss now the occasional vulgarity and weakness which appeared to me in them. He seems entirely master of himself and his resources and capable of carrying out his great intentions without a flaw.[23]

On returning to London from Littlehampton, Hubert and Maude determined to give up the lease on their house in Cranley Place, but Maude could not be persuaded to move to Hubert's area of choice – Bedford Square – and so instead they went down to Highnam for a month prior to Hubert's departure for Bavaria.

Bayreuth was a revelation. That first encounter with the full force of Wagner's artistic vision, not only in music and libretto, but in architecture, lighting and acting style, was overwhelming. Dannreuther, who had attended the first *Ring* cycle and whom Hubert, *en route* to Bayreuth, met at Neuenmarkt going home, *had* been overwhelmed:

> He had been taken ill and felt obliged to go. He said the music and the excitement were altogether too much for him, and I can well understand it. I give up all attempts to describe my own feelings. I never was so perfectly satisfied with my life. *Rheingold*, first of all, was perfect to my mind. Then *Die Walküre* came up to my expectations, which were of the very highest. *Siegfried* I found certainly hard to understand, and I did not enjoy it so much as the others at the time, but on looking back upon it I got to enjoy it more, and the impression afterwards became very strong. As for *Götterdämmerung*, it utterly surpassed my expectations. I was in a whirl of excitement over it, and quite drunk with delight. The First Act satisfied me most with its three great climaxes piled one on another like Andes or Himalayas. Before the performance I met Otto Goldschmidt in the street, and he was rather pooh-poohy about it. After *Götterdämmerung* he came into the restaurant with a very solemn face and said, 'I suppose it must be the finest thing since *Fidelio*.[24]

The descent from Valhalla to the thankless business of house-hunting in London was a dreary one. After long searching a decision was made to purchase Lincoln House in Lower Phillimore Place – again in Kensington – but Maude's health had not improved in Hubert's absence. Dr Black was deeply concerned about her, and advised that they should return to Littlehampton for several weeks before taking possession of their new home in the middle of November.

---

23 *Ibid.*
24 *Ibid.*

The landlady was less than welcoming, expressing the hope that Hubert would not wish to play the piano as often as before; for several days the weather ranged from dismal to 'diabolic'; and much of Hubert's time was spent in taking care of his wife. But the weather and Hubert's mood lightened, Littlehampton had become 'our beloved Littlehampton', and it was with great reluctance that they set off back to London on 30 October.

Still Maude's lung refused to heal. Dr Black called in Sir William Jenner for an opinion, and he recommended that they escape to a warm climate for the winter: a cruise on the Nile would be ideal! Maude, a poor sailor, hated the idea of a long voyage, and so it was decided that they should go to Cannes instead. On 24 November they settled into their rooms at the Hôtel Paradis, where for the next five months Hubert was torn between a sense of unwanted exile and an appreciation of the beauty around him. Incessant interruptions, including the crying of Dorothea, rendered work almost impossible, and Hubert was constantly worried by Maude's condition – a worry compounded when Dorothea too fell ill. Dorothea, affectionately nicknamed 'Dolly' by her parents, had contracted croup. But even here Hubert was able to make music: he befriended a gifted young Italian violinist, Guerini, and took an active part as performer and composer in his chamber concerts.

Maude was not fit enough to travel home until 19 April 1877, and when, five days later, the family arrived back at Upper Phillimore Place it was to discover that Hubert's business affairs at Lloyd's, which he had for so long neglected, were in a critical position. McDonnell had been forced to break their partnership agreement by borrowing money, and Hubert decided that the time had come to wind up the business. His personal investment in it already amounted to £3,000, and at least half as much again was required to settle outstanding debts. It was, he wrote, 'a sad ending to the connexion between me and one of my best friends'.[25] But it was also the shedding of an impediment. He would at last be able to give his undivided attention to composition, to his lessons with Dannreuther, and to his work with and for Grove – and the year 1877 also marked one of the great musical highlights of Hubert's life: the visit to London in May of Richard Wagner.

The celebrated series of Wagner concerts at the Albert Hall were arranged in an unsuccessful attempt to recoup part of the large deficit made at the Bayreuth Festival of 1876. The musical direction of the concerts was shared by Hans Richter and Wagner himself, and during their visit Richard and Cosima Wagner were Dannreuther's guests at his home in Orme Square. It was there, on 2 May, that Hubert met the great man for the first time:

> Of his personal impressions of Wagner at their first meeting he has left no record, but it is clear from subsequent references that he was far more interested in the musician than the man. Thanks to Dannreuther he was enabled to attend many of the rehearsals, and derived as much enjoyment from them as from the actual concerts. At the rehearsal on May 4 'the hero was there in good humour: Richter conducted wonderfully and drilled the incompetents with vigour' On the following evening at Dannreuther's house

---

[25] CHHP, *Diary 1877*, Shulbrede archive.

'there was a goodly company of artist folk to see Wagner, who was in great fettle, and talked to an open-mouthed group in brilliant fashion'. Hubert Parry, who was still going on with his German lessons from Dr. Althaus[26], confesses that Wagner talked so fast that he could catch but little of what he said. He spent the whole morning at the Albert Hall on the 7th:

'Wagner's conducting is quite marvellous: he seems to transform all he touches; he knows precisely what he wants and does it to a certainty. The *Kaisermarsch* became quite new, and supremely magnificent. I was so wild with excitement after it that I did not recover all the afternoon'.[27]

Hubert, as a member of the Wagner Society committee, was given the frequent task of escorting or finding suitable escorts for Cosima Wagner, and on Sunday 13 May the lady herself, accompanied by Mrs. Dannreuther, called on the Parrys at Upper Phillimore Place:

She is certainly a very remarkable woman and was very pleasant and kind. She told us that George Eliot was with them yesterday at the performance, and seemed to enter into it very much. The poetical parts seemed to affect her especially, and she wept plentifully over the heavenly scene between Siegmund and Brünnhilde.[28]

After years of seeming indifference to music, Maude, much to Hubert's pleasure and relief, reacted enthusiastically to the music of Wagner.[29] On 18 May Hubert and Maude attended the rehearsal for a concert which included extracts from *Tristan und Isolde*:

I enjoyed them fully and so did Maudie, who is keener about Wagner's music than I ever saw her about anything except the Rights of Women. We sat with George Eliot and Madame Wagner... Wagner got into a charmingly unsophisticated rage at some of the band for beginning badly; and threw down his bâton and seized his coat and comforter and put them on (for no ostensible reason except the need to do something) and walked up and down the platform in front of the orchestra till time and the appeals of those of the orchestra more in favour had cooled him down a bit.[30]

Throughout the weeks of the Wagner concerts Hubert had worked in every spare moment that he could find, and when they were over he asked only for peace and quiet in which to re-double his efforts, but peace and quiet were hard-won commodities in Victorian London. Not only was he constantly distracted by the practising of an amateur pianist who lived next door, the noises from the street were both loud and annoying. Moving traffic generated surprisingly high volumes of penetrating noise: the clatter of iron-shod hooves and iron-rimmed wheels on hard, granite street surfaces. Barrel-organs were to be heard everywhere; the poet Coventry Patmore complained on a visit to

---

[26] Friederich Althaus, Professor of German Literature at University College, London, from 1875 till his death in 1897.

[27] Graves, *op cit,* p 177.

[28] CHHP, *Diary 1877.*

[29] Ethelinda Gambier Parry wrote to Hubert after the death of Wagner in 1883: 'We thought [Maude] seemed to take her friend Wagner's death rather quietly! but I daresay many people would say and feel, that it was better he should die whilst his genius and fame were at their height – a few more years might have found him failing in powers of mind – and consequently in popularity'. (Shulbrede archive).

[30] CHHP, *Diary 1877.*

London that there were never less than three of them playing beneath his windows: 'The incessant varying roar of carts, carriages and organs, to me, who have never lived in London, is indescribably maddening'.[31] So it was for Hubert, who, on one typical day, began work at 8.45am, was called away until 9.45am, and was then unable to escape the pounding of his neighbour's piano:

> So I practise a bit also. Stop at 11. He is still hard at work at his pet flourishes. Stop again at 12. Oh Joy! the neighbour has finished. I take my paper and pen again, write two notes only and a barrel-organ immediately begins a joyful strain in the street outside. Another start at 12.45 with half a dozen notes. My neighbour, who has evidently plenty of time at his disposal to-day begins to extemporise. 1 o'clock, luncheon, so there's an end of it for the present.[32]

Under conditions such as these Hubert was able to complete his Piano Trio in E minor, to work consistently hard at his articles for Grove's *Dictionary*, and to spare as much time as possible for Maude. A diary entry for 9 July 1877 reveals something of the tension in his life:

> Little walk with Maudie – entailing an aggravating incident, which is so typical of the annoyances of this life that I quote it. I went into a shop to buy a soft hat, and Maudie sat down to wait. The man pulled out big boxes full of hats and strewed them all over the counter for me to choose from – when suddenly Maudie gets up and says she feels faint and we had to walk straight out of the shop leaving the bewildered and astonished shopman to put all his hats back again and wonder at the strangeness of our behaviour. It wasn't her fault at all, poor little girlie, but its the sort of mischance that riles one.[33]

On the following day Hubert and Maude went down to Littlehampton by train from Victoria, Maude pregnant again:

> Maudie well propped up with cushions and leg rests… [she] bore the journey wonderfully, and seemed delighted to be back at her dear little sea side place again. She at once ate a first rate luncheon, and went out for a bit of a walk after and sat on the seats on the esplanade. It all looks much the same as before, and the renewal of dependant disturbed hotel life does not put me in the best of tempers. Had a little walk to Rustington mill.[34]

At the end of August, Maude went to stay with the Morrisons at Roehampton, while Hubert returned to London for a few days before travelling down to Highnam in time for the Three Choirs Festival at Gloucester. This was the first Festival under the direction of Charles Harford Lloyd, appointed to replace S S Wesley, who had died in the previous year, and, as usual, standards of performance varied widely, shortcomings generally resulting from wholly inadequate rehearsal. Hubert noted that a performance of Schumann's *Paradise and the Peri* was bad; that of Beethoven's *Mount of Olives* the worst he ever heard; but Bach's *St. Matthew Passion* and Brahms's *Ein Deutsches Requiem* were splendidly

---

[31] See Donald Read, *England 1868-1914* (Longman, 1975), p 63.
[32] CHHP, *Diary 1877*.
[33] *Ibid.*
[34] *Ibid.*

done, as were the traditional performances of *Messiah* and *Elijah*. It was a couple of years since Hubert had been told by Robin Benson about a rising man in the musical world, the organist of Trinity College, Cambridge, called Stanford who, Hubert noted, 'according to him must be a tip-top man'.[35] Just *how* tip-top he was able to judge for himself when Charles Villiers Stanford appeared at the Three Choirs Festival for the first time in 1877, conducting his own *Festival Overture*.

Maude remained at the Morrisons' for several more weeks, and when Hubert returned to Phillimore Place from Highnam the house was empty and cheerless. 'It is horrid this loneliness', he wrote, 'not a soul to speak to, or to look into their eyes and catch a gleam of sympathy'.[36] For the remainder of the year his priority was in work for the *Dictionary*, but he also persevered in compositional experimentation, and by 22 September had completed a striking *Concertstück* in G minor for orchestra in which the influences of Beethoven, Weber and Liszt bend, overwhelmingly, to that of Wagner.[37]

Hubert's long solitary stretches were broken by walks to Roehampton, where he would sometimes lunch with Maude, take her out in her wheel-chair for 'little walks', and have 'great games with the Morrison children who were very uproarious and nice'.[38] And following a visit from Willie Baker, who came to tell him that 'Possie & Co, were at Bayfordbury and would I go down there', he travelled down to Hertfordshire. Hubert had not seen his father for four years but found him looking just the same, back from Italy and 'smelling even stronger of tobacco'. A few weeks later Gambier Parry sent Hubert an essay by Clinton on 'Cosmic Emotion' which he had received from his eldest son, still a patient of Dr Fermè's at Stratton St Margaret:

> He does not make a word of comment in sending it to me but Clin writes to me that he had received a furious letter from Possie about it, which Clin describes metaphorically as 'foaming at the mouth'. The article is very poetical-philosophical, full of Clin's old warm-hearted breadth of feeling, but contains many allusions to advanced views of utilitarianism, biology and references to modern Philosophers, quoting them with approval; which of course raised Possie's High Church ire to a terrible degree.[39]

Hubert had continued to maintain a correspondence with Clinton throughout his elder brother's exile, receiving not only letters from him but compositions for comment and 'emendations'; he had also done his best to send comfort to Clinton's long-suffering wife. 'You are the *only one* of the family', Florence wrote to him, 'who ever writes to me in a really affectionate way, and you have always been the same to me'.[40]

At last, on 15 October, Maude and Dorothea came home. The house in Phillimore Place was now, with the assistance of the Garretts, beautifully

---

[35] CHHP, *Diary 1875*.
[36] CHHP, *Diary 1877*.
[37] See Bernard Benoliel, *Parry before Jerusalem* (Ashgate Publishing Ltd., 1997), p 55 for information on the re-discovery and preparation of a performing edition of the *Concertstück*.
[38] CHHP, *Diary 1877*.
[39] *Ibid.*
[40] Florence Parry, letter to CHHP, 25 August 1878. Shulbrede archive.

decorated, and Hubert had spent a good deal of time and effort on fitting it out comfortably, but a major problem remained. The drains had been troublesome from the outset; on 17 October they were condemned. The whole system required urgent replacement. After only two days in the house Maude and Dorothea had again to be sent away, this time to the Majendies at Hedingham:

> At present [the drainage system] is absolutely breathing poison through every vent hole in the house and it will take quite a fortnight to do and cost a lot of money. So does evil fortune always dog us... went to bed with the impression that it had been the longest day I had ever lived. Poor Maudie was very much distressed about it.[41]

Once again the Garretts came to the rescue, supervising the replacement of the drains, and on 5 November Hubert and his family were again united under their own roof. Domestic harmony was in prospect, good progress was being made on the *Dictionary* articles, even if, as on 23 November, Hubert's ideas were not always absolutely in harmony with those of Grove:

> In the afternoon to 'G' to finish our grind over the 'Form' article. First of all we went and had some oysters and porter and then some coffee at Gatti's extraordinary restaurant near the Soho Bazaar in which I had never been before, and then to work. We fought a good bit over it, and 'G' said that many sentences were so badly expressed as to be quite unintelligible to any but an expert, but in many cases, finding the ideas too tough to be expressed otherwise, had to leave them unchanged. I couldn't see what was the matter with them myself, which was unfortunate. However, we were very cheery altogether.[42]

Rather more than harmony had developed in Hubert's relationship with Dannreuther, whose admiration for him had accelerated at the same pace as Hubert's clearly discernible advance in compositional inventiveness and verve. On 11 December he writes: 'Dannreuther alarmed me a good deal by expressing a very high opinion of what I ought to do as a composer. I am afraid he will be disappointed'.[43] And two weeks later:

> At the end of my lesson he made a declaration which moved me so much that I could not make answer. He said he had been so lonely for so long, and I might be a brother to him and help him on in life and he would not let me consider myself as having lessons from him any longer, and so on. I can't write all the sweet things he said. They almost hurt me because I felt I was unworthy, and it might so wound him in future if, after having put his trust in my abilities, he found me wanting.[44]

Christmas day found Hubert more at ease with himself than for a very long time. 'In the afternoon', he wrote, 'I settled myself comfortably down with my big pipe and read from George Sand's *Malgré Tout* – which is a truly noble work'. Frank Pownall called round and sang Schubert. 'Maudie and I spent a nice bit of time together, and with a bit of reading of Palestrina in the evening we

---

[41] CHHP, *Diary 1877.*
[42] *Ibid.*
[43] *Ibid.*
[44] *Ibid.*

bring to a close the happiest Christmas Day I ever spent'.[45] And he was delighted to see that Dorothea was 'now getting to the delicious age when character really begins to show itself', a quality to be discovered by Lady Herbert two days later when they visited her at Wilton:

> Mama begins early to try to impress Dolly with the beauties of the R.C. superstitions. She marched her into Chapel and took her up to a place where there was a figure of the 'infant Jesus', expecting it to produce some devotional impression on her, but Dolly discomfited her and treated the figure with easiest familiarity saying 'there's a baby'... She said to Maudie today, 'I shall make Dolly be fond of me by giving her lots of things'.[46]

*   *   *   *   *   *   *

For Thomas Gambier Parry, 1878 was a year of two ceilings: that in the baptistery of Ely Cathedral, and the nave vault at Tewkesbury. The work at Ely, his last there, is dull and disappointing; that at Tewkesbury, a triumph of restraint. Sir George Gilbert Scott, who died in 1878, had consulted Gambier Parry when between 1868 and 1873 he had taken charge of the restoration of the choir at Gloucester Cathedral, and came to him again when employed on the choir roof at Tewkesbury Abbey. As Ernest remembered:

> Father always maintained that gold properly used was at once beautiful and effective, while if laid on in masses the very effect that was desired was at once lost. As at Gloucester, so at Tewkesbury, Scott's work has been marred by the heavy use of gold, the bosses on the groined roof, especially at Tewkesbury, being gilded all over and the beauty and their design and workmanship consequently lost. Scott's work at Tewkesbury has been generally considered as unworthy of the Abbey, and when the nave roof was to be taken in hand father was earnestly pressed to continue the decoration, as he saw fit, to the west end. The vaulting of the roof and the many precious carvings had been so overlaid in the course of ages by the constant and liberal application of lime white, that, in many instances, even the subjects of some of the carved bosses could not be made out. Father consented to take the matter in hand, and by degrees the roof was scraped, cleaned and restored. I remember father's delight from time to time at the 'finds' that were made under the countless layers of whitewash as the work progressed, and how eager he was to show these up by the application of gilding and colour. During 1878 and 1879 he was constantly backwards and forwards to Tewkesbury, often staying there a few nights at a time; and when the work was finally completed there were, I understand, no two opinions about its success, though father himself is said not to have been satisfied with it.[47]

Gambier Parry's work on the nave vault at Tewkesbury stands as testament, as Peter Burman has written, 'to Gambier Parry's sensitivity to architecture as well as to painted surfaces'; it also demonstrates, by sharp contrast, just how unfortunate it was that Gambier Parry was not called in earlier and asked to decorate the choir roof also:

---

[45] *Ibid.*
[46] *Ibid.*
[47] GPM pp 180/1.

The celebrated early fourteenth century bosses [in the nave vault] are lightly gilded so that particular aspects are emphasised (eg wings, crosses, harps, and so forth); much is left plain, and the bosses have been given a ground of a particularly satisfying red... The severies of the vault have featherty open work borders in green, again nicely understated. Too strong a decorative scheme would have caused too great a visual separation between the zone of the sensational Romanesque arcades and the zone of the richly carved vault of some two hundred years later. As it is, they are made to seem more closely integrated, a considerable achievement.[48]

*   *   *   *   *   *   *

On 6 February 1878, exactly nine months after the series of Wagner concerts in London, Maude gave birth to a second daughter, Gwendolen: a name once more chosen from a novel by the Parrys' friend and companion at those Wagner concerts, George Eliot; this time from her last book, *Daniel Deronda*. Partly, at least, for the sake of his father, and in an effort not to upset Maude, Hubert reluctantly agreed to attend the baptism, confiding in his diary none the less that: 'It really is an absurd pitch of constraint that I should not only yield to the baby's being jabbered over and splashed by a parson in the interests of "the Church" for the sake of other people's feelings, but also have to endorse his nonsense by my presence – and yet I was absolutely driven to it by the unforseen force of circumstances'.[49]

For reasons as yet to be explained, Hubert's financial situation improved markedly from about this time, and before the end of the following year he had taken the decision to build a house at Rustington. There is no hint in correspondence with his father that Gambier Parry had provided a significant sum. Could it be that Maude's family were the beneficiaries and that Hubert's presence at Gwendolen's baptism, along with the possible insistence that he reign-in his outspoken and unconventional opinions on religion, was the price demanded for their assistance? Hubert, reflecting on his thirtieth birthday on 27 February, concluded that it was 'enough to make one tender-hearted to all men who are getting on in years to think of the gradual opening of the mental eye to what life is, through which they must all have gone'?[50]

Although it might have been possible for him to maintain a discreet silence about his religious views, Hubert's attitude to politics, in spite of the fierce opposition of most of his social circle, remained uncompromisingly anti-Tory. At the end of February he took part in a pro-Government demonstration in Hyde Park at which 'the mob must have numbered many thousands and wouldn't hear a word the Liberals had to say'.[51]Maude and the two children had both been ill since Gwendolen's birth. To escape London, the Parrys went down to Wilton for Easter, but political differences with George Pembroke and his wife, Gety, and Sidney Herbert made the stay an irritating one for Hubert:

---

[48] Peter Burman, *op cit,* p 24.
[49] CHHP, *Diary 1878.* Shulbrede archive.
[50] *Ibid.*
[51] *Ibid.*

The violence with which the family… talk about Gladstone is perfectly astounding. As Eddie [Hamilton] said, it is quite indecent. According to their views everything Gladstone does is for the sake of popularity. They make out by some round-about process that the present war is owing to him. Their way of talking is so extraordinary that I can only listen with gaping mouth and answer not a word, for I simply don't know what to say to such a torrent of invective. If one attempts to say a word in his defence one is gaped at as if one were a lunatic. They cannot understand that it can be possible that a word can be said for him by an honest man.[52]

Maude went on down to Littlehampton, to be joined by Hubert in the middle of May. He had just completed his third String Quartet (inG) and for the next several weeks whilst working on a Fantasie Sonata in B major for violin and piano he divided his time between London and Littlehampton, delighted to see that, as before, Maude's condition visibly improved the longer she remained in this favourite corner of Sussex. If she could be happy there, and Hubert could find the peace and quiet so essential to his work, then surely it would be sensible to find a house in the district? After much fruitless hunting, in the middle of July a suitable place, Cudlow House at Rustington, was found and rented. To add to Hubert's pleasure, the Dannreuthers were holidaying at Littlehampton: a spur to embarking upon a detailed study of *Tristan und Isolde* and, in contrast, revisiting the keyboard music of Bach: a fitting prelude to the composition of his Theme and Nineteen Variations in D minor for piano. Rustington, 'dear little Rusty', had begun to work its magic. Swimming, tennis, excursions with friends to Highdown Hill, Leominster water meadows and Arundel Park; searches for botanical specimens; blackberrying and mushroom-hunting.

The bliss of Rustington coincided exactly with, and was clearly contributory to, a peak in Hubert's creative development. During that summer at Cudlow House, as well as the Theme and Nineteen Variations, he worked at a Fantasia and Fugue in G major for organ, begun in the previous year, and scored an Overture entitled *Guillem de Cabestanh,* inspired by Franz Hueffer's *The Troubadours,* which was subsequently performed at the Crystal Palace; completed the outline for his Piano Concerto in F sharp minor, and, most significantly, began to sketch a Piano Quartet in A flat. He was also deeply absorbed in reading, as always, a wide variety of literature, including Darwin's *Descent of Man,* Tennyson's *Harold,* Swinburne's *Songs before Sunrise,* and – lighting a shining beacon in his mind – Shelley's *Prometheus Unbound.*

The artist William Blake Richmond, who had first met Hubert at Oxford in 1869, was among the many friends who would become regular visitors to the Parrys in Sussex in the coming years. Richmond regularly spent the summer with his family in Littlehampton or with Hubert and Maude at Rustington. In London, Hubert and Richmond were often in each others' company, sharing both intellectual interests – Richmond was a fine amateur musician as well as an artist

---

[52] *Ibid.*

of great distinction – and more leisurely pursuits, such as when, in the harsh winter of 1871, the two had delighted in skating together on the frozen surface of the Thames. In 1874 Richmond had completed a large mythological painting for exhibition at the Royal Academy, *Prometheus Bound*, a work received very favourably by the critics, the *Athenaeum* considering it 'an exceptional work in every respect'.[53] No doubt Hubert had seen the painting, and may well have discussed it with Richmond, continuing to turn over in his mind the idea of a composition based on a Promethean theme, but setting it aside until his technique was worthy of the subject.

In the Greek myth Prometheus is chained to a rock for his defiance of Zeus, symbol of evil and intolerance, but the two are eventually reconciled. The Greek tragedy of Aeschylus, of which only the first part survives, is based upon this myth; But Shelley, in his four-act drama of 1820, substitutes the Latin Jupiter for the Greek Zeus, and rejects the notion of a reconciliation between Prometheus and his tormentor. In Shelley's interpretation of the myth, Jupiter is overthrown; Prometheus is unchained by Hercules, the embodiment of strength; love emerges supreme; powers and principalities, gods and prisons fade into the past, and all mankind rejoices in equality and freedom. The twilight of these gods parallels that of Wotan and his retinue in the epic *Ring* cycle, and, as myth, its theme could empower Hubert, as it had Wagner, to break free from the limitations of history. It presents a vision entirely in accord with Hubert's own liberal and humanitarian principles, and it could hardly have failed to inspire him.

Returning to Phillimore Place in December 1878, Hubert continued to immerse himself in the flood of composition which had begun in Sussex. Setting aside the sketches for the Piano Concerto, and in spite of the constant aggravations of street bands, organ-grinders and the noisy next-door neighbour, he was soon totally absorbed in the Piano Quartet in A flat. It was to be a turning point, the crowning achievement of Hubert's early association with Dannreuther, and his finest contribution to the chamber genre. The myriad of teutonic influences which had for so long mingled in the crucible of Hubert's creative imagination were at last successfully fused with a wholly personal ore – and the resultant ingot bore an English hallmark.

Dannreuther was delighted with the Piano Quartet, especially the outstanding Scherzo, and included it in a recital at Orme Square on 13 February 1879. Writing of the rehearsal on 11 February, Hubert allowed himself an uncharacteristic burst of real enthusiasm about his own work:

> Of course it gave them [the performers] a great deal of trouble, but they seemed much pleased with it. And with this expression of approval I was utterly happy. I was strangely intoxicated with much of it myself and astonished at the tone and richness which appeared. One thing pleased me especially. The effect of the Scherzo had been doubtful before. But this time it went, and Dann, at the end turned quickly to the others and said loudly, 'Superbe Satz'. The slow movement they expressed emphatically 'magnifique',

---

[53] See Simon Reynolds, *William Blake Richmond, An Artist's Life, 1842-1921* (Michael Russell Publishing Ltd., 1995), pp 106/7.

'ganz himmlisch' and so I was wild with delight. The end of the last movement went like mad.[54]

The Piano Quartet was heard by a larger audience in a concert given at Arthur Balfour's house in Carlton Gardens on 1 April, in which the programme consisted entirely of Hubert's works. The critic of the *Pall Mall Gazette* was both enthusiastic and perceptive:

> The compositions of Mr. C. Hubert Parry, who is already known to the public by a recent performance of his overture, *Guillem de Cabestanh, Troubadour*, at the Crystal Palace, have been from time to time heard in the Musical Evenings given by Mr. Dannreuther at his house in Orme Square. The favourable impression they created has led to a performance being given, of Mr. Parry's compositions only, at the house of Mr. Balfour, M.P., in Carlton Gardens, where a large audience was invited to hear them – an experiment that would prove fatal to anything short of real power of composition, demanding three hours' continuous attention to the works of one composer... In Mr. Parry's works we have the inspiration of a composer supported by the learning of an earnest and eclectic student who is no less at home in Bach than in Wagner. 'In polyphonous treatment', says a writer who has made a careful study of Mr. Parry's compositions, 'and continuousness in his thematic work, avoiding formal cadences, he ranges himself with the most recent school of composition; breaking away entirely from English ideas, which, submitted to the influence of Mendelssohn, have not dared or cared to look beyond the limits that master may be said to have defined... This performance has taken him out of the category of mere amateurs, and future public opportunities will no doubt enable us to recur to his works and criticize them from the only possible standpoint... on the real merits they display as music appertaining to the English school, in which Mr. Parry promises to take a leading place.[55]

The performance of *Guillem de Cabestanh* on 15 March had gone badly, 'a complete fiasco' in Hubert's estimation, and so the enthusiastic response to the Carlton House concert was doubly gratifying. Even so, there were many to complain of the influence of Wagner on his music: an influence seen as pernicious by those rooted in past traditions:

> He declares that he does *not* write 'ill-considered reflections of Wagner', and though he feels the impress of Wagner's warmth and genius strongly, is 'not tempted to tread in the same path in regard to construction, because what is applicable to the province of *dramatic* music is entirely alien to *instrumental* music.[56]

Dramatic music such as might be appropriate for *Prometheus Unbound* perhaps?

At precisely the moment in which Hubert seemed poised for artistic success, his elder brother began a final descent into the abyss. On 1 May Hubert met Clinton in London. He was horrified by what he found:

> His humours alternated between violence and swearing and crying, extravagant demonstrations of affection for me, and collapse. When I got him to Phillimore Place

[54] CHHP, *Diary 1879*. Shulbrede archive.
[55] *Pall Mall Gazette*, 12 April 1879.
[56] Graves, *op cit*, p 201.

I found I could not manage him. He was perfectly wild for more drink and my only chance seemed to get him down to Swindon [*to Dr Femè's clinic at nearby Stratton St Margaret*]. I had to hold him always as he seized every opportunity to try and get after more drink. Altogether he was a piteous and sickening spectacle.[57]

On 8 September 1879, under the care of his brother-in-law, Claude Hinde, Clinton was committed to an asylum at Ilfracombe: the same small Devon village to which, as an eleven-year-old boy, he had sailed by steamer from Bristol, summoned to join his doting father on honeymoon with the unfamiliar woman who had taken his mother's place. How changed were the circumstances now, twenty-three years later. 'Claude Hinde is the only person who seems to have any power with him', Gambier Parry told Hubert, 'As far as I can judge from very slight acquaintance and from what he does, C.H. must be an excellent fellow'.[58] Clinton's marriage was now at an end. He had shown such violence and brutality to Florence that any idea of reconciliation was out of the question, and in agreeing to accompany Claude Hinde he also promised not to attempt to visit her at Tunbridge. But Clinton refused to stay in Ilfracombe for more than a few months; his future was as unsure as ever.

*   *   *   *   *   *   *

Gambier Parry, his work at Tewkesbury finished, set out in 1879 on one last continental tour, visiting Annecy and Aix-les-Bains. Hubert and Maude returned to Rustington for the summer, and there in the first week of August, happily undisturbed, and in spite of 'excruciating trouble'[59] with the structure of the flowingly lyrical slow movement, Hubert completed the scoring of his Piano Concerto. Dannreuther pronounced it Hubert's finest work to date, and the anti-Wagnerian August Manns, who had condemned the overture *Guillem Castebanh* as 'a downright bad piece of music from sheer want of proper self-criticism on his part', agreed to conduct the concerto at the Crystal Palace in April 1880.

In 1879, too, the first volume of Grove's *Dictionary of Music and Musicians* was published, bringing the work of Hubert Parry to the musical world at large, but as writer, not composer. Hubert's articles explained the formal and technical aspects of music with rare clarity, and remain as models of lucidity and accessibility. At least one aspiring composer, as yet unknown beyond his native Worcestershire, found everything in the new *Dictionary* of enormous value and interest; but, wrote Edward Elgar later, 'the articles which have helped me most are those by Hubert Parry...'.[60]

Early in November Hubert started work on a Cello Sonata, which Dannreuther had agreed to include in one of his Orme Square recitals in February 1880. December brought ice to the big pond near Angmering – and

[57] CHHP, *Diary 1879*.
[58] TGP, letter to CHHP, [?] 1879. Shulbrede archive.
[59] CHHP, *Diary 1879*.
[60] *The Strand Magazine*, May 1904, p 539.

with it the delights of skating. In spite of the severe winter, Hubert continued bathing in the sea until 19 December, a day upon which he also skated! And two days later, he and a neighbour, Colonel Matthew, 'went out in the afternoon… to look at some land with a view to building'.[61] 1880 promised to be a busy year: not only was there a house to be built, but Hubert had also received an invitation from Charles Harford Lloyd at Gloucester to compose a major choral work for the Three Choirs Festival in the following September.

The prospect of two such major undertakings brought a recurrence of Hubert's old heart trouble. The problem, he wrote, was 'an extraordinarily irregular action of the heart which hardly gave me an hour's peace. During the fits work was impossible, as it was almost unendurable except by walking rapidly round the room'.[62] These palpitations were a manifestation to the sufferer that he was driving his restless, creative self too hard. But his doctor's advice to rest failed entirely to restrain Hubert now or throughout his life from a self-imposed regime of physical and mental exertion.

The first performance of the Piano Concerto, given at the Crystal Palace on 3 April under the direction of August Manns and with Dannreuther as soloist, was successful enough, albeit that it was received without much enthusiasm by the audience, added to which Manns was a little grumpy about the difficulty of presenting his orchestra with the complex key of F sharp major! Happily, Richter agreed to include the Concerto in a concert which he was to conduct on 10 May, after which Hubert received two hugely encouraging letters, one from Frederick Corder:

> I must write and thank you… for demonstrating in your Concerto (I must consider last night as its *first* performance) that there are English composers who can write. I was impressed by the slow movement even at the Palace, and a proper rendering makes it perfectly charming. The last movement has great 'go', but if I may venture to find fault, the cadenza is a little long, though you have so much to bring into it that I'm sure I don't see how you could shorten it.[63]

The other letter was from Hubert's father who, for the first time, had travelled to London to hear a performance of his son's music:

> I write to congratulate you on your success last night. Write and tell me by and by whose the best and truest critique is… I was delighted with it all… though I confess to be old fashioned enough to long for more of the pathos and loving restful beauty than the deep mysterious intellect of the advanced school condescends to allow. It is grand, glorious, emotional, passionate – and sweeps on with a flood of mingled meanings, which I find it difficult to interpret. I want none of the sensuous melodies of the Italian opera – nor old fashioned 'tuny' music – but I feel a want of something to leave some form and feature, some clearly drawn effect even if it be of colour only, like those a painter lingers on in external nature, which have form enough in all their indefiniteness of beauty to leave a clear image on the memory – something that one can rest upon and love. There seems to me so much of unsettlement of heart in modern art. All this I have no intention to apply to your concerto – but generally to the advanced ideal of the day.

---

[61] CHHP, *Diary 1879.*
[62] CHHP, *Diary 1880.* Shulbrede archive.
[63] Letter from Frederick Corder to CHHP, 11 May 1880. Shulbrede archive.

In short, it is time for me to be snuffed out! I have gone very far with the art of modern times in thorough appreciation if not in thorough understanding – but while I love its dreaminess and mystery I feel that it has lost outline. I have no sympathy with its restlessness and vague humour of discontent. I want less devil and more angel in it – and without any loss of mystic power and passionate emotion. I want more of the poetry of frankness, confidence, purity and peace.

'Then, my dear old father', you will say, 'I think you had better shut up' – So I do. God bless, enlighten, draw and prosper you and yours, you dear boy! I glory in your grand and beautiful talent – and hope you will remember in all your future works the needs and cravings of poor human hearts as much at least as the demands of the intellect, and thus win in them *both* the noble place which your genius and accomplishment deserve.[64]

Such warmth and acknowledgement of his gifts, after so many years of antagonism to any idea of his finding a career in music, can hardly have failed to move Hubert; nor would he have been surprised by his father's resistance to 'the new music'. But there was more behind Gambier Parry's approval of his son than the understandable satisfaction of witnessing the realisation of his potential as a composer. The 'noble place' which Hubert's accomplishment deserved was in large measure due to his having proved that it *was* possible to be taken seriously as a composer, to earn money from his art, and yet to continue to enjoy the reputation of a gentleman. For the first time in class-conscious Victorian society, the role of professional composer was seen as socially acceptable. Gambier Parry knew this now but could never have conceived of such an outcome at an earlier time, when, fearful of social consequences, he had forbidden Clinton and discouraged Hubert from answering Euterpe's call.

And what of Clinton now? What of his standing in society? Claude Hinde had failed to persuade him to stay in Devon, and, to ensure that Florence and the children remained unmolested, it was decided that he must again be sent to the colonies. Like the Flying Dutchman, doomed to travel endlessly, Clinton was put aboard the *SS Crusader* on 29 June, bound for New Zealand. Hubert was at the quayside to see his brother off: a deeply emotional interlude in the midst of his work on *Prometheus Unbound* for Gloucester.

Dannreuther had, from their first discussion about it on 29 February, shared Hubert's enthusiasm for a 'Dramatic Cantata' based upon Shelley's *Prometheus Unbound,* an epic drama described by George Bernard Shaw as 'an English attempt at a Ring'.[65] A scheme in five scenes was decided upon, and as each scene was completed Hubert sent it to Dannreuther for comment. All went well – very well – until the end of June, Clinton's departure, and the last chorus approached. With too little time remaining to make changes, Hubert, to his dismay, recognised that the last chorus was 'an utter hodgepodge of jumpy and unassimilable sections':

I had not realised the general effect in totality before and it came upon me suddenly. There is nothing to be done now as there is no time to rewrite it, but to face it and

[64] TGP, letter to CHHP, 11 May 1880. Shulbrede archive.
[65] G B Shaw, *The Perfect Wagnerite* (London, 1898), p 230.

despair. It appears to be the fault of having taken such a helterskelter of disconnected choice songs which nothing can even make into a continuous musical whole – as far as I can see at the present. It is heartbreaking after such a persistent and heavy grind as I have had.[66]

Even the reassurance of Dannreuther failed to dispel Hubert's gloom, and his mood of despair was only intensified when by 28 August, as he wrote to Dannreuther, he had 'only one set of fiddle parts up to the end of the Jupiter and Demogorgon scene and wind parts to match', and they were 'cram full of mistakes'.[67] He would not now see the remainder of the parts until he got to Gloucester in the week before the Festival itself – and when they did arrive, they too were full of mistakes. Hubert knew that he would be allowed only one preliminary rehearsal with the Festival Chorus, on the Thursday, before the full rehearsal with orchestra on the following Monday, 6 September: the day before the opening of the Festival, always grimly known as 'Black Monday', the day into which rehearsal of every work had to be crammed. Nothing augered well.

In 1869 Otto Goldschmidt, still smarting from the failure two years earlier at Three Choirs of his oratorio *Ruth*, a disaster which he attributed to insufficient rehearsal, had written a cautionary note to Arthur Sullivan, who was to conduct *The Prodigal Son* at Worcester that year:

> In the case of Hereford two years ago, the chorus – numbering about 160 – came from Hereford, Worcester, Gloucester, Bristol, Bradford [and] London. They had not come together until the general rehearsal [for both choir and orchestra] in the Cathedral on the Monday. Your choruses may be so well written and easy that this single hasty rehearsal is sufficient. As a rule I should say it was not. Certainly it did not prove so in my case. I had again asked for one joint rehearsal, but the answer was that it was impossible… Experience, however, has shown me that though the chorus may not be able to meet collectively before the Monday noon, they *can* meet after, *viz*. in the evening of that day… You will know how to profit by this friendly hint.[68]

Facing a similar situation, but with a far more complex work than either Goldschmidt or Sullivan could have conceived, Hubert faced Black Monday with foreboding. 'The rehearsal of *Prometheus* in the evening… was literally agonizing', he wrote. 'Not time to do much more than go through it. Everything at sixes and sevens and chorus literally bewildered. Everbody tired with rehearsing other things all day, and general misery all round'.[69] The members of the chorus, two hundred and fifty strong, were drawn from London, Huddersfield, Oxford and Bristol, as well as Gloucester, Hereford and Worcester. What Hubert did not know was that the Huddersfield contingent, who were unlikely to have been present at the chorus rehearsal on the previous Thursday, would volunteer to rehearse again on the Tuesday morning, the day of the performance. Their Yorkshire pride and determination to give of their best saved *Prometheus* from an embarrassing collapse.

---

[66] CHHP, *Diary 1880*.
[67] CHHP, letter to Dannreuther, 28 August 1880. Shulbrede archive.
[68] Arthur Jacobs, *Arthur Sullivan, A Victorian Musician* (Oxford, 1984).
[69] CHHP, *Diary 1880*.

Whatever the musical quality of Hubert's work, there was never any question that *Prometheus Unbound* would receive its first performance in Gloucester Cathedral. At a time when the Dean and Chapter would tolerate only works set to biblical or liturgical texts, so powerful an expression of humanitarian ideology would most certainly not have been permitted to cross the threshold of the cathedral. Instead, *Prometheus* was heard at a secular evening concert in the city's Shire Hall. The programme began with Beethoven's *Fidelio* Overture, followed by four arias by Mozart, Gluck and Gounod, and then came *Prometheus*, conducted by Hubert himself. After the interval, a long evening continued with a Mozart symphony, several more arias, and Gounod's Jupiter Festival March from *Polyeucte*.

Players, singers and audience were all weary. They had performed or listened to *Elijah* in the afternoon; the parts were peppered with mistakes and difficult to read in the dim gaslight; Frank Pownall, singing the title rôle, was out of his depth; but thanks to the Huddersfield chorus and the magnificent singing of Anna Williams and Edward Lloyd, the performance held together, and it was with a considerable degree of pleasure that Hubert was able to write to Dannreuther:

> I am very glad you did not take the long journey here on your own account, though I should on my own part have felt much more happy for your presence. The rehearsal at Gloucester exceeded my worst expectations, and we were so driven for time that in most cases we could only go straight through and call attention to mistakes in the execution and trust to 'Provy' for their being rectified at the performance... The band was more obliging [than the chorus] but very rough, and after the rehearsal and all next day I felt utterly hopeless. It was very hard on them. I think my rehearsal came on after they had been rehearsing for seven or eight hours in the Cathedral; and though they all tried their best it was as much as they could do to keep their attention to it. However, next day after the performance of the *Elijah* a large contingent of the chorus which came from Huddersfield got together of their own free will and had a private rehearsal under their own Chorus Master without telling me till just before the performance, and the result was astonishing. The first Chorus went admirably, and the constant crescendo up to the *ff* sounded all I could wish. But still more astonishing was the Fury Chorus. Almost directly they started I felt we were quite safe and went ahead without hesitation; and though it was pretty rough, it had lots of go and sounded furious, and there was no question for a moment of coming to grief. Some of the Spirit Chorus sounded better than I expected, but I was very much put out with the Confusion at the end... Anna's [Anna Williams's] was the best thing of the evening and I think sounded almost best in the band of anything in the whole. The only terrible grief was in Jupiter's scene... I felt woeful and disheartened. But Anna sang so superbly that she put me in heart again and I got 'my pecker up'... The last part went like mad and made a most exciting row. Edward Lloyd behaved angelically and was most kind and generous to me about it. All the first part of his scene went admirably and he sang it splendidly.[70]

The critics took up positions which ranged from the generously defensive to the pointedly hostile, anti-Wagnerians expressing the most antagonistic views. Not that Wagner was the sole influence in Hubert's realisation of *Prometheus*.

---

[70] CHHP, letter to Edward Dannreuther, 11 September, 1880. Bodleian Library, Oxford, MS Eng. Letters e.117.

Conscious of the tastes of a Three Choirs audience never weary of *Messiah* and *Elijah*, Hubert absorbed Handelian and Mendelssohnian strands into the work, and, surprisingly, contrived that Wagner should share the same table as his polar opposite, Brahms.

This very diversity of influences, the lack of a unifying personal imprint, and the resultant unevenness of *Prometheus* as a whole, rule out the probability of its succeeding to enter the regular choral repertory today. But this is to look back with the benefit of hindsight to a time before Elgar, Vaughan Williams, Holst, Finzi and Howells. Hubert Parry, who inspired all of these, was striding into an arena peopled by the likes of Barnby, Cusins, Barnett, Armes and Caldicott: dullness personified. *Prometheus* contains much that is exciting, animated and involving; it has, as the violinist Prosper Sainton put it, the *'étincelle électrique'*,[71] a refreshing quality described by Ernest Walker as 'instinct with a sort of youthful and yet deep emotional thrill';[72] and it was Ernest Walker, too, who asserted that 'if we seek for a definite birthday for modern English music, September 7, 1880, when *Prometheus* saw the light at Gloucester and met with a distinctly mixed reception, has undoubtedly the best claim'.[73]

---

[71] See Dibble, *op cit*, p 194.
[72] Ernest Walker, *A History of Music in England* (Oxford, 1924), p 300.
[73] *Ibid.*

XII

The Last Angel

On his return to Rustington from Gloucester, Hubert was preoccupied with progress on the new house, showing as much concern for the welfare of the building workers as for the quality of their work. Fortunately, the quality was sufficient for the structure to withstand the near-typhoon gales of November 1880, and as calm returned he gained pleasure in watching the steady rise of a place which, for the first time in his life, he could call absolutely his own. Additional pleasures came with the delivery of a new telescope and the excitement of peering into the heavens:

> I first got a good view of Jupiter and saw his cloud belts clearly. Then to Saturn and was beside myself at the sight of him. It appears at first sight to me as the very strangest thing in the universe. I went on looking again and again with a sort of feeling of amazement akin to the feeling one has when some one tells a thing beyond the range of experience. Then I took a look at Sirius which blazes and sinks and blazes again. Then at the great nebula in Orion, which amazed me almost as much as Saturn. Four such sights were enough for one evening, and I went to bed thereupon.[1]

In the previous month Novello had accepted *Prometheus* for publication. Hubert set about making very necessary revisions, but even after publication would continue to have further thoughts about the work: there are a number of pencilled amendments in his own copy of the printed vocal score.[2] He was also working on articles for Grove's *Dictionary* and for the *Saturday Review*, and at the end of November was at the Crystal Palace to hear the First Symphony of Brahms. For up to two years Hubert had considered attempting a symphony of his own but had set the idea aside; but at last, on 23 December, he began work on the first movement of a Symphony in G, dedicated to Maude.

The first weeks of 1881 brought sub-zero temperatures, skating, and, on 18 January, snow-drifts up to nine feet deep to fill the Rustington lanes and force

---

[1] CHHP, *Diary 1880*.
[2] Highnam archive.

Hubert on to the roof of his rented house with shovel in hand. Far away in New Zealand, Clinton, trying to make his way on Fred Williams's sheep-station at Kukutua, Wanganuï, faced a far more terrifying face of nature On 21 January he wrote to his to his brother:

My dearest Hubert   'Eben! fugaces Posthume, Posthume,
                                'years glide away and are lost to me, lost to me',
'Nec pietas moram, virgis et instanti senecta, Afferet… Non si trecenis…'[3]
nor were I to kill 300 of Williams' sheep daily (to paraphrase Horace) should I stay resistless Time; which like the irresistable river Wanganuï (in front of my window), forces its way towards the Pacific of Eternity, with a mighty impetuosity!!!! Which being interpreted means that I have just been thinking that I have been nigh 7 months away from England, am well into 3rd week of 1881, and past the Rubicon of 40 which event occurred off Kerguelan Island on board the 'Crusader'.

Here am I now on Williams' sheep-station, in the land of gorges, forests, volcanoes, and *earthquakes*! We have had two of the latter since I have been here. The first was while we sat at luncheon, but though one felt the direction of the earthwave, N to S, it looked on the sunny grass like a sudden breeze passing. The second. Ah! I had been out early chopping wood for the days consumption – Fred Williams was away and I was entirely solus. I had got very hot, and before cooking my breakfast at 8 am had determined on a big wash – engaged on this I suddenly heard and felt what at the moment I *really* believed to be one of our big bulls in the kitchen. At that moment my window burst open, – crash, crash, two panes of glass went, the whole room rocked, the wooden house creaked and groaned – 'Earthquake, by Heaven!' I shouted to myself, and slipping on a pair of trousers dashed into the verandah. Yes, there it was, the dull, hideous, subterraneous roar, the perceptible shaking of everything in sight at intervals of about 5 minutes. When all was still again, and the dull roar had faded away Pacific-wards, I returned to the house – I caught sight of my face in the glass – I *was as white as a sheet*. Yes – the mighty monster that lies under Tongariro was turning in his sleep. Did Poss send you my letter about my expedition to the Murumutu plains, through the Mangamaho forest? That was an affair to be remembered through life. The plains, about 50 miles in diameter, are encircled by a ring of about 30,000 square miles of well-nigh impenetrable forest, for there are only 3 horse tracks at intervals of about 50 miles. The rest is just about impossible. The plains are fertile, but no one hardly lives there because of the remoteness and difficulty of access. I saw the wife of the man I went to there, who was a Gloucestershire (Stroud) girl, who told me she had seen no other lady for 3Ω years, since she had married Hazelden and come there.

The scenery of course is grand, but you cannot live upon grand scenery. Man, *and especially woman*, is gregarious – requires sympathy. At the end of the plain stands the volcano Togariro and his brother Ruapehu. Fancy – 2,000 feet of forest at base, to 8,000 feet of snow above!!!! (The snow-line of the Southern Hemisphere is for no reason yet accounted for lower than in the Northern Hemisphere).

How glad I am that for 10 years I have been an early riser (after having in my younger days been such a sluggard). What recollections I have of lovely summer morning walks between 5-6 a.m. in England. And of numberless winter mornings in

---

[3]   Alas, Postumus, Postumus
        The fleeting years glide by nor will piety
        bring delay to wrinkles and advancing old age
        and unconquerable death -
        no, not if with three hundred bulls [*i.e. three hecatombs of bulls*] each day that passes you
        should essay to appease the tearless Pluto.

        (Horace, *Odes 2. 14*)

Wiltshire or Devon – hard frost, when the high road rings beneath one's iron-shod boots, while yet the stars seem to twinkle 'with a crystalline delight' – ere yet the blood-red winter sun peers over the bare downs. Recently I kept a register for one month of the time I rose. I found at the end, that I had never once been in bed after 5 a.m. Do you remember Jean Ingelow's pretty 'For me the freshness of the morning hours' *etc.*, or better still Theophile le Viault (*temp.* our James 1st and Charles)

> '*Tout le plaisir des jours est en leurs matinées*
> *La nuit est déjà proche à qui passe midi.*'

All this preamble is to prepare you for what I saw one morning on the 'Plains'. The Hazeldens had fixed up a little tent for me, as their house was so small. I rose one morning at 4.30. The time was near midsummer at the end of November. I opened the fly of the tent and stood barefoot on the dewy grass. There I saw the ink-black plains of Murumutu; there I saw the 2,000 feet of ink-black forest at the base, and there *a crimson cone of 8,000 feet of snow,* where topmost Ruapehu 'stood up and met the morning' – a crimson cone cleaving a cloudless sky of apple green. I stood, and shook, and trembled with delight, and the tears came into my eyes. Well were it worth the 100 miles of river-crossing, of forest-wandering, of being without food for 29 hours, of sleeping in the rain all night, lost, – for one half-hour of such a noble sight as this. It is stamped deep in my brain, in my heart, never to be effaced.

While on the 'Plains' I was initiated into the mysteries of the Stock-driving craft; it is hard exercise and hard work, often dangerous work, for the cattle are mostly wild, particularly the bulls, which charge. Next to Gnu hunting in Africa as I had it in the *Oranje Vrij Staat* it stands as exciting fun. I stayed at Hazelden's but a short time. (Unfortunately for me who, for certain reasons, was much disappointed).

Upon my return to Wanganuï (NB There is a river, a district and a little wooden built town all Wanganuï) I heard of Fred. Williams, and came to his sheep run to help him and live here for a time. I have been here going on for 3 months. When we are together we are lonely, but as he does a great deal in buying and selling cattle miles away I am frequently left utterly alone for 2, 3, or 4 days a week, even 5 I have been. Then, as we have never kept any servant till we got a German boy of tender years ten days ago, we have of course to do everything for ourselves. I declare it takes me sometimes an hour and a half to get my lonely dinner; to chop the wood, light the fire, boil the kettle, peel the 'tatoes, cook the meat, lay the cloth, *etc., etc.* And what weary work it is when you come home at evening after having been in the saddle all the blazing hot day; to have to do this. You may think it fun – Try it for a few months, when you *must* do it, weary or not weary, if you want some food…

It so happened that on Friday afternoon 31st December '80 Williams went away many miles to see some friends, and left me till Monday evening January 3rd. 1881 (evening of the day of the earthquake). That anticlinal axis, so to speak of 1880-81 *was* lonely. I took an hour or so cooking myself an especially good tea to cheer myself up. I killed a fowl and curried it, I fried eggs and potatoes, and got some beans and peas, and boiled myself, (for we *boil* tea here, our only beverage) a strong cup of tea, and afterwards took a rocking chair and pipe into the verandah, and watched the summer sun fade out its crimson glories Pacific-wards. The hills across the Wanganuï were blue-black against the sunset… As Goethe says in his introduction to Faust, 'The images of the days that have passed away, and many well-loved shadows arise around me'. Sad ghosts of wasted opportunities – melancholy memories of utterly mis-used time – misdirected, wasted energies of years – unintentional unkindnesses and pain-causing thoughtlessness and selfishness with regard to others. As the moon came out, and one great star, I thought of Floëy, the boys, Lillie, and dear impulsive affectionate Blue [Florence, Lilian and Isabel]. Then Possie's dear, noble face – Highnam, the woods, Muz [Ethelinda], the sisters – I scarcely care to confess my cheeks were wet with tears. I could not sleep, but wandered about the empty, deserted house and into the verandah and watched the stars till they paled before the new born dawn, and went out one-by-one. Such was my anticlinal axis of 1880-81. Sad enough you'll say. Aye – scarcely to be borne.

Yet I think in many ways this everlasting having to do everything for yourself, from catching your horse on the run if you want him, through cooking, down to sweeping your own room, and blacking your own boots and cleaning your own bridle, *etc., etc., etc.* is a kind of tonic. And it *is* wonderful considering the life I have led, that at 40 I sleep so well, digest anything, and feel so elastic, cheery, strong, and what is more wonderful *young*. In some sunny valley here alone, the haunt of the bee and the grasshopper, I sometimes whirl my arms about and shout to the solitude 'How fair is this bright world,
Thank God that I'm alive!!!' (Alex. Smith).

I think if I return alive to England – please God in August next – I shall be very different in many ways – I know this for certain, that I am utterly different from what I was in Africa. I should not wonder if it were true what a Lady in England said of me one day last year *'You'll make a most charming old man'*. Anyhow I have gained in self-mastery and self-reliance here, even in these few months. But at times the longing, the intense longing for home is well-nigh overwhelming. 16,000 miles of stormy sea, across the 'broad back of the sea' [*this phrase is written in Greek*]...

I had such an enthusiastic letter about you from a Lady who went to hear your Prometheus. How I glory in your triumphs. Don't your ears ever burn? She thought your music so glorious, and you so graceful and handsome. Poss appears to have held a plate somewhere, for she mentions it, and says 'I looked hard into his eyes, but he could not know that one of his son's greatest friends was there'. I have written to our beloved Poss to advance me money to return. I don't think he can refuse – In fact I deserve it.[4]

It is not difficult to read between the lines, and whilst it is startling to find that so erudite a letter should have come from the pen of a man brutalised by drink, it is also clear that Clinton was just as much adrift as ever. It needs little imagination to visualise the 'certain reasons' which prompted the isolated Hazeldens to send him away from them, and can it be possible that *tea* was the only beverage to pass Clinton's lips in Wanganuï? The money to return was refused and the drift continued. On 27 September Gambier Parry wrote to Hubert to tell him of a letter which he had received from Clinton:

giving much detail of the way he had been going about in all directions, with perpetual disappointment about getting occupation. He describes the colony in a state of economical panic, with heavy debt – and hundreds of men discharged from every sort of public or government work and office. So in despair he is off to Australia.[5]

Throughout that summer Hubert's main preoccupation had been with the completion of work on the new house, which he and Maude had decided to call 'Knight's Croft' after the name of the piece of ground upon which it had been built. Problems of detail, both large and small, had been legion, and Maude's health had been particularly worrying throughout. Inevitably, the Garrets had been called upon to advise on furnishings and décor. At last, on 22 July, they had moved in and celebrated with a party for the forty-six workmen

[4] Clinton Parry, letter to CHHP, 21 January 1881. Shulbrede archive.
[5] TGP, letter to CHHP, 27 September 1881. Shulbrede archive.

who had laboured to realise their dream. When the door finally closed behind this small army and quietness descended Hubert 'felt quite woeful and fit to cry at parting from them':

> We have been such good friends all through, and they have done their work so well, so readily and patiently, and I shall never see any of them in such congenial circumstances again. I felt too depressed to do anything after they were gone.[6]

A quite different mood had lightened the spring and early summer. On 26 April there had been a great family gathering in London for Ernest's marriage to Evelyn Palk, the younger daughter of Baron Haldon of Exeter, at St. Paul's, Knightsbridge; and, to Hubert's great pleasure, Stanford had agreed to conduct *Prometheus* at Cambridge in the following month. Hubert had gone over for rehearsals a couple of times in the previous January, and was absolutely delighted by the performance on 17 May, which quite dispelled the painful memory of some of the more woeful aspects of the Gloucester première:

> People seemed much pleased, and (what pleased me most) especially my friends, who were there pretty numerously, such as 'G' [Grove], and Eddie [Hamilton] and Spencer Lyttelton, *etc.* Stanford all along was marvellously kind and genial. He has the Irishman's characteristic sweetness in companionship and is evidently worshipped almost universally at Cambridge; as it seems with good reason.[7]

Hubert's joy flowed over in a letter to Eddie Hamilton, who had ensured that Maude knew of her husband's triumph: 'It was a performance indeed! I never hope to hear anything finer than Anna Williams or King in their respective parts. And how the band did play! and the Chorus sing! And everybody was so overwhelmingly kind, and you most especially; Maude was so wild with delight over your telegram that she told me that bad as she was, she got up and jumped about the room'.[8]

During the last weeks of 1881 and the first two months of 1882 Hubert devoted as much time and energy as possible to the orchestration and completion of his Symphony in G and, with some trepidation, approached Richter with a view to his including it in his 1882 series of London concerts. On 9 May the two men met to read through the MS, and Richter agreed to do it; a rehearsal was fixed for 13 June:

> Unfortunately, great part of the band did not come. No first clarinet, no 3rd Horn and great part of the strings absent. We struggled on roughly for a long while, against heaps of mistakes in the parts and finally it became evident that with the one rehearsal which only is possible, Richter could not make it go and so it was given up. A good deal of it sounded well; but even the men who were there were tired and not up to the mark and shirked their work. Dann came and supported me nobly in the trying ordeal.[9]

---

[6] CHHP, *Diary 1881*. Shulbrede archive.
[7] *Ibid.*
[8] CHHP, letter to Edward W. Hamilton, 18 May 1881. BL Add. MS 48621. See also Dibble, *op cit,* p 196.
[9] CHHP, *Diary 1882*. Shulbrede archive.

Months of concentrated work seemed to have been wasted. Hubert's disappointment in Richter was immense – but all was not lost. Spencer Lyttelton's brother, Robert, an Eton contemporary of Hubert's who was working in Birmingham, had heard about the symphony and persuaded the committee of the Birmingham Festival that the première should be included in their programme for the following August. And to further dispel Hubert's chagrin, May and June brought a positive feast of Wagner to London. He not only attended *Tannhäuser, Lohengrin, Der Fliegende Holländer, Tristan und Isolde* (twice), and *Die Meistersinger* (four times, plus a rehearsal) at the Theatre Royal, Drury Lane, but also the whole *Ring* cycle at Her Majesty's Theatre – and went a second time to *Siegfried* and *Götterdämmerung. Meistersinger* far exceeded his 'utmost expectations', and Hubert's delight in it was more than doubled by the presence of his father – who was genuinely enthusiastic. What had Gambier Parry told Hubert he wanted of music: 'something to leave some form and feature….something that one can rest upon and love'? He found all that and more in *Meistersinger.* And then, on 21 July, Hubert and Dannreuther set out for Bayreuth – and the première of *Parsifal.* They attended all three performances, and that stunning music would not quit Hubert's waking thoughts for several weeks after his return to England:

> All the singers did better than I ever heard them do before… Scenic management and tableaux supremely effective and all the difficult points, I had dreaded – the swan, the flower-maidens, the washing of the feet and the dove – were all just perfect. As a work of art it is at the very highest point of mastery. The religious element makes it seem to me a little hollow, and I was not satisfied with the climaxes of the first and last Acts being chiefly scenic and not humanly emotional. But the impression was very great.[10]

Hubert and Dannreuther attended a splendid reception at the Wagners' house before hurrying home for the first London rehearsal of the Symphony in G on 9 August. The result, under Hubert's own bâton, was fairly good, but later rehearsals were lack-lustre and unsatisfactory. The subsequent rehearsals in Birmingham were, if anything, worse still, and the first of them on 26 August was 'listened to with absolute coldness and the band showed no signs of anything but indifference throughout'.[11] And yet the performance itself on 31 August was very fine, marking a new beginning for the English symphony, albeit that it appeared in the same year as Frederic Cowen's third symphony, the 'Scandinavian', and Cowen was thought then to be England's finest symphonist.

Already possessed of a strong grasp of symphonic form, Hubert was clearly influenced in the first movement by Schumann, and especially by the *Rhenish* Symphony; in the second by Wagner; and even raised his hat to Dvorak in the Presto and the opening of the Allegretto. But the Symphony in G is much more than a pastiche of continental models. Hubert was able with supreme confidence to draw together the many disparate elements of his inspiration and to forge from them a distinctive and individual symphonic voice, born of English

---

10 *Ibid.*
11 *Ibid.*

earth; and, especially in the Andante, to give voice to that profoundly English emotion which, though rarely allowed to surface in our everyday lives, is planted deeply in the national consciousness and emerges, proud and glistening, when stirred by that indefinable quality, 'Englishness' in music; a quality which, for all his technical brilliance and melodic invention, Frederic Cowen's music lacks.

Hubert was loudly applauded as he stepped down from the rostrum, and although remaining convinced that most of the enthusiasm had been 'evoked by the good nature of the steward and my friends', he was

> especially moved by the approbation of old Sir Julius Benedict who 'after all, was the pupil and familiar of Weber, and often saw Beethoven and Schubert in the flesh' [Benedict was also Cowan's teacher]. The best Germans in the band were equally kind; Gounod 'buttered' him to the utmost, though not very acceptably; Stainer, Hueffer (of *The Times* [and a supporter of Cowen]) and Prout (of the *Athenæum*) were all very encouraging, and the great Mr. Joseph Bennett of the *Telegraph* came up and said: 'I didn't believe in you before, but I do now. You have converted me'.[12]

Stanford, too, was deeply supportive; and amongst those applauding most loudly was Thomas Gambier Parry. The next day he wrote to Hubert from Highnam Court:

> It was but a tantalising sight of you yesterday! We caught a glimpse of Maude in the gallery – and saw that some of the Lyttelton party were about perpendicularly above us. We were not well placed, being partly under the side gallery. The sound did not reach us *fully*. It was what a picture is, not in a perfectly good light, but with just a shimmer of glaze, which *takes the bloom off.* Linda got a little better into the open, in a seat temporarily vacant just when your music was being performed. As all I can do to express myself as to music is by feeling and not by knowledge, I do not pretend to any criticism, – but I must not let a day pass without just a word to say how deeply Linda and I were impressed with your work. It is a great work – and can only be properly appreciated by being perfectly known. It will surely be given again – and I do hope indeed to be within reach, to hear it. You must have had the hearty congratulations of all who were capable of hearing it.[13]

What greater contrast could there have been between the achievements of Gambier Parry's two eldest sons? Hubert had given proof of his industry and genius, and his father was justifiably proud. His elder brother, on the other hand, washed up on the shores of Australia, was unemployable in any capacity. Writing to his father from Sydney on 18 September, Clinton confessed to his failure to find employment:

> However, I am by no means idle. But my life here is a very quiet one. I get up and have a shower bath; then breakfast at 7.15 or 7.30; I have been an early riser as you know for many years. After breakfast I go to the public gardens, and stay till the public library is open. There, in the public gardens, I pay visits to my pets, for there are lots of animals. There is one little musk deer, with lovely large eyes and little horns not bigger than the

---

[12] Graves, *op cit,* p 235.

[13] TGP, letter to CHHP, 1 September 1882. Shulbrede archive.

prongs of a fork; he is about the size of a 3 months pig and very fat. He allows me to scratch his forehead. Then he eats out of my hand, as does also a wallaby, an emu, and some ducks. After this, public library till 12 when I dine. After dinner reading or original writing till about 2 when I go out and walk miles and miles. I 'tea' at 6; public library till 10 pm and then bed.[14]

In other words, had it not been for his allowance of £500 per year Clinton would have become a vagrant, and in spite of claims to have a 'large acquaintance' in Sydney, at that time a town of two hundred thousand souls, it is clear that he was already a social outcast.

*　　*　　*　　*　　*　　*　　*

After an autumn holiday in Ireland with Hugh Montgomery at Blessingbourne, Hubert and Maude returned to Rustington. Hubert was already at work on a Symphony in F major, requested by Cambridge, no doubt at the prompting of Stanford. The death of Rhoda Garrett on 23 November and her funeral at Rustington were deeply distressing to the Parrys; but at the beginning of December Hubert set off for a couple of days as the guest of the Stanfords in Cambridge. 'It was altogether a happy visit, and memorable in its results, since it led, at Stanford's suggestion, to the commission to write the music for *The Birds* [of Aristophanes] in the following year, and opened up a new field of composition which proved his greatest musical recreation and kept him to the end of his life in close touch with successive generations of the "blessèd young" at Cambridge and Oxford'.[15] In later years Hubert composed incidental music for Oxford performances of *The Frogs*, *The Clouds* and *The Acharnians*, and for Cambridge the *Agamemnon* of Aeschylus in 1900.

On New Year's Day, 1883, Hubert received a letter from George Grove, now Director of the newly-founded but not yet opened Royal College of Music:

> Temporary Offices,
> Duchy of Cornwall Office,
> 1, Buckingham Gate,
> London, S.W.
> Royal College of Music
>
> December 30, 1882

My dear Parry,

I write by desire of the Prince of Wales to ask if you will assist him in his great experiment by taking the Department of Musical History with a seat on the Board of Professors. It is our wish to make lectures an important part of the College course, and into no hands could those on the history and development of music be put with more propriety than yours. As the College grows I hope that there may be some other opportunity of turning your great abilities to account – as in Composition etc. but the lectures will be your cardinal occupation.

---

[14] Clinton Parry, letter to TGP, 18 September 1882. Shulbrede archive.
[15] Graves, *op cit*, p 238.

I must tell you that we must begin the College on the same low rate of remuneration to the Professors that the National Training School proceeded upon during its whole existence:- namely for the Professors who form the Board 15/- an hour. When we come to our full strength, I am not without hope that that rate may be increased; but at first it must rule; and I trust that it may not deter you from accepting His Royal Highness's invitation. He hopes to open the College in April or May.

yours ever sincerely,

G. Grove

Director[16]

Further acknowledgement of Hubert's appointment to the Board of the Royal College and his achievement as scholarly writer for Grove's *Dictionary* came from Macfarren, who invited him to act as the external examiner for the Cambridge Mus B and Mus D examinations in February; further professional recognition was to follow soon afterwards – his admission to Trinity College, Cambridge, and the conferring upon him there of an Honorary Doctorate. Ethelinda's letter of congratulation was less than warm: 'I hope people won't think it necessary to call you *Dr. Parry!*', she wrote. But Hubert's father was hugely proud:

I heartily congratulate you on your honours which you thoroughly deserve. I am delighted at the whole affair. You say that you are already admitted to my old College – Trinity – fancy that! *but how?* I have no recollection of any reasons of transfer from an Oxford Coll. to one at Cambridge but by taking the *ad eundem* degree – your old university owes you something – mine alas! owes me nothing – I only took an inglorious 'Poll'!

Williams [Charles Lee Williams], organist at Gloucester, and I suppose future conductor of the Festival next September (some day in the first week) asked me whether you had anything *within our scope* that you particularly wished to be done here – something already written – sacred for the morning or secular for the evening. The system adopted by the Stewards is to invite 2 modern composers to write specially. They invited Stanford and Stainer. The former offered to finish specially a Mass Service – which, to be written specially for our Cathedral, was seriously objected to – an old mass, as a *study* of music of established high class for sacred purposes was placed in a totally different category. We cannot regard such matters merely and nakedly from the musical side alone. We much regret Stanford not caring to produce anything else – unless it be a Symphony which would be somewhat beyond our ability for want of time and means of rehearsal – so another composer has promised something.[17]

The 'other composer' was Dr G B Arnold, the organist of Winchester Cathedral and Charles Lee Williams's teacher. Arnold conducted his cantata *Sennacherib*, of which not even Williams could say more than that 'the composer's great knowledge of fugal writing and elaborate counterpoint was apparent throughout';[18] *The Musical Times* judged it simply tedious. Stainer's contribution was *St. Mary Magdalen*, thereafter know as his 'Gloucester Oratorio'; Stanford conducted the second performance of his *Elegiac* Symphony; and Hubert

[16] George Grove, letter to CHHP, 30 December, 1882. Shulbrede archive.
[17] TGP, letter to CHHP, 20 February 1883. Shulbrede archive.
[18] See Anthony Boden, *Three Choirs: A History of the Festival* (Sutton Publishing, 1992), p 119.

provided *The Glories of our Blood and State*, a setting of James Shirley's poem *Death the Leveller*, dedicated to the memory of Rhoda Garrett. The intervening months saw the opening of the Royal College of Music on 7 May and the première of Hubert's Second Symphony in F, appropriately named 'The Cambridge', given an 'excellent performance' under Stanford in the Guildhall of that city on 12 June 1883.

The Symphony in F, completed after considerable 'wrastling' with it, marked a further advance in Hubert's compositional maturity and attracted altogether favourable reviews. It remained one of his favourite compositions, and in 1887 he revised it thoroughly for a London performance under Richter. Grove, to whom Stanford had played through the first movement, was delighted with it: 'I can't help telling you of the *very great impression* it made on me. It is splendid – so clear and tuneful and fresh, and so like your own dear self'.[19] Precisely. The personality of Hubert Parry is clearly stamped upon this symphony; the influences of others might be detectable, but the structure and voice are unmistakeably his own.

Only Maude's habitual illness marred Hubert's complete happiness in the success of the 'Cambridge':

> The Symphony got fair consideration, and in the afternoon went most admirably and sounded to me well. It was wonderfully well received, and the friends I like to please seemed well delighted with it. On account of Maude's weakness we had to hurry away before the end of the concert, and the worry incident to getting away and leaving so many people I wanted to see and so many things I wanted to do at Cambridge spoilt a very great deal of my pleasure. We got back in time for dinner and Maude did not seem much the worse.[20]

The enjoyment of the summer months were considerably enhanced for Hubert by the presence nearby on holiday of William Blake Richmond, his wife Clara, and their six children: Francis (Checco), Helen, Herbert, Ernest, John Sebastian (Chunks) and Arthur. Nothing gave Hubert greater pleasure than sharing in the games of children, and as well as Dorothea and Gwendolen, the Richmond children were his 'constant playmates' in the warm summer of 1883. Helen Richmond, a lively thirteen-year-old, 'filled to the brim with girlish glee', shared Hubert's love of the sea, and adored to be taken sailing in his little canoe, often getting 'well-ducked' but enjoying it thoroughly. Knight's Croft had already become 'Parrydise' to Helen, and Hubert delighted in her refreshing spirit and humour.

But summer's end brought dreadful news from Gambier Parry:

> …I little thought when I wrote a rather scrambly note to you on Sunday afternoon that I should receive such a letter as this morning's Post (Aug 29) has brought me from Sydney (Australia). Our dear Clinton is no more. He died on the 7th of July. He appears to have been long ill – the last letter received by any one of us was to B. [Beatrice] dated as long ago as about the middle of last December. She did not keep this letter. The previous letter had mentioned his being ill. He was then however better after a

---

[19] George Grove, letter to CHHP, 28 February 1883. Shulbrede archive.
[20] CHHP, *Diary 1883*. Shulbrede archive.

considerable illness. He spoke of trouble from erysipelas. He appears to have been in the care of the mistress of his lodging house about whom I have also letters from friends of poor Clinton and from a Sydney solicitor, who writes an exceedingly nice letter. I will send you the letters on their return from Claude Hinde, to whom I write enclosing them. They tell of the care and kindness of that woman as it is hardly possible to exaggerate. It is too long a story to write now… About your coming here, all this must make no difference – especially as it is most necessary for you to go through your Cantata with the Conductor… the Conductor spoke of the originality of your work making it very difficult to deal with without your help or explanation.[21]

Hubert travelled to Gloucester, reflecting sadly on the dreadful loneliness of his brother's last months. Clinton's death certificate records the cause of his death as *'Morbus Cordis & Oedema of the Lungs'*: his heart had simply given up. 'What an end to such abilities and such a genial widely sympathetic nature', Hubert wrote in his diary.

At Highnam his father was inconsolable. The performance of *The Glories of our Blood and State* on 4 September was very good, albeit that the audience failed to warm to its sombre tone; but what must Hubert and his father have been feeling in response to Shirley's words?

> The garlands wither on your brow;
>> Then boast no more your mighty deeds!
> Upon Death's purple altar now
>> See where the victor-victim bleeds.

Nor was that an end to pain and sadness for Clinton's family. Florence remarried but failed to find happiness; Isabel, little 'Bluebell', died in January 1885, five months before her nineteenth birthday; and Owen, who was extremely bright and showed great promise, followed his sister in October 1888 at the age of twenty. Lilian, on coming of age, fled to the continent . At the end of April 1903 Hubert was horrified to receive the following letter from the British Consul in Munich:

> I beg to inform you that a certain Frau A. Praechter, Augustenstrasse 76/0, Munich, called on me this morning showing proof – a medical certificate, cheque book etc. – that your niece, Miss Lilian Clinton-Parry, is seriously ill and has been taken in by the said Frau Praechter, as your niece is entirely without means; she was on her way to Paris and was found in a fainting condition in the street.
> I have been asked to write to you on behalf of Miss Clinton-Parry, in order to see whether you are willing to send this young lady some means of subsistence, either directly or through me.[22]

Hubert was the only sympathetic member of her family to whom Lilian could turn; four months later she was dead. Only one of Clinton and Florence's children remained, Noel, and he, like his father before him, went out to Australia, and there, in 1946, ended his own life by cyanide poisoning.

---

[21] TGP, letter to CHHP, 29 August 1883. Shulbrede archive.
[22] Letter from British Consul, Munich, to CHHP, 29 April 1903. Shulbrede archive.

Hubert and Maude, probably through their friendship with the Garretts and with William Blake Richmond and his family, had made the acquaintance of the De Morgans, the Morrises and the Burne-Joneses. By 1883 these associations had developed into friendships and, additionally, Hubert was a frequent visitor to musical parties at the beautiful London home of Lord Leighton, of whom Richmond was a fervent admirer. Something of the flavour of this circle, of William Morris the mercurial idealist and of Lady Maude the thoughtful realist, is captured in a diary description by Maude herself following a dinner party at the Richmonds' home, Beavor Lodge, in Hammersmith:

Dinner with the Richmonds. Sat next to W. Morris who made such a noise that he nearly deafened me. A German lady on the other side apparently irritated him so that he bawled more than usual. We talked of Ibsen's *Doll's House* which Morris admired immensely. The German lady thought Norah should not have left her children. 'Why not', screamed Morris, 'her husband was a cur. Why should she stay with him?' 'No woman has a right to leave her children', returned the German. 'But a man may', returned Morris, 'for any national cause or duty, and a woman is an individual just the same, therefore she may'. I tried to tell them that Ibsen felt that Norah was not morally fit to bring up the children, and that the nurse was. The German maintained that the husband was no worse than the generality of men, which, if I believed, I should cut my throat at once.

But I found most people agreed with her. One man said indeed that he [the husband] was not at all a bad man, but a kind good fellow, and that it was a great want of gratitude in Norah to leave him.

Mrs. Richmond said she thought the play so immoral that she wouldn't go and see it. And that Norah must have been either a fool or a knave, which showed how little she knew about it. Afterwards Morris talked of Bismark. He said he felt him to be the most unmitigated rascal in the whole history of mankind and that the Germans were a most immoral race to stand him.

Here the German lady vigorously protested. She said Bismark wasn't a rascal, and that Germans were a very moral race, though she thought them wanting in individualism and character. She defended Bismark's system of mouchards, and said the Empress was the most indiscreet and traitorous woman possible, and that as she was most intimate with her, and saw her nearly every day, she was bound to know. I would say, 'defend me from my friends'. Then she asked Morris if he approved of the new German socialistic law of providing for poor people in their old age, and said it was very bad for trade.

'If it is bad for trade', replied Morris, 'I should certainly approve of it; anything that is bad for trade is a blessing. I look upon all trade as thieving. Everybody steals – all capitalists are thieves. The judge who condemns the poor man for thieving is a greater thief himself. As a boy I did not think it very wrong to steal, and I think it less wrong now.' I said of course that I felt that if a poor person were in want of food they were justified in stealing. Morris agreed, and quoted an old saying, that the English were a better race than the French because so many more hundred men were hung every year for stealing. 'When an Englishman wants a thing, he has the pluck to take it'.

I asked Morris how he would like to live in a common house sharing with everybody alike. 'Not at all', he had the honesty to reply. He defined himself as a parasite feeding on the rich, as the poor couldn't afford to buy his goods. Then he started the startling paradox that the labourer ought to be better paid than the skilled artisan because we could live without the latter, but not without the former. The German lady here remarked that there were plenty of arguments to be adduced on the other side. 'Yes', he replied, 'but I shan't stop to argue with you, neither will the labourer – he will just cut your throat, that is what he will do – he won't stop to hear all your arguments.

Here, fortunately, strawberries and cream arrived, which calmed Morris's ardour a little. He grunted at intervals, 'we must all eat – the labourer just as much as you. What is the use of this bottle?', catching hold of Mrs. Richmond's elaborate water jug. 'We can do without the man who made this, but we can't do without the labourer'. He says socialism is increasing. He approves of Co-operation but does not think it will do everything.

And he seems to be all against poor people saving.[23]

An almost equally extraordinary opinion, but on a totally unrelated matter, was expressed by August Manns after a rather unsatisfactory rehearsal of Hubert's Symphony in G at the Crystal Palace in April:

> He says the men are always in bad order on Monday morning: they smoke too much and kiss their wives and sweethearts so much that the lips of the wind-players are all out of order. But by the Saturday it was another story. The room was very empty, but the performance was superb; lots of friends came over and I think all were pleased. Maude came and sat in the corner in the gallery and I held her hand nearly all the time. That was sweet.[24]

Sweet too was the success of Hubert's Second Symphony in F, performed for the first time by the Cambridge Musical Society on 12 June under Stanford's excellent direction. Hubert's first professional priority was now the Royal College of Music. But at the end of the year he began work on a String Quintet in E flat, completed in February 1884, the year in which he also composed his Piano Trio in B minor and agreed to contribute a series of biographical essays to *Every Girl's Magazine*; a series which three years later was drawn together into a single volume by Routledge under the collective title *Studies of the Great Composers*. Written for young people, the essays, in Hubert's words, did 'not attempt to deal with the profounder and more abstruse questions which are of interest to advanced musicians and students, and professed masters of artistic policy'.[25] None the less, to quote only one example, there is surely a timeless truth for any composer in the central precept of the preamble to Hubert's essay on Robert Schumann:

> In art, just as in the circumstances of outward life, it is always more inspiring to adventure into new lands and open them for the first time, than it is to cultivate and improve them when some one else has discovered and conquered them. When great material resources are at the command of many people, there are plentiful opportunities for average men to make themselves useful, but less for individual men to tower into rare eminence above their fellows. The sum of work done may on the whole be greater than what was done in earlier stages of history, but it is more diffused, and more hands have a share in it. Individual greatness may show itself still, but its signs and tokens seem less clearly marked out, and to depend on subtler conditions, and to have less of monumental and isolated conspicuousness about them. Men have to use what

---

[23] Lady Maude Parry, *Diary* 29 June 1889. Shulbrede archive.
[24] CHHP, *Diary 1883*.
[25] CHHP, *Studies of Great Composers* (Routledge, 1887), Preface.

has been used before, and do what has been done before, and their individual prominence depends chiefly upon the way in which they can adapt themselves to phases of mind and action in their time, or the manner in which they use established forms so as to illustrate the taste and characteristic modes of feeling of their generation. They may rise to eminence as illustrators, as many painters do; or they may revive and combine different branches of art; or they may become great critics, and by appreciating thoroughly what has been done in the past, find out also where there is something which has not been done, or at least not done in the sense which appeals most powerfully and naturally to the people of their own time. The mere copying of other people's ways of expressing themselves can never be of much use to the world. People who only write blameless symphonies and sonatas after the accepted models, with nothing of their own to mark them by, might just as well let composing alone. They are only taking up time which would be better employed in attending to the original masterpieces.[26]

One man in whose music Hubert found little to admire was also a man to whom he owed a considerable debt of gratitude. Charles Villiers Stanford had, after all, willingly championed Hubert's work. Writing to his friend Francis Jenkinson ('Jinks'), the classics scholar of Trinity College, Cambridge, Hubert confided that 'It wouldn't be fair to say I don't praise C.V.S.'s music; only I rarely get to that pitch of boiling enthusiasm which is necessary to produce complete satisfaction in others'.[27] When in July 1884 Stanford's opera *Savonarola* flopped at Covent Garden, Hubert felt obliged to defend it against adverse press criticism – but by then he had already completed the first act of an opera of his own, a project which had been in his mind for two years. Where Stanford had failed, might Hubert Parry be able to write something which would appeal 'most powerfully and naturally to the people of his own time'?

George Grove had suggested to Hubert that the ideal librettist for his opera would be Una Taylor, committed devotee of Wagnerian music drama and daughter of the author Sir Henry Taylor. At this same time in Italy another composer equally influenced by the harmonies of Wagner was embarking upon the composition of *his* first opera; but even if Hubert had possessed the innate sense of dramatic structure which was the great gift of Giacomo Puccini, Una Taylor was no Illica. Hubert had determined to draw his subject from Arthurian legend, as had Wagner in *Lohengrin, Tristan* and *Parsifal*, a huge challenge for any librettist. Towards the end of her life Una Taylor recalled her struggles with what was to become Hubert Parry's *Guenever*:

My ignorance of the stage was complete – it was my only excuse – and I caught at the idea. Hubert Parry, whom I had not met before, came to talk things over with me and discuss the subject he had chosen – Lancelot and Guenevere. His conception of the story and mine differed. As you know, the *Morte* is a medley of various versions of the stories it tells, and it seemed to me one could legitimately base our plot on a less commonplace one than the generally received tradition, and make Gareth's death, not Guenevere's faithlessness, the main motive in the tragedy. After Hubert Parry had read up the chapters in the *Morte* which I thought justified this rendering, I think he agreed willingly to work on those lines. My impression at that time was that his ignorance of

[26] CHHP, *op cit*, pp 289/290.
[27] CHHP, letter to F J H Jenkinson, 2 December 1885. CUL Add MS 6463. See also Dibble, *op cit*, p 227.

the practical requirements of the stage was almost as great as my own. I remember asking if we had not best call in a stage carpenter to help. But he had Dannreuther behind him, under whose supervision every page was re-written. Hubert Parry had absolute confidence in his judgement, as naturally I also had...

As to the music, I was at that time not qualified to judge. Wagner's influence was, I suppose, paramount, and I could not help thinking, from the little I knew or have been told, that you may find qualities in Hubert Parry's opera which are totally absent from his later compositions. I should say – only *please* remember my impressions, as I recall them, are the crude impressions of inexperience and enthusiasm – that he was working under very strong emotional stress. In fact I should have said aesthetic emotionalism was one of his most characteristic gifts, balanced, or should one say distracted, by his absorbing interest in literature and life at large.[28]

The opera was finished in the spring of 1886 and sent to Stanford, who was much more than simply enthusiastic: 'I have just finished playing it through, and I think it's quite superbo, *really* superbo. Dramatically and every way I bet my hat on its success'. But it was doomed from the outset. Stanford's very best efforts to interest Carl Rosa and continental opera houses in *Guenever* met with rejection. Hubert, after two years of work on the opera, set it aside, leaving only a vocal sketch and skeletal scoring. His collaboration with Una Taylor, whom he described as 'one of the most singular miniatures of cleverness and silliness', had been 'thoroughly uncongenial'.[29] It was her libretto, above all, which ensured that *Guenever* would be sunk without trace. And yet it is surely the case that many a great opera composer's first attempt ended in failure. Would we remember Puccini for *Le Villi* or Strauss for *Guntram* if nothing had followed?

The stress under which Hubert was working, accurately sensed by the unfortunate Una Taylor, had also contributed to the failure of *Guenever.* It was simply impossible for him to give the project his undivided attention. His responsibilities at the RCM; lecturing and examining at Cambridge; lecturing at Oxford, where he had been appointed Choragus, and at Birmingham; intensive work on the *Dictionary* and *Studies of the Great Composers*; travelling to and fro between London and Rustington; and continuing concern for Maude's health, all took their toll. The drudgery of academic life had, by the beginning of 1885, begun to weigh heavily upon him: the creative spirit chained by conformity occasionally seething inwardly, as when obliged to be present at the 'exercises' of vocal students who 'look such idiots with their mouths wide open howling nothings!'.[30]

A poor review for a performance of *Prometheus* given by the Bach Choir in February left Hubert in an uncharacteristically gloomy mood:

Being very tired and out of sorts I fell into low spirits. I know it is stupid. But it is cruel to struggle vainly on and have to endure these vile sneers.[31]

---

[28] Graves, *op cit*, Vol II, pp 210/211.
[29] CHHP, *Diary 1886*. Shulbrede archive.
[30] CHHP, *Diary 1885*.
[31] *Ibid.*

Further knocks came with the news from Highnam that Gambier Parry was suffering acutely from the effects of the 'great depression' in agriculture. Six out of the thirteen gardeners had been dismissed, one groom, one lady's maid, one footman – all had been let go. Much was in a sad state of disrepair, and barely enough horses remained for the family's needs. Worse still, Ernest had been invalided out of the army and was seriously ill at home. Hubert's usual response to adversity, even greater physical and mental exertion, now only exacerbated his heart condition, and by June had become sufficiently worrying for Dr Black to instruct him to 'knock off' all exercise and to stop smoking:

> At this juncture Hugh Montgomery and Sedley Taylor opportunely arrived with the proposal that he should go on a sea voyage with Sedley Taylor, who was in much the same condition. Hubert went off at once to find a ship for the west coast of South America, and after two failures secured passages in one of the Pacific Mail Company's liners which was sailing direct to Valparaiso. Throughout the whole business Robin Benson was invaluable in procuring information and introductions – he was indeed the good genius of the trip and its sequel. The next week was spent in a rush of preparations, shopping, etc., and Hubert nearly collapsed from a heart attack at his last lecture at the College. A few days at Rustington, which was looking lovely, and a last sail [in his small yacht, the *Ornis*, built by Harvey of Littlehampton in the previous year] made the wrench of parting all the greater. On the 13th Robin Benson gave a farewell dinner in his honour, attended by the Burne-Joneses, Spencer Lyttelton, Alfred Lyttelton and his wife, and Lady Lonsdale – all very kind and friendly. More rushing and good-byes at the College followed, and on the 16th, after a final 'play at Bach' with the Lushingtons he saw Lady Maude off at Victoria:
>
> 'It was grievous. I watched the train till it disappeared with a horrid ache in my throat and a miserable morbid dread in my mind; though it is not so much for myself getting back to her as for anything happening to her at home'.[32]

Hubert and Sedley Taylor left Liverpool aboard the *Aconcagua*, Hubert condemned to spend the voyage in 'the worst and noisiest cabin' in the entire ship. They sailed down via Pauillac and Lisbon to face the great Atlantic; landing first at Pernambuco – 'full of colour, fruit and parrots' – and on to the even more exciting Bahia; to Rio – 'a series of enchanting sights, the sun blazing, the water blue with great rollers crashing on the shore'; Montevideo, then a 'large, modern, unkempt, dirty and shabby town' which Hubert left without regret; through the Straits of Magellan, 'one magnificent view succeeding another for hours and hours'; Coronel 'in splendid midnight'; but on reaching Valparaiso the return of troublesome heart symptoms served only to remind Hubert 'of the uselessness of their voyage'.[33] His homesickness increased as the journey continued; fellow passengers became ever more irritating; at St. Vincent the 'fussy quarantine arrangements of the Portuguese' tried his patience sorely; and as Portugal itself came once more into sight on 11 September Hubert was not alone on board in 'gazing eagerly to lose no atom of the joy it seemed… to see Europe again'.[35]

---

[32] Graves, *op cit*, Vol I, p 253.
[33] CHHP, *Diary 1885*.
[35] *Ibid.*

Maude brought Dolly and Gwen to the station at Littlehampton on the afternoon of 18 September to welcome home a bearded 'Feyjey', the affectionate name which the girls used for their father, and the Richmonds came out to welcome him on the road to Rustington:

> But the strange feeling is present all the while since landing that everything is exactly the same as when I went away. The people just on their ordinary course; places just as if I had left them yesterday. More and more it is as if I had squeezed a long queer dream in between yesterday and to-day, and yet the inner being is not quite the same. The experience makes some effect, though it cannot alter constitutional indolence, hastiness and irritability.[36]

The voyage had been a mistake. Dr Black was able to detect only a slight improvement in Hubert's health. On 2 October he underwent a minor operation for the removal of a cyst on his neck; and when in the following month he saw his specialist, Sir Andrew Clarke, Hubert was advised that the one thing which he did *not* require was enforced rest. Inactivity, he was pleased to be told, merely served to increase his anxiety and thus exacerbate the strain on his heart.

Throughout his life, art-songs formed an important part of Hubert's compositional output, and by 1885 he had already set over three dozen poems. In that year and the next, the first two volumes of what were to become twelve sets of *English Lyrics*, many of high quality, true English Lieder, were published by Stanley Lucas, the second volume including one of Hubert's finest songs, 'O mistress mine' from *Twelfth Night* (memorably recorded by Dame Janet Baker and the incomparable Gerald Moore). Released from enforced idleness once more, Hubert immediately set about revising a separate collection of four Shakespeare Sonnets for publication and, at the same time, began a set of *Characterstic Popular Tunes of the British Isles* for Dolly and Gwen to play as piano duets. Above all, it was *Guenever* which now became the principal focus of his creativity, occupying every spare moment until the middle of 1886. But spare moments were all too few: lectures at the College resumed on 28 October.

The failure of *Guenever* was a bitter blow; too bitter even to be committed to Hubert's diary. But, as Una Taylor remembered:

> What remains clearer than any impression is the memory of the courteous consideration, the never-failing tact and patience, as well as the intense enthusiasm which he brought to the work, and which made one feel that no amount of labour in re-writing, correcting, re-casting, and amending was wasted in the attempt to get the effects and results at which he aimed.
>
> When Carl Rosa's ultimate refusal came I believe he was almost as sorry for my disappointment as for his own.[37]

The hurt remained, even to the last year of Hubert's life, when he wrote:

---

[36] *Ibid.*
[37] Graves, *op cit*, Vol II, p 211.

Opera is the shallowest fraud man ever achieved in the name of art. Its invariable associates are dirt and tinsel. Its history is falseness, intrigue, shallowness, levity and pretension. It is the appanage of wastrels, the home of humbugs. No composer who is worthy of any reverence at all ever wrote an Opera.[38]

Even so, it is tempting to imagine how very different a course Hubert's compositional ship might have taken if Stanford's assessment of *Guenever* had been shared by Carl Rosa. Dannreuther, with gross over-optimism, hailed *Guenever* as 'the real English Opera for which we have waited so long', but had Hubert only felt sufficiently confident to release himself from the now needless imprimatur of his mentor, and to have followed the dictates of his own intuition, a truly British post-Wagnerian masterpiece might have been ours. But to do it he would have required a Hoffmansthal by his side.

$\ast$ $\qquad$ $\ast$ $\qquad$ $\ast$ $\qquad$ $\ast$ $\qquad$ $\ast$ $\qquad$ $\ast$ $\qquad$ $\ast$

In the three years following the death of Clinton, Thomas Gambier Parry plunged himself into the task of recording, in a series of essays, the most important aspects of his accumulated knowledge in relation to fine art: of the history of mosaic, of glass painting, of the adornment of sacred buildings, of archaeology, of colour in sculpture and wall painting. Some of these essays had been written previously; some already delivered in lectures to professional bodies and specialist groups. He wrote lovingly of the builders and buildings of the Abbey of St Peter at Gloucester, now the Cathedral, and he also included in the series his description of the method of spirit fresco painting, first published in 1880 at the request of the Secretary of the Science and Art Department, South Kensington. But in the three leading essays, establishing the dominant theme of the entire series, he set down the ruling philosophy of his life in art: The Purpose and Practice of Fine Art, The Ministry of Fine Art to Common Life, and The Ministry of Fine Art to Spiritual Life. The essays were, he wrote in the dedication, 'but sketches, and pretend to be no more, of arts which best minister to life's happiness by leading it aside to look beyond it'. The collection was completed in June 1886 and published by John Murray in the following year under the title, *The Ministry of Fine Art*.

'Fine art comes of the union of love and labour, for without love it has no sufficient motive, and without labour it can have no success', he wrote, but, more importantly, 'What is the purpose of fine art?' Is there, he asks, 'any purpose assignable as the basis of its existence that distinguishes it from all other subjects?'

> It is the element of beauty that characterises all fine art... In external nature, where man has not marred it, all is beautiful, in calm or storm, in fertility or in desert. So too in much of animal life, and in the exquisite cosmos of all created things. The sense of moral or physical beauty is the source of all art's motive. That beauty gained the artist's

---

[38] CHHP, *Notebook* [?1918]. Shulbrede archive.

love, and his labour realised it. The purpose of all fine art is *the expression of the sense of beauty.*

> …The existence of art is at once a testimony and an appeal; it is the witness to and the appeal from that, which, by its irresistible force, obliges us to recognise it as a reality, a reality irrespective of time and space, of life or death, always urgent for attention – a witness to a power beyond mortal grasp or range of sense, a power that asserts itself as commanding our respect, an appeal like a voice ever sounding in our ears, as from a living source, that we cannot refuse to listen to; its existence is a mystery; but mysteries inexplicable exist as facts, and this one of art's existence is so; and as a fact it is that man in every age and in every condition has been and is its pupil, its servant, its disciple, commanded by it, blessed by it, benefited by it, *because the voice of it, the voice of spiritual and physical beauty,* is one that he has no power to resist, for it comes from the divine source of his own self and of all things else, and speaks, calls, appeals to him from and for a higher life than that of sense, and stirs him in the deepest depths of his being. It is that sense of divine beauty that masters him; and his art is the feeble expression of his sense of it; his acknowledgement and his worship of that which has cast across his path of mortal toil the light of its life and the shadow of its reality.[39]

If the artist is compelled to express himself, consciously or unconsciously, as an act of faith, it follows that 'the source of art's immortal fire is in the hearts of men; and the beauty of external nature is the symbol of that Divine light which illuminates both it and them'.[40] And if the beautiful and the good are interconnected, surely there must be a moral obligation to do good with art? 'Art's highest sphere', believed Gambier Parry, 'is the sphere of national service, by which the cultivation of a whole people is affected; and, whether observed or unobserved by themselves, their interests and pursuits, their labour and their recreation are supplied and enlightened by it':

> But we have a very mixed multitude to deal with. There are classes among our fellow-men over whom the shadows seem to have settled impenetrably, and the dullness of their dreary homes has driven them to drown their weariness in vice. It would be a worthy work to open the eyes of such as they are to their own relief, and to show them how close it is within their reach. We believe that by the narrow wedge of counter-attractions we may introduce elements of interest and occupation that will raise the tone and purify the motives and habits of our people, and shaming them away from evil, may induce some brighter thought and hopefulness of life to disperse its shadows'.[41]

Quite how the 'narrow wedge of counter-attractions' would compensate for the lack of bread in the hovels of the hungry and downtrodden poor is, of course, omitted from Gambier Parry's logic. Little wonder that on his visits to Highnam, Hubert, 'increasingly out of sympathy with the uncompromising Conservative champions of society and aristocracy',[42] found it best to keep his radical political views out of conversations with his Tory father. None the less, *The Ministry of Fine Art* is a scholarly and valuable book, and if Gambier Parry

---

[39] TGP, *The Ministry of Fine Art* (John Murray, 1887), pp 7/ 8.
[40] TGP, *op cit*, p 19.
[41] *Op cit*, p 28.
[42] Graves, *op cit*, Vol I, p 265.

were alive today he would probably be introducing the wonder of fine art to a television audience of millions. The moral of his story was that:

> The foundation of all fine art lies in that *relationship* which exists between the things of material and the things of spirit; and the degree of its perception and the power of its use is the gauge of all art's genius. By force of that relationship Fine Art testifies to that Divine life which underlies the whole sphere of man's mortal state. She testifies to the utter inadequacy of all material things to measure the range, or to satisfy the aspirations, of that which is itself illimitable – the human soul. She is herself that soul's interpreter. Her greatest works are but symbols. She is conscious of her own feebleness, and of the impenetrable clouds which dim her mortal sight. But she is conscious also of that light which shines beyond those clouds; and by an impulse of desire and faith she stretches out her arms to the heavens, and, silent, she binds around her lovely brow this motto: 'What is not seen is eternal.' [43]

And Hubert would surely have been able to say 'Amen' to that. In spite of his rejection of religious orthodoxy he recognised that ordered civilisation was entirely dependent upon an ethical framework; recognised the vital necessity for a spiritual dimension in the life of man; recognised no conflict between that dimension and his humanist convictions; and delineated clearly between the unsurpassable beauty of the language of the Authorised Version of the Bible and the need to subscribe to the doctrines of any Church. If opera was not to be his chosen art-form, then oratorio, so fixed in the public consciousness in combination with the Christian religion, and the passport to acceptance at the great Victorian music festivals, could surely not satisfy his deeply-felt need to give an unfettered ethical meaning to his work?

Delius was entirely wide of the mark in claiming that, given half a chance, Hubert Parry would have set the entire Bible to music. By the age of sixteen Hubert had read the whole of the Bible; he loved its language as literature; it was cemented into his consciousness; and it was central to his culture as it was central to the culture of the nation to which he belonged. His choice of biblical texts in works such as *Judith*, *Job* and *King Saul*, even though they possibly failed to kindle his most deeply creative fire, presented contemporary audiences with the comfort of familiarity and, at the same time, ensured a ready welcome by the deans and chapters whose cathedrals provided the principal platforms for performances of large-scale symphonic-choral works.

However, Hubert chose secular texts for his choral works rather more often than texts from the Bible or the liturgy, and almost always these resulted in his best work, *L'Allegro ed Il Penseroso* (Milton), *The Lotos-Eaters* (Tennyson), *Invocation to Music* (Bridges), and *A Song of Darkness and Light* (Bridges) amongst them. Hubert's search for a successor to the oratorio through which to express his philosophical and artistic ideals was to lead to the composition, between 1898 and 1908, of six works which he termed 'Ethical Cantatas'.[44] For one of the most successful of these, *The Soul's Ransom* of 1906 (A Psalm for the Poor), he turned again to the Bible, choosing to conclude the second section with a quotation

---

[43] TGP, *op cit*, p 362.
[44] *War and Peace* (1903), *Voces Clamantium* (1903), *The Love that Casteth Out Fear* (1904), *The Soul's Ransom* (1906), *The Vision of Life* (1907), and *Beyond These Voices There is Peace* (1908)

from St. John, iv, 24, an unequivocal statement of his own profound spirituality: 'God is a Spirit: and they that worship him must worship him in spirit and in truth'. For the final chorus he supplied words of his own:

> Truth will not die,
> In every soul of man it lives;
> The Sprit cannot lie!
> To each and all the choice it gives
> To rate the tempting world aright
> And to esteem it light;
> To ward the ransomed soul from stain,
> And make it worthy to attain
> To flawless harmony, divinely pure,
> With that which was, and is, and shall for evermore endure.

Six years later, in what is arguably his finest choral-orchestral work, *Ode on the Nativity*, and after a life-time of experimentation in the form, Hubert wrought perfection from a song of unquestioning faith by William Dunbar (1465-1520?):

> All *Gloria in excelsis* cry!
> Heaven, earth, sea, man, bird and beast, -
> He that is crowned above the sky
>   Pro nobis Puer natus est.

And Thomas Gambier Parry would have said 'Amen' to that!

*   *   *   *   *   *   *

Hubert's work at the Royal College continued to eat further and further into his time during 1886: a problem which was to beset him for the rest of his life. One of his students, Emily Daymond, readily volunteered to ease his burden slightly by taking over the task of Dolly and Gwen's piano lessons, thus becoming yet another of the adoring young women who came under the spell of Hubert's charm. Indeed, Hubert's personality was such as to engender the worship of many who came into contact with him, both male and female, but Emily Daymond's loyalty was long-lived and unvarying. She was of enormous help to Hubert, especially in his later years, when her assistance was invaluable. She herself, as Dolly put it, was 'ugly, sentimental and good'.[45] She was a constant visitor at the Parrys' London home and at Rustington or Highnam in the holidays, and she was never able to do enough for the man whom she affectionately called 'Pedagogue'. As she wrote to Dolly in 1913, 'I always feel that the only thing I can do for him at all is proofs! So I do proofs as hard as ever I can! It makes me so fearfully glad that I can help, in that, because he has always

---

[45] Dorothea Ponsonby, *Diary 1914*. Shulbrede archive.

done such *thousands* of things for me ever since I was a child almost, and I only wish to goodness there was more I could do. But there isn't'.[46]

But not all of Hubert's colleagues at the Royal College accepted him with unquestioning admiration. In an apparent attempt to provoke his dismissal in May 1886, Joseph Barnby, one of the Board of Examiners, launched a severe attack against Hubert's teaching methods in an address to his fellow examiners. This at a time when at least two of Hubert's composition students, Charles Wood and Hamish MacCunn, had proved the efficacy of his approach. And even though the attack was not supported in the College, it was inevitably deeply distressing to Hubert.

Whenever he could escape to Rustington from the claustrophobic atmosphere of the College, Hubert's chief recreation was sailing. Facing the challenge of the open sea had become a passion, and a doubly exhilarating one when conditions were rough; mill ponds were not for him! Having outgrown the *Ornis* he bought a small sailing boat, the *Kitta* ('magpie' in Greek), and in the summer of 1886 purchased a little yawl of 7-tons, the *Hoopoe*, which, in October, he sailed from the builder's boat-yard in Southampton to Rustington. 'Ornis', 'Kitta' and 'Hoopoe' are all characters in Aristophanes's *The Birds*; 'Hoopoe' was the prince who chose to *become* a bird – and at the tiller of his boat Hubert too became as free as air. In that autumn of 1886 he was 'constantly out in the *Hoopoe*' with Dolly, Gwen and the Richmond children, or with friends. Of one sail with his skipper, Roach, he wrote: 'a big sea on; the tail end of one of the equinoctials which would have swallowed up the *Ornis*, but the *Hoopoe* hardly took a drop over'.[47] Little wonder that Hubert became one of the earliest – and fastest – motorists in Britain, and one of the first to have his licence endorsed for speeding. He revelled in speed!

> Speed you conjure
> With a crook of your finger;
> Speed which your touch
> On a core, on a master-bit,
> Breeds for your use;
> As Man's hand on a tiller
> Gives brain to a boat;
> As Man's hand on a pen
> Turns the poor, workaday
> Labourers of language Straight into insolent,
> High, living Song;
> Speed—
> *Speed in the Lap of the Lord!*

(W. E. Henley (1849-1903), from *A Song of Speed*)

The Roach family were particularly associated with Hubert's sailing exploits throughout his life, and Roach senior, his first skipper, was succeeded in

---

[46] Emily Daymond, letter to Dorothea Ponsonby, 25 December 1913. Shulbrede archive.
[47] CHHP, *Diary 1886.*

later years by his son. The artistic creativity which Mary Oakes had brought to the Parry family was in Hubert's blood, but so too was the salt-sea which had flowed in the veins of his great-grandfather, Thomas Parry. Hubert owned a number of boats over the years, the largest of which was the *Wanderer*, as Captain Roach remembered:

> The *Wanderer* came to Littlehampton on November 23, 1900. She was then a ketch-rigged vessel, built for a Humber pilot and called the *Humber*. Sir Hubert bought her, pulled her all to pieces inside and fitted her up as a yacht in 1901. After cruising in her for some time he had her hauled up on Mr. John Harvey's slip, had her cut in halves, and ten feet added in the middle; she was then 61 tons. This made the accommodation much larger – a fine large saloon with state-room, three spare rooms in the lobby, a nice ladies' cabin, a good sized galley and pantry, and a large forecastle with cots and two berths and every convenience. Sir Hubert cruised with her for some time and then had her hauled up on the slip again. This time he had the short counter cut off and a yacht's counter built on, which made the *Wanderer* look much smarter; and in 1911 he had the old mast taken out and a much larger one put in with entirely new rigging... In the *Wanderer* we used to go for long cruises for a month or so to the S.W. of Ireland and the Skelligs, a favourite cruise of Sir Hubert's, or up St. George's Channel to the N.W. of Scotland, or down in the Bay of Biscay sailing all the time, night and day. The crew was seven all told... In the year the War broke out Sir Hubert had a 33-horse-power Thorneycroft motor put in to go through the canals of Sweden and Norway, but we were prevented going by the War.[48]

* * * * * * *

In the closing weeks of 1886 the Parrys once again changed their London address, moving from Phillimore Place to 17 Kensington Square. It was not long before Hubert was able to write that 'the new house and garden are an indescribable blessing and make our lives quite different. We seem to have cause to bless the change many times every day'.[49] Christmas was spent at Wilton, and on 30 December, alone in his bedroom, he began to work once more at a piece for which, twenty years earlier, he had sketched an opening: *Blest Pair of Sirens*.

The opening pages of *Blest Pair of Sirens* have been ranked as the most thrilling in all English music, and the splendidly assured scoring for eight-part chorus and orchestra, with its powerful and stately climaxes, matches perfectly the mood and metre of Milton's verse. In this setting, dedicated to Stanford and the Bach Choir, Hubert demonstrated vividly his ability to write an addictively memorable tune and proved himself master of that characteristic and elevated style, exemplified by a nobility of manner, which speaks directly to the English heart, and which Elgar was later to adopt and to label *nobilmente*.

The first performance of *Blest Pair of Sirens*, given by the Bach Choir under Stanford, was a triumph and a landmark. It brought Hubert national recognition, and the piece rapidly became, and remains, a popular favourite with choral societies all over the country. It is interesting to note that within a couple of years it had been performed so frequently that one festival director thought it

---

[48] Graves, *op cit*, Vol II, p 279.
[49] CHHP, *Diary 1887*. Shulbrede archive.

prudent to ask Hubert to confirm his intentions regarding correct tempi. The reply was characteristic:

> With regard to your question about the 'tempi', I cannot give you a Metronomic answer, as I don't possess a Metronome. But certainly the passage 'Jarred against nature's chime' should be quite slow. The 'ritardando' in the two previous bars should be very strong, and I should guess (with the help of my watch) that the crotchet in the $\frac{3}{4}$ would be between 60 and 64 to the minute... I remember by the bye that most conductors take the latter part beginning 'To live with him' too slow for my feeling. It should be very vigorous 'Alla breve'.[50]

*   *   *   *   *   *   *

The summer of 1887, the year of Queen Victoria's Golden Jubilee, was a golden one for Hubert Parry. On 7 July he and his father attended Robin Benson's wedding in London. William Blake Richmond was there with his family, and Helen, now a shining seventeen-year-old, noted in her diary that 'Pupsy' (her father) introduced her to Thomas Gambier Parry: 'such a funny little old man with a wig, which does not look a bit like a wig. He jumped about in the funniest way, and said Mr. Parry [Hubert] was "the dearest boy in the world".'[51] Four weeks later the Richmonds were in Rustington for their holiday; hardly a day passed when Helen was not in Hubert's company, albeit never alone. She and her brothers Ernest and 'Chunks' lay on the grass watching Hubert and Phil Burne-Jones playing tennis, or she paddled in the sea whilst Hubert and Robin Benson bathed, or was enchanted when, after dinner at Knight's Croft, Hubert played Bach, Brahms and Beethoven. The young Lady Carmarthen was also a guest at Knight's Croft that summer and, years later, had still not forgotten the alchemy which the place, and especially Hubert, worked upon her:

> I shall never forget my first visit to Rustington, when I was very young, ignorant and mad about music, books and so on, and what a revelation it was to hear him talk on these subjects. I can honestly say he gave me my first glimpses into real music, real art and real poetry. He had a wonderful unusual gift of putting order into the chaos of one's enthusiasms, without knocking out the enthusiasm itself, and it was all done without any condescension. Every night the first time I stayed at Rustington he played Bach and Beethoven to teach me something about form in music, about which I had told him I was puzzled, and I put that experience amongst the best I ever had... I well remember rowing from Arundel to Littlehampton when he was so carried away by telling us the story of *Burnt Njal* that he forgot time and tides and we were stranded on the mud. he dined with us one night early in the War, and I was amused to see my daughters falling just as much under the spell as I had done more than twenty-five years before.[52]

On 22 August William Blake Richmond returned to London and Hubert took Helen, Gwen, Ernest and Miss Coghlan, who had come down with the

---

[50] CHHP, letter to a Dr. Campbell, 22 February 1889. Property of Mr. Graham Lloyd.
[51] Helen Richmond, *Diary 1887*. Property of Mr. Christopher Walker.
[52] Graves, *op cit*, Vol I, p 282.

Richmonds, for a river trip. Helen had to steer with an umbrella as there was no tiller on their little boat:

> But in spite of my steering and all our fooling, we got past Arundel and nearly to the Black Rabbit, when the boat drifted into the reeds and we had luncheon. Miss Coghlan and I cut ham sandwiches, and the others opened the ginger beer bottles and we were all very festive. We all went on shore for a few minutes and ran up into the wood between the Rabbit and Swanbourne Lake, which looked about as lovely as it could. After our turn on shore, we went up an arm of the river where none of us had ever been before, and where we came upon a railway bridge only a foot or two above the water, so our heads were nearly taken off...
>
> As soon as we got into the real river I began to row, and managed to keep my tongue in! Miss Coghlan rowed too, and Ernest took my place just after Arundel Bridge, and they rowed a good way; Gwen also had a turn... Ernest poured out questions. When he asked why there were so many windmills, Mr. Parry said that there was once a man called Bill, who had a grandson, Tom, who possessed $2^1/2$d. and invested it in Consols, which brought him in 2 per cent. A few years later, a fortune of 4/6d. was left Tom, so he invested that also in Consols, and in ten years it brought him in $3^1/2$d. dividends. Then he went to America, and saw a savage who said, 'You look nice and fat'. 'Well', Tom replied, 'I am pretty well covered'. 'You would be very nice in a pudding', says the savage. So they ate him, and 'that's the reason why there are so many windmills', says Mr. Parry.
>
> We got back at 6.30. Dolly had been to Angmering on the tricycle with Chunks, and had been in a field where there were bulls. So she too had a fine time, but not equal to ours I bet.[53]

Two days later Hubert took the Richmond children out to sea in the *Hoopoe*:

> We sailed out and inspected a small schooner of only 100 tons which was going to Mauritius. Denyer had rigged her and said she was built for slaves, but I'm not certain if Mr. Parry was humbugging us or not when he told us.
>
> We then sailed down to Kingston, and dangled our feet in the water and caught fishes, and I steered while Mr. Parry packed our basket. Coming into the harbour we saw a small boy lose his ball, and Mr. Parry sent Ernest and me off in the little boat to get it for him. We felt tremendous masher ones rowing alone after the ball, which we got after rowing round and round it several times.[54]

On the last full day of her holiday, 16 September, Hubert was about to set sail when Helen again appeared. He took her aboard:

> Oh, it was scrumptious. We sailed in the *Kitta* to Littlehampton. Regardless of sore throats, I took my stockings off and enjoyed myself. We had to go about constantly as we were going against the wind, and had to row at last so as to get over the Works before the tide got too low. I pulled for a a good time, 'good, long, slow, steady strokes' they were, like the man in 'Punch', but my legs did not go up quite so high. We cleared the Works, and then got into difficulties in the harbour as the tide was going out too fast, and there was too little wind to allow of us sailing in. So we went outside again, and sailed about a bit, and finally decided to run ashore on the beach. Mr. Parry put me

---

[53] *Ibid.*
[54] *Ibid.*

ashore. I came back inland as it was raining, and tucking my dress up round my waist, scooted back as hard as I could go.

Sat. Sep 17th The fatal day arrived for leaving the Parrydise, and a very horribly wet one too. Much packing had to be done, for Mother was very tired, and I had to do the boys' as well as my own.

The boys and I went to say goodbye at Knight's Croft. It was truly awful, Lady Maude was such a dear, and Dolly and Gwen I know sorry to lose us. The dear man drove with us to Littlehampton and saw us off. The train was so full that we had to come 2nd. It was *disgusting* saying goodbye to the dear man, and when he put his hand into the carriage, we all tried to shake it at once, and when the train had started, waved our hats and arms to him out of the window as long as we could see him, with tears pouring down our faces and trickling off the tips of our noses![55]

With a steady inevitability, through summer after blissful summer, Helen began to think of Hubert as something more than a close family friend. 'Mr. Parry' gives way in her diary to an affectionate nickname, 'the Pirrieman'; she experiences the euphoric torture of an adolescent crush, sufficient once to have her conceal herself near to Knight's Croft in the hope that Hubert would emerge, and to continue waiting even though it begins to rain, only to wait in vain. And as she grows to beautiful young womanhood, to find her ardent glances returned by the object of her affections. A hopeless and despairing sexual tension holds her fixed as though frozen. And when Helen eventually marries in 1902 it is to find herself locked into a loveless relationship.[56]

'Mr. Parry is to write *the* big thing for Birmingham next year', recorded Helen Richmond in her 1887 diary. And the big thing was *Judith*, a conventional oratorio which consolidated his fame but about which Hubert himself was never enthusiastic, having been obliged to work at it spasmodically and more often than not without inspiration. 'It's poor stuff, sugary and thin, I am too done up to do better', he wrote. But, of course, it was exactly the sort of thing to appeal to the regional festivals and to be received enthusiastically by choral societies.

Judith fell short of Hubert's own ideals, and George Bernard Shaw was highly critical of it, but at least one of its numbers has gained lasting popularity. Hubert's first intention, mercifully dropped, was to call the oratorio 'The Regeneration of Manasseh'. In it, the ballad 'Long since in Egypt's plenteous land' is sung touchingly by the wife of King Manasseh, Queen Meshullemeth, to her children, who respond in the final verse, reminding them of how God led the Israelites to safety. Known today by every church choir in the land as 'Repton', set to words by J G Whittier, it has been voted the nation's number one favourite hymn, 'Dear Lord and Father of Mankind'.

*   *   *   *   *   *   *

---

[55] *Ibid.*

[56] Memories of Mr. Christopher Walker, Helen Richmond's grandson.

In August 1888 Hubert arrived at Highnam in readiness for the Three Choirs Festival at Hereford, where he was to conduct *Blest Pair of Sirens*. He found the atmosphere of his old home dispiriting, as he explained in a letter to Dolly:

Darling Little Doll,

Thanks for your nice letter, and the nice little picture at the top. I find Highnam rather melancholy. It has a way of reviving my memories of old times, and a sort of life that can never come back; when Possie was hearty and lively, and there were many people we loved that have either taken their departure from the world, or changed in time into something quite different. They had a garden party yesterday, but I kept out of the way till the last half hour. The people looked pretty nice some of them from a distance. But when one gets into that sort of thing one gets tackled by the people who don't look nice and one hasn't time to draw out any of their niceness, and altogether the world don't adapt itself quite to one's wishes or inclinations...

Goodie bye my own dearest little Doll

Your ever loving

Feyjey.[57]

Ernest was one who had 'changed in time into something quite different' since Hubert had seen him off at Southampton thirteen years earlier. In 1885, the year in which General Gordon was slaughtered in Khartoum by the followers of the Mhadi, Ernest, by then a Captain, transferred to the 1st Royal Devon Yeomanry Cavalry, was based at Suakin on the Sudan coast as a Special Service Officer. In his book, *The Pageant of My Day*, Ernest described graphically the day on which, soon after dawn, bugles sounded the 'Fall-in', and all the regiments in the barracks marched out into the white heat of the desert:

He is mounting now higher into the heavens, and shadows on the ground draw in. The solid blocks of sand-coloured men are breaking up, wheeling to right and left, and gradually resolving themselves into an immense hollow square in the glare and the dazzle of the heat. A thousand camels, burdened with water-tins and trusses of forage, are driven, a vast herd, into the open space thus formed, and these are followed by guns, and other pieces man-hauled by jolly sailors...

A slight rise in the ground has been reached, and from your horse you can see some distance. In one direction a peaceful landscape is spread out again for you to marvel at. Here are blue trees in rows, and water and waving reeds, and, as if to deceive you further, a bird's note, like that of an English lark, is to be heard, followed by another where the bush is thickest [On more than one occasion in the Sudan, the natives were known, afterwards, to have made use of bird-calls as preconcerted signals]. The blue landscape and the waving reeds appear closer than before, and seem now to be moving towards you. Your men are lying down resting, and you look over them – look, and look again. Of a sudden there is a shot, and all jump to their feet and clutch at their rifles. There are shouts at the same time from all directions. A riderless horse passes an opening in the bush, and then you see, for the first time, that what you took for trees, are mounted men, looking twice their height, too, in the mirage; while the waving reeds

[57] CHHP, letter to Dorothea Parry, 24 August 1888. Shulbrede archive.

have transformed themselves into the lances and pennons of scattered horsemen. They are coming in at a gallop, endeavouring to clear the front. And close behind them is a running crowd, dressed in white *galabiehs*, or naked as they came into the world, brandishing spears and swords and shields of every size and shape, shouting and waving strange flags; those with rifles firing wildly. There is little time to look at them. They are coming on like an angry wave, and the sound as they come is as the sound of a roaring sea.

There are shouts to stand to arms. In some cases rifles had been piled, and the men were opening their haversacks, or drinking from their felt-covered bottles. They are up in an instant. Bullets are flying thickly, and some have found their billets among the camels. These, stung by their wounds, break their lines, and charging in all directions with their unwieldy loads, throw the rest into confusion and create a general stampede among the transport. A vast column of dust, visible for many miles, rises skywards as they go, and soon they are enveloped by the oncoming host that drives them all ways, and hacks and hews and butchers them at will. Meanwhile, it looks for a moment as if, by this stampede, all order had been destroyed: in more than one place the formation has been altogether broken up: the companies are divided: some are unable to reach their rifles: men are running in every direction, and officers are filling gaps with any that come to hand. In the dust and confusion it is impossible to see far. Many have evidently been shut out from the square, and these have formed themselves into groups outside and are firing independently, while the sailors have already got their Gatlings into action and are pumping lead into the bush and the on-coming tide of fighting men that nothing seems capable of checking. Every one is loading and firing as rapidly as he can, and the din of the fight becomes a general roar. But still above it all, rises the volume of sound of the Dervish onrush.

Many have charged right up to the muzzles of the rifles and are clutching at the bayonets; and many more have got between the faces of the square and the groups outside. A few have even penetrated the square itself; and officers are using their revolvers. Men are falling on our side, and not all hit by Dervish bullets; but many more are falling on theirs. Their bodies lie scattered thickly on the ground; but again and again numbers of them are only stopped to rise once more and charge on as before. Some, in their cool indifference, appear to bear the charm they were promised by the Mhadi, and pass, unhurried and unscathed, through the storm of lead that is kicking up the sand and cutting the branches from the cruel thorns...

Even in all that you have to do, in the din and the dust and the heat, you have still time to look, for an instant, and marvel at what you see. A thousand impressions that you will never lose are being stamped every instant on your memory. Wounded and dying are borne past you to the centre of the square; a horse rears up and tumbles backwards with its rider, shot through the head; a man falls close beside you, going down with the rattle of fire-irons; there are scarlet stains on the sand at your feet; and wretched camel-drivers – poor mangled creatures of another race – crawl in through the lines, calling, in different tongues, for 'water' – 'water' – 'water!' that will not reach them while they live.[58]

Ernest was cut down. Drifting into and out of delerium impressions, half-remembered, half-imagined, lingered in his mind: of the gentleness of the men who came to his aid, of the long voyage home, of his return to Highnam, and of his father:

He is asking you questions, and telling you many things you want to hear about. But now and then you notice that the gladness in his face goes out; the tone in his voice alters,

[58] Ernest Gambier-Parry, *The Pageant of My Day* (London, 1910), pp 202-207.

and you see him pass the back of his hand across his chin and move his feet… This was one who used to talk to you of reverence, and what it meant, as you strolled together in the fields, in the season when hope denied you nothing. He had, you knew, built everything on your success, as you came to man's estate… You can recall the very smile there was upon his face on such occasions, and the way in which he took your arm in his. There was never any doubt of his love; and yet you had sometimes held it cheap!… He was sitting by you now: you could see him plainly – the keen, alert look in the face, the smile that had so often come into your dreams.

'Yes,' he said – 'I suppose it was. Well, any way, we have got you back now, and we shall all see what we can do'.[59]

Ernest was awarded the rank of major 'for services', along with the Sudan campaign medal with clasp and Khedive's star, but he was physically broken. Skilled as an artist, several of whose pictures were exhibited at the Royal Academy, a musician, and gifted as a writer, his potential had been great when the Sudan brought him to what he described in the words of Heine as 'a mattress grave'. His wife, Evelyn, nursed him devotedly at Highnam for five pain-racked years, but even when physical suffering came at last to an end the mental burden remained. The Sudan put something upon Ernest which, as Hubert observed, 'affected his nerves and his judgement', he had grown to 'exaggerate sentiment in the most abnormal way, without having any genuine healthy feeling at the base of it'.[60]

Although a dozen of his books were published, Ernest never achieved literary success of the first rank. Apart from two biographies, of Reynell Taylor and Ainslie Gore, his subject matter tended to the narrow, parochial path. His *Annals of an Eton House* still captures the attention of those concerned with the history of the school; but in such titles as *The Combat with Suffering* and *Day-Dreams, being thoughts from the note-book of a cripple*, his skilful and impressive prose is turned to the service of cloying sentimentality.

∗   ∗   ∗   ∗   ∗   ∗   ∗

Nearly twenty years after Thomas Gambier Parry had completed his work on the St Andrew's Chapel in Gloucester Cathedral he was asked to decorate the great tower-buttress that crosses obliquely the arched entrance to the Chapel. Ernest, confined to his bed, remembered his father's determination to complete this task, in spite of the heart trouble which now dogged his old age:

> His scheme was a very happy one: the buttress was to bear a fresco of Jacob's vision of the ladder set up to Heaven, with angels ascending and descending it (Genesis xxviii, 12); and the shafting and moulding that frame the arch were also to be coloured to make the entrance more in keeping with the interior of the Chapel.
>
> Father was no longer able to mount a scaffolding so the work was begun at Highnam. It is on canvas, and though alas! never quite completed, it was, so far as the main subject was concerned, very nearly so. All the angels were finished, but not the sleeping figure of Jacob. Father had a huge drawing-board set up in the drawing-room

[59] Ernest Gambier-Parry, *op cit*, pp 221/2.
[60] CHHP, *Diary 1888*. Shulbrede archive.

with a large wooden cylinder fixed obliquely to one side. The canvass was rolled up on this cylinder and unrolled bit by bit as required, being cut exactly to the plan of the great buttress, or rather, perhaps, having the plan of the buttress marked out on it. Father was engaged on this painting, whenever he could find time, up to the last – that is up to the very day he died.[61]

On the last evening of his life, 28 September 1888, the eve of St Michael and All Angels, Thomas Gambier Parry was reading *The Renaissance in Italy* by John Addington Symonds. Ethelinda, Ernest, Linda and Beatrice, who was sitting at the piano, were with him. Looking up from his book he said, 'I have finished my last angel'. Beatrice was playing something familiar, and when she finished it her father said, 'Oh, do play that again'. It was Clinton's *Remembrance*. Within an hour, still sitting in the same chair, he died.[62]

The next morning, a Saturday, Hubert received a telegram from Ernest. 'Utterly bewildered', he travelled down to Highnam with Maude by the first available train. Sunday was 'a most painful day'. Hubert 'went to church so as not to pain the family more than need be; and felt even more disgusted than usual at the totally senseless forms of modern conventional religion'.[63] 'The death of that dear old father of mine hit me rather hard', he wrote to Dannreuther:

> I scarcely realised how fond I was of him till he departed, and it seems to me now as if the attraction he had for me was different from that of any other person in the world. Though we disagreed, as you know, about many things, the last year drew us together more than ever before. I never was more drawn to him, nor was he ever more loving to me than in the last few months; and his going made me strangely lonely.[64]

The hopes which Gambier Parry had held for Clinton and Ernest had been shattered and, probably to his great surprise, Hubert, the son who as a small child had seemed to him the least likely to succeed, had proved himself the very one who would bring honour to the family for whose good name he had strived so hard. The laurels which were yet to come to Hubert would surely have astonished his father. In 1894 he was appointed Director of the Royal College of Music, followed by a knighthood in 1898, the chair of music at Oxford in 1900 and, in 1903, a baronetcy, an honour which brought with it his own coat of arms: the addition of three clarions to the ancient arms of the Parrys of the Golden Vale. The motto beneath the arms remained unaltered, *tu ne cede malis*, 'yield not to evils' or, as Hubert would have it, 'never chuck up the sponge'!

Directorship of the RCM inevitably entailed a level of strains and demands which for most men would have been burden enough. But for Hubert, who some years earlier had written in his diary: 'Verily, man that is born of woman hath but a short time to WORK',[65] no waking moment was ever to be

[61] GPM p 176. The 'Jacob's Ladder' canvas is now lost.
[62] GPM p 150.
[63] CHHP, *Diary 1888.*
[64] CHHP, letter to Edward Dannreuther, 26 October 1888. Copied in full in Graves, *op cit,* Vol I, p 287.
[65] CHHP, *Diary 1879.* Shulbrede archive.

wasted. Always reluctant to delegate any part of his responsibilities, Hubert imposed an extraordinarily heavy administrative load upon himself. And yet many of his finest compositions were born out of this pressure, including three symphonies; the superb Symphonic Variations (1897); the coronation anthem *I Was Glad* (1902); *The Soul's Ransom* (1906), arguably, as Bernard Benoliel has pointed out, the link work between Elgar's *The Dream of Gerontius* (1900) and Vaughan Williams's *A Sea Symphony* (1909)[66]; *The Vision of Life* (1907), for which Hubert wrote both words and music, and which was a work greatly admired by Elgar; *Ode on the Nativity* (1912); and, of course, *Jerusalem* (1916). He was, said Herbert Howells, 'and for years had been – a human dynamo of tireless energy: not the energy of "a Lascar let loose in a power-house", but that of a limitless sensibility and comprehensive culture in a man of myriad activities, wide interests and commanding creative achievement'.[67]

In the autumn of his life Hubert's creative energy even bloomed afresh. Although demoralised by the War, wearied by the capriciousness of his wife, strained by tensions at the Royal College of Music, deeply disappointed by Macmillan's refusal to publish his book *Instinct and Character*, and increasingly troubled by deteriorating health, Hubert gave expression to his profound inner loneliness, and to a faith which was both unorthodox and unshakeable, in six unaccompanied *Songs of Farewell*. The first motet, 'My soul there is a country', a setting in four parts of the poem *Peace* by the metaphysical poet Henry Vaughan 'the Silurist' (1622-1695), is the best-known and most frequently performed. And in choosing this text Hubert was unwittingly reaching back to his ancient ancestry. Amongst the Parrys who served Elizabeth I, none was more loyal than her faithful cofferer and Controller of the Royal Household, Thomas Parry (d1560). But Thomas was not actually a Parry at all. He was a Vaughan, one of the great-grandsons of Sir Roger Vaughan of Tretower (half-brother of Sir William Herbert, First Earl of Pembroke) whose family were linked in marriage with the Parrys. Thomas had chosen, rather than 'Vaughan', to use his father's patronymic – and Henry Vaughan 'the Silurist' was of the same blood.

A mood of valediction pervades the other five motets: 'I know my soul hath power', a setting, also in four parts, of two stanzas from the poem *Man* by Sir John Davies (1567-1626), concluding with the poignant words 'I know myself a Man, which is a proud and yet a wretched thing'. For the gentle 'Never weather-beaten sail' by Thomas Campion (1567-1620) the parts increase to five, and to six for 'There is an old belief' by John Gibson Lockhart (1794-1854), which was sung at Hubert's funeral at St Paul's Cathedral on 16 October 1918.

'At the round earth's imagined corners' is a seven-part setting of one of John Donne's *Divine Meditations* in which the poet stands in awe of the Last Judgement; and surely at the words 'Despair, law, chance hath slain, and you, whose eyes shall behold God and never taste death's woe', Hubert's vision was that of his father's great *Doom* at Highnam. For the final motet, set for double choir, Hubert turned

---

[66] Bernard Benoliel, *op cit*, p 97.
[67] Herbert Howells, *Hubert Parry*, from text of the Crees Lecture delivered at the Royal College of Music on 7 October 1968.

again to the Bible, to Psalm 39, 'Lord, let me know mine end': a confession of the uselessness of riches and vanity, an acceptance of the brevity of life, and a plea for forgiveness: 'Hear my prayer, O Lord, and with Thine ears consider my calling, hold not Thy peace at my fears! For I am a stranger with Thee and a sojourner as all my fathers were. O spare me a little, that I may recover my strength before I go hence and be no more seen'.

The affection and reverence in which Hubert Parry was held by his students is legendary, and his interest in them went far beyond the formalities of lecture and tutorial. Ivor Gurney, brilliantly gifted as both poet and composer, was just one of those many students whose departure to war caused Hubert so much sorrow. 'Sir Hubert is a great man, and my admiration for him has been great from the first. He speaks with authority, not as one of the scribes', wrote Gurney to Marion Scott, Registrar of the RCM, in January 1918.[68] Hubert took time and trouble to write to Gurney several times during the war, and presumably to others in the trenches too. 'Sir C.H.H.P.'s two letters have arrived, and very nice too. But niceness makes me yearn' Gurney wrote from the Somme in February 1917. Two months later he confessed to Marion Scott that 'Pain rules so much and so continually in the sight of one who bears Pain hardly'; but on hearing from her a few days later of Parry's reaction to his magnificent setting of Masefield's *By a Bierside*, composed whilst he was 'at rest', Gurney's morale was instantly boosted: 'Did Sir C.H.H.P. really say my song was the most tragic thing he knew? If so, what an enormous praise! I shall be very proud of that, if it is so; and could desire no other or higher praise'.[69]

*　　*　　*　　*　　*　　*　　*

Hubert Parry died on 7 October 1918. Few who came into contact with him failed to be struck by and to admire his essential qualities. As a father he was genuinely adored. 'My father', wrote Gwendolen, 'stood pre-eminent and alone as both the loved centre and the training-ground of our lives. His was the spirit to whom we owed our first recognition of loveliness, the first intimations of beauty spoke through him'.[70] Gwendolen's husband, the baritone Harry Plunket Greene, remembered his father-in-law as a man whose bluff exterior concealed a fierce fighting temperament kept firmly in leash, a definite shyness – a lonely man. To counter that shyness his ice-breaking technique was emphatic: 'He did not pat people on the back', wrote Charles Graves, 'he thumped them'!

Maude lived on until 1933. 'Mercifully', as Dorothea's husband, Arthur Ponsonby, wrote, 'Hubert Parry was spared the watching of cruel decay which overcame her in the last years of her life'. And perhaps the most perceptive summary of Hubert Parry the man was that written by Arthur Ponsonby, with whose family, at their Shulbrede Priory home in Sussex, Hubert was able in later life to find some of his deepest happiness:

[68] R K R Thornton (ed), *Ivor Gurney, Collected Letters* (MidNAG Carcanet, 1991), p 391.

[69] Thornton, *op cit*, p 245.

[70] Gwendolen Greene, *Two Witnesses* (J.M. Dent & Sons Ltd., 1930), p 11.

Of all the people I have met in my life Hubert Parry stands out as the most remarkable. Admiration for his wide equipment of knowledge and admiration for his musical genius although ever present were not as a matter of fact the basis with me of his inspiring influence. Nor indeed even was our close relationship. Nor again was it his artistic temperament because that is unaccountable and often capricious. It was his character. Here was a man... who knew how to dismiss the superfluities and unrealities and unnecessary trimmings of life and could reach the realities, the fundamentals and the things that counted. I was attracted too by the fact that although he had been brought up in the surroundings of a rich country gentleman at Highnam and although by his marriage he had been drawn into high and luxurious society, he elected to carve out a career of his own as a professional in a field despised at that time and against much opposition. But beyond those considerations I have never come across anyone with a higher standard, a more faultless sense of quality and a more profound reverence for the spiritual. This last drew me to him as much as anything because I saw – and other instances came my way – how goodness and recognition of goodness could exist in a high degree without any links whatever with the supernatural or the dogmas of any religion. I think he was the most religious man I have known but he showed me how institutional religion of any description prevented the development of the spiritual which always became overlaid either by superstition or by religious observances which generally became quite perfunctory. He greatly appreciated the beauties and some of the grandeur whether in music, art or architecture which the churches had inherited. He knew large parts of the bible by heart and understood its magnificence far better than all the clergy I have met put together. He took it as his theme in much of his music. But anything in the nature of superstition made him fiercely intolerant...

Hubert Parry inspired great adoration – too much. I think it bored him. He liked a rough path very much more than a smooth. One day on board ship in the Mediterranean I expressed admiration and content at the sunshine and the smooth sea. He told me he greatly preferred a rough sea and was looking forward to the coming squall. In fact in his life, his nearest approach to complete happiness came to him when he was on his yacht with his hand on the tiller steering it over waves and through shoals and going on impossible journeys to impossible places. There was an extraordinary and one might say unique charm in this combination of the hardy bluff joy in the relentless buffets of the waves and the storm and the delicate hyper-sensitive appreciation of the most elusive beauty and the highly enlightened spritual capacity to create it. A most unusual combination. His hands curiously enough illustrated this. They were as hard as iron. He might have spent his time handling ropes judging by the toughness of his palms. Yet when he sat down to the piano his touch was so delicate that he could produce effects which were nothing short of ethereal. With Eton, with Oxford, with country houses he had been steered into easy waters where he might have with many others have drifted, had it not been that within him there was an ever growing refusal to accept the ready made when it was presented to him whether materially or intellectually and an innate preference for the rough stone of life on which alone he knew he could sharpen the blade of his personality...

His wife could not distinguish God Save the Queen from Rule Britannia...But music was very rarely heard at Rustington or Highnam. Other people strumming on a piano would have driven him mad and he himself very rarely used one for his composition. His powers of concentration were quite abnormal. He never relaxed indoors. He would go to his table with the door open and noises from the house coming in or he would sit with his papers on his writing table or on the dining room table while a meal was being laid, and with a cap which he always wore on his bald head and a pipe in his mouth he would with the tough seaman's hand rapidly fill in a complicated score in very neat writing. Every five minutes was used, he was an indefatigable worker. He did not soar away beyond one by getting up at 6 or going to bed at 2 but showed what could be done within the compass of a normal man's normal day. Watching him made me think; his stray words gave me the right hint; his shout gave me the proper warning and his wonderful soft smile and twinkling eyes gave me the needed encouragement. Yes, I really do not believe now that I am getting on towards the end that one learns very much from sitting down to long talks, 'having it out', listening to sermons and advice, in fact being *consciously* taught, encouraged or admonished. I have learned much more by detecting, noticing, watching all my unconscious models, comparing the bad with the good and the good with the better and seeing the passing glints of illumination. It is only my own eyes that are to blame that I have not seen more. Many of the passengers on my road have been worth watching. None more than Hubert Parry.[71]

*   *   *   *   *   *   *

In the months following his father's death, Hubert Parry completed two symphonies, No 3 in C ('The English') and No 4 in E minor, dedicated to Hans Richter, who conducted the first performance at the St James's Hall on 1 July 1889. The 4th Symphony is a stunning work, enriched by the brilliance and heroic sweep, the rhythmic hesitation, and the elegiac sound-picture which we have come to recognise as 'Elgarian'. And Elgar, still an unknown at the age of 34, was in the audience at the première of Parry's 4th. He encountered the work of a master and took note. Shortly afterwards, and significantly, the Worcester organist, William Done, agreed to include, for the first time, one of Elgar's own compositions in the programme of the Three Choirs Festival; and following the première of *Froissart* in 1890 Elgar set out with sure foot upon the path to greatness.

When in April 1891 Hubert Parry travelled to Worcester to conduct a performance of *Judith*, Elgar was playing in the orchestra. Before Hubert mounted the platform, Elgar crept up to the conductor's desk, placed his own bâton on it, and then slipped quietly back to his accustomed place amongst the violins. In later years Elgar would envelop this small act of homage in protective humour: 'Oh! Parry did all those', he would say, pointing out all the knocks along the length of the bâton, 'I played first fiddle then and put my stick on his desk. I wanted to make it immortal.'[72]

[71] Arthur Ponsonby, *Brief Glimpses: Hubert Parry*. Shulbrede archive.
[72] *The Musical Times*, 1 October 1900, p 647.

Epilogue

A visitor to Highnam Court in the late nineteen eighties would have detected decay long before reaching the house: a dilapidated and deserted gate-house, a rutted carriageway, and once elegant gardens overgrown and choked with weeds. And in the house itself, stripped of Thomas Gambier Parry's treasures, a number of strategically-placed buckets and tin baths tinkled on rainy days to the depressing sound of water leaking through the roof. For over sixty years the decline had been both harsh and unremitting.

In his will, Gambier Parry left the Highnam Court estate and the whole of his personal estate upon trust for Ethelinda for life, followed by Hubert for life, and then Ernest for life, and then in tail for Ernest's sons. Throughout the remaining years of his step-mother's life Hubert had taken little interest in the management of the estate. Ernest and Evelyn continued in residence at Highnam, with Ernest acting as squire on his mother's behalf, assisted by an excellent and loyal estate manager, Sowray. But when, on 24 May 1896, Ethelinda died and Hubert came into his inheritance, he soon realised that he was also heir to a considerable financial burden. In the last quarter of the nineteenth century British agriculture was in slump. By 1879 corn prices were falling steadily due to American imports, rent returns at Highnam were tumbling, and hundreds of arable acres were being laid down to permanent grass.

Hubert suggested to Ernest that some retrenchment must be faced, perhaps by selling off land. Ernest, who held a controlling interest in his late father's trust, was appalled. Within a fortnight of his mother's death he wrote to Hubert:

> Your letter this morning has filled me with the kind of horror which I cannot describe… There are to me – to us all, I think – traditions here so sacred, that to touch them seems almost sacrilege. I have been round and round, month by month, year by year, doing this, doing that; and it seemed to me always that I was pointing father's walls, guarding father's trees: they were his, *his* – he did it all, and I was only the family's servant who was sent to guard them – nothing else. And while I acted thus, I swear its truth, I added always – 'his work shall not go back, no stranger shall ever touch it, Hubert shall find it nice – clean, undamaged, free from debt, as father left it! I worked for you, I tell you, and I never thought of self or son. One aim alone had I in my mind – to keep father's handiwork safe and secure, that these walls and these walks should know only the voices he knew and the tread of the feet that had tried hard enough to follow in the course he set… There is only one thing that I could not see, it may be weak to say so –

I could not see a strange foot here and live. *Somehow* the family must go on, and I will sacrifice all I have in the world to keep the stranger out.[1]

When next Ernest wrote to Hubert it was to include a detailed breakdown of the estate accounts and to suggest that Hubert should ease the situation by making an annual net contribution of several hundreds of pounds. Hubert, already committed to the expense of maintaining Knight's Croft and 17 Kensington Square, refused. Ernest and Evelyn moved from Highnam to live at 'Elmcroft', Goring-on-Thames, and for the rest of his life Ernest refused so much as to open the letters he received from Hubert. His obsession with his father's memory and his determination to 'keep the stranger out' flew in the face of financial prudence. And those same passions destroyed the precious affection of a lifetime.

Even though Maude disliked Highnam, never sleeping well whilst there, Hubert assumed his rôle as the squire of Highnam, conscientiously playing his part in the community even to the extent of, in spite of his many other commitments, taking the place expected of him as a local magistrate. He also played an active part in the musical life of Gloucester, and provided both the energy and the funds to improve the Shire Hall, converting the interior into a fitting concert hall of one thousand seats for the city and giving £1,500 of his own money, a huge sum then, towards the scheme. The work was completed in 1910, and as Herbert Brewer, the then organist of Gloucester Cathedral, remembered:

> At the secular Concert of the [Three Choirs] Festival the Mayor presented Sir Hubert Parry with an address of gratitude for his generous gift for the enlarging and improvement of the Hall, which Sir Hubert acknowledged with a speech in which he tried characteristically to persuade the audience that most of the thanks were due to other people.
>
> I had hoped that the gratitude of the city would take a more tangible form and that the Freedom of the City would have been conferred on Sir Hubert. I took steps to bring this about, but unfortunately Parry's political views were very pronounced and he had recently appeared on the political platform and spoken in no uncertain voice [*in support of a Liberal candidate*]. Party feeling, alas, runs very high in Gloucester as in most cathedral cities, and as these views did not coincide with those of the party in power at the time, I was unable to achieve my project and secure this recognition of Parry's munificence.[2]

In 1922 a plaque in memory of Sir Hubert Parry was unveiled in the south-west corner of Gloucester Cathedral. Over seventy-five years later it looks rather forlorn, tucked among the displays in the cathedral shop, which is situated in that very corner. But no other fitting recognition of Parry the man, his generosity or his genius exists in the city even now; and the concert hall, scene of so many important musical occasions, including the historic first performance of Parry's *Prometheus Unbound*, was sacrificed in the nineteen fifties to provide space for County Council offices!

---

[1] Ernest Gambier-Parry, letter to CHHP dated 3 June 1896. Shulbrede archive.
[2] Sir Herbert Brewer, *Memories of Choirs and Cloisters* (London, 1931), p 140.

For Ernest and Evelyn misfortune seemed to be without end. Although both of their children were gifted intellectually, neither was able to marry. Thomas Robert, 'Tom', was sent to Eton, but in 1897 acute spinal disease necessitated his being taken away to live an invalid life for some years. Mark was sent to Eton too, and went on to Oxford, but his profoundly introspective personality was such that by 1911 Ernest despaired of his younger son ever finding employment. 'Mark, poor dear boy', he wrote, 'he tries his best and is as anxious to earn as we are that he should'.[3] However, in 1913, Mark, who was particularly fascinated by eighteenth-century history and possessed considerable ability as a writer, published a very successful biography of the wife of the illustrious financier whom Louis XVI called in to right his exchequer, *Madame Necker*.

Evelyn continued to correspond with Hubert. In August 1915, whilst working at the Voluntary Aid Hospital in Goring, she wrote:

> I would give all I possess to bring you two together, but that will never be in this world, so it only remains to accept the fact, deplorable though it is… [Ernest] has had two rather bad breakdowns – nervous breakdowns which always terrify me – but I think he has hardened up a bit since then. Mark has at last got some definite work, thank goodness, nothing very wonderful but something which to start with went very much against the grain, so in a way it is meritorious. He is running the Tobacco Fund for the Oxford Military Hospital, which means he has to carry round a huge basket to supply 23 wards, on every other day. He sees and hears most terrible things, but it is very good for him.[4]

The reconciliation for which Evelyn longed never came, but after Hubert's death Ernest emerged from his self-imposed exile and returned with her to Highnam. He had not seen the house for twenty-two years but slipped back to the manor born as though he had never been away. There was much for him to do. In 1915 ferocious gales had blown down one hundred of the best elms and many specimen trees in the *pinetum*, and then the War Office had demanded the felling of trees for rifle butts, but even this was not enough – in 1917 Hubert had received orders for yet further felling. Herbert Howells recalled a conversation which he had with Hubert Parry at the Royal College of Music in October 1917:

> It happened to be my birthday: he knew that somehow. So in his own high-spirited, joyous way he talked of anniversaries – mine, anybody's – and of the chronological antics of time. Then, in serious mood, spoke of his own next birthday, his 70th, called it 'the last milestone', adding that he had only one major fear – not of death, but just that, being gone, his successor at Highnam might cut down some of the rare and lovely trees there. And maybe he did. So indeed did the war in Sir Hubert's last four years: trees and men, cut down by the million in and beyond Europe, in a scourge that cast a

---

[3] Ernest Gambier-Parry, *Diary 1911*. Highnam archive.
[4] Evelyn Gambier-Parry to CHHP, letter dated 6 August 1915. Shulbrede archive.

devastating shadow over Parry's mind and heart, but drove him in sheer genius and in hunger for consolation to his paramount creative achievement – the *Songs of Farewell.*[5]

Before war came again Ernest was to know very real anguish. Evelyn, who for years had coped heroically with his obsessive and unstable temperament, slowly descended into insanity. On 6 November 1928 she was, as Mark put it, 'ejected ignominiously from her home and shot willy nilly into the nearest mad house'.[6] Then, in the following year and in an attempt to keep his wife's condition secret, Ernest purchased a house, 'Littlecroft', in Jack Straws Lane on the outskirts of Oxford, an isolated spot at that time. Here, out of sight and out of sound, Evelyn was nursed until her death in 1935. During those 'six terrible years' it was Mark who was made to carry the greatest burden of responsibility for his mother, the strain of which resulted in his being troubled with asthma and skin rashes for the rest of his life. But more than Mark's health was to suffer. In 1925 he had published his most ambitious work, *Studies of Childhood and Youth*, accounts written with great insight and sensitivity of the early years in the lives of Châteaubriand, Lamartine and George Sand. After his experiences at 'Littlecroft' Mark did not publish anything more.

Ernest's elder son, Tom, recovered sufficient health to read Modern History at Magdalen College, and remained in Oxford, where he was made a Senior Assistant in the Bodleian Library. In spite of continuing poor health he became a student of Sanskrit, and made a catalogue of the collection of Sanskrit manuscripts in the Bodleian. In 1931 he was made Keeper of the Oriental Department of the Library and shortly afterwards of the Indian Section. An authority on numismatics, he bequeathed his valuable collection of coins to the University; but his greatest pleasure was in the study of botany, and he was in the first rank of the field botanists of England.

Ernest's sister Geraldine died on the first day of 1934, and in 1935 he suffered a terrible double blow: Evelyn died on 10 February; Tom five days later. 'I still can't realise that my precious two are gone', Ernest wrote in his diary, 'and each day I frequently repeat to myself – "They are dead": "they are dead".'[7] One month later, Ernest's sister-in-law, Sidney's wife, Grace, also died. On 23 March 1936 his sister Linda died too; and on 15 April 1936 Ernest himself followed, leaving Mark the sole heir to Highnam Court.

*   *   *   *   *   *   *

At the time of his father's death, Mark was living in a flat at 5A King Edward Street, Oxford, bequeathed to him by his brother Tom. His sole income of £120 was derived from the rent of the shop on the ground floor of these premises and, quite content with his lot, he had no desire whatsoever to move to Highnam Court. It was a considerable shock to him, therefore, when within a week of

---

[5] Herbert Howells, *Hubert Parry*, from text of the Crees Lecture, delivered at the Royal College of Music on 7 October 1968.
[6] Mark Gambier-Parry, letter to Alfred Eels dated 3 November 1936. Highnam archive.
[7] Ernest Gambier-Parry, *Diary 1935*. Highnam archive.

Ernest's passing he received a letter from his Uncle Sidney, Ernest's executor, asking him to pay £500 into Lloyd's Bank, Gloucester, in order that the estate manager, Alfred Eels, who was Sowray's son-in-law and successor, might be able to pay the wages of the estate servants. Sidney, at the age of seventy-seven and living comfortably in Surrey, had no interest in inheriting Highnam himself, probably considering it an expensive millstone. Mark was therefore left with no alternative other than to draw upon the residue of his brother's estate, a sum not greater than £830. His problems were rapidly compounded when it became clear that as a result of the nature of his father's will, in which Highnam had been entailed to Tom, he was liable for double death duties on the estate caused by the deaths in close succession of his elder brother and his father!

Eels assured Mark that sufficient funds would be available for the needs of the estate once probate had been granted on his father's will, but sales of land and property were essential to settle the death duties. With great reluctance, Mark began to make periodic visits to Highnam from Oxford, remaining there for as few hours as possible; but no matter how short the visit, each one occasioned a recurrence of his skin rashes. One particular room depressed him beyond measure: his father's study, 'that dreadful room' as he described it to Eels. 'I shall like to discuss the question of colours for that hateful study. I am quite determined to make it as unlike it ever was before as possible! None of the pictures nor furniture that used to be in it shall ever be seen there again in *my* lifetime',[8] he wrote, and also ordered the destruction and replacement of most of the bedroom furniture. Could such resolve, such absolute abhorrence, have been prompted merely by his distaste for the décor of these rooms? Surely not.

Mark, a recluse and a misogynist, was positively afraid to mingle in company with others: 'I can no longer remain in a crowded room, church or indeed any other place of assembly', he wrote to Eels.[9] With two exceptions, he was entirely without close friends. Those exceptions, Lord Wharton and Nigel Browne, both lived far from either Oxford or Highnam, but Mark visited the latter, his 'best and oldest friend', at his home in Swanage often, and it was by no means unusual for their frequent letters to each other to exceed fifty pages. And when Mark eventually decided to move into Highnam Court it was only Nigel Browne's visits which were able, as he put it, 'to beguile my loneliness there'.

Certainly, with the exception of his Aunt Hilda's husband, Edgerton Cripps, Mark wanted nothing to do with his close family. Cripps had been energetic in sorting out Mark's finances, securing a legacy for him from Beatrice's estate, and helping with the settlement of death duties. Mark's particular *bête noire* was his Uncle Sidney's son, Michael Denman Gambier-Parry (an army officer who rose to the rank of Major General), who, Mark was convinced, wished to wrest Highnam Court from him. 'I have been so outrageously treated by my relatives throughout, with the exception of Captain Cripps, that in future I am quite determined to employ the Oxford University Solicitors to insist that my

---

[8] Mark Gambier-Parry, letter to Alfred Eels dated 5 July 1936. Highnam archive.
[9] Mark Gambier-Parry, letter to Alfred Eels dated 30 April 1937. Highnam archive.

interests are properly attended to',[10] Mark told Eels, who, apart from Browne, had become his only confidant.

At the outbreak of the Second World War the stables and grounds of Highnam Court were requisitioned by the War Office for billeting and manœvres. When British troops were replaced by Americans, Mark, afraid that they might also move into the house, reluctantly decided that he must take up residence there to protect the property and, more especially, his grandfather's art collection. He had already deflected any suggestion that he would dispose of art treasures to ease his financial difficulties, as he explained to Eels before the war:

> I am being pestered by a London art dealer... to sell several of the art treasures. Of course I turn a stone deaf ear to such proposals. On the other hand, I am very much annoyed to have discovered that in quite reputable art circles in London the rumour is being freely circulated that some of *my* pictures are shortly to be sold! Who started such a preposterous notion I cannot imagine. Once more I place on record my fixed intention of disposing of the very last rood of land before any of the irreplaceable art treasures.[11]

As the years passed Mark became ever more melancholic, lonely and manic. The remnants of a large household staff had gone soon after his arrival at Highnam, and Mark was looked after by a single housekeeper, Alice Smith, who saw it as her duty to protect him from the world. He rarely went out, and outdoor staff caught only occasional glimpses of him. Reginald Davis, for instance, Mark's forester for ten years, met his employer only twice in that time.[12] Even within the house there were areas which he shunned, believing them to be haunted by the ghost of a little grey woman, 'grief-stricken and closely veiled' which had been seen by several members of the family over four generations.

In the last few years of his life Mark, who by then was suffering from pernicious anaemia and lived entirely in the servants' quarters, gave to one unrelated family five ninety-nine year leases at rents ranging from £150 a year to 5p a year, on two cottages, the stable block, the estate manager's house and even a wing of the main house at Highnam. In an effort to avoid further death duties, he also passed five farms on the estate during his lifetime to his first cousin, William Cripps. He assured William and his wife Kate that it was they who would inherit the whole estate, but when, some time later, William visited Highnam, Mark, convinced that he detected the smell of beer on his breath, instantly disinherited him – not the first relative to be cut out of Mark's will on a whim! Soon after, William's son, Timothy, was killed in a motor-cycle accident, reopening the question of who should succeed Mark at Highnam. Again on a whim, Mark decided to leave the estate to Thomas Fenton, the youngest son of William's sister, Margaret ('Peggy') Cripps, who had married Lieutenant Commander (later Captain) James Fenton in 1937. It appears that young Tom Fenton, when a small boy, had shown some affection for his Uncle Mark, and

---

[10] Mark Gambier-Parry, letter to Alfred Eels dated 3 November 1936. Highnam archive.
[11] Mark Gambier-Parry, letter to Alfred Eels dated 8 February 1937. Highnam archive.
[12] Memories of the late Molly Davis.

that was sufficient for him to become heir to a large mansion, 9 acres of gardens, a 50-acre park, 250 acres of woodland, and nineteen cottages!

Mark, concerned above all that his grandfather's art treasures should remain as an intact collection, had, at first, offered the house and collection to the city of Gloucester. This was declined, and soon after the war he wrote to Samuel Courtauld offering Highnam Court, park and collection to the University of London. For practical reasons the University found it impossible to accept the offer of the house and park, but, determined to adhere to his central idea, Mark offered to bequeath the collection alone. So it was that on his death in August 1966 the collection left Highnam under heavy guard for London.

At eighteen years of age Tom Fenton found himself possessed of a crumbling mansion, a run-down estate, and nineteen cottages all needing new roofs and sanitation but with tenants paying an average of 50p per week under controlled tenancies. The liquid assets available to him to pay death duties amounted to no more than £78,000, while the amount that had to be found in cash was over £100,000. Meanwhile, the art collection was hailed by the press as 'the most important bequest made to the nation in recent years', placed on display in the Courtauld Institute Galleries, and valued at £750,000!

The last remaining woodlands and some of the house furnishings at Highnam were sold off to pay death duties and for urgent repairs for dry and wet rot in the house, and in 1977 Fenton sold the house and gardens to a local musician, Roger Smith, who wished to found an arts and music centre. This scheme failed, as did Smith's much grander concept of a 600-seat opera house in the Highnam grounds, to be financed by the building of 300 houses on the estate. 'Not put off by massive public opposition', wrote Fenton, 'he pursued the application until finally refused at a public inquiry in July 1988'.

> Next, in 1991, came his [Smith's] 'Arts Houses Hotel' scheme, with another opera house incorporating audio-visual recording studios, corporate hospitality suites, 18-hole golf course and a polo ground. When the funding for this was not forthcoming and Mr. Smith's own finances were in a serious state, he was forced to consider losing personal control of the house's management. In 1991, while still hoping to be involved in a proposed Zen Buddhist study centre, Roger Smith suddenly died and, with the house now in a seriously neglected state, shortly afterwards the nationwide Building Society took control, putting Highnam Court and 32 acres on the market for only the third time in recorded history, at an asking price of £900,000.[13]

Highnam Court remained empty for five years, the gardens, including the water gardens created for Thomas Gambier Parry by James Pulham, becoming ever more tangled and overgrown, whilst vandalism and the theft of garden vessels also took their toll. But Tom Fenton remained at Highnam, living in the Old Rectory, and determined that the church built by his great-grandfather, which had also suffered the ravages of time and damp, would at least be restored. From 1987 to 1994 Fenton spearheaded an appeal which raised the necessary £200,000 required to restore the building and save the frescoes, which were

---

[13] Thomas Fenton, from a lecture given at a seminar, *The Future of the Country House*, at the Institute of Advanced Architectural Studies, York University, 22-24 November 1993.

blackened by soot and severely damaged by water. The Church of the Holy Innocents at Highnam may once again be fully appreciated, as John Betjeman recognised, as the most complete Victorian gothic church in England.

Hard on the heels of this great accomplishment came the purchase of Highnam Court by Gloucester businessman Roger Head, who, with equal determination and with expert advice and assistance, set about the task of restoration. He too has achieved a remarkable success. Highnam Court again stands proud, a comfortable family home, a beautiful and rare example of a country house of the Commonwealth period; and in its gardens Thomas Gambier Parry's vision is revealed afresh.

*　　*　　*　　*　　*　　*　　*

The Gambier Parry Collection remains in the care of the Courtauld Institute Galleries, where, at Somerset House, several of the finest paintings and other items are on permanent display. But the family portraits, including those of Thomas Parry, his daughter Harriot, daughter-in-law Mary Parry, and others, remained in Gloucestershire. Amongst these was one far older than the rest, but which was the most recently acquired.

When Bishop Henry Parry of Worcester died in 1616 his portrait, painted two years earlier, when he was aged fifty three, was passed down through his family to the only surviving son of the Revd. John Parry of Aston Somerville (see Chapter I), Joseph Parry (1680-1763), who lived at Clifford Chambers in Warwickshire. Joseph's grand-daughter, Elizabeth Harris (1760-1829), married a certain John Nash (1760-1837) of Sidbury in Devon, and after Elizabeth's death, Nash married Susanna Bourne – who lived to the astonishing age of 100 years and 11 months, and even took a second husband before her death in 1879!

Memorials to the Parrys adorn the walls and pass beneath the feet in the churches of both Aston Somerville and Clifford Chambers, and the treasured portrait of their eminent ancestor remained in the continuous possession of this branch of the family until one day soon after the First War, when a Colonel Bourne arrived with it at Highnam Court and presented it to Ernest to ensure that it remained in the hands of those Parrys of the Golden Vale who shared a common ancestry with Bishop Henry Parry of Worcester.

The portrait, which now hangs in the palace of the Bishop of Worcester at Hartlebury, remained at Highnam until Mark Gambier-Parry's death, and it was hanging in the dining room there when, in September 1939, he received a visit from Her Majesty Queen Mary, accompanied by her niece, the Duchess of Beaufort, and Lady Cynthia Colville, her lady-in-waiting. It was an occasion which Mark was unlikely ever to forget:

> As a connoisseur of eighteenth-century plasterwork, the Queen was particularly interested in the Music Room, and so I was glad to be able to tell her that its wall decorations dated back to that period.
>
> Considering the value of its contents – perhaps for that very reason – the adjoining room failed to make much impression. After examining the lovely little Holy Family by

Garofalo, the Queen seemed much more attracted by the dreadful flower-encrusted urn standing on the marble topped chiffonier close by.

As there were so many other things more worthy of admiration, notably the Louis Quinze *garniture de cheminée*, what in the world could she find so attractive in that mid-Victorian monstrosity, I wondered? Had it not been an heirloom, I might doubtless have begged her graciously to accept it as a memento of the occasion, but that I dared not do.

…Knowing her acquisitive tendencies, I had, only that morning, locked up all the china cabinets and handed the keys to the steward, instructing him to hide them away without telling where he intended to put them.[14]

Moving on from the gold drawing-room into the library, the Queen made few comments, but Mark could see 'that she fully realized the beauty and value of certain pictures'. But it was in the dining room, where some of the family portraits were hanging, including that of Bishop Henry Parry, that the Queen 'seemed very much in her element'. When she reached the bishop's portrait she paused, gazed at it for a moment, remembered that he had been domestic chaplain to Elizabeth I and, turning to her niece, said, '*That* is the family'!

---

[14] Mark Gambier-Parry, *Highnam Memoranda*. Highnam archive.

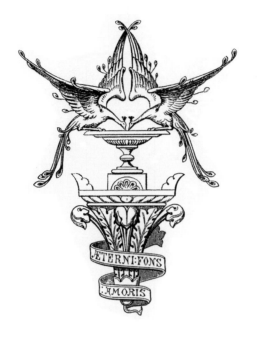

Thomas Gambier Parry: cover design for *The Ministry of Fine Art* (1887)

Genealogical Tree I

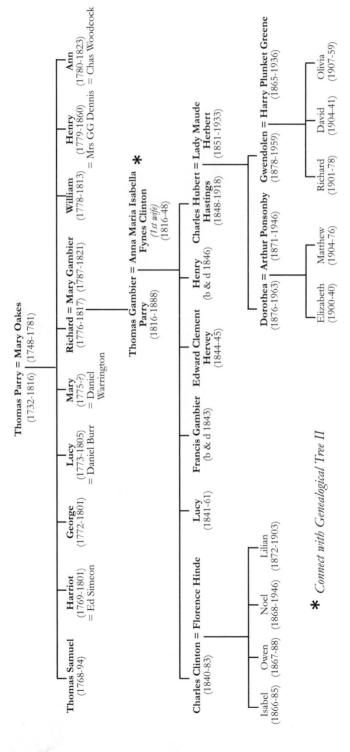

Thomas Parry = Mary Oakes
(1732-1816) (1748-1781)

Thomas Samuel (1768-94)

Harriot (1769-1801) = Ed Simeon

George (1772-1801)

Lucy (1773-1805) = Daniel Burr

Mary (1775-?) = Daniel Warrington

Richard = Mary Gambier (1776-1817) (1787-1821)

William (1778-1813)

Henry (1779-1860) = Mrs GG Dennis

Ann (1780-1823) = Chas Woodcock

Thomas Gambier = Anna Maria Isabella Fynes Clinton
Parry (1st wife)
(1816-1888) (1816-48)

*

Francis Gambier (b & d 1843)

Lucy (1841-61)

Edward Clement Hervey (1844-45)

Henry (b & d 1846)

Charles Hubert = Lady Maude Hastings Herbert
(1848-1918) (1851-1933)

Charles Clinton = Florence Hinde (1840-83)

Isabel (1866-85)

Owen (1867-88)

Noel (1868-1946)

Lilian (1872-1903)

Dorothea = Arthur Ponsonby (1876-1963) (1871-1946)

Gwendolen = Harry Plunket Greene (1878-1959) (1865-1936)

Elizabeth (1900-40)

Matthew (1904-76)

Richard (1901-78)

David (1904-41)

Olivia (1907-59)

* *Connect with Genealogical Tree II*

238

Genealogical Tree II

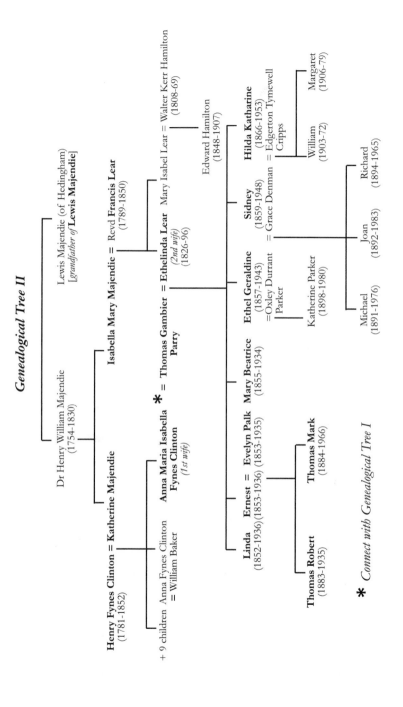

* *Connect with Genealogical Tree I*

BIBLIOGRAPHY

Mildred Archer, *Company Drawings in the India Office Library* (HMSO, 1972)

Bernard Benoliel, *Parry before Jerusalem* (Ashgate Publishing Ltd, 1997)

Anthony Boden, *Three Choirs: A History of the Festival* (Sutton Publishing, 1992)

Charles Angell Bradford, *Blanche Parry, Queen Elizabeth's Gentlewoman* (London, 1935)

Anthony Blunt, *The Gambier Parry Collection* (Provisional Catalogue, Courtauld Institute of Art, 1967)

Anthony Blunt, 'Thomas Gambier Parry: a great art collector'. *Apollo* (April 1965), 288-295

Herbert Brewer, *Memories of Choirs and Cloisters* (London, 1931)

Peter Burman, Dennis Farr et al, *Thomas Gambier Parry (1816-1888) as artist and collector* (Courtauld Institute Galleries, University of London, 1993)

Peter Burman, 'Thomas Gambier Parry. Country Gentleman, Artist and Collector', *The British Antique Dealers' Association Handbook 1990*, 36-40

Nicholas P Cushner, *Documents Illustrating the British Conquest of Manila 1762-1763* (Royal Historical Society, 1971)

Charles Deering (ed G Ayscough), *Nottingham Vetus et Nova* (1751)

Jeremy Dibble, C. Hubert H. Parry – *His Life and Music* (Oxford, 1992)

Edward Elgar (ed Percy M Young), *A Future for English Music and other lectures* (London, 1968)

Dennis Farr (ed), *100 Masterpieces from the Courtauld Collections* (1987)

Dennis Farr & John Newman *Guide to the Courtauld Institute Galleries at Somerset House*, Courtauld Institute Galleries (London, 1990)

Thomas J Fenton, *A History and Guide to the Church of the Holy Innocents, Highnam, Gloucestershire* (Gloucester, 1985)

Eliza Foy, *Original Letters from India* (Calcutta, 1817)

Roger Fry, 'Pictures in the Collection of Sir Hubert Parry, at Highnam Court, near Gloucester'. *The Burlington Magazine*, NoV, Vol II, July 1903, 117-131

Ernest Gambier-Parry, *Annals of an Eton House* (London, 1907)

Ernest Gambier-Parry, *The Pageant of My Day* (London, 1910)

Linda Gambier-Parry (ed), *A Book of Angels* (Longman, 1906)

Mark Gambier-Parry, *Madame Necker* (London, 1913)

Mark Gambier-Parry, *Studies of Childhood and Youth* (London, 1925)

Charles L Graves, *Hubert Parry*, 2 vols (London, 1926)

Gwendolen Greene, *Two Witnesses* (London, 1930)

Geoffrey Grigson (ed), *William Allingham's Diary* (Centaur Press, 1967)

G H Hodgson, *Thomas Parry: Free Merchant of Madras 1768-1824* (Madras, 1938)

Imogen Holst, Holst (Faber, 1974)

Valerie Hope et al, *The Freedom, the Past and Present of the Livery, Guilds and City of London* (Barracuda Books, 1982)

Arthur Jacobs, *Arthur Sullivan, A Victorian Musician* (Oxford, 1984)

Joan Johnson, *The Gloucestershire Gentry* (Sutton Publishing, 1989)

Tresham Lever, *The Herberts of Wilton* (John Murray, 1967)

Daniel Lysons et al, *Origin and Progress of the Meeting of the Three Choirs of Gloucester, Hereford and Worcester* (Gloucester, 1895)

Thomas Babington Macauley, *The History of England in the Eighteenth Century* (Folio Society Edition, 1988)

Robert Bernard Martin, *Tennyson – The Unquiet Heart* (Oxford, 1980)

Arthur Oswald, 'Highnam Court, Gloucestershire. The Home of Mr. T. M. Gambier-Parry', I & II, *Country Life*, CVII (12 and 19 May 1950), 1376-8, 1462-66

Christopher Palmer, *Herbert Howells* (Novello, 1978)

Hubert Parry, *The Art of Music* (London, 1893)

Hubert Parry, *Johann Sebastian Bach* (London and New York, 1909)

Hubert Parry, *Studies of Great Composers* (London, 1887)

Hubert Parry, *Style in Musical Art* (London, 1911)

Thomas Gambier Parry, *The Ministry of Fine Art* (John Murray, 1887)

Thomas Gambier Parry, *The Adornment of Sacred Buildings*. A Paper read at the Annual Meeting of the Associated Architectural Societies, held in the County Assembly Rooms, Lincoln, 17 June 1868, Lincoln Diocesan Architectural Society published as *Reports and Papers read at The Meetings of the Architectural Societies of the Diocese of Lincoln...during the year MDCCCLLXVIII* (Lincoln, 1868), 141-53

Thomas Gambier Parry, *The Relation of Fine Art to Social Science*. An address delivered at the Social Science Congress, Cheltenham, October 1878 (London, 1878)

Thomas Gambier Parry, *Spirit Fresco Painting. An Account of the Process* (London, 1880) [Takes the form of a letter to the Secretary, Science and Art Department, South Kensington, 30 March 1880]; 2nd ed, 1883

C H Philips, *The East India Company 1784-1834* (Manchester, 1961)

J H Plum, *England in the Eighteenth Century* (Pelican, 1986)

Lady Sophia Raffles, *Memorials of the Life of Sir Stamford Raffles* (John Murray, 1830)

Donald Read, England 1868-1914 (Longman, 1975)

Simon Reynolds, *William Blake Richmond, An Artist's Life 1842-1921* (Norwich, 1995)

N A M Roger, *Naval Records for Genealogists* (HMSO, 1988)

John Ruskin, *Modern Painters*, 2nd edition in small form (George Allan, 1898)

George Bernard Shaw, *The Perfect Wagnerite* (London, 1898)

Leonard Thompson, *A History of South Africa* (Yale University Press, 1995)

R K R Thornton (ed), *Ivor Gurney, Collected Letters* (Mid NAG Carcanet, 1991)

G M Trevelyan, *History of England* (Longman, 1934)

Ursula Vaughan Williams, *RVW – A Biography of Ralph Vaughan Williams* (Oxford, 1964)

David Verey, 'The Building of Highnam Church', *Country Life*, CXLIX (13 May 1971), 1160-62

Ernest Walker, *A History of Music in England* (Oxford, 1924)

INDEX